THE
CHICANO
HERITAGE

This is a volume in the Arno Press collection

THE
CHICANO
HERITAGE

Advisory Editor
Carlos E. Cortés

Editorial Board
Rodolfo Acuña
Juan Gómez-Quiñones
George F. Rivera, Jr.

*See last pages of this volume
for a complete list of titles.*

THE MEXICAN SIDE

OF THE

TEXAN REVOLUTION

[1836]

BY THE

CHIEF MEXICAN PARTICIPANTS

GENERAL ANTONIO LOPEZ DE SANTA-ANNA
D. RAMON MARTINEZ CARO (Secretary to Santa-Anna)
GENERAL VICENTE FILISOLA
GENERAL JOSÉ URREA
GENERAL JOSÉ MARÍA TORNEL (Secretary of War)

TRANSLATED WITH NOTES

BY

CARLOS E. CASTAÑEDA

ARNO PRESS

A New York Times Company

New York — 1976

Editorial Supervision: LESLIE PARR

———◆———

Reprint Edition 1976 by Arno Press Inc.

THE CHICANO HERITAGE
ISBN for complete set: 0-405-09480-9
See last pages of this volume for titles.

Manufactured in the United States of America

———◆———

Library of Congress Cataloging in Publication Data

Castañeda, Carlos Eduardo, 1896-1958, comp.
    The Mexican side of the Texan Revolution.

    (The Chicano heritage)
    Reprint of the ed. published by P. L Turner Co.,
Dallas.
    Includes bibliographical references and index.
    1.   Texas--History--Revolution, 1835-1836--
Personal narratives. I.   Santa Anna, Antonio
López de, Pres. Mexico, 1795-1876. II.   Title.
III.   Series.
[F390.C317   1976]   976.4'03   76-1215
ISBN 0-405-09487-6

THE MEXICAN SIDE
OF THE
TEXAN REVOLUTION
[1836]

BY THE
CHIEF MEXICAN PARTICIPANTS

GENERAL ANTONIO LOPEZ DE SANTA-ANNA
D. RAMON MARTINEZ CARO (Secretary to Santa-Anna)
GENERAL VICENTE FILISOLA
GENERAL JOSÉ URREA
GENERAL JOSÉ MARÍA TORNEL (Secretary of War)

TRANSLATED WITH NOTES
BY
CARLOS E. CASTAÑEDA
Latin-American Librarian, University of Texas

P. L. TURNER COMPANY
PUBLISHERS
DALLAS   TEXAS

FOREWORD

THOUGH in recent years a great deal of material concerning the history of Texas has been made available, the Spanish sources for the Texas Revolution still remain inaccessible except to those who can read Spanish. Since many of these sources are extremely rare even in Spanish, the present translations have been undertaken in order to give to the public the accounts of the Texas campaign of 1836 as related by five of the chief participants, who present the Mexican side of the campaign.

The five documents presented show clearly how a series of coincidences that may almost be called providential, united to give the victory to the Texans and to make possible their independence. Without detracting from the merit of the patriots who risked everything to make this great State independent and who laid the foundations of this great commonwealth, they show that the traditional sins of Mexico, dissension and personal envy, were more deadly to the Mexican army than the Texan bullets.

In translating the present documents great care has been exercised to render with all accuracy the thought of the Spanish originals, but no attempt has been made to give a literal word for word rendition. Notes have been added wherever it was thought they might make the meaning clear or throw light upon debatable questions.

Special acknowledgments are due Dr. E. C. Barker for helpful advice and the courtesy of permitting the reproduction of the original surrender of Fannin; to Mr. E. W. Winkler, Librarian, for useful suggestions; and to Mrs. M. A. Hatcher, Archivist of the University of Texas, for reading most of the manuscript.   C. E. C.

CONTENTS

ILLUSTRATIONS

MANIFESTO

WHICH

GENERAL ANTONIO LOPEZ DE SANTA-ANNA

ADDRESSES TO
HIS FELLOW-CITIZENS

RELATIVE TO HIS OPERATIONS
DURING THE TEXAS CAMPAIGN
AND HIS CAPTURE 10 OF MAY 1837[1]

---

[1] This *Manifiesto* was first printed at Vera Cruz, 1837, by Antonio María Valdés. It was reprinted by Genaro García in *Documentos para la Historia de México*, XXIX. This reprint was used for the present translation, though the text was verified with the first edition in the García Collection, University of Texas.

MANIFIESTO

QUE DE SUS OPERACIONES

EN LA CAMPAÑA DE TEJAS

Y EN SU CAUTIVERIO

DIRIGE

A SUS CONCIUDADANOS

EL GENERAL

ANTONIO LOPEZ DE SANTA-ANNA.

VERACRUZ:

Imprenta Liberal à cargo de Antonio Maria Valdes

1837.

THE MEXICAN SIDE
OF THE TEXAN REVOLUTION

NEVER has the ambitious thought of obtaining universal approval for my actions entered my mind; nor have I been so pusillanimous that the fear of the disapproval of a few, or even of many, could have prevented me from acting in a certain way when convinced, even though erroneously, of the propriety of my action. In the palace of Mexico as in this humble hut, in the midst of the applause of a free people the same as amidst the insolent hisses of the Texans who loudly called for my death, I have realized that my conduct would always be criticized, for who has not at least one enemy if fate has raised him above his fellow-citizens and placed him in the public eye? I was not surprised, therefore, to see the triumphs of Béxar and the Alamo tainted by the tireless and venomous tooth of that envy which I have always despised, nor the defeat of San Jacinto horribly portrayed by the unfaithful and disloyal brush of an unjust animosity; much less was I surprised that by these means a great part of a nation, zealous as it should be of its honor and anxious that the cost of sustaining it should be reduced to a minimum, should have been made to doubt the propriety of my war measures if not to condemn them outright. But my misfortune having reached its limit, this ill opinion has gone one step further, and, although I expected as much, it has been all the more painful to me. Thus, when I placed foot upon the soil of my native land, evoked as it were from the grave, after having suffered for its cause, the most sacred of causes, a painful imprisonment, a cruel separation, a great misfortune, the judgment of my compatriots would like to banish me. This ill-deserved judgment has not failed to inflict a mortal wound to my heart, in spite of the fact that I recognize its noble origin in some cases. Still I expected, yea, I flattered myself in the midst of my sorrows, that I would obtain the compassion of my compatriots and that upon hearing me they would accept my justification.

It was my purpose, as I looked upon the chains that held me prisoner, to show as an offering to my country, the marks left upon me, if I ever succeeded in breaking them. To-day even the fact of having broken them is imputed to me as treason. I would have explained to my fellow-citizens the cause of our common misfortune; my tears would have flowed and mingled with theirs; my story would have excited their noble passions just as my misfortunes the friendly sympathy of brothers. I now have to speak not of my personal misfortunes but of those that it is thought have befallen our country exclusively because of me, in order to prove my innocence rather than to mitigate my mortification. More unfortunate than Manlius, accused before the Romans, the wounds received for our country, far from securing for me an undeserved absolution from a proven crime, are themselves the accusations from which I must vindicate myself. My imprisonment and my freedom, these are the two things which I must explain; and the laurels of victory that I won before, whose glory has not been sufficient to safeguard my name, will avail me but little now as I raise my voice in protest, though it be shielded by reason.

I must speak, nevertheless, for my honor belongs to my country, just as my arm and my soul have always been hers. Hers is the innocence that encourages my heart in this great misfortune. Why, may I ask, must reason and sincerity this time go unheard? Let no one answer me in the affirmative! Let no one, in pity's name, offer me so cruel a disappointment! If it be a false illusion, let no one dissipate it. Let me persist in an error which now pours a health-and-life balm upon my lacerated name.

I shall lead my compatriots by the hand to the margins of the San Jacinto and there among the very ruins where they wish to bury my glory, in the very deserts where it is said that its

OF THE TEXAN REVOLUTION 7

luster was dimmed, by the deep rivers still tinted red with the
blood shed in a righteous war by Mexicans and the invaders of
Texas, but now laid upon my head, there I will show them how
far I steered from that treacherous path imputed to me. We
shall enter the port of Velasco and from my enemies and those
of my country themselves they shall hear the testimony of a firmness that brought down upon me threats of death while many
in Mexico accused me of a weakness that I well might have
shown. Santa Anna, whether conqueror or conquered, whether
free or in chains, yea, I swear it before the world, did not in
Texas debase the Mexican name in which he glories and takes
pride.

At the age of thirty-five my military achievements had long
since carried me to the highest military rank, thanks to the
liberality with which my services were repaid. I held the first
place among Mexicans by their own generous vote. My name
was known beyond the limits of Mexico and a competent fortune
assured me against poverty. To what else could the ambition of
a man who had just refused a dictatorship offered to him, and
who had fought those who had dared to make such an offer,
aspire? What else could he desire who, though able to live in
a palace in luxury and plenty surrounded by never-failing cour-
tiers, dwelt in a simple country home where his pride could only
be flattered by the sincere love of his wife and the innocent games
of his children? I was wrested from this peaceful life by my
love for my country. I had sworn that my sword should always
be the first to strike the blow upon the daring necks of her
enemies, and the news that came from Texas regarding the plight
of General Don Martín Cós, besieged in Béxar by the Texans,
late in 1835, made me realize that they were the most formidable
enemies that threatened our country at that time.

Some journalists had tried to compare my campaigns to those
of Napoleon and my enemies hoped that that of Texas would be
as disastrous to me as that of Russia was to the Corsican hero.
My friends, while cursing the prophecy, feared to see it fulfilled,
and I, myself, was never so blind as to be unaware of the

difficulties of the enterprise, arising from the circumstances. This word, which by dint of applying it to such varied uses and to objects so different, has now amongst us no meaning, was to me an endless source of unquiet reflection. The administrative system of the nation had just been changed,[2] and the basis of the new fundamental law had scarcely been established, always a critical moment for any people and particularly for ours at a time when resentment still burned high and the efforts to influence the future of the nation succeeded each other. The creation of a formidable army appeared to me a serious evil at this time because of the danger that a considerable part of it might be induced to take an active part in determining the national institutions which should be the outcome of free and calm meditation. The honor of the country, however, demanded that such a danger be faced and that every attempt be made to minimize it, as was fortunately done, the soldiers of the republic giving in this instance an irrefutable proof of their prudence and patriotism.

It was necessary to attend immediately to another difficulty of considerable importance: that the creation of a force capable of defending the integrity of the nation should not hinder the leaving of a sufficient force in the most important points of the country both to preserve internal tranquillity and to stop or combat any attempt to disembark troops, such as the enemy practiced later. The national law regarding militia that occasioned a civil war did not permit the raising of the necessary troops to meet the exigencies of the moment and our battalions were mere companies. Without ignoring this problem, national decorum demanded that war be waged against those who wished to betray the territory of Texas. A cause more just could not be found. It was necessary practically to improvise an army to defend it.

Who does not know the condition of our public finances? Not only was it sad, but the only hope of obtaining money for the war was the very doubtful and dilatory system of direct

[2] The federal system was changed by special decree of Congress on Oct. 23, 1835. The provisions of this decree established a strongly centralized government.

taxation that might also serve as a pretext for uprisings and popular protests. It was not, therefore, proper to adopt it. Even the system of forced loans contracted by the government that had drained the public treasury to such an extent were difficult because of the very frequency with which it was necessary to recur to them. The income of our customs houses, the only guarantee which up to that time had been given as security, were mortgaged for a long period. The government, in spite of the authorization given by Congress for that purpose in November, 1835 (Document No. 1) was unable to secure the necessary funds for this campaign; and up to the time of my arrival at San Luis, they were so insignificant that part of the army gathered in that capital had to go without pay for five days before I succeeded in getting ten thousand pesos by giving my personal security. Authorized to negotiate a loan by the government as a result of the decree mentioned, I was obliged to try to effect it under these disadvantageous circumstances for the nation, fearing that later on the urgency would be greater and consequently the terms more disadvantageous. Finally I concluded a loan with Messrs. Rubio and Errazu (Document No. 2) by the terms of which four hundred thousand pesos, half in silver and the other half in bonds, were to be turned over to me, and furthermore, all supplies necessary for the army were to be delivered at Matamoros at their own expense and cost, these sums to be repaid with the proceeds of the forced loans of the department of San Luis, Guanajuato, Guadalajara and Zacatecas and the remainder by import duties at the customs houses at Matamoros and Tampico where the receipts for the delivery of the supplies were to be accepted as currency. This contract, which was subject to the approval of the government, who finally ratified it (Document No. 3), and which presented by itself seems ruinous to the nation, but the advantages of which are evident if it is compared with other transactions of similar nature executed by the government itself, was the only means by which the troops were equipped and the Texas campaign opened. In this campaign, the small sums of the forced loans

and other remittances made by the government to increase somewhat our resources, demanded a strict economy that has not
escaped censure but which, after the reverse of San Jacinto, left
a sum of more than a hundred and fifty thousand pesos in
Matamoros. Nevertheless, the contract was disapproved by Congress and I, filled with astonishment, surprised, and overcome by
the fearful consequences which I foresaw, had to struggle against
my better sense to rise above such a blow and to continue directing, though filled with the bitterness of these circumstances, an
enterprise in which new difficulties were met at every turn. I
would have found myself in a most embarrassing situation on
account of this disapproval, with the army already on its way to
San Antonio de Béxar, had it not been that the money-lenders,
whom I had not known before and to whom no interested motive
could incline me, generously sent me the funds that had been left
deposited with them after the contract was made, realizing with
all certainty the enormous loss they would suffer, as experience
later demonstrated. I could not help but complain in a friendly,
yet bitter tone to the president *ad iterim*.[3] Shortly before, the
mine of Fresnillo in Zacatecas had paid the government one million pesos that were absorbed with incredible speed by a prodigious multitude of outstanding obligations. A dark horizon,
indeed, that foretold the storm!

I went to Mexico, therefore, in November, 1835, to take
charge of a war from which I could have been excused, for the
fundamental law of the country offered me a decorous excuse
that my broken health made all the more honorable. Nevertheless, aware of the adverse circumstances I have expressed, I still
desired to try to serve my country. In a few days I gathered
six thousand men, clothed and equipped. At the cost of immense
sacrifices, rising above obstacles that seemed insuperable, this
force set out from San Luis towards the end of December, 1835.
The difficulties arising from the need of securing food supplies
sufficient for the army while crossing four hundred leagues of

[3] Miguel Barragán was acting president from January 28, 1835, to February,
1836. He died early in March, 1836.

desert lands, and those attendant upon its conveyance, as well as the transportation of other equipment, arms, munitions, etc., were all difficulties that, though not pressing at the time of organization, were, nevertheless, of the utmost importance, particularly since the cost of transportation was extremely high in that long stretch. Hospitals had to be located and protected; a great number of rivers had to be crossed without bridge equipment, without even a single boat; the coast had to be watched and the ports kept open to receive provisions and to prevent the enemy from receiving reenforcements or from retreating—all of this with only one serviceable war vessel—and lastly, we had to raise a reserve force to come to our help in case of a reverse, a frequent occurrence in war, when, in order to complete the number of those deemed necessary for the campaign, we had had to use raw recruits.

When a general is given command of an army and everything that is necessary is furnished to him and placed at his disposal, he should be held strictly responsible if he departs from the established rules of war. The government has said, and with truth, that all the resources at its command were placed at my disposal in this campaign, but these being so few, could it have given me many? Could they have been sufficient to carry on a war according to usage when all those resources which are necessary for such an undertaking were practically lacking? The army under my command consisted of only six thousand men when it left Saltillo [4] and of these at least half were raw recruits from San Luis, Querétaro and other departments, hastily enlisted to fill the ragged companies. The people of Nuevo León and Coahuila, at the instigation of their worthy and patriotic governors, donated food supplies to the army. These, added to those that were brought, made a considerable amount that in a country so vast, where all transportation is done on mule back, was ex-

[4] Many years later, while in exile, Santa Anna said, referring to the number of men, "I gathered and organized the expeditionary army of Texas, consisting of eight thousand men, in the city of Saltillo." *Diario de mi vida política y militar* in *Documentos para la Historia de México*, II, 33.

tremely embarrassing to me, although indispensable for our needs. In order to transport it, I made use of extremely heavy ox-carts, a means of transportation never used by armies but which because of the lack of the necessary equipment, and in spite of the most active efforts made to secure it, I was obliged to use. Our needs had been foreseen and that was all that could be done, for to meet them all was an impossibility. The great problem I had to solve was to reconquer Texas and to accomplish this in the shortest time possible, at whatever cost, in order that the revolutionary activities of the interior should not recall that small army before it had fulfilled its honorable mission. A long campaign would have undoubtedly consumed our resources and we would have been unable to renew them. If the only four favorable months of the year were not taken advantage of, the army, in the midst of the hardships of a campaign, would perish of hunger and of the effects of the climate, upon those who composed the army under my command, who were accustomed to a more temperate climate. In order that the soldier by means of repeated marches and frequent battles should forget the immense distance which separated him from his family and home comforts; in order that his courage might not fail; and, in short, to maintain the morale which an army obtains from its activity and operations, it was of the utmost importance to prevent the enemy from strengthening its position or receiving the reenforcements that the papers from the North asserted were very numerous. In a word, the government had said to me that it left everything to my genius, and this flattering remark became an embarrassing truth, making it necessary in this campaign to move with all diligence to avoid the many difficulties that delay in action would undoubtedly bring about. This realization established the norm for all my operations and I always tried earnestly to shorten them. Had we been favored by victory to the last, this policy would have shown a surprised world our occupation, in sixty days, of a territory more than four hundred leagues in extent and defended by the enemy.

Béxar was held by the enemy and it was necessary to open the door to our future operations by taking it. It would have been easy enough to have surprised it, because those occupying it did not have the faintest news of the march of our army. I entrusted, therefore, the operation to one of our generals, who with a detachment of cavalry, part of the dragoons mounted on infantry officers' horses, should have fallen on Béxar in the early morning of February 23, 1836. My orders were concise and definite. I was most surprised, therefore, to find the said general a quarter of a league from Béxar at ten o'clock of that day, awaiting new orders. This, perhaps, was the result of inevitable circumstances; and, although the city was captured, the surprise that I had ordered to be carried out would have saved the time consumed and the blood shed later in the taking of the Alamo.

Having taken Béxar and the proceeds of the small booty having been sold by the commissary department to meet its immediate needs, all of which I communicated to the government (Document No. 4), the enemy fortified itself in the Alamo, overlooking the city. A siege of a few days would have caused its surrender, but it was not fit that the entire army should be detained before an irregular fortification hardly worthy of the name. Neither could its capture be dispensed with, for bad as it was, it was well equipped with artillery, had a double wall, and defenders who, it must be admitted, were very courageous and caused much damage to Béxar. Lastly, to leave a part of the army to lay siege to it, the rest continuing on its march, was to leave our retreat, in case of a reverse, if not entirely cut off, at least exposed, and to be unable to help those who were besieging it, who could be reenforced only from the main body of the advancing army. This would leave to the enemy a rallying point, although it might be only for a few days. An assault would infuse our soldiers with that enthusiasm of the first triumph that would make them superior in the future to those of the enemy. It was not my judgment alone that moved me to decide upon it, but the general opinion expressed in a council of war, made up of generals, that I called even though the discussions which such councils give rise to have not always seemed to me appropriate. Before undertaking the assault and after the reply given to Travis who commanded the enemy fortification, I still wanted to try a generous measure, characteristic of Mexican kindness, and I offered life to the defendants who would surrender their arms and retire under oath not to take them up again against Mexico. Colonel Don Juan Nepomuceno Almonte, through whom this generous offer was made, transmitted to me their reply which stated that they would let us know if they accepted and if not, they would renew the fire at a given hour. They decided on the latter course and their decision irrevocably sealed their fate.[5]

On the night of the fifth of March, four columns having been made ready for the assault under the command of their respective officers, they moved forward in the best order and with the greatest silence, but the imprudent huzzas of one of them awakened the sleeping vigilance of the defenders of the fort and their artillery fire caused such disorder among our columns that it was necessary to make use of the reserves. The Alamo was taken, this victory that was so much and so justly celebrated at the time, costing us seventy dead and about three hundred wounded,[6] a loss that was also later judged to be avoidable and charged, after the disaster of San Jacinto, to my incompetence and precipitation. I do not know of a way in which any fortification, defended by artillery, can be carried by assault without the personal losses of the attacking party being greater than those of the enemy, against whose walls and fortifications the brave assailants can present only their bare breasts. It is easy enough. from a desk in a peaceful office, to pile up charges against a general out on the field but this cannot prove anything more than the praiseworthy desire of making war less disastrous. But its

[5] "To the proposals to surrender he replied always that every man under his command preferred to die rather than surrender the fort to the Mexicans." Genaro García, *Documentos*, II, 34.

[6] "Not one remained alive but they disabled over a thousand of our men between dead and wounded." *Ibid.*, 35.

nature being such, a general has no power over its immutable laws. Let us weep at the tomb of the brave Mexicans who died at the Alamo defending the honor and the rights of their country. They won a lasting claim to fame and the country can never forget their heroic names.

The enemy, discouraged by this blow that left fateful memories, fled before our forces. Our flanks, however, were, nevertheless, constantly molested by guerrilla bands,[7] which, favored by their intimate acquaintance with the country, the thickets of the woods, and the effectiveness of their rifles, caused daily losses to our troops. It became necessary to remedy this evil. The slow and embarrassing march of the whole army as a unit could have availed but little for such a purpose, for the fact of being together could not stop this evil. Nor was it advisable that our whole army should stop to combat the small guerrilla bands that were almost invisible, allowing the main army of the enemy, now fleeing, to perfect a plan of defence. Brevity was the ruling principle of all my operations, and for this reason I divided the troops available into three divisions, leaving at Béxar a sufficient force under the command of General Don Juan José Andrade to fall back upon.

The first division on our right, under the command of General Don José Urrea, was to operate in the district of Goliad, El Cópano and the whole coast. Its orders were to fight the small groups that were gathering to prevent their acting in concert and becoming a menace, and to clear and free the coast of enemies as far as Brazoria. This division was to rejoin me at San Felipe de Austin, which, situated on the margin of a river, in a central location, and well provided with food, seemed to me very appropriate as a point from which to direct the campaign.

Another division under the command of General Don Antonio Gaona was ordered to our left for the same purpose. With the same objects in view as the first, it was to scour the entire line from Béxar to Bastrop. Although at first he had instructions to

---

[7] There seems to be no evidence in the English accounts of the campaign that the Texans resorted to the use of guerrilla bands.

continue as far as Nacogdoches, it was always my intention, upon his reaching Bastrop, to have him come to San Felipe, as I did in the end.

Each one of these divisions was in itself sufficient to give battle to the enemy; and, assured now that the army was well protected on its flanks, I had to look for a crossing on the Colorado. The officer whom I sent for this purpose with troops, supplies, and other resources at my command sent me a dispatch that made me believe he was in a serious situation. I issued orders for both the divisions, Urrea's and Gaona's, to march to his assistance, and I myself started out to join him. This I did at the pass of Atascosito on the 5th of April. The enemy who was defending it fled, and the central division of the army crossed the Colorado while the two flank divisions received counter orders instructing them anew to meet me in San Felipe towards which place I was marching.

It is necessary, before proceeding, to pause and review the operations of General Urrea. All of them were brilliant and fortune crowned all his efforts. Dr. Grant was overcome by his division; the coast was cleared of enemies; and those defending Goliad under the command of Fannin abandoned it and fled to Guadalupe Victoria, being forced to surrender at El Encinal in the plain of Perdido.[8] All this contributed in no small manner to the well-earned reputation of that general in the Texas campaign. To me, however, the last incident has brought grave consequences; and it is necessary, therefore, that I be allowed to digress here in order to speak of this matter.

Let it be said now in order to avoid repetition: the war against Texas has been as just on the part of the Mexican government as the lack of the slightest attempt on the part of those who forced it upon Mexico has been to try to justify their action. Few of the colonists, properly speaking, have taken up arms in the struggle. The soldiers of Travis at the Alamo, those of

[8] "Fannin, who occupied the town of Goliad, went out to meet General Urrea with 1500 filibusters and six pieces of artillery." "Diario de mi vida politica y militar" Genaro Garcia, *Documentos*, II, 35.

Fannin at Perdido, the riflemen of Dr. Grant, and Houston himself and his troops at San Jacinto, with but few exceptions, were publicly known to have come from New Orleans and other points of the neighboring republic exclusively for the purpose of aiding the Texas rebellion without ever having been members of any of the colonization grants.

Some Mexicans,[9] partisans of a former system of government, thought, perhaps in good faith, that the only effect of fanning the fire of war in Texas would be a political change in accord with their opinion. Their shortsighted ambition must be a terrible lesson to them as well as a source of eternal remorse. Too late, they now deplore having placed in jeopardy the integrity of our national territory.

Our country found itself invaded not by an established nation that came to vindicate its rights, whether true or imaginary; nor by Mexicans who, in a paroxysm of political passion, came to defend or combat the public administration of the country. The invaders were all men who, moved by the desire of conquest, with rights less apparent and plausible than those of Cortés and Pizarro, wished to take possession of that vast territory extending from Béxar to the Sabine belonging to Mexico. What can we call them? How should they be treated? All the existing laws, whose strict observance the government had just recommended, marked them as pirates and outlaws. The nations of the world would never have forgiven Mexico had it accorded them rights, privileges, and considerations which the common law of peoples accords only to constituted nations. (Document No. 5.)

Up to this time I had enjoyed among my fellow-citizens a reputation which I preferred to that of being brave: that of being generous in victory. It was necessary, in order that my misfortune should be complete, that even the only virtue that my most bitter enemies never denied me should now be questioned. I am made to appear more ferocious than a tiger, I, who in a country

_____

[9] Santa Anna is hinting at Zavala, who left Mexico City and joined the Texans. He was the first vice-president of Texas.

the most generous and humane, pride myself on being known for my clemency. Because of the execution of Fannin and his men [10] I am accused of being barbarous and sanguinary. I appeal to those of my fellow-citizens who have exercised the profession of magistrate. They shall say how many times their trembling hands have signed a death sentence, the letters of which were blurred by their tears. Law commands, and the magistrate has no power to mitigate its rigor, for him it is to put into execution. If, in the execution of law, no discretion is allowed a judge, can a general in a campaign be expected to exercise greater freedom? The prisoners of Goliad were condemned by law, by a universal law, that of personal defence, enjoyed by all nations and all individuals. They surrendered unconditionally, as the communication of General Urrea (Document No. 6) shows. How could I divert the sword of justice from their heads without making it fall upon my own? Let it be said, if you want,— I confess that it is not my opinion—that the law was unjust, but can there be greater blindness than to impute the crime to the dagger and not to the hand that wields it?

The prisoners greatly embarrassed the commander of Goliad. They had, before fleeing, set fire to the town and no building had been left except the church now being used by the sick and wounded. The guard consisted only of the garrison which was much inferior in numbers to the prisoners, while the food supplies were barely sufficient for the most essential needs of the troops. Without cavalry, with every soldier needed for the campaign, the prisoners could not be conducted to Matamoros. All these considerations transmitted to me by that officer had undue weight upon my determination. Perhaps even in civilized Europe, in a war between nations, these circumstances might have resulted in the execution of similar prisoners and not been the only example of such a sacrifice to the imperious laws of necessity and self-preservation.

[10] In the *Diario* already cited Santa Anna quotes Urrea as follows: "Adventurers who introduce themselves into Texas armed to favor the revolution of the colonists being outlawed, the prisoners have been executed." Genaro García, *Documentos,* II, 35.

How my arbitrariness would have been exaggerated, and to speak the truth with justifiable excuse, if by pardoning, as I desired, those unfortunate wretches I should have dared to violate the law. I would have taken to myself the most enviable attribute of sovereignty and exposed that detachment of troops to a surprise that might have easily been attempted by the prisoners. I could not, therefore, pardon those unfortunates. It has been said that they were protected by a capitulation, and, although the communication of General Urrea denies such a statement, I have asked the supreme government that an investigation be instituted (Document No. 7), to prove that neither officially nor confidentially was I notified of such a capitulation. Had any such existed, even though General Urrea had no authority to grant it, it would have afforded me an opportunity to petition, in the name of humanity, the indulgence of Congress for Fannin and his soldiers.

With less reason, and taking advantage of their professional knowledge, several physicians saved themselves, as well as forty prisoners who, because of the usefulness of their trade, were spared to construct flat boats. Likewise, eighty-six men who were taken at El Cópano were not executed because I ordered an investigation to be instituted to determine if it were true that they had not made use of their arms nor caused damage in any way to our country in order that I might intercede with Congress in their behalf, in spite of their having been taken under arms. It has since been asserted that those at Goliad were executed with cruelty. Upon this point I have asked in the document already cited that the military commandant at that point should be made to give a detailed account of his acts. I cannot be held responsible for the manner in which that officer carried out the law. What I know to be true is that in my imprisonment I was guarded by some of those that escaped from the firing squads who carried out the execution without order or concert. I was cruelly treated by them, to the extent that on several occasions they tried to assassinate me and to excite against me a fierce hatred that almost led to my being taken to Goliad for execution. The news printed in the capital, particularly some of which seemed to be worthy of credit, in which it was stated as true that Fannin concluded a capitulation that was violated by my orders, contributed in no small way to this danger. I trust, however, to the good judgment of my fellow-citizens, and I feel certain that since up to now they have deemed me humane and generous, their opinion may not be changed by an order that I was unable to avoid without breaking a law whose observance the government had just recommended in an emphatic circular. The desire to minimize, if possible, what might be considered the most cruel part of that law made me consult the government on this point (Document No. 8). The reply to this fell into the hands of the enemy, tying my hands in a manner as painful as is the horror that the shedding of blood after the heat of battle has always inspired in me.

The capture of the Alamo, in spite of its attendant disasters, and the quick and successful operations of General Urrea gave us a prodigious moral prestige. Do not expect to hear any more details of battles. Our name terrified the enemy, and our approach to their camps was not awaited. They fled disconcerted to hide beyond the Trinity and the Sabine. The ruins and devastation they left behind were the only signs seen by our soldiers as evidence of the presence of the invaders of Texas. The attainment of our goal was now almost certain. It was then, with sorrow on the part of the troops, that thought was given the need of garrisoning that vast territory in order to hold our conquest; and the mere idea of remaining in Texas dismayed the triumphant soldier more than defeat. Our campaign was a military parade; but to remain in Texas, perhaps forever, what a misfortune! Such was the general clamor that reached my ears and this not from the common soldiers alone. Some of the officers will remember my reprimand on so delicate a point. The evil spreading, however, in spite of all of my efforts, it would have been an unpardonable fault not to try to encourage the dejected soldiers. Perhaps it would have been an equal sin to have tried energetically to suppress the disturbance. This and not the conviction that the campaign was over, was the cause for

the general order of the twenty-fifth of March by which some of
the troops were instructed to hold themselves in readiness to return together with the wagons which were to start out for San
Luis. I had definite information, however, that the enemy was
not undertaking a retreat but was in full flight. I learned later
that, in order to stop the number of desertions among their
troops, the enemy had to resort to the ruse of assuring them that
I had returned to Mexico and of declaring that a new revolution
had broken out. In spite of these impostures, there remained
with Houston, out of 1500 men, only the 800 with which he surprised my camp at San Jacinto. It could not be otherwise, a very
considerable number having perished at Béxar, the Alamo,
Goliad, and the plain of Perdido. In short, this was shown by
the proclamations of the so-called government of Texas, in all
of which appeals were made in desperate terms for the sympathy
of the Americans to come to the rescue of their defeated hosts,
since the colonists, either voluntarily or forced by circumstances,
persisted in taking refuge beyond the scene of war. In spite of
all this, it was not an excessive confidence in these facts but a
pertinent distrust of the dangerous discontent of the army under
my command that, with no intention of carrying it out, made me
issue the aforementioned order, never put into effect, about whose
terms or the conduct of the campaign, I never heard a remonstrance, much less a protest. Colonel Almonte has assured me
that he does not remember his having been instructed to make
any such known to me. I have been thought dead [11] and, placing confidence on the silence of the tomb, the facts have been distorted and attributed to very different causes.

At San Felipe de Austin we found only the ashes of what had
been a town and it was now impossible for the army to encamp
there without serious inconvenience. The enemy, with the help
of a steamboat, had taken refuge at Groce's crossing, placing the
Brazos between their soldiers and victory as well as a small for-

[11] Bernardo Couto wrote José María Mora, from Mexico City, on August
3, 1836. "It seems it is true that Santa Anna was executed on the 4th last,
at Nacogdoches." Genaro García, *Documentos*, VI, 6.

tification held by one hundred and fifty men at that point, and another detachment at Thompson's Crossing which they also tried to hold. I looked for another crossing and succeeded in taking Thompson's,[12] where I ordered the army to reunite. There several colonists, among them a Mexican with his family, gave me positive information that the enemy's troops had taken refuge in the thick woods above the already mentioned crossing at Groce's, the leaders of the rebellion remaining in Harrisburg. The president, the cabinet members of the so-called government of Texas, and the chief leaders of the revolution were gathered there, where a single blow would have been mortal to their cause. Such a blow depended on the rapidity of my movements and it appeared to me—and I believe rightly—too important an opportunity to abandon or to allow to escape on account of our slow motion.

I, therefore, decided to reach Harrisburg by forced marches without waiting for the rest of the army, for I really did not need it to attack a point entirely devoid of troops. We traveled all night but the enemy fled immediately after I crossed the river, astonished at an advance they believed impossible, as some Texans later confessed to me. In spite of all of my diligence, the fear that our blow upon Harrisburg might be frustrated was realized. The town was abandoned by the officers of the so-called government of Texas and we found half-written letters that our sudden and unexpected approach did not permit them to finish.[13] Some printers there were able to tell us only that they had fled towards Galveston, assuring us that the fire that was consuming the town had been accidental. What should I do now? What should be my next move? The enemy adopted that infallible means of defence that devastated the country without stopping

[12] "We were obliged to surprise the detachment at Thompson's Crossing, an operation which was well executed and permitted us to cross the river comfortably with the help of the flat boats we captured." Genaro García, *Documentos,* II, 36.

[13] In the *Diario,* written about thirty years later Santa Anna merely states that in the office of President Burnett "we found some letters of Houston." See Genaro García, *Documentos,* II, 37.

to give a single battle. It was of the utmost importance to force
a fight and the only way possible was to cut off their retreat.
For this purpose I hastened my march as much as I could, the
natural obstacles I had no means to overcome causing me untold
impatience. The printers already mentioned assured me that Houston's
force did not exceed 800 men. This was not the only source of
information that I had regarding it, but it was confirmed by another report absolutely reliable, that was given me by Colonel
Almonte from New Washington, where I had sent him with
fifty mounted men to reconnoitre. That officer succeeded in
capturing a large train of supplies from the enemy, consisting, in
the main, of food supplies that were essential to us. His force
being so small, I believed it expedient to march to his aid and
to insure the safety of the supplies he had captured that were so
important for us. Keep this fact in mind in order to examine
later in the light of sane criticism, the probable number of the
main army of the enemy. I arrived then, at New Washington
the 18th of April, having sent, under the command of Captain
Marcos Barragán, an advance guard to Lynchburg to observe
the movements of the enemy, who, whether it made its way
towards the Trinity or towards Galveston, would have to pass
in sight of that point, where it was my intention to attack it.
For this purpose, having dispatched the food supplies to New
Washington under an adequate guard and having destroyed those
that it was not possible to take in safety, I marched upon Lynchburg on the 20th. I had already asked my second in command,
His Excellency, General D. Vicente Filisola, to send me five
hundred *picked* [14] men with General Martín Cós. I stressed the
word *picked* purposely, in order to avoid his sending me the
recruits that I well knew made up the greater part of our army.
While on the road, Captain Barragán came to inform me that
the enemy was approaching Lynchburg. As a matter of fact,

[14] "I instructed . . . General Filisola, my second, to dispatch the battalion
of sappers, full strength, with orders for its commander to join me immediately . . ." *Ibid.*, 37. There is no mention here of *picked* troops.

being desirous of an engagement, I had the satisfaction of seeing it, of confirming the information I had of its strength, and of observing that it had taken a disadvantageous position in the low lands of the angle formed by the junction of Buffalo Bayou and the San Jacinto just before they enter Galveston Bay. The communication about this last march (Document No. 9) gives enough details. Let it suffice to say that it never crossed my mind that a moment of rest, now indispensable, should have been so disastrous, particularly after I had issued orders for strict vigilance to insure our safety. It was, however, overconfidence that lulled the zeal of those in whom I trusted. My sleep was interrupted by the noise of arms, and upon awakening I saw with astonishment that the enemy had completely surprised our camp. In vain I tried to repair the evil. The confusion of my feelings during those unfortunate moments was equal to the misfortune itself. I exhausted all my efforts trying to turn the tide. A moment before they might have still given us victory, now, it was too late.

The hand of destiny was still at Thompson's Crossing which I tried to reach. The division of the army that accompanied me now dispersed, I saw in the main body of our army the avenger of our misfortune. In order to reach it, I made my way through the enemy with the greatest difficulty as far as the head of Buffalo Bayou, beyond which, my retreat would be safe, but pursued constantly, it was impossible for me to reach this last anchor of salvation. A mere accident permitted me, on the following day, to change my wet clothing in an abandoned house where I found some others cast off. To that same good luck I owe my not having attracted the attention of those who pursued us, who a few hours later overtook me and believing that I was an officer of the Mexicans army made me appear before the Chief of the Texans, Sam Houston, on the very battlefield of our engagement.[15]

I have given a summary of all of my operations during the

[15] "When the filibusters surprised my camp . . . as I opened my eyes I saw myself surrounded by men who threatened me with their rifles and took me prisoner." *Ibid.*, 38–39.

campaign in spite of the fact that the Supreme Government has
received and printed all my communications regarding it. I now
add to them that of the last disastrous engagement, in order that
by turning our eyes back we may contemplate all of them from
a correct point of view and without the partial bias under which
they have been considered.

Few of the colonists, if any, have taken part in this war, as
I have stated before, and even the greater number of them
found themselves forced to abandon their homes and set fire to
them against their will. This is an evident fact known by the
whole world. At Béxar and the Alamo a great number of the
armed adventurers from New Orleans had perished, and it was
not possible that those that remained could equal in number the
army under my command, composed of six thousand men. The
aim of the Texans was, and should have been, not to risk in a
single battle the success of their undertaking which from the
second of March was, openly and without disguise, independence.
The character of the country, on the other hand, favored this
type of warfare, one that among ourselves, during the first
struggle for independence, gave such happy results to our small
number, enabling a handful of poorly clad and undisciplined
sharpshooters, with no other advantages than their acquaintance
with the country and its fastness, to take immense trains of provisions and to hold in check for months at a time large divisions
of the Spanish army. The memory of this fact, always present
in my mind, and the necessity of always choosing dispatch rather
than any temporary advantage, which I believe I have proven,
determined me to divide my forces, after the capture of the
Alamo, since our numbers permitted it, but in such a way that
each division in itself should be able to cope with the enemy,
whom I believed and now know positively, could not be
numerous.

Without a fleet to cooperate with the army, to guard the
coast, and to prevent the enemy from retreating or from receiving aid, the troops under my command had to supply this de-
ficiency, and it was neither prudent nor plausible that, in order

not to divide our forces, the coast should remain unprotected and the army flanked on the right by the enemy. The other alternative was for our whole force, remaining together, to attend to this necessity, in which case without avoiding the evil, the war would be prolonged by the ponderous march of our troops, all in a body. Our army would have suffered numerous losses on account of the prevailing sickness in the coast region, especially during the last April; and finally, as a result of this and the small bands of the enemy who would have constantly harassed our left flank, all our soldiers would have perished, uselessly fatigued by the hardships.

If the army was to move always as a unit, it would have been possible only by going from Béxar to Gonzales to cross the Guadalupe at that place, then to the crossing of the Colorado at the place where Señor Ramírez Sesma and I crossed it, then to San Felipe de Austin in order to cross the Brazos. But, in spite of the fact that by this means both our flanks and the coast remained constantly exposed and our march would have been extremely slow, it left Goliad as a rallying point for the enemy, who, reinforced, would have fallen upon my rear guard. Our troops, finding themselves faced on the front by those swollen and impassable rivers, on their flanks by skirmishers, and on their rear by the enemy, who, perhaps, without offering formal battle, could still cut off our retreat and our land communications, left us without a port to our name through which we might receive supplies. What would have been the fate of the army then? At present it has suffered only a partial defeat while in search of victory and while trying to force the enemy to fight, a common occurrence in the hardships of war. Had it adopted another policy as a result of a childish fear of dividing its forces when its numbers permitted it, all would have perished of hunger or by the lead of invisible enemies.

It is not the division of an army as executed by me under the circumstances explained and for the reasons presented, that prove the inefficiency of which I am accused. I repeat that I am not in favor of discussions in councils of war to determine military operations. Thus, the object in dividing the army into three divisions was no other than to facilitate the rapidity of its marches, to protect it from the guerrilla bands, to insure our flanks, to expedite our retreat, to secure food supplies through the ports, and to destroy any enemies that might appear. This policy was successful as far as the Brazos, where, having accomplished our purpose, the army should have been reunited in order to fight the enemy who was fleeing, and was to be found only on our front. Where was the mismanagement? There were troops and there was courage. The organization of our army enabled it to use its courage successfully; its plan, its system, its order, and the cooperation of its divisions succeeded in making the enemy flee out of sight upon hearing of our approach; our troops, amidst privations and hardships, were infused with an unlimited enthusiasm that made them conceive an utter disdain for an enemy whom it had defeated and the remnants of which, after great threats and boasts and in spite of their large stature and heavy rifles, did nothing but flee constantly after the Guadalupe was crossed. The means adopted insured our communication with the interior, the receipts of our food supplies through the ports, and cleared the whole country of enemies between the San Antonio and the Brazos. The organization and the division of the army accomplished all this in the short space of a month and a half, since on the 15th of April, they should all, or the greater part of them, have been reunited at San Felipe de Austin.

No means have been spared to represent me as a being so unreasonable as to risk the greatest interests of the country in unadvisable and rash operations. For this reason before going any further, it is necessary to review the position of the two belligerents on that very 15th day that has been chosen for my incrimination. The enemy we were going to fight was facing the army; Béxar, Goliad, and El Cópano on the route to the San Antonio River; Gonzales and Victoria on that to the Guadalupe; and the Colorado was guarded by the detachment of Matagorda. All of them could help each other and receive reenforcements from the main army in the remote case of an attack by the enemy should it be reenforced by a landing on the coast, a contingency that their reduced navy, the small number of their forces, and the growing need of their concentrating made most impracticable. Therefore, whatever the distance may be between these various points and San Felipe, it cannot be said with justice that it is inadvisable for an army to cover the most important points of the country left in the rear with more or less numerous detachments. Otherwise, it would either have had to abandon them or have had to remain all together at the first place occupied —Béxar in this instance. The war we were engaged in was, from its very nature, offensive. Can it be claimed that the detachments should have been smaller? Would it not have been thought then that they were in a precarious situation? It has been necessary to criticize and all censure has, of necessity, been directed against me.

When the concentration of the army was necessary, as it appeared to me at the crossing of the Colorado, in order to help General Sesma, I issued orders for that purpose and it could have been accomplished with ease. As it was not necessary, however, the army did not remain so widely divided as it has been made to appear by exaggerating the distances in our case (and minimizing them in regard to the enemy). Señor Gaona should have been at San Felipe on the fifteenth and Señor Urrea at Brazoria or Columbia, leaving a garrison at the port of Matagorda. Thus, the position of the army on that day should have been as follows: Generals Filisola and Gaona at least as far as San Felipe; Señor Sesma at Thompson's Crossing, a distance of twelve, not sixteen, leagues from the first at the most; and I on the road to Harrisburg, twelve leagues from Thompson's Crossing. If General Gaona lost himself in the desert from Bastrop to San Felipe can that accidental misfortune be argued as proof of the mismanagement of the army? And if General Urrea, either for the same reason or some other excusable cause, was not able to be at Columbia as it happened, can a general be accused of not having a plan, just because he is unable to carry it out as the result of circumstances foreign to his will and not easily foreseen?

My orders were responsible for the concentration of the army after the twenty-first of April. Because of them General Gaona was at Thompson's Crossing by the twentieth and General Urrea was at Brazoria on the same day, part of his division having advanced as far as Columbia. Therefore, on that day the position of the army was this: Generals Filisola, Gaona, Sesma, Tolsa, Woll, in a word, all those that on the twenty-fifth were at the house of Mrs. Powell at Thompson's Crossing (except General Urrea), were six leagues distant from Columbia and twelve from Brazoria where General Urrea himself was, only ten from New Washington (which is only fifteen from Thompson's) where I was. Why was not this day chosen to point out the scattered position of the army?

The operation undertaken against Harrisburg, besides being necessary and urgent, as I have pointed out, had been viewed by me in the light of its full importance in case of success. When this was frustrated, believing myself obliged to attack the enemy without waiting for the concentration of the army previously arranged, I foresaw all the contingencies as we shall soon examine.

The enemy had occupied the thickest part of the woods at Groce's Crossing since before the fifteenth with a force not exceeding eight hundred men, fearing to be attacked every minute, and it had a few detachments, very small in number, in addition to those at the crossings of San Felipe and of Thompson, at Velasco, which I ordered occupied, and at Galveston. Evident proof of its weakness and reduced numbers was the abandonment of the chief officers of the government of Texas at Harrisburg, which, for that very fact and various others, it should have held and defended as the capital if it had had sufficient forces; its failure to attack the divisions of our army on the fifteenth, as Houston could have done with mine, the force under my command being made up of a little more than seven hun-

dred men, including fifty, not seventy, mounted troops of my
escort and the artillerymen of a six pounder that I had; likewise the divisions of Generals Filisola and Gaona could have
been attacked; the abandonment of a point as important as New
Washington worthy of being protected not only as a port but
still more because of the considerable deposit of all kinds of supplies, especially food, that was located there and which was taken
by Colonel Almonte; lastly, the irrefutable news from all sources
that confirmed the flight of the Texan troops toward the Trinity.
Was it likely or credible that they could be so numerous as it
has been incorrectly supposed, to the extent of giving them as
much as two thousand men? Was it proper to stop or to retreat
in our advance even if that had been their number?

It was not, therefore, an inordinate desire for glory nor an
immoderate impatience for it that determined my operation
against Harrisburg and made me direct it in person after serious
consideration. I had more than seven hundred men and, supposing that Houston had eight hundred, I believe our soldiers,
chosen soldiers such as I had, were able to fight and to overcome
eight hundred Texans. If national pride blinded me, I believe
that it is excusable, especially since from this error of mine no
serious consequences followed but rather with that very force,
I was able to fight the enemy on the eve of our misfortune. The
blow upon Harrisburg failed. The enemy having fled, and New
Washington being occupied by Colonel Almonte, I considered
that if they attempted an attack upon New Washington from
Lynchburg, Colonel Almonte by himself would be in a precarious situation, and I marched to his rescue. But in spite of
the relative equality of our forces, I may almost say superiority,
I did not want to risk a battle, so I asked, as I have stated
before,[16] for a reenforcement of five hundred *picked* men with
which I would have outnumbered by one-third or more the enemy
troops. Was there lack of foresight as it has been supposed?

In view of Houston's march communicated to me by the ad-

16 Compare with note 14.

vance guard at Lynchburg I was now in a position to choose the
location for battle; and I shut up the enemy in the low marshy
angle of the country where its retreat was cut off by Buffalo
Bayou and the San Jacinto. Their left was opposed by our
right, protected by the woods on the banks of the Bayou; their
right covered by our six pounder and my cavalry; and I myself
occupied the highest part of the terrain. Is this position com-
patible with the fatal lack of foresight of which I am accused?
Everything favored our country and the cause which we were
defending in its name. Lastly, in order that nothing be lacking
to our good luck, the enemy was repulsed in a skirmish on the
evening of the twentieth, and it did not believe that the troops
brought by General Cós were really reenforcements, but took
them to be a ruse by means of which we were trying to make our
troops appear larger by causing a detachment sent out the night
before to march back to camp.

If, then, everything was favorable, if everything had been
foreseen, and the operations well conducted, what was the cause
of the fateful defeat of San Jacinto? It was the excessive number of raw recruits in the five hundred men under the command
of General Cós. As is well known, such recruits contribute
little in sustaining a battle, but cause the very grave evil of intro-
during disorder with their irregular operations among tried
veterans, especially in a surprise. A cargo of supplies I had
ordered not to be brought, and the guarding of which reduced
the five hundred men that I asked for to a bare hundred was also
a cause. The capture of an order that was sent to me from
Thompson's [17] as well as that of the officer bringing it, was likewise a cause. The fatigue and lack of food of the five hundred
men of General Cós and of my escort, an imperious necessity
that made me allow them time for their rations, was no less a
cause. The disdain with which a constantly fleeing enemy was
generally viewed by our troops, well deserved up to this time

[17] "The disobedient Filisola had sent one of his aides with correspondence
from Mexico, who, before reaching my camp was intercepted, submitted to
torture, and made to declare everything he knew." *Ibid.*, 38.

though carried to an extreme, was another cause. The very inaccessibility of the ground we occupied was itself a cause, for without a close vigilance such as I had emphatically ordered, it permitted the enemy to occupy successfully the woods to the right, as it did in an act of desperation. None of these causes was the result of neglect on my part or of acts immediately emanating from me. I, therefore, can only be held responsible for having a sickly and weak body,[18] on account of which, after having spent the previous day marching, the night watching, and the entire morning on horseback, I yielded to a repose that unfortunately the time allowed the troops brought up by General Cós made possible and which in moments of greater danger, however, I would not have indulged in. As general-in-chief I fulfilled my duty by issuing the necessary orders for the vigilance of our camp, as a man I succumbed to an imperious necessity of nature for which I do not believe that a charge can be justly brought against any general, much less if such a rest is taken at the middle of the day, under a tree, and in the very camp itself. This proves also that I did not abandon myself immoderately to the comforts and pleasant well-being that our human condition requires, a failing which the greatest men of our age, including the military men of our century, have not been able to escape, without being accused of carelessness or lack of foresight.

It was fate, therefore, and fate alone, that clipped the wings of victory that was about to crown our efforts. Though I do not flatter myself that my operations are above reproach, in spite of what has been briefly stated, I do not believe that persons of judgment and sane criteria and thinking military men who are free from bias will fail to admit how unfounded have been the charges by which it has been attempted to represent me before the world as a conceited and overproud general, without knowledge, without a plan, without foresight, without caution, and,

---

[18] "He was of a robust nature" says Col. Manuel María Giménez, an aide and intimate friend of Santa Anna in his *Vida Militar*, Genaro García, *Documentos*, XXXIV.

in a word, without any of those qualities that adorn a military leader of my kind, who, in other campaigns, has known how to be victorious; but whose name, now that misfortune has placed his very life in jeopardy, is dishonored, while the nation that confided its defense to him is accused of having exercised little judgment at least in so doing.

We were overcome at San Jacinto, and I was taken before the chief of the Texans, Houston,[19] on the 22nd. I endured untold sufferings of all kinds but, as I have had the sorrow of learning, only by ending my life could they have placed me beyond the recriminations of my fellow-citizens. In their opinion, the tomb was the end pointed out by honor; and, at the same time that I am accused of being daring and imprudent I am accused of being pusillanimous to the point of treason just because I still live and breathe the free air of my country. They expected of me more victories, and, misfortune having overtaken me, death should have been my glorious end. This optimism, for which we look and which we expect of others in whom we criticize anything short of sublime romanticism—if I may be allowed to use this expression—more than once, has led us into error; and perhaps this shall not be the last time that it carries us to the brink of injustice, all the less palpable, and for that reason more dangerous as the principle on which our blindness rests is the more noble, the more heroic. As the extremes usually meet, since I was not a tragic hero in my misfortune, I am branded as a traitor. The distance between one and the other is immense. I have not risen to the superhuman virtues of a God, neither have I sunk to the depths of perpetrating a crime, the most horrible that can be committed. Let the distance be measured impartially and I will have been judged correctly.

It is a great consolation for me, however, that the prejudice of my fellow-citizens should rest in part on false appearances that I myself have partially been obliged to create. But by assuring them, now that I am free, that I am not bound by dishonorable treaties against my country, I have dissipated those appearances

[19] Cf. note 15.

by confirming the truth. If after explaining my acts and the
circumstances that determined them, suspicion and calumny still
excite their venomous tooth against me, it is not for me to prove
their error. I shall not be able to disprove a negative, the very
nature of which is not susceptible of proof. Time alone shall
bear the evidence and I would intrust my justification to its care,
having no other friends in my defense, if, as I have already said,
I did not owe an explanation of my actions to my country and to
my honor.

The first duty during my imprisonment was to demand the
treatment and considerations due a prisoner of war. The word
talon which I overheard Houston utter made me enter into a discussion, to draw a parallel, daring as it was in my position, as to
the justice of the war and its character as waged by both belligerents, Mexico and the Texans. The son of Don Lorenzo Zavala
was serving us as interpreter and finally their effrontery went as
far as to demand the practical surrender of the entire army under
my command. The idea was as preposterous as it was highly
offensive to our national honor, and my indignation must have
been shown so clearly in my face that Houston himself blushed
and changed the nature of the proposal, contenting himself with
the retirement of the army.

Do not think that I pretend to assume greater importance
than that to which my position as general-in-chief entitles me. I
foresaw that my troops, on account of my imprisonment, would
experience a discouragement that would need much tact to
dispel. Never, however, did I imagine what happened. I tried
to make the best of the situation which doubtlessly was to save
the lives of my companions and mine from the present misfortune and the danger of that first moment of exultation, and to
give the troops that made up the army time to decide upon a plan
and mature their operations. It was apparent to me that if, in
the first instance of confusion that a misfortune of such dimen-
sions as that of San Jacinto produces, the operations of our
troops were suspended, the heart of the soldier, reacting to the
honorable idea of avenging the recent insult, convinced that both

justice and superiority were on his side, a new attack upon the
enemy could and would be attempted successfully. At the sight
of a force three times larger, such as could have been mustered,
and by virtue of an intimidation that should have been practiced
but was not done, our lives undoubtedly would have had to be
spared. Having been abandoned to the clemency and interested
motives of our opponents, such a thing seemed incredible,
though our lives were actually spared.

Nevertheless, the retreat of General Filisola could have had
no other origin than a concept on this point diametrically opposed
to mine. Thus in his reply to my communication of the 22nd he
said that he was acting only out of consideration for the safety of
my person, a desire to save my life and that of the prisoners,
although he realized the advantages that might befall our army
from a continuation of hostilities. So noble a motive, as this
must have appeared to me, was engraved with indelible gratitude
upon my heart. Although afterwards that general, in view of
the public disapproval of his movements, has attributed his
actions to other causes, the only true one is, in my judgment,
the former; and a respect for this would keep forever within my
heart my opinion upon the matter had not my honor been
offended afterwards by attributing the sad plight of the army
under my command to other causes.

Much importance has been attached to the lack of resources.
I am ashamed to admit that, because of lack of food, it was not
thought advisable to undertake a march upon San Jacinto by an
army that was sixteen leagues distant, an army that has always
been justly admired for its endurance of all kinds of privations,
though it had meat and other provisions in abundance and was
also expecting to receive others, that, if not of fine quality, were
sufficient to keep it from starving. It had, however, enough for
a retreat as far as Matamoros, that is to say, to retreat almost
two hundred leagues.

Two days would have been sufficient for the forces gathered
at Thompson's alone to have given a blow to the enemy that
would have repaired easily the misfortune of the 21st, leaving

orders for General Urrea to protect the crossing, or if the entire army wished to be concentrated by ordering the said general to cross the river at Brazoria. The position of the army beyond the Brazos would have been exempt from the obstructions presented by the country on its retreat after the rains of the 27th, by which time the enemy should have been destroyed and the food that I brought from New Washington and that fell into its hands should have been in our possession. Even if for no other reason, this last one, in my judgment, should have decided the general that succeeded me in command to try an attack; and I flatter myself, even risking to appear presumptuous, that if I had been able to reach Thompson's as I wanted, victory would have returned to our troops within three days.

It was not without surprise that I later heard the news of the retrograde movement so precipitately undertaken contrary to my real desire. Allow my self-esteem a comparison, the odiousness of which shall fall upon he who first made it. The twentieth of April the greater part of the army that had crossed the Colorado was together. Two of its divisions were sufficiently numerous to have engaged the enemy and to help each other had it not been for a chain of unfortunate coincidences. We had had food, munitions, and other war supplies in plenty and even in excess of our needs. We had been victorious in every encounter; our line was covered both on its rear and on its flanks. Yet the moment I fell a prisoner the army retreated, the food became short, our positions were abandoned and the army concentrated itself two hundred leagues from the place where it should have been and where it had left six hundred prisoners in the most complete abandonment, entirely to their own resources. When did the army fulfill its object and its duties better?

I foresaw, therefore, the confusion of the moment among the troops of our army and I took advantage of the opportunity afforded by Houston's proposal, succeeding, as I have already stated, in giving the said army the time necessary for its reorganization as the result of an armistice that I concluded but which our troops used only to retreat unmolested.

All that was done in favor of the prisoners on the part of the general on whom the command fell was reduced to sending General Woll as emissary, not to conclude an armistice, or rather, to make one as it was proper, since a prisoner was the one who had drawn it up, but only to ask for instructions and to deliver the treaty in person. When that general was detained and treated without consideration for the mission on which he came, not even the slightest protest was made, and his treatment was completely ignored so that he had to depend only on the efforts of a general who was himself a prisoner to make himself respected. To that same general I gave instructions by word of mouth in order not to compromise him as to what should be done by the army according to my judgment. In this I counted, of course, on the fact that the enemy was not going to allow itself to be robbed of its triumph, consequently I gave the said general a paper which stated that credence should be given to whatever he said on my part. Nothing was thought of, however, except a retreat, their fear reaching such an extreme as to set free or allow the Texan prisoners that were in our army to the number of more than one hundred [20] to escape without trying to arrange an exchange for those who had fallen prisoners at San Jacinto, and even abandoning our sick, in such a way that the proximity of the army, its actions, the dignity of its commander who should not have been discouraged by a mishap, everything in short that might have encouraged those who were prisoners and enabled them to raise their voice in defence of Justice was wanting, and we were left to the mercy of the conquerors, an undisciplined mob although justly proud of so important but uncontested a triumph.

In all justice it must be confessed, however, that the Texan general, Sam Houston, is educated and is actuated by humanitarian sentiments. I am indebted to him for a treatment as decorous as the circumstances permitted while he was in Texas.

[20] "I sent an order to General Filisola on the 22nd of April to set them free, but can it ever be thought that this order was to be carried out without even trying an exchange, though unsuccessful? [Note of the original.]

and for my liberty after he returned from New Orleans where he went to have a wound that he received at San Jacinto treated. There were, nevertheless, before this solution, transactions of which I am going to speak, the obscure aspects of which have been used by critics in order to defame me.

The nation has seen in print the agreements that I signed at Velasco on the fourteenth of May, revealed only as a disgraceful weapon against me by an infamous betrayer who served in the office of my secretary, taken up and published by the papers that carried on a most advantageous and disloyal war against me as conclusive and irrefutable proof that I sacrificed everything to the pusillanimous terror, the cowardly fear of death. Neither my previous constant service in favor of the independence and liberty of Mexico, nor those that I had just rendered in Texas, not obligatory on my part, were able to outweigh the opinion of my adversaries with regard to an incredible report. As the facts were presented without considering the circumstances, without being aware of the unheard of exactions demanded by the officers of the government of Texas, the agreements were regarded as uncalled for. In short, as duty to one's country is as delicate as the honor that dictates it, by playing upon this chord so highly pitched among my fellow-citizens it has been possible to make my name sound in their ears that had just listened to my proclamation as benefactor of the country like that of a monster of ingratitude and infamy.

Nevertheless, to my part in the action of San Jacinto I have wished to add the principal testimony as to my actions after it, confident that the good judgment of my compatriots, once they read it will save me the greater part of the painful task of vindicating myself which, in itself, would involve involuntary self-praise. The proposals that were transmitted to me by the so-called Cabinet of Texas have doubtless been read, and the sight of them must have surely dissipated in great part, if not entirely, the immense amount of evil that was thought to be contained in the agreements of the fourteenth of May.

The Directory of Texas, let us call it thus, arbiters of my life and of six hundred Mexicans, wished to see our entire expeditionary force lay down its arms and become prisoners; that Generals Filisola, Gaona, Urrea, and Ramirez Sesma be considered by me and obliged to admit themselves confessed prisoners of the Texans; that they sign with me their infamy by offering, though free, not to take arms against Texas. I converted this idea into a personal promise on my part of not making war, one from which no prisoner can save himself. It was desired that my influence should be used upon the entire nation, armed in so just a struggle, to make it lay down its arms. I changed this proposal to a negative, that is, I promised not to use my influence for the continuation of the struggle. But do the Mexicans need my guidance in order to have a country, to love it, and to know how to defend it heroically? They wished the independence of Texas to be recognized from that very moment and the limits fixed; that a petition by the army should force the government to approve this transcendental proposal, leaving to the nation only the negotiation of a treaty of commerce, the prisoners taken at San Jacinto to remain as hostages. I brought this daring proposal to an honorable conclusion for me, one free of embarrassment for the nation. I did not even try to implicate any of the officers of the army in the matter. I honorably refused to recognize Texas as a nation or to determine its limits. I showed, it is true, a desire to terminate the struggle through friendly and peaceful means but I left the government free to judge if it was suitable to the nation, for if the recent and fateful retreat of our troops did not give me flattering hopes in warlike operations, I did not wish that the hope of the nation should end with mine. I did promise *to try* to get a hearing for the Texas Commissioners, but this in itself did not bind the government to receive them, nor if they were received did it have to accede to all their pretensions. I, in short, gave no other guarantee of my promises than my personal responsibility, but not with the official character of President of the Republic, for I was not acting in that capacity at that time. Neither did I pledge myself as a plenipotentiary of the government, much less as general-in-chief. My imprisonment, if I may express it that way, afforded me the one advantage of making it impossible for me to harm my country by my acts, or better said by my promises, even supposing I had been willing. If by my promises I did not save my unfortunate companions from their chains as I so ardently desired, having obtained my first desire, that they be considered prisoners of war, I saved their lives. Such was at least my idea of the alternative, characteristic of all games of chance, either to leave the promise to the discretion of those who accepted it, or to see if a promise so highly offensive in our case as the recognition of Texas would be fulfilled. The respect for private property and its restitution to the owners that I promised was not only useless but very different from the complete indemnification demanded.

In brief, I offered nothing in the name of the nation. In my own name I pledged myself to acts that our government could nullify and I received in exchange the promise of being set free without delay. Where is the treason? Where the pusillanimous cowardice I have been thought guilty of?

My voice has always been raised in support of the rights of my country and of my own honor and it is not necessary for me to give a detailed account to make it evident that a prisoner over whose head the sword of vengeance was suspended constantly could not, without putting aside all fear, have withstood the threat of the sword for twenty-two days and have flatly refused at the end of this time to subscribe to the most essential demands that formed the base of the pretensions for the clemency of his conquerors.

Such are, however, the stability of the government of Texas, its moral strength and its principles of righteousness that it feared to exercise them in public. It feared that the soldiers might destroy its work, overthrowing its power and, perhaps, making an attempt against those who claimed to be its depositories. For this reason it was necessary to stipulate the terms of my release in a secret treaty, as a result of this fear. Frequently such secret agreements hide great evils; and, the public being disposed to judge as fearful, terrible and astonishing that which is hidden from sight, it has been thought that in my case the mysterious agreement could hide only treason. In truth, that crime committed by a man whom his country has favored so lavishly, who has labored so faithfully for its glory, whose name is met at every turn in the history of Mexico, where it is mentioned with honor even by those who oppose him, would have been a great crime, terrible and unimaginable. However, this secret hid nothing of which I might be ashamed under the circumstances; but fatality had written that from the very failings of my enemies calumny should draw the venom with which to poison its arrows.

I should not have wasted so much time analyzing those agreements for I do not owe my liberty to them. It is true that their terms were partially put into effect, and as a result I was placed on board the *Invincible* on the first of June, but one hundred and thirty volunteers that arrived from New Orleans made the so-called *nation* break its pledge. One hundred and thirty volunteers demanded my death, and the government of Texas, whose troops were not attacked on the twenty-first of April because of fear on the part of three thousand men was obliged to give way before the ferocious and tumultuous petition of one hundred and thirty recruits from New Orleans. The moment that I was taken off the vessel and delivered into the hands of the military I asked pleadingly for my death, and at that same instant any obligation on my part entailed by the condition of my immediate release was broken also, and could not have been otherwise.

The subsequent acts of the Texans only served to confirm me in this opinion, universally recognized by the common law of peoples. I endured exposure to the cowardly insults and affronts of the soldier-like mob; I endured the closest confinement; I endured the severe vigilance of those who were most enraged against me, the prisoners that had escaped from Goliad; I endured a succession of attempts to assassinate me; I suffered them to place a heavy ball and chain upon me; and, lastly, on

the 30th of June, I suffered them to order me to march to Goliad
to be executed in the place where Fannin and his men had died.[21]

I saw death approaching without regret. The only regret
that I felt in addition to the sorrow of leaving my wife and my
children was the thought that Mexico was not happy. Notwithstanding, life was offered to me; and, convinced that its sacrifice
on the scaffold would not benefit my country, I listened to the
generous advice of the colonist, Stephen F. Austin, whom I had
favored in Mexico, and who, more grateful, on seeing me a
prisoner and at the point of death, remembered in Texas favors
infinitely smaller than those that had been forgotten entirely in
the capital, and decided to save me. The only means of saving
myself in his opinion (and my opinion could not be contrary to
his under the circumstances) was to invoke the name of the
President of the United States, Andrew Jackson.

His character, the conviction in which we have all lived and
which was confirmed more than ever, that the Texas War was
but a result of his policy, or at least, of his tolerance in sympathy
with the wishes of many of his citizens—an opinion that without
disguise the Texans themselves expressed; and lastly, the force
that a favor so marked as that which Austin proposed to me
carries with it, determined me to write a letter to that gentleman
on the fourth of July in the terms advised by Austin. In it I
flattered the favorite pretension of the Texans without risking
anything positively, stating that I was desirous of seeing the war
ended and of seeing Texas enter its claims to be a nation
through peaceful channels and negotiations. I flattered the distinguished gentleman whom I addressed by hinting the possibility
of this outcome if Mexico and the United States cooperated
mutually towards that end. The only question which I formally
stated in my letter was that he secure my liberty through his in-

[21] In his *Diario*, Santa Anna says nothing of the order for his execution
or march to Goliad. He merely states that on Houston's return he was
notified by him that he was free on condition that he pay a visit to General
Jackson. Genaro García, *Documentos*, II, 40.

fluence and by virtue of the now annulled agreement of the fourteenth of May which I again offered to renew.

A copy of this letter was delivered to our minister, Señor Gorostiza, by that government. This letter was published in the newspapers of the North, from one of which it was very poorly translated and printed in those of Mexico as the most shining proof of my treason. The Texas revolutionists whom I fought, the revolutionists of Mexico, who have defamed me, and the speculators of the North together with their sympathizers, all voice this opinion, a singular coincidence of which I cannot be ashamed. In spite of the loud protestations of my enemies, the judicious majority of my fellow-citizens will see in that document the results of an unavoidable necessity at the time it was written. They will see that the generalizations that appear favorable to the Texans do not exceed the bounds necessary to avoid the issue, proposing a peaceful solution as *possible* but nothing more. They will be convinced that on the way to the scaffold it was not prudent to display a vain boastfulness against those who had raised it; and they will agree, in short, that I could not have used any other language to ask a personal favor of General Jackson.

The terms in which he conceived his reply at the same time that they confirm how correct I was in addressing myself to that official prove that the general statements were erroneously taken for explicit demands, for, instead of acceding to the request to interpose his influence in behalf of my liberty—the only definite, clear and unmistakable object of my letter as I explained it—he replies by reminding me of my position, which I could not have ignored, refusing as an inevitable consideration in view of the circumstances, his interference in the affairs of Texas in the name of the United States. I do not know how such a pretension could be inferred from the statements in my letter. Thus, General Jackson, having erroneously understood my petition, has replied under a false assumption which my enemies have not stopped to examine but rather following in the same error as the President of the United States, they have made use of these statements as the basis for my denunciation.

A misfortune reduced me to the position of a prisoner in Texas; and this notorious fact should, in the light of sane criticism, make valueless whatever statements I may have made as to the freedom under which I celebrated the agreement of the 14th of May or as to my conviction of the futility of continuing the war, a conviction that cannot be arrived at correctly while in chains.

If the idea of the discouragement of the army during the first moments following the 21st of April forced me to agree to an armistice, subsequent events led me to believe that because of other obstacles, independent of the well-known valor of our soldiers, the war would not be renewed for some time. When speaking among foreigners of our resources and enthusiasm, I shall always believe it more decorous to declare myself convinced that it is not expedient to make use of our resources nor to allow our enthusiasm to have free play than to risk the slightest doubt as to the existence of the former, since that of the latter can never be doubted. I believe that the language I adopted on that occasion was the only one that could accomplish my object without dishonor to the nation.

And what advantage could have resulted from my expressing a desire that the war should continue, or even from my assertion that it would, when the army, without which it is impossible to wage war, had just undertaken a retreat? It was precisely because the hope of being able to continue the war at the time seemed to me so remote that I was obliged to adopt, as the only course left to me to secure my liberty, the declaration that I was convinced of the advisability of terminating the question peaceably by means of a treaty. Whatever might have been the true cause of the retreat of the expeditionary army as far as Matamoros, the Texans saw, in spite of their ill-dispelled fear after the recent victory, a possibility of such a conclusion, an idea that I thought I could take advantage of to put an end to my sufferings by merely flattering their hopes.

I acceded, therefore, to the idea of a treaty, not to be celebrated by me but by the nation; and that is what was stipulated
in the agreement of the fourteenth of May which I assured the
President, General Jackson, in my letter I was ready to fulfill.
The imminent evils I stated in that letter that I wished to avoid
were not those of war, for in spite of the false report of the
advance of our troops under the command of General Urrea, I
did not believe it would take place soon. Although I spoke of
deep concern for an early settlement, I took care not to allow
myself to be more explicit than to offer that I would try to
secure a hearing for the Texans before the government of our
country, as stipulated in the agreement, which is as far as my
duty went. I stated that if the friendship between Mexico and
the United States was enhanced, if both nations became interested
(and that alone and not the free President of one and the imprisoned General of the other could do it) in giving stability and
protection to Texas, it was evident that it would have to be as
an act of their free will. The moment I tried to get a hearing
for the commissioners of Texas, whether they were received or
not, my only pledge would cease. It is essential, therefore, to
fix our attention closely on the fact that the celebration of the
treaties that would give Texas being and stability could only be,
and was, presented by me as a *possibility,* and not as a certainty,
this being the most compromising point which can be cited
against my letter, and even this possibility, I said, could only be
the outcome of a national move prompted by humanitarian
sympathy for the prisoners who were on the threshold of the
scaffold after our troops retreated, and whose situation would
exercise a prodigious influence.

In the meanwhile Austin circulated my letter among the
Texans who considered my life valuable as a result of the hopes
with which I flattered them; and my march to Goliad was suspended; but the idea already disseminated among them of a possible agreement between Mexico and Texas, which they believed
guaranteed by the intervention of their protector, facilitated my
freedom which I secured later without, however, being bound

either by the agreements of May or the letter of the fourth of July. It has been shown how the agreements were annulled and how the reply given by General Jackson to my letter while it imputes to me ideas that I have not entertained, much less expressed, is for me a weapon of defense all the more powerful as it is the same with which I have been attacked.

It was written on the fourth of September and it is evident that the President of the United States believes that the principal object of my letter is to put an end to the disasters of civil war in Texas and to ask the intervention of the United States for that purpose. He believes that the agreements signed on the fourteenth of May were negotiated by me as a representative of Mexico and that I asked for the intervention of his country to uphold them. It is only necessary to read my letter in order to realize that it is a private letter in which I express my wishes of seeing the struggle terminated by peaceful negotiations but without reaching the ridiculous extreme of establishing such negotiations, leaving them to the nation. It is seen that my letter is addressed to an honorable man, beloved by the Texans, and very influential because of the position he occupied, to ask him to use his influence to secure my liberty, but not in an official capacity; that there is not a single word in it that suggests the intervention of the United States either for that purpose or in order to put an end to the war; and that it is nowhere asserted that in the agreements concluded I acted as a representative of Mexico, or that in order to fulfill them I requested the intervention of the Union or anything of the kind. In short, I shall always repeat that I asked only for the interposition of his personal influence in behalf of my liberty.

I cannot allow myself, however, to fail to show how unjustly a part of the hostility which the cabinet in Washington feels for our nation is attributed to me. It is a known fact that the diplomatic correspondence had assumed a very marked character of hatred and hard feelings. The conduct of some of the officials of the United States with regard to Texas was far from being as loyal and disinterested as might have been expected of the functionaries of a nation attached to ours by good faith and sincerity. As early as the 20th of June last, the Mexican minister was advised, through the Secretary of State, that, if a very long and unjust list of claims was not satisfied within a very limited period of time, he would return with the passports of his legation. Consideration was already being given to the alarming message of February last that took me so completely by surprise, since, in passing through the capital, I had just learned of that of December in which, by virtue of the report of the commission sent to Texas, and because of very pertinent considerations for the harmony and good faith due Mexico, the President did not hesitate to express his opinion against the recognition of Texas and to give the greatest assurance of a peaceful and friendly disposition towards my country. Why then turn to me in order to look for and determine the cause of a break between Mexico and the United States? Is it not true, national pride being hurt by the duplicity and the interested motives displayed by that cabinet in favor of the Texan rebels, that there has sprung up in the heart of every Mexican a noble resentment against the bad faith with which we have been treated?

Can it be doubted, after reading the communications published by our worthy minister, Señor Gorostiza, that to that fatal policy and that alone, without my connivance or concurrence, the hostile threat is due?

I have been fortunate amidst so many troubles in that the claim decreed by the Congress of the United States as a result of that alarming message, and which is soon to be presented is evoked by the diplomatic correspondence of Mexico, proving beyond a doubt that the war with which we are threatened has not been a machination of mine, and that, without my trip to Washington, everything that has happened would have happened.

At any rate, the end of my public career has arrived. If it is extremely painful to me that it has not been crowned by glory, if in its stead my military fame and all that can be pleasing and dear to a Mexican has been torn to shreds, if instead of a feeling of pity which the misfortunes of a prisoner well deserve, few of my enemies have failed to make fun of me to the extent of printing in the capital the writings of a Mirabeau Lamar and to speak of my death as an event worthy of national rejoicing, I have the consolation that my conscience affords me, assuring me that these misfortunes have not been deserved. If he who reads this writing with impartial attention, convinced of my innocence, does not consider me unworthy of being called a Mexican, I shall then be happy in my peaceful retreat. Herein is centered all my hope. A constitution has just been published; its ratification during my imprisonment has proved that the abolition of the old system was not the work of my influence. As I voluntarily take a pledge to the new law I elevate to Heaven my most sincere desire for national happiness under its rule. Peace, that precious gift of Heaven, superior to the dreams of optimism and the barbarous pleasure of vengeance, must be dearly appreciated and closely guarded by us as without it [there is no happiness possible].[22] Let me perish before the fatal day arrives in which the enemies of public order may gather the bitter disappointment of the realization that Mexico cannot be happy except in peace.

I am second to none in my desire for the welfare of my country. No one, I believe, can with greater justice claim to have been offended and insulted than I. I could have returned to the honorable position that was wrested from me, for even the most merciless of my enemies have turned their eyes towards me. Their vengeance against a defenceless man would be easy. The least disturbance, however, would be contrary to my invariable determination to preserve peace and, therefore, I have sacrificed everything: complaints, power, influence, all for her sake. My voice has been a continuous echo of my heart, exhorting my friends and my enemies to be reconciled. This is the only service, I believe, that I can now render my country. Time alone can tell its true worth. In the meantime, without forgetting that my duty is to fly to the national ranks whenever the nation is unfortunately attacked, I do not fear in this refuge either that my fellow-citizens will be unjust or that in recording the Texas

---

[22] A phrase is missing at this point in the text of the first copy printed in Veracruz and also in the one published by Genaro García. This omission makes the last sentence meaningless.

campaign history will make my country and my descendants ashamed of my actions.

Antº. Lopez Santa Anna [23]

MANGA DE CLAVO,
May 10, 1837.

[23] Antonio López de Santa Anna was born in Jalapa, June 13, 1792. His parents were of noble descent but poor. He received an education such as conditions in colonial days in Mexico permitted. Very early he showed a disposition for a military career. He enlisted as a cadet in a regiment at Veracruz, June 9, 1810. His promotion was rapid, for by 1821 he was a lieutenant-colonel in the Spanish army and was made commander of a district near Veracruz. He enjoyed the friendship of Field Marshal José Dávila and of the viceroy. Notwithstanding, he declared himself for the *Plan de Iguala*, March 28, 1821. He was instrumental in bringing about the fateful interview between Iturbide and O'Donoju that resulted in the treaty of Cordoba and gave the final triumph to the Mexican Revolution of 1810. When the national government was established, however, he was only promoted to colonel, while many others received higher honors. He resented this action of Iturbide. In October, 1822, as reward for his services during the mutiny of Veracruz, he was made a brigadier general. In December of the same year he took up arms against the government of Iturbide and launched himself on his colorful career which was to lead him to the presidency of Mexico six times only to be deposed and banished three distinct times. He returned to Mexico after his last exile in 1874 and two years later died in Mexico City, a broken and forgotten man. He is buried in an unpretentious grave in the Tepeyac Cemetery, just outside of the national shrine of Guadalupe. For a popular account of the life of this man who exercised so profound and sinister an influence on the history of México, see C. R. Wharton, *Life of General Santa Anna*.

DOCUMENTS

No. 1

MINISTRY OF FINANCE
First Section

His Excellency, the President *ad interim* of the Mexican Republic has transmitted to me the following decree:

The President *ad interim* of the Mexican Republic to its inhabitants, know that Congress has passed the following decree:

"The government is authorized to raise as much as five hundred thousand pesos in cash by the least burdensome means, this sum to be used exclusively for the expense of the war.—*José M. del Castillo*, President.—*José de Jesús D. y Prieto*, Secretario.—*José Rafael Olaguíbel*, Secretario."

I command, therefore that it be printed, published and circulated for its due observance.—National Palace of Mexico, November 23rd., 1835.

I transmit it to you for your information and guidance.

GOD AND LIBERTY
VALLEJO

MEXICO, November 23, 1835.

No. 2

MINISTRY OF FINANCE
First Section

Proposals made by the undersigned to His Excellency, General Antonio López de Santa Anna, President, to relieve the needs of the Army of Operations under his command:

1st. I will deliver in cash.............	200,000 *pesos*
Likewise in printed bonds.........	200,000 "
	400,000 *pesos*

2nd. As payment for this amount there shall be delivered to me:

First. The total proceeds from the forced loans of the departments of San Luis, Zacatecas, Guanajuato and Guadalajara.

Second. The war subsidy of the four said departments.

Third. This loan shall be liquidated four months from date, the certificates of the commissaries of the four departments showing the amounts received, and the balance still due to be considered as cash, allowing me an equal amount on the printed bonds. The total amount due me shall be made up by warrants on the maritime customs houses of Tampico, Veracruz and Matamoros, to be taken as specie and in full payment of all kinds of duties without requiring any cash. The bonds of which I speak in the first proposal will be delivered to the sub-commissary in this city before the expiration of the said four months.

Fourth. Of the one hundred and forty-seven thousand *pesos* which I am presenting in sworn warrants issued arbitrarily by the officials of the customs house of Matamoros before the arrival of the order of the government on the subject, evident from the warrants themselves, the said customs house shall credit the firm of Messrs. Rubio Brothers and Company to the amount of forty-seven thousand *pesos* cash. San Luis Potosí, December 15, 1835.—Joaquín M. Errazu.

General Headquarters at San Luis Potosí, December 16, 1835.

Accept the present proposals. Inform the supreme government through the Minister of Finance for its approval. Issue instructions to the commissaries of the four departments for the fulfillment of their part of the contract. Señor Errazu may deliver without delay the two hundred thousand *pesos* which he offers to the subcommissary of this city.—*Antonio López de Santa Anna.*

This is a copy of the original.

MEXICO, May 8, 1837.

DOMINGO DUFFO

No. 3

MINISTRY OF FINANCE

Most Excellent Sir:

His Excellency, the President *ad interim,* apprised by your communication of the 19th last and the copies inclosed of the contract celebrated with D. Joaquín María Errazu, agreeable to which Señor Errazu is to deliver two hundred thousand *pesos* in cash and an equal amount in printed bonds, subject to the terms and conditions expressed; and aware of the orders which you have issued on the subject, he has seen proper to approve the said contract and to reissue the corresponding instructions to the commissioners of Zacatecas, Guadalajara, Guanajuato and San Luis that they may hold the amounts collected as a result of the forced loans and the special war subsidy at the disposal of those designated by Your Excellency without using them for any other purpose. The officials of the maritime customs houses of Veracruz, Tampico and Matamoros have been likewise instructed to honor all orders that may be drawn upon them agreeable to the contract. The officials of the last customs house named have already been instructed to honor to the amount of forty-seven thousand *pesos,* the one hundred and forty-seven thousand issued as sworn warrants by that office without demanding cash. I have the honor of having replied to your mentioned note restating the sincere expression of my respect.

GOD AND LIBERTY
VALLEJO

MEXICO, December 31, 1835.

To His Excellency, President of the Republic, the General-in-Chief of the Army of Operations.

(This was transmitted to Sr. Rubio, Jan. 25.)

No. 4

Commissary of War
of the
Army of Operations

Most Excellent Sir:

Upon my arrival, last year, in San Antonio de Béxar, on the 10th of March, Your Excellency immediately instructed me to make an inventory of the goods that had been taken from the colonists when the army occupied that city and which were deposited in the house adjoining that of Your Excellency, in order to determine their value and place them on sale, the proceeds to be applied to the needs of the commissary general of the army. I informed Your Excellency that, since my illness prevented me from carrying out your instructions, I would have to commission the clerk, D. José Robelo, to execute your orders. At the same time I asked Your Excellency to have this act legalized by the presence of a person of your confidence who should witness the inventory in order that detractors might have no occasion at any time to mar the good reputation I have earned in the public service.

Your Excellency acceded to this just request, appointing your secretary, D. Ramón Martínez Caro, for the purpose; and completely satisfied all my desires by witnessing the inventory personally and helping to appraise the above mentioned goods. These amounted in all to three thousand five hundred ninety-four *pesos* and six *reales,* including a barrel and a half of pecans as shown in the corresponding balance sheet.

The prices fixed on some of the goods being too high, Your Excellency later ordered verbally that the corresponding reductions be made. These were specified in the new inventory which D. Nicolás Arredondo made before he left. He was appointed by Your Excellency together with D. José Terroba to sell the said goods. The lack of time, the detailed character of the inventories and the desire not to delay my reply prevent me at this time from enclosing a copy of them, but I offer to send one as soon as possible. You may rest assured that any charge that may be brought against Your Excellency on account of this matter is dissipated before hand, for in compliance with one of the duties of my office, I transmitted the monthly balance sheets of the commissary department of the army to the Minister of Finance who made the following notation on the one corresponding to March last: "Informed by D. José Terroba of the goods taken from the enemy at this (that) place, sold by order of His Excellency, the President, and the proceeds having been applied to the expenses of the army, due credit has been entered for one thousand nine hundred fourteen *pesos,* one *real,* nine grains."

I took charge of the balance, amounting to one thousand six hundred eighty *pesos,* four *reales,* and three grains, which came in the following April, and Your Excellency will see how they were spent and by what branches of the army in the general reports which I am preparing agreeable to an order of the supreme government. I shall have the honor of transmitting a copy of these reports to you in compliance with your letter of the 11th of March last in which you ask me to give you an account of the expenses of the army from the time Your Excellency took charge of it at San Luis Potosí until the engagement of San Jacinto. To prove the legal expenditure of the public money will be an added pleasure to me, for I flatter myself that no fault will be found in any of the items listed, down to the smallest of them.

As to whether General Castrillón and Colonel Batres, deceased, paid into the commissary general of the army certain sums that were to bear four percent interest monthly, and if so, why, I must inform Your Excellency that Señor Batres did not make any such deposit; but Señor Castrillón paid in a thousand dollars of his own, agreeable to an order of Your Excellency of January 1st of last year, dated in the capital of the department of San Luis Potosí. This payment was in the character of a loan, with a monthly premium of four percent for a period of four months in conformity with the law of November 5th, 1835, and it had a special mortgage on the share of the government in the Fresnillo transaction and on other securities listed in the general provisions stated by the second article of the said law, all subject to the approval of the Supreme Government, whom I notified on the 2nd of the said month. On the 9th it was approved by the Government as shown by the communication sent to me by the Minister of Finance.

Subject to the same terms, on the same date, and by previous order of Your Excellency, D. Juan María Errazu, a merchant of San Luis Potosí, turned in six thousand *pesos,* the transaction receiving a similar approval from the Executive. This amount also belonged to General Castrillón, deceased, as shown by the letter which he delivered to me before he left Béxar with Your Excellency. In this letter Señor Errazu declares that the money and its interest belong to the above mentioned general for which reason I gave him a receipt on the 30th of March last in order that he might try to collect both of these sums and their interest from the government, since the commissary of the army was unable to pay them because of its notorious lack of funds.

I have replied to your esteemed note of the 26th of March last with all due consideration and respect.

GOD AND LIBERTY

José Reyes López

Mexico, April 5, 1837.

To His Excellency, General Antonio López de Santa Anna, President and Benefactor of his Country.

No. 5

Ministry of War and Marine
Central Section
Desk No. 1.

Circular

Most Excellent Sir:

Under this date I have notified all commandants-general and the principal governors and political chiefs of departments and territories as follows:

"The supreme government has positive information that in the United States of the North public meetings are being held with the avowed purpose of arming expeditions against the Mexican nation, of helping those who have rebelled against this government, of encouraging civil war, and of bringing upon our territory all those evils attendant upon civil war. Some expeditions have already been organized in that republic—our former friend—such as the one conducted by the traitor José Antonio

Mejía to Santa Anna [24] in Tamaulipas and others on their way to the coast of Texas. All kinds of war supplies have been sent to the said coast; and, due to this censurable procedure, the rebellious colonists have been able to carry on a war against the nation that has showered so many favors upon them. The supreme government has the most positive assurance that these acts, censured by the wise laws of the United States of the North, have merited the consequent disapproval of that government with which we maintain the best understanding and an unalterable harmony. The speculators and adventurers have succeeded in evading the punishment that awaited them in that republic, but we hope that it will still overtake them. His Excellency, the President *ad interim,* who cannot see with indifference these aggressions that attack the sovereignty of the Mexican nation, has seen proper to command that the following articles be observed with regard to them. 1st. All foreigners who may land in any port of the republic or who enter it armed and for the purpose of attacking our territory shall be treated and punished as pirates, since they are not subjects of any nation at war with the republic nor do they militate under any recognized flag. 2nd. Foreigners who introduce arms and munitions by land or by sea at any point of the territory now in rebellion against the government of the nation for the purpose of placing such supplies in the hands of its enemies shall be treated and punished likewise. I have the honor of transmitting these instructions to you for their publication and observance."

I have the honor of transmitting the foregoing circular to Your Excellency for your information, assuring you of my sincere affection.

GOD AND LIBERTY

José María Tornel

Mexico, December 30, 1835.

To His Excellency, the President, General-in-Chief of the Army of Operations, Antonio López de Santa Anna, Benefactor of his Country.

---

[24] A small town in Tamaulipas, located near the coast.

No. 6

MINISTER OF WAR AND MARINE
Central Section
Desk No. 1.
Division of Operations

Most Excellent Sir:

On the 19th Inst., the fort of Goliad was abandoned by the enemy after an attempt to fight this division. The said fortress is, therefore, at the disposal of the supreme government. The leader, Fannin, and his companions with more than three hundred soldiers (who capitulated) [25] that were garrisoning the said fortress are likewise at its disposal. When these men left their fortifications, they carried with them nine pieces of artillery, about one thousand rifles, and plenty of ammunition. With a little more than three hundred men, infantry and cavalry, I overtook them at the Plain of Perdido. I drove them out of a fine live oak thicket which they defended by a lively cannonade, and attacked them in spite of the superiority of their force, equipment, and artillery—I myself being entirely deprived of the latter. The engagement was hotly contested; and, because of circumstances which I shall explain to Your Excellency in detail whenever opportunity offers, it was dangerous for us. But the valor of our army was brilliantly displayed in the engagement. When the light of day failed, I gathered my force in columns but remained facing the enemy, less than two hundred paces distant. Thus we spent the night, and the following day, yesterday, as soon as two six-pounders I had ordered from Goliad arrived, I placed my battery one hundred and sixty paces from the enemy.

[25] There is a contradiction here. Santa Anna emphatically states in the *Manifiesto* that there was no capitulation. Furthermore, Urrea in his *Diario*, published immediately after the *Manifiesto*, says "the phrase in the parenthesis has been altered, for I wrote *Que se titulaban* [who called themselves such] and there is a vast difference between the two phrases evident from their very meaning, but specially so, given the circumstances." This document is reproduced in the appendix to the *Diario* under the same number. It was published in the *Diario del Gobierno*, México, April 13, 1836, and also in the *Alcance* of *El Mercurio*, Matamoros, April 3, 1836. In both instances the phrase in question appears as "que se titulaban."

I prepared for a new attack; but the enemy, who had strengthened his position during the night by digging a rectangular trench, being already intimidated by the intrepidity of our soldiers, surrendered at discretion the moment we renewed our fire as shown by the enclosed document relative to the proposals made by the enemy officers and the reply I gave them. My terms having been accepted, they are all in my power with their arms and a large supply of munitions.

In spite of the fatigue of the troops, I marched immediately with two pieces of artillery to this place to keep the enemy from reenforcing it to obstruct our crossing of the river. The movement was very opportune, for I met a party of about eighty men of the enemy already here. They fled the moment I ordered a charge upon them, just as I was entering the town. The party took refuge in the thick woods along the river and made good its escape, but another party of twenty which was coming to this place fell into my hands. I took seven of them prisoners, the rest, together with their officer and his aide, having been killed in the skirmish.

Early tomorrow morning I shall occupy a private port on the La Baca lake which is frequented by the enemy. As I have been assured that the food supplies are kept there, and that a ship was seen in the port of La Baca day before yesterday, I may find some troops at that place.

There is another ship anchored at Cópano, and I have learned from two Americans who were taken at the mission of Refugio by the troops left there that it has eighty men aboard and some food supplies. I have issued instructions to make certain of everything but I am not very hopeful, for we do not have a single boat to our name.

At this place I have taken twenty barrels of flour belonging to the enemy, as well as other things, of all of which I shall render a report later.

Our active operations should be continued, I believe, unless Your Excellency decides otherwise, because the enemy seems to be intent on fortifying itself at the Colorado. For this reason I have sent instructions to-day to Colonel Juan Morales at Goliad, a copy of which I am accompanying to Your Excellency. I shall act in accordance with the resolutions of Your Excellency and agreeable to circumstances, without compromising the honor of the nation or that of the army.

It only remains for me now to commend, in general, the

bravery and daring of the gallant officers and soldiers who, with so much honor and courage, added luster to the characteristic valor of the Mexican army in the brilliant engagement of the 19th.   Immediately upon the surrender of the enemy, their fury was changed to the most admirable indulgence.   This show of generosity after a hotly contested engagement is worthy of the highest commendation, and I can do no less than to commend it to Your Excellency, at the same time begging you to have due regard for the families of the brave combatants that fell in defense of the rights of their country.   I shall soon send Your Excellency the details of the action.

I congratulate Your Excellency and the supreme government for the triumphs obtained by the army under your command in this most just and honorable war.

I again present to Your Excellency my most distinguished considerations of affection and respect.

GOD AND LIBERTY.—Victoria, March 21st., 1836.— *José Urrea.*

To His Excellency, the President, Antonio López de Santa Anna, General-in-Chief of the Army of Operations.

This is a copy.   Mexico, March 9, 1837.

IGNACIO DEL CORRAL

COLONEL FANNIN'S CAPITULATION ON THE COLETO

March 20th, 1836

The original, of which this is a reproduction, was discovered in the Archives of the War Department in Mexico City by Professor Eugene C. Barker, of the University of Texas, and with his permission, is now reproduced for the first time.

[Handwritten Spanish text reproduced below:]

Rendicion de la fuerza que se hallaba en Goliad á las ordenes del S. D. James W. Fannin Jr.

Articulo 1º. Habiendo puesto la tropa Mexicana á distancia de ciento sesenta pasos la batería y amontado á romper sus fuegos, pusimos una bandera blanca, y al momento vinieron el Coronel D. Juan Morales, Coronel D. Mariano Salas y el Teniente Coronel de Ingenieros D. Juan José Holzinger y les propusimos medianos á discreción á lo que quedaron conformes

Articulo 2º. Que á los Heridos y al comandante Fannin sean tratados con toda la consideración posible Proponiendoles el entregar todas las armas

Articulo 3.º Todo el destacamento sera tratado como
prisioneros de Guerra y puestos á disposic.ⁿ
del Supremo Gno

Campo sobre el coleto entre Guadalupe y
la Bahia Marzo 20/836   B.C. Wallace Com.

Approved   J.m. Chadwick Adjt.
Com.

M Fannin
J⁰ Col Com.

Como cuando se puso la Vandera blanca p.ʳ el
enemigo mandé manifestar el gefe a ella: que no
tendria mas acomodam.ᵗᵒ que el de q.ᵉ se rindiera á
discrecion; sin otra circunstancia y se convino en
ello p.ʳ conducto de los S.S. gefes q.ᵉ quedan expre-
sad₂, no tiene lugar los otros pedidos
q.ᵉ hacen lo q.ᵉ suscriven esta rendicion: así lo he manifestado á ellos
y quedaron conformes, pues ni devo ni
puedo ^ ninguna Conceder otra cosa.

José d'uría

MINISTRY OF WAR AND MARINE
        Central Section
        Desk No. 1.

Surrender of the force at Goliad under the command of James W. Fannin

Art. 1. The Mexican troops having placed their battery one hundred and sixty paces from us and the fire having been renewed, we raised a white flag; Colonel Juan Morales, Colonel Mariano Salas, and Lieutenant Colonel of Engineers Juan José Holzinger came immediately. We proposed to surrender at discretion and they agreed.

Art. 2. The commandant Fannin and the wounded shall be treated with all possible consideration upon the surrender of all their arms.

Art. 3. The whole detachment shall be treated as prisoners of war and shall be subject to the disposition of the supreme government.

Camp on the Coleto between the Guadalupe and La Bahía, March 20, 1836.—B. C. Wallace, commandant.—I. M. Chadwick, Aide.—approved, James W. Fannin.

Since, when the white flag was raised by the enemy, I made it known to their officer that I could not grant any other terms than an unconditional surrender and they agreed to it through the officers expressed, those who subscribe the surrender have no right to any other terms. They have been informed of this fact and they are agreed. I ought not, cannot, nor wish [26] to grant any other terms.—*José Urrea.*

This is a copy. México, March 7, 1837.

IGNACIO DEL CORRAL

No. 7

Most Excellent Sir:

One of the strongest causes for the resentment, whose fatal effects I was on the point of suffering in my captivity while a prisoner of the Texans, was the assertion that a capitulation [27]

[26] The terms of surrender are reproduced also in Urrea's *Diario,* but the last phrase "nor wish" is omitted. It reads "I ought not, nor can I, grant any other terms."

[27] This debated question has caused much hard feeling and misunderstanding. The truth of the matter seems to be that Fannin and his men proposed to surrender on terms; that these were not accepted by Urrea, who nullified all the proposals by his note added at the end of the said terms; and that, due to the fact that all the negotiations were conducted through an

had been drawn up before the surrender of Fannin and his men at Goliad and that in violation of its terms they had been executed. This assertion was common not only among the Texans but in many papers of the United States and even in some of the capital. Although the official report of General José Urrea, published and printed in various papers, belies such a statement, I shall deem it a great favor for the supreme government to order Colonels Juan Morales and Mariano Salas and Lieut. Col. Juan José Holzinger to declare and explain before the competent authorities everything that happened, giving testimony in due form, since they were the mediators in the surrender. In case that from their declarations it should appear that some agreement guaranteeing the life of the prisoners was signed, let them declare whether, officially or unofficially, I was ever informed of it. If I had heard of such an agreement at the time it would have been scrupulously investigated; and if its existence had been proven, even though celebrated without authority, I would have explained the circumstances to Congress and obtained, perhaps, a pardon for those unfortunate wretches.

Likewise it is said that the execution of those prisoners was carried out in an inhumane and cruel manner, shooting them without order or concert, in such a way that some were able to escape. These formed part of the guard that kept watch over me for many days. The commandant at Goliad, Lieut. Col. José Nicolás de la Portilla, is responsible for the cruel and inhumane manner of carrying out the execution to the nation, to the world, and to God. I do not doubt that, since its own honor is involved, the supreme government will also order an investigation of his acts, advising me as to the findings.

I have made war like a soldier. My pride is founded on my never having soiled victory with murder, and my having been always adjudged humane and just, as I am in fact. If during the last campaign, one in which we were not fighting against a recognized nation, I was forced by law and by the strict orders of the supreme government to apply to the delinquents a penalty which though severe was legal and from whose application I could not excuse myself, I am none the less sensitive to the attacks made upon my good reputation, one that I believe I deserve. I flatter myself that the president will accede to my petition out of consideration for me, for the army, and for the nation in order to help me clear myself of this accusation, and

interpreter, many were left under the impression that the surrender had been on terms, and not unconditionally.

⁺o blot out a stain that involves the whole nation. I, therefore,
beg Your Lordship to communicate this petition to His
Excellency.

I reiterate the assurances of my esteem.

GOD AND LIBERTY

Antonio López de Santa Anna

Manga de Clavo, May, 1837.

To His Excellency, the Minister of War and Marine.

No. 8

Ministry of War and Marine
Army of Operations

Most Excellent Sir:

The army of operations under my command being already
on its march to Béxar, which I expect to occupy before fifteen
days, I am going to find myself embarrassed if the supreme
government does not send me opportunely the necessary instructions as to the policy that I am to observe in dealing with the
colonies after order has been restored. I believe, therefore, that
it is necessary for the executive, together with the legislative body,
to give its attention to the reorganization of the government of
those colonies without delay; and that the instructions sent to
me ought to be definite, clear and ample in order that when the
time comes I may act in the most convenient manner for our
national interests. Otherwise we will have gained but little by
the painful march which our army has undertaken; and the large
sums that have been spent, and must be spent, will go for nothing
if we fail to take this splendid opportunity presented to us to
insure the integrity of the territory of the republic, unfortunately
neglected for such a long time that to-day its conservation is
costing us ten times more than if we had looked after it more
opportunely. With these considerations in view and moved by
the deepest concern for the propriety of the measures that may
be adopted I will proceed to explain briefly the points I believe
ought to be kept in mind in view of the experience I have acquired concerning this country.

The campaign being over, it is but natural that the causes
that gave rise to it be analyzed. As it is evident from these that

it was the colonists who unjustly provoked it, and it is a known fact, on the other hand, that in war the aggressor is responsible for the consequences, it seems certain that the rebels of Texas will have to pay the expenses incurred by the march of the army to the frontier. How, then, must the payment of this debt due necessarily to the nation, be met? Upon this point it is necessary that I be given a definite answer. The next question that arises is what shall be done with the prisoners, Mexicans or Texans, who are taken either in action or by capitulation or by unconditional surrender? What shall be done with the property of these and that of their families? What shall be the fate of those colonists, Anglo-Americans or Europeans, who have not taken an active part in the revolution? Will they be left on the frontier and on the coast, or will their property be appraised and other vacant lands or money given them as compensation? There are also many foreigners who have introduced themselves without passports or permission from the constituted authorities of the republic, and these, in my opinion, should be treated as invaders, or at least, they should be immediately expelled from Mexican territory.

There is a considerable number of slaves in Texas also, who have been introduced by their masters under cover of certain questionable contracts, but who according to our laws should be free. Shall we permit those wretches to moan in chains any longer in a country whose kind laws protect the liberty of man without distinction of cast or color? Here are some points that it is important to solve beforehand and upon which I wish definite instructions to be dictated in order not to fall again in error as when the Anglo-Americans were permitted to colonize in Texas. In my judgment, those lands have a recognized value both in America and in Europe and there is no need of giving them to foreigners when we ourselves are capable of settling them. Military colonies such as those established by Russia in Siberia, by England in East India, and even by Spain itself in this country would be the most convenient for Texas, in my opinion. It would also be opportune for the national Congress to occupy itself in forming a plan, instead of drawing up a new colonization law, by which the salaries of both civil and military employees might be capitalized by those who chose to do so, each one receiving two-thirds in land and one-third in silver to encourage the establishment of settlements. It is understood that the government will take proper steps to counteract any abuses

and to promote the desired end. From such a plan the nation
would reap many advantages, it seems to me, the first one being
a decrease of the annual budget; the second, the population of
Texas by Mexicans; and the third (perhaps the most important)
the preservation of the integrity of our territory. Let it not be
said that there would be no industrious Mexicans capable of
establishing themselves in the confines of our frontier, for while
on my way from Mexico to this place I have observed in all the
country states and cattle ranches the greatest desire to go to the
frontier on the part of the poor and hard-working people who
are, to a great extent, mostly farmers and herders. The riff-
raff of our great cities would, of course, be incapable of undertaking such an enterprise both because they are accustomed to
a different life and because, unfortunately, they are too demoralized. I do not believe that this class, in spite of its poverty, can
be used for anything but the establishment of manufacturing
enterprises in the future.

If both civil and military officials who capitalize their salaries
according to the proposed plan are obliged, therefore, to settle
their land with Mexicans, the result will be that every official and
his family who goes to Texas will bring with him a multitude of
industrious and useful settlers. Otherwise, if Texas is settled
entirely by Europeans, or if it is left unpopulated, it will be
necessary to maintain a large number of troops there, constantly
exposed in the first case to continuous plottings, for after all
foreigners, whatever be their nationality, more readily take on
the customs and interests of the neighboring nation than ours,
especially when they find themselves such a long distance from
the government of their new allegiance. In the second place, our
troops would find themselves without the necessary food supplies
as a result of the want of settlers. In any case, I am firmly convinced that we ought not to risk allowing either Anglo-American
or European colonists to remain on the frontier, much less along
our coastline. Even if some of those settled there did not take
part in the present Texas revolution, a rare coincidence indeed,
prudence warns that they be removed to the interior of the republic in order not to expose ourselves, as at present, to the sad
experiences of our inadvertence, a lesson that is costing us so
dearly. It should be added to this that the wars waged by the
savage tribes in the frontier departments are encouraged by the
colonists who buy the stolen booty from the said tribes, giving
them in exchange arms and munitions. In this manner they

carry on a trade at the expense of the Mexicans which though wicked is nevertheless very lucrative to them. These are considerations that, in my judgment, the supreme government must present to the legislative body when the definite policy in regard to Texas is formulated. All of them could easily be enlarged upon by the numerous details of our sad experiences. In the future it should be kept in mind that all foreigners admitted into the territory of Texas ought to be required, in addition to their compliance with all other requisites of our laws, to reside for at least ten years in that territory and hold title to well-defined property before they can hold public office. Otherwise, it will not be possible to avoid the introduction of evil foreigners who will contaminate those already established in the country with their revolutionary ideas. The execution of the plan proposed will involve but a small portion of the territory of Texas. What shall be done with the rest of the vacant lands of that vast and beautiful province? Supposing that the territory adjoining the frontier and that along the coast is settled strictly by Mexicans as I have indicated, I would be of the opinion that the rest of the lands be surveyed in acres or *fanegas,* a Spanish unit of measure with which we are acquainted and which we understand better. This done, an agency to be known as the *land office* should be opened, such as that of the United States of America, which constitutes one of the principal sources of income of that republic. In that country, the minimum price per acre, as provided by a decree of Congress, taking it on an average, that is to say, of the best and the poorest, is ten *reales.* Why, then, could we not sell a *fanega,* the equivalent of the acre, for a peso, when our lands are known to be superior to theirs in every respect? I am convinced that it could be done; and I believe that, if the sale of those lands was decreed, the nation would not only discover new resources to replenish its exhausted public treasury, but would be able, at the same time, to carry our civilization to those far away places, with which, on the other hand, frequent communication could easily be maintained through the Gulf of Mexico. If we are to judge by the printed maps and the accounts of some of the travelers who have crossed Texas in different directions, its territory must include at least one billion *fanegas.* From this fact alone, its importance is evident. But in order to neutralize the influence that Europeans who acquire lands may exercise, disregarding the Anglo-Americans who must be entirely excluded, it would be advisable, for example, not to sell to the French settlers more than five million *fanegas*, a similar amount to English settlers, a little more, perhaps, to Germans. No limit need be placed on those nations where our language is spoken, for no Columbian, or Cuban, or Canary Islander, or Spaniard would be very anxious to settle in our country. There is nothing to lose in such a plan, but there is much to gain. Why, then, should we not try to put it into execution? If it answers our purpose, that is to say, if definite advantages result to the nation from its operation, we may apply it to the Californias, New Mexico, Colima, Coatzacoalco, etc., and by these means, at the same time that we would increase our population, we would increase the resources of the nation without giving away its lands or mortgaging still further the strained credit of the country. The plan is feasible, for the lands of Texas already command a definite market value everywhere as evidenced by the last revolution, undertaken in the main for the purpose of speculation with its lands. It is for Congress, therefore, to ponder over such a measure, upon which I do not believe I ought to be more explicit in consideration of the well-known wisdom of its members.

I will now discuss another point, perhaps the most important under the present circumstances. I say under the present circumstances because upon its solution depends, perhaps, the amount of resistance offered by the rebellious Texans, whose interests are involved. I want to refer to the grants made by the legislature of the state to various individuals, both Mexicans and foreigners.[28] How must these grants be regarded? As forfeited by the rebellion of the grantees, or as annulled by this act? Is there any possible right that legalizes the sale of lands that has been made in the United States and that gives title to the buyer though he has not complied with the requisites of the Colonization law? I do not think so; but at this time, I believe that it is very important for congress to make a declaration on this matter, or at least to give me detailed instructions in order that I may not be embarrassed in reviewing any of these grants. I must also consult the government about several tribes that have migrated from the United States into our territory and that could be advantageously used by the republic if lands were

[28] Immediately prior to the Texas Revolution, a number of large grants were made as the result of two acts of the legislature of Coahuila y Tejas, whose constitutionality was questioned by the national government. For a full account see E. C. Barker, "Land Speculation as a Cause of the Texas Revolution," *Texas State Historical Quarterly*, X, No. 1, 76-96.

assigned to them. One of these tribes, the Cherokee, rendered important services to the nation in 1827; and it holds, as I understand, the solemn promise of the government to give them lands upon which to establish themselves, a promise that has not been fulfilled up to the present. What shall be done in regard to these tribes? Are they to be left without any definite agreement, exposing ourselves by that very fact to their hostility? Or shall we request them to leave the country? All of this, I repeat, must be solved ahead of time if we are not to walk blindly. On the other hand I will do everything that I can to secure the best possible solution, but without the help of the government and congress I may, perhaps, find myself in an embarrassing situation.

As a tribute to justice, I believe I am duty bound, before finishing this letter, to suggest to the government the convenience and advisability of establishing a land bounty for those officers and soldiers who may voluntarily want to remain in Texas, making such grants only to those that may be deemed advisable. It seems unnecessary for me to emphasize the utility of such a measure, for it is evident on the face of it, that the further removed a military man is from his family and those comforts he has a right to expect, the greater the effort that should be made to keep him pleased. Nothing that may contribute to this end should be omitted for the highest success of the mission intrusted to him depends upon it. I believe that a square league for the staff officers, half a league for other officers and a *solar* for each soldier would be enough for the purpose. The amount, in my opinion, is unimportant, the thing that matters is that bounties be established. I will not finish this letter without calling the attention of the supreme government very particularly to the conclusion of the treaty of limits with the United States of America which has so often miscarried and which is so important to bring to an early termination. The extraordinary mission which, as I understand, is going to Washington will offer doubtlessly a good opportunity of securing the desired end, in view of the known wisdom of the negotiator that has been chosen.[29] The march of the army towards the frontier on the other hand will facilitate the demarcation of the boundary line.

The statement on the part of the president of the United States of America that it will be useless to extend the time limit stipulated at the last negotiation celebrated with Mexico two years ago should not be taken, in my opinion, as an excuse.

[29] The extraordinary mission sent to the United States was headed by M. E. Gorostiza, a very able diplomat.

This is all that occurs to me as worthy of being presented to
the supreme government relative to Texas, surrounded as I am
by numerous duties. I hope that the points suggested will immediately be taken under consideration and submitted, if necessary, to the legislative body.

I again present to you the assurances of my personal
esteem.

GOD AND LIBERTY

ANTONIO LÓPEZ DE SANTA ANNA

General headquarters, Villa de Guerrero, February 16, 1836.

To His Excellency, the secretary of War and Marine, General José María Tornel.

This is a copy. Mexico, March 7, 1837.

No. 9 [30]

MINISTRY OF WAR AND MARINE
Central Division
Desk No. 1

Most Excellent Sir:

Considering the Villa de San Felipe de Austin a suitable
point from which to direct the subsequent operations of the army

[30] This document is followed by twenty-five letters designated numerically
in the first edition of the *Manifiesto,* but alphabetically in the Genaro García
reprint. Since most of these letters are unimportant, adding little informa-
tion; and since many of them are available in English they have been omitted
in the present translation. They are: (A) Santa Anna to the Minister of
War, Béxar, March 28, 1836; (B) Santa Anna to Ramírez y Sesma, Béxar,
March 8; (C) Santa Anna to Sesma, Béxar, March 23; (D) Sesma to Santa
Anna, Rio Colorado, March 25; (E) Santa Anna to Sesma, Béxar, March 29;
(F) Houston to Burnet, April 25; (G) Santa Anna to Filisola, San Jacinto,
April 22; (H) Santa Anna to Filisola, San Jacinto, April 22; (I) Santa Anna
to Filisola, same date; (J) Filisola to Santa Anna, San Bernardo, April 27;
(K) Santa Anna to Filisola, San Jacinto, April 30; (L) Treaty of Velasco,
May 14; (M) Public Treaty, same date; (N) Private Treaty, same date; (O)
Letters of Seguin and Ampudia published in the *Telegraph,* Sept. 21, 1836;
(P) Santa Anna to Burnet, Velasco, May 17; (Q) Burnet to Santa Anna,
Velasco, May 20; (R) Farewell of Santa Anna, Velasco, June 1st; (S)
Santa Anna to Captain of the *Invincible,* June 4; (T) Santa Anna to Burnet,
Velasco, June 4; (U) Burnet to Santa Anna, same date; (V) Santa Anna
to Burnet, Velasco, June 9; (W) Santa Anna to Jackson, Columbia, July 4;
(X) Santa Anna to Minister of War and Marine, Manga de Clavo, March
11, 1837; (Y) a translation of Jackson's reply.

under my command, I decided to establish my headquarters there. I notified Your Excellency that I would depart from Béxar on the 31st of March.

Before setting out, I instructed General Joaquín Ramírez y Sesma to march with the division under his orders and occupy the said villa. He was to operate in combination with Generals José Urrea and Antonio Gaona against the enemy, pursuing it continuously in order to prevent it from gathering in any considerable number. For this purpose the division commanded by General Eugenio Tolsa which had joined his command was to operate against Bolivar, West Bay, Chocolate, Hall's Bayou, Harrisburg, Lynchburg, and as far as the San Jacinto, and Goose and Cedar creeks. General Urrea had been instructed to march by way of Victoria, Lavaca, Carancaway, Matagorda, Raft, Mrs. Neils, Brazoria, Columbia, and Orazimba as far as the Brazos, north of San Bernardo river. General Gaona, as soon as he arrived in Nacogdoches, was to undertake operations against Angelina, Natchez, Little Alabama, and Zavala, while waiting for the landing at Galveston of the troops that were to campaign in East Bay, Double Bayou, Anáhuac and Liberty.

The need of helping General Ramírez y Sesma at the Colorado made me order General Gaona to change his route and turn to San Felipe de Austin. For the disembarcation at Galveston I had issued orders that the schooner of war *General Bravo* and the merchant ships that were to conduct food supplies from Matamoros to El Cópano help in the enterprise.

The cavalry brigade, some of whose horses died from exposure to the cold while others were disabled, was unable to take an active part in the campaign with the exception of a few detachments detailed to conduct cattle and supplies, there being no way of replacing the horses. I consequently ordered General Juan Andrade, its commander, to remain with his brigade at Béxar. Several detachments of infantry together with the baggage of their respective units, the hospitals, the artillery and surplus munitions, etc., were also left there.

The divisions having set out,—one under General José Urrea, with more than thirteen hundred men, another under General Joaquín Ramírez y Sesma with fourteen hundred men, and a third under General Gaona with several hundred, each one strong enough to give battle to the enemy,—I left Béxar on the appointed day with my staff and an escort of thirty dragoons. I do not include a statement of the relative strength of these divisions because I have suffered the loss of my baggage where I had these data and other documents.

On the 3rd day I overtook a battalion of sappers and one of regulars of Guadalajara under the command of Colonel Agustín Amat, in the outskirts of the burnt town of Gonzalez, on the Guadalupe. They were marching to reenforce the division under Ramírez y Sesma.

D. Pedro Ampudia, who was two days' journey behind us was bringing up the artillery, the digging implements, the breastwork materials, the munitions, and the food supplies for the above mentioned division.

The waters of the Guadalupe being high, it was not possible for the troops and the above mentioned train to cross with the speed desired, and we were necessarily delayed for three days. The dispatch sent to me by General Ramírez y Sesma, who was facing the enemy on the Colorado, gave me some concern and decided me to send him assistance as stated in my reply to his note. For this reason I ordered General Vicente Filisola, whom I thought best should accompany me as my second since I had left General Juan Andrade at Béxar, to remain to expedite the crossing, leaving instructions for everything to be moved forward with all possible speed under his command. I hastened my march, and on the 5th., I arrived at the Atoscosita Crossing, on the said river. I found the division of General Ramírez y Sesma on the other side of the river. He informed me that, the enemy having retired to the Brazos, he had been able to cross without opposition. Seeing that there was but a single canoe, I ordered the battalion of regulars of Aldama under command of General Adrian Woll to construct flat boats to facilitate the passage of the division that had remained under the command of General Filisola.

General Gaona was supposed to have been on his march toward San Felipe de Austin, according to his reply from Bastrop, a town located on the east bank of the Colorado, thirty leagues west of San Felipe de Austin; while General Urrea was supposed to be marching toward Brazoria, situated on the west bank of the Brazos, twenty-five leagues south of the above mentioned San Felipe. I, therefore, continued towards the San Bernard with the division of General Sesma on the 6th, and early on the 7th arrived at San Felipe de Austin. This town, located on the west bank of the Brazos, was no more, for the enemy had set fire to it and forced its inhabitants to flee to the interior as it did at Gonzales. An Anglo-American who was

arrested among the ruins, declared *that he belonged to a detach-*
ment of about 150 men that had been detained to defend the
crossing on the opposite side of the river; that the towns were
burnt in order to deprive the Mexicans of all supplies as com-
manded by General Sam Houston, who was now in the woods
at Groce's Crossing, fifteen leagues distant to our left; that he
had only eight hundred men, and that he intended to retire to the
Trinity if the Mexicans crossed the Brazos.

When our forces came in sight of the said detachment, it
opened fire from behind a redoubt. I ordered a trench to be
made facing the redoubt; and, placing two six pounders behind
it, we returned the fire without interruption, suffering no loss on
our part. I immediately reconnoitered the river for a distance
of two leagues to our right and left in order to find a crossing
to surprise the enemy during the night, but it was all a useless
effort. The river is wide and deep, the water was rising, and
there was not a single boat to be found. The great rivers that
water that country present insuperable obstacles to an expeditionary army. They are all large and subject to floods in the
spring, occasioned by the melting of the snows in the mountains
and the sudden showers. The latter cause considerable delay in
the movements of an army.

On the 8th, I ordered the construction of two barges (flatboats) the lumber for which had to be brought from distant
houses. After the work was started, it was found that it would
take from ten to twelve days to finish, due to the lack of carpenters, and that it would require three or more additional days
to place them where they were to be used. This loss of time
seemed to me an irretrievable mishap, considering the circumstances of the army and of the republic which made it so important that the campaign be terminated before the rains began,
as I shall soon explain to the nation.

General Filisola had not arrived at the Colorado and General
Gaona, who should have joined us ere this, had not said when he
would be able to do so. The situation of the enemy leader was
no longer unknown to me. Intimidated as he was at the sight of
our rapid advance over a territory that naturally presents almost
insuperable obstacles, and suffering from want and constant
desertion, he was compelled to look for his safety only in a retreat such as he was undertaking, all of which proved beyond a
doubt that the most advisable policy was to pursue him and make
him fight before he could improve his condition.

We were unable to cross the Brazos at San Felipe. In view

of these circumstances, I decided to reconnoiter the right bank of the river for ten or twelve leagues, taking for granted that this flank was covered by the division of General Urrea, who, as I have stated before, was on his way to Brazoria. On the 9th, I left San Felipe for this purpose with five hundred grenadiers and riflemen and fifty mounted men, leaving General Ramírez y Sesma with the rest of his division to be reenforced at any moment by that of General Gaona. Three days later, after painful marches and counter marches, during one of which I walked for five leagues, I took possession of Thompson's Crossing in spite of the efforts of a small detachment of the enemy that tried to defend it but succeeded only in wounding one grenadier and our bugler. As a result of this unexpected operation I also succeeded in capturing from the enemy a fine flatboat and two canoes. The staff, the officers, and the troops conducted themselves in this engagement with bravery and courage. Fortune was still on our side. General Ramírez y Sesma joined me on the 13th, agreeable to my orders, but General Gaona did not appear.

Through some of the colonists taken, among them a Mexican, I discovered that the heads of the Texas government, Don Lorenzo Zavala, and other leaders of the revolution were at Harrisburg, twelve leagues distant on the right bank of Buffalo Bayou; and that their arrest was certain if our troops marched upon them without loss of time. More important than the news was the rapidity of our march, which, if successful, would completely disconcert the rebellion. Without confiding in anyone, I decided to take advantage of the opportunity. I made the grenadiers and riflemen who had captured the crossing, the battalion of regulars of Matamoros, the dragoons of my escort, a six-pounder well supplied with ammunition, and fifty cases of small ammunition cross the river; and I started with these forces towards Harrisburg the afternoon of the 14th. I left General Ramírez y Sesma with the rest of the troops of his division at Thompson's and gave him sealed orders for General Filisola.

I entered Harrisburg the night of the 15th, lighted by the glare of several houses that were burning, and found only a Frenchman and two North Americans working in a printing shop. They declared *that the so-called president, vice-president, and other important personages had left at noon for the island of Galveston in a small steamboat; that the families to whom the houses belonged were making their way to the same place; that the fire had been accidental, they having been unable to put it out; that the families had abandoned their homes by order of*

Houston, who was at Groce's Crossing with 800 men and two four-pounders.

The arrest of the leaders of the rebellion having been frustrated, and knowing the location of the enemy and its strength, I ordered Colonel Juan N. Almonte with the 50 dragoons of my escort to make a reconnoiter as far as the crossings at Lynchburg and New Washington in order to be better able to decide upon my subsequent operations. From the last mentioned place the said colonel told me among other things *that several colonists found in their homes uniformly asserted that General Houston was retreating to the Trinity by way of Lynchburg.*

To intercept Houston's march and to destroy with one stroke the armed forces and the hopes of the revolutionists was too important a blow to allow the opportunity to escape. I decided to take the crossing at Lynchburg before his arrival and to avail myself of the advantages afforded by the country. The first question was to reenforce the division that accompanied me, composed of one cannon, 700 infantry and 50 cavalry, in order to make it superior in number to that of the enemy, which it surpassed in discipline. I issued instructions to General Filisola to stop the march of General Cós to Velasco, ordered in my previous instructions, and to send me immediately under the command of the said general 500 *chosen infantry* which were to join me as soon as possible. This order was taken to him with all speed by my aide-de-camp, Lieut. Col. José María Castillo y Iberri. Colonel Almonte was at the port of New Washington, on the shores of Galveston Bay, exposed to the enemy ships that might arrive; and it was necessary to insure the large amount of food supplies that he had succeeded in taking. I, therefore, marched toward that point the afternoon of the 18th. When I arrived, a schooner was in sight, which, because of the lack of wind, could not get out to sea. I tried to capture it in order to make use of it when the time came against the island of Galveston, but just as the boats and barges that Colonel Almonte had secured were being made ready a steamboat came and set it on fire.

In the early morning of the 19th, I sent Captain Marcos Barragán with some dragoons to the crossing at Lynchburg, three leagues distant from New Washington, to keep a lookout and to give me timely notice of the arrival of Houston. At eight o'clock, the morning of the 20th, Captain Barragán came to me and told me that Houston was approaching Lynchburg. All the members of the division heard of the approach of the enemy with joy; and, in the highest spirits continued the march already started towards that place.

When I arrived, Houston had taken possession of the woods on the banks of Buffalo Bayou, whose waters join the San Jacinto at that point and flow into those of Galveston. His position would force him to fight or take to the water. The enthusiasm of my troops was such that I immediately engaged him in battle; but although our fire was returned, I was unable to draw him from the woods. I wanted to draw him out to a place that suited me better. I retired about one thousand *varas* and camped on a hill that gave me an advantageous position, with water on the rear, heavy woods to our right as far as the banks of the San Jacinto, open plains to the left, and a clear front. While taking our position, the cannonade was kept up by the enemy and Captain Fernando Urriza was wounded. About one hundred mounted men sallied forth from the woods and daringly threw themselves upon my escort placed on our left. For a moment they succeeded in throwing it into confusion and seriously wounding one of the dragoons. I ordered two companies of riflemen to attack them and these were sufficient to rout them, sending them back to the woods. Some of their infantry had also started out; but, on seeing their cavalry retreating, they turned back to the woods. It must have been about five in the afternoon, and the troops needing both food and rest the remainder of the day was spent attending to these indispensable necessities. A good watch was kept during the night. I occupied myself with the best distribution of our forces and the construction of a parapet that would afford more protection to our cannon, placing it in a more advantageous location. This was the disposition of our camp: The woods to our right were defended by three chosen companies; in the center the regular battalion of Matamoros in battle formation took its place; and to the left was our cannon, protected by the cavalry and a column of chosen companies under the command of Lieut. Col. Santiago Luelmo who was to act as our reserve. At nine o'clock on the morning of the 21st, in full view of the enemy, General Cós arrived with four hundred men from the battalions of Aldama, Guerrero, Toluca and Guadalajara. He left one hundred men under the command of Colonel Mariano García to bring up the baggage that was detained at a bad crossing near Harrisburg. These men never joined us. I immediately saw that my order with respect to the five hundred *chosen* infantry had been disregarded, for the greater part of the reenforcement was made up of recruits that had been distributed among our troops from San Luis Potosí and Saltillo. In view of the circumstances that made me superior to the enemy, this serious disobedience instantly caused me the greatest displeasure, realizing that the reenforcement so anxiously awaited and with which I expected to inflict a decisive blow to the enemy was insufficient.

Nevertheless, I tried to take advantage of the favorable impression which I noticed reflected in the countenance of the troops at the arrival of General Cós. He explained to me, however, *that forced to march continuously in order to arrive quickly, the troops under his command had neither slept nor eaten in twenty-four hours; that while awaiting the arrival of their baggage, which should take from two to three hours, the troops should be permitted to rest and prepare for battle.* I granted his request and consented to the troops resting and eating.

I placed my escort, reenforced by 32 men mounted on officers' horses, in a strategic position from which it could observe the enemy and give protection to the already mentioned baggage. Hardly had an hour passed since the last disposition when General Cós came to me to ask me, in the name of Captain Miguel Aguirre, commandant of the escort, *that he be permitted to allow his troops to eat* and to water and feed the horses which had not been fed since the day before. The pitiful tone in which this petition was made moved me to grant it, warning him, however, that as soon as the men were through Captain Aguirre should immediately take up his position as ordered. His failure to do so contributed to the surprise that the enemy succeeded in effecting.

Fatigued as a result of having spent the morning on horseback, and not having slept the night before, I lay down under the shade of some trees while the troops ate their rations. I sent for General Manuel Fernández Castrillón, who was acting as major general, and I ordered him to keep a close watch and to advise me of the slightest movement of the enemy. I also asked him to wake me up as soon as the troops had eaten, for it was necessary to take decisive action as soon as possible.

As fatigue and long vigils provoke heavy slumber, I was sleeping deeply when the din and fire of battle awoke me. I immediately became aware that we were being attacked and that great disorder prevailed. The enemy had surprised our advance guard, a party attacked the three chosen companies that guarded the woods to our right and took possession of them, increasing the confusion with their unfailing rifles. The rest of the in-

fantry of the enemy was making a front attack, protected by
their two cannon, while their cavalry charged our left.

Although the evil was done, I thought for a moment that it
might be repaired. I ordered the permanent battalion of Aldama
to reenforce that of Matamoros which was sustaining the line
of battle; and hurriedly organized an attack column under orders
of Colonel Manuel Céspedes, composed of the permanent battalion of Guerrero and detachments from Toluca and Guadalajara, which simultaneously with the column of Colonel Luelmo,
marched forward to check the principal advance of the enemy.
My efforts were all in vain. The front line was abandoned by
the two battalions that were holding it, notwithstanding the continuous fire of our artillery, commanded by the brave Lieutenant
Arenal. The two newly organized columns were dispersed,
Colonel Céspedes being wounded and Captain Luelmo killed.
General Castrillón, who ran from side to side to restore order
among our ranks, fell mortally wounded. The recruits bunched
themselves and confused the tried soldiers, and neither the first
nor the second made any use of their weapons. In the meantime
the enemy, taking advantage of the opportunity, carried their
charge forward rapidly, and shouting madly, secured a victory
in a few minutes which they did not dream was possible.

All hope lost, with everyone escaping as best he could, my
despair was as great as the danger I was in. A servant of my
aide-de-camp, Juan Bringas, with noble kindness offered me the
horse of his master, and earnestly pleaded that I save myself. I
looked about for my escort and was told by two dragoons who
were hurriedly saddling their horses that their companions and
officers had fled. I remembered that General Filisola was at
Thompson's Crossing, sixteen leagues distant, and, without
hesitation, I tried to make my way to that place through the
enemy's ranks. They pursued me and overtook me a league
and a half from the battlefield at a large creek where the bridge
had been burnt.[31] I turned my horse loose and with difficulty took
refuge in a grove of small pine trees. The coming of night permitted me to evade their vigilance. The hope of rejoining the
army and of vindicating its honor gave me strength to cross the
creek with the water above my waist, and I continued on my

<hr />

[31] In his *Diary* Santa Anna says he was captured the day of the battle.
His memory doubtless failed him, for Houston in his report to Burnet, dated
April 25th, states that Santa Anna was taken prisoner on the 22nd. The
bridge referred to is the famous Vincent bridge burnt by Deaf Smith.

route afoot. In an abandoned house I found some clothes which I exchanged for my wet ones. At eleven o'clock of the 22nd I was overtaken again by my pursuers just as I was crossing a plain, and thus I fell into their hands. Not recognizing me because of my clothes, they asked me if I had seen General Santa Anna. I replied that he was ahead of me and this happy thought saved me from being assassinated on the spot as I found out later.

Your Excellency will see at once, from what I have stated, the principal causes of an event that has, with justice, astonished the nation, and for which I alone have been held responsible. I have been thought dead, and consequently unable to present the facts as they were. But since, fortunately, I find myself alive and enjoying freedom, I am obliged to present the facts so that the causes may stand out clearly as the light of day, in order that justice may render its verdict. I esteem too much a reputation won by dint of long and costly sacrifices to permit it to be soiled with impunity, especially by those who should be the last to impugn it. Limiting myself to those faults committed by some of my subordinates that were, directly or indirectly, the cause of the lamentable catastrophe I am discussing, I will ask Your Excellency to keep in mind that General Filisola sent me a reenforcement made up of recruits when he could have sent me seasoned soldiers. He had with him the battalion of sappers, made up of veteran troops in its entirety, but he did not send me a single man out of it. Being able to have selected the best men from the regular battalions of Guerrero, Aldama, Activos de México, Toluca, and Guadalajara, he failed to do so. Thus, he disregarded the very spirit of my instructions, for, if I distinctly ordered him to send me 500 *picked men,* it was because I wanted no recruits to be sent, aware as I was that there were many among our troops. Had not this been clearly my purpose I would have used some other phrase.

The sending of Captain Miguel Bachiller with special mail that had arrived from that capital, dispatched to me by the supreme government, and which was intercepted, was no less a cause. As a result, the enemy acquired positive information regarding our forces [32] at a time when it was retreating, wondering what it could do, astonished by our operations and triumphs. Thus it became aware that I was at New Washington, it learned

[32] This statement is confirmed by Houston's report to Burnet, made on the 25th of April.

the number that made up the division that was operating in that region and the situation of the rest of our forces, all of which cleared the confusion in which it found itself as a result of our continuous offensive and the appearance of our victorious columns at the points least expected. From the dispatches, it learned everything that it desired; and, coming out from the uncertainty that was making it retreat to the Trinity, it gained new courage. This could not have happened without knowing that my force was inferior to theirs. The arrival of the reenforcement under General Cós was regarded by the enemy as a ruse, believing it a party sent out during the night before, to return in the morning in full view. This was told to me by the enemy afterwards. Such was the terror that prevailed throughout Texas as a result of the operations of the army under my command that in order to dissipate it, General Thomas J. Rusk, acting secretary of war of the government of Texas, told me that he had had to go to the camp where his forces were and *assure them that General Santa Anna had returned to Mexico as a result of an internal revolution in the republic; that he did this to stop the desertion of many of the volunteers that had come from the United States whom he was unable to hold.* It is to be particularly remembered that General Filisola had no instructions to send me any correspondence. If he had wanted to insure its safe conduct, he could have sent it to me later with General Cós. I do not see how the fatal results that would follow the falling of such important correspondence into the hands of the enemy can have escaped him.

General Gaona, who did not join me as he should—the cause of whose delay I have not yet learned—prevented me from setting out from Thompson's Crossing with twice the force I had. I took only 700 infantry in order to leave General Ramírez y Sesma the necessary force for the protection of that point. In view of this fact, I asked for the above-mentioned reenforcement in order to make my forces superior to the enemy.

General Cós reduced his 500 men by leaving 100 near Harrisburg as an escort for the baggage he was conducting. I can see no reason for his bringing this baggage when I had asked General Filisola to send me only fifty cases of ammunition. General Cós brought only part of these munitions, but he brought all the baggage belonging to the troops that had remained at Thompson's, this in spite of the fact that a called reenforcement is supposed to march as lightly equipped as possible in order not to be unduly burdened for it is known that excessive baggage slows up the march. The reenforcement was thus reduced by one-fifth, and 100 men were left seriously exposed, saving themselves by mere chance.

Lastly, the conduct of General Castrillón and of the other officers to whom the vigilance of our camp, in full view of the enemy, was entrusted, contributed considerably to the already mentioned misfortune. I regret to have to discuss an individual who is dead, one whom I always regarded with esteem. Likewise, I regret to have to speak of others who are still living, but duty obliges me to relate the facts such as they were. I have positive evidence to prove that all the time I was sleeping the said general occupied himself with making his toilet and changing his clothes; and that when the enemy attacked and surprised our advanced guards, he was whiling away his time in a party with other officers of my staff. He did not inspect our outposts a single time, and his example was followed by the other officers. Thus, part of the troops were sleeping, while those who were awake, not being vigilant, permitted the enemy to carry out a surprise that could not have been more complete had it taken place in the middle of the night. As a result, it was easy for the enemy to take possession of the woods on our right with only 116 men, in spite of being defended by three chosen companies. Though they outnumbered the enemy, they offered no resistance. This was the source of the encouragement that enabled the enemy to continue the charge, as well as the cause of the confusion in our camp, increased by the panic that possessed the recruits, who, unable to use their arms, permitted the enemy to assassinate them in cold blood. It is true that General Castrillón conducted himself with extraordinary bravery, as I have stated, during the last moments of the engagement, but his efforts then were useless; and, before he breathed his last, his remorse must have been great if he paused to think how he neglected his duty at a time when he should have attended to it.

My duties as general-in-chief did not forbid my resting, for no general is forbidden this necessity, nor can it be expected that he should not succumb to natural needs, particularly under the conditions and at the time of day that I did. I confided, as I had a right to do, in that my orders would be observed. A general-in-chief cannot discharge the duties of a subaltern officer, or those of a soldier. Each class has its respective duties and attributes assigned. If the failings of inferiors cannot be taken as an excuse by their superiors in general, there are exceptions such as the case in hand, especially if the circumstances explained are taken into consideration.

They have, perhaps, tried to accuse me of being incautious because I did not march with all my troops in a body, but chose to advance with only a small division as I did. In the first place, it is necessary to keep in mind, in order to destroy this objection, that I left Thompson's Crossing to execute an important operation whose purpose was to surprise and capture, with a single blow, the directors of the revolution who were but a short distance away. As soon as I discovered that the enemy was retreating by way of Lynchburg, I asked for reenforcements in order to make my force superior to theirs. Lastly, there was no advantage to be gained by the army marching along a single route, and in a body; because, after having driven the enemy from all points, there was no enemy force to fight except that found at the point and place indicated. Since the direction followed by the enemy showed clearly that it intended to retreat beyond the Trinity, it was necessary, in order that no one be left to fire a single shot from the Rio Bravo to the Sabine, to cut off its retreat and to force it to fight rather than to attack the rear guard. The march of the whole army would have been adverse to this important plan that would put an end to the question with a single blow. The slowness with which the army would have had to move as a result of its baggage, trains, etc., would have permitted the enemy to get so far ahead of us that we could not have overtaken it, considering the obstacles presented by the country and its large rivers.

The force under my command was superior in quality to that of the enemy; it was well supplied with food and munitions, and it held an advantageous position; that of the enemy was inferior in number; it was cut off by Buffalo Bayou and the San Jacinto, and occupied a disadvantageous position. The enemy was without food. An attempt to draw it into battle had been made on the previous day, before the arrival of our reenforcement, but the challenge had been refused. Who, under such conditions, would have waited to mobilize a whole army, losing precious moments in the meantime? Who could have doubted victory? I appeal to the impartial judgment of the intelligent classes, feeling confident that, far from siding with envy and malice in imputing carelessness, precipitation and lack of foresight on my part, they will admit that judgment, foresight, and discretion were exercised in considering the circumstances and that if these did not result in victory as it was expected, it was through no lack of plan, nor failure of coordination in the operations, nor the dispositions of the general-in-chief.

Having demonstrated, as I have done, that the catastrophe of San Jacinto was caused purely by the faults and carelessness of some of my subordinates and the disregard of orders by others, there remains nothing for me but to deplore my participation in the engagement. My regrets are mitigated, however, when I remember that I did everything that was in my power, exceeding the duties of a general-in-chief, to serve my country well. I find no other excess in my conduct than my zeal for the interests of the country, placing them above my own and subordinating everything else to the desire to defend them well and to cover with glory the arms intrusted to me.

Fortune turned its back upon me at the very moment when my efforts were to be crowned with success, preventing me from having the satisfaction of presenting a new laurel to the nation, and leaving my desire unknown.

Having presented these facts, I will continue the narrative of the incidents experienced during my imprisonment. These have not escaped either malignant interpretation nor the most bitter recriminations, without consideration for the sad plight of our country and without my being heard.

Taken before Houston on the 22nd of April, the day I was captured, I was received with marks of consideration when I disclosed my identity. Someone proposed a salvo to celebrate my imprisonment, but Houston rejected the idea and showed displeasure. We began a conversation at once with the help of the son of Don Lorenzo Zavala as interpreter. He was acting as aide to that chief. He proposed to me *that I issue orders for the surrender of the troops immediately under my command,* but I refused emphatically to accede. After speaking to me *of his resources to make Texas independent and of the difficulties of the Mexicans to preserve such a vast extent of territory, he expressed his willingness to reach a suitable agreement. He stated that in order to save my life and that of the other prisoners, as he wished, it was indispensable to avoid an engagement between my troops and his.* This statement, in the difficult situation in which I found myself, was as a ray of light to a lost traveler in a tempestuous night by which he finds the way. I feared that my misfortune would discourage the army, and I took advantage of the opportunity afforded me by Houston's reasoning to try to avoid its ill effects by making my existence known to the troops. By reviving their courage, an attempt to vindicate the honor of our arms could yet be made successfully. Such was the occasion for my first orders to General Filisola who replied to me in an official note brought by General Woll. He was admitted as a commissioner on the 30th and should have first addressed himself to Houston demanding from him a formal guarantee, which he might have secured, had he not agreed at once to observe my orders as he did, without trying to make a demand or adopt some measure favorable to us. Such an attempt might have been crowned with success, considering the critical situation of the enemy, the proximity of our forces, and their superior number. Our lives would have been guaranteed then, and our sufferings as well as those of other prisoners, who would not now be as they are abandoned to their fate, would have been helped. All of this could have been secured with ease, for on the 23rd, Major General Wharton proposed to Houston that he be commissioned to go to the camp of General Filisola in order to draw up an armistice. Although Houston gave his consent, the proposal was not put into effect because other officers,—the more radical—were opposed to this measure. Nevertheless, it proves the willingness of the enemy to negotiate, born of a feeling of weakness from which great advantages could have been derived. Great was my grief when, upon the arrival of General Woll, I learned that everything had been confusion after the first news of my misfortune,—a common occurrence in war—and that instead of attacking the enemy, a retreat had been decided upon with the intention of continuing as far as Matamoros.

Nevertheless, as the above-mentioned reply of Señor Filisola [33] simulated dignity, and General Urrea gave expression to the high spirits of the army in a letter that he addressed to me, Houston was unable to discern the true intentions of General Filisola. He feared the respectable force that could easily destroy him, and he redoubled his flattering proposals. I pretended confidence and signed the order for the proposed retirement of our forces. With this I saved the honor of the army— and appeased the arbiters of the fate of more than 500 Mexicans

[33] There is a discrepancy between the date of Filisola's letter and that of Urrea's letter, the first being dated on April 28, while the latter bears date of the 27th.

—I one among them—who had been abandoned and who were about to be left in a trying position, for I had no illusions as to the policy that would be pursued.

General Woll conducted himself with the greatest dignity and is, therefore, entitled to all praise. Having been instructed by me as to what he should say to General Filisola in order that he might act as his duty dictated without embarrassment on account of my previous communications, General Woll asked for permission to return to his camp. He carried a piece of paper signed by me in which I stated *that due credit should be given to whatever he said.* He was detained, however, on pretext that *he should take back with him the proposed agreement for the termination of the war and the guarantee of my liberty,* but in reality because they feared he would disclose the strength of the conquerors.

The attentions shown me by General Houston at the time, his phrases, and the sincerity that I thought inspired him exercised such an influence on my spirit that I gave credence to his promises. The so-called president of Texas, his cabinet, and Don Lorenzo Zavala, the vice-president, arrived at this time, and, in several meetings, expressed similar ideas. They took me in a steamboat to the port of Velasco to finish the armistice proposed by Houston, as they said, making me accompany them for that purpose. They permitted Colonels Juan N. Almonte and Gabriel Nuñez, as well as Don Ramón Caro, my clerk, to accompany me.

General Houston was getting ready to leave for New Orleans where he was going to have a wound that he received in the battle treated. In his farewell he assured me that the cabinet of Texas would settle everything as he had agreed. The already mentioned secretary of war, Thomas J. Rusk, took over the command of the army; and, with 800 men and three pieces of artillery—the entire available force of Texas at that time,— took the field. He visited me first, however, and repeated the promises of his predecessor, leaving me several articles written in his own hand as proof of his good faith. *All this took place before I was placed on the steamboat.*

There were several serious conferences at Velasco regarding the articles of the said Rusk, but it was not until May 14th, that I was able to reduce their unreasonable pretensions to those expressed in the agreement signed on that day. For political reason, or rather in order to keep the clause relative to my immediate release from the soldiery and the populace, the treaty was divided into two parts: one public and one secret. In the first it was stated that I would be set at liberty whenever it was deemed convenient. A careful analysis of the said treaties plainly show that they reduce themselves to a suspension of hostilities favorable to the army, the setting at liberty of the prisoners and myself, and lastly in order to obtain the terms stated to flatter the enemy with the hope that I would use my influence to secure a hearing for its commissioners. I thought, perhaps wrongly, that my freedom would be favorable to the army, to the nation, and to its cause. My promise to use my influence to secure a hearing for their commissioners would not contribute in any manner to the favorable or unfavorable outcome of their pretensions. When I accepted the terms of the agreement, I had taken into consideration that if my fears of a precipitous retreat by our army, as the result of the failure to restore its courage, were confirmed as indicated by the information I had of the abandonment of even the sick, the enemy would be prevented by the very terms of the agreements from pursuing it and making the catastrophe greater. General Woll, losing all hope of carrying the said agreements, left San Jacinto with the new general, Mr. Rusk, expecting to reach his own camp. A few days later he was brought to Velasco under a guard by order of Rusk. I was very much surprised to see him; and, upon hearing of the outrages to his person and an officer who accompanied him—having gone as far as to declare both of them prisoners of war—I officially protested to the president of Texas, as shown by my letter. Agreeable to the note also cited, a passport was issued to General Woll for his safe conduct. His extreme delay in leaving, though it aroused suspicion, did not cause the general-in-chief to investigate his conduct or to try to take possession of his person.

Consequently, on the 1st of June, with all tranquillity and in full view of the town of Velasco, I embarked on the *Invincible*, which was to take me to Veracruz, having first taken care to address a farewell to the people, whose publication produced the desired effect.

Two days after I had gone on board, the captain of the ship, J. Brown, notified me that *he had orders to take me back ashore.* I immediately protested in writing but he replied verbally by saying that *he was disposed to use force for the execution of his orders.* This action was occasioned by the arrival of 130 volunteers from New Orleans on that day, the 4th, under the command of the so-called General Green, who with threats and violence demanded that I be delivered into their hands.

I immediately wrote to Mr. Burnet an official communication which I concluded by saying *that I was determined not to leave the ship alive.* Several persons came on board with his reply, who assured me *that my confinement would last only a few days, and that my person would be respected.*

I was taken ashore and shown as a spectacle to those who had demanded my disembarkation, after which I was turned over to the military and thrown into prison. Captain William Patton, who had come from Victoria specially for the purpose, took charge of me and conducted me to a small house in the outskirts of Columbia, where I was kept for a month and a half.

Irritated by such treatment, I protested against the failure of the Texans to observe the terms of the agreements. Consequently, and without taking into account the duress that determined all my acts after my imprisonment, the agreements were nullified by their conduct and I was left at the mercy of fate.

The exaltation that caused my being brought ashore continued to increase to such an extent that every private felt himself called to assassinate me. On the 27th of June a pistol was fired at me through a window near my bed and almost caused the death of Colonels Almonte and Nuñez. Finally, on the 30th of June, orders were issued for our removal from Columbia to Goliad where we were to be executed in the place that Fannin and his men had been shot. A prominent colonist, Stephen F. Austin, whom I had befriended in Mexico, moved by my unfortunate condition, wanting to return the favor, told me that *if I would write a letter to General Jackson flattering the hopes of the Texans, even if I only used courteous phrases, the very name of that official, from whom the Texans expected so much and whom they heard with the greatest respect, would restrain popular fury and facilitate my salvation.* I did not believe the loss of my life was indispensable to the welfare of my country. The army, who even the enemy agreed should try to save me, did nothing for me, and I lost all hope of being saved. I signed the letter couched in the terms that Austin himself suggested and the reply to it is known. Public sentiment being appeased by the reports circulated about my favorable disposition towards the Texans, Houston was able to follow his kind plan with regard to my person. He arranged for me to go by way of Washington, accompanied by three Texan officers, in order to keep the hotheaded from becoming suspicious and reenacting the scenes of

June 4th. Although the journey, in the middle of the winter, was very painful to me, I had to be satisfied as there was no other way out of the danger.

I had been taken to Orazimba before, where, as the result of the denunciation *of a plan to escape from prison* by my clerk, Don Ramón Caro—as I was afterwards informed—a heavy ball and chain was placed on me the 17th of August, and on Colonel Almonte on the 18th. We wore them for fifty-two days.

It is easily seen that the reply of General Jackson, when compared with my letter, is founded on a misinterpretation. I only asked him to use his influence with the Texans to secure the fulfillment, on their part, of the promise to set me free, in view of the fact that I had complied with my part of the agreements and was willing to observe the clause that still remained pending if called upon to do so. But his negative reply put a definite end to this matter; and my freedom was not due either to his reply nor to the agreements of May 14th, but rather to the spontaneous free will of the said Houston. If, in view of the news about my country, Houston thought that my presence there might be the cause of a new revolution favorable to the Texans, he neither told me so, nor did he express any other motive for his actions than a generous impulse for which I am grateful, and nothing more.

There were three powerful reasons for my journey to Washington, two of which were, as a matter of fact, essential, while the third was one of public convenience. It was necessary not to alarm the Texans but rather to try to confirm the opinion of my willingness to favor their plans. It was neither safe nor prudent to go to New Orleans where I would expose myself to being subjected to new insults, since that port has been the center of activity for the rebellious colonists. I could not return directly to Veracruz because there was no communication between that port and the rest of Texas. Lastly, it was very expedient that I should approach the cabinet at Washington to observe at close range its real attitude towards Texas and towards us.

The six days of my stay there were used for this purpose. General Jackson expressed to me his desire of continuing the friendly relations that bind the two nations, and very kindly furnished me transportation in a war vessel. We spoke very little, and that by mere accident, about the correspondence sustained while I was a prisoner. He told me that he had given copies both of his letter and mine to Señor Manuel E. Gorostiza. I arrived at the port of Veracruz in the above mentioned war vessel, communicating this fact to Your Excellency at the time.

The haste with which I have had to prepare this report, the difficulties entailed by the disorder of my papers as a result of my journey and attendant circumstances, and the poor state of my health may have resulted in some errors, which I shall correct if pointed out. I must state to Your Excellency that I do not attach the documents covering our movements from the time I left Thompson's to the 21st because all my belongings fell into the hands of the enemy and were lost.

In closing this long narrative I cannot but, in all justice, commend to the graces of the supreme government the very worthy Colonel D. Juan Nepomuceno Almonte for the good behavior observed throughout the campaign and the propriety with which he conducted himself while a prisoner. Furthermore, he was a most faithful companion during my bitter days and served me as an interpreter whenever I needed him.

Personally, I have endured privations, sufferings, insults, and calumny. Posterity and my country, whom I have served as the duties of a citizen demand, will doubtless render me justice. I expect no less of the supreme government.

Your Excellency will be pleased to make known to the most Excellent Señor Presidente *ad interim* what I have transmitted to you for his information. I reiterate the assurances of my consideration and esteem.

GOD AND LIBERTY

Mango de Clavo, March 11, 1837.

To His Excellency, the Secretary of War and Marine.

A TRUE ACCOUNT OF THE FIRST TEXAS CAMPAIGN

*And the Events Subsequent
to the Battle of San Jacinto*

BY

RAMÓN MARTÍNEZ CARO [1]

---

[1] Ramón Martínez Caro was the secretary of Santa Anna during the Texas campaign. [C. E. C.]

VERDADERA IDEA

DE LA

PRIMERA CAMPAÑA

DE

TEJAS

Y SUCESOS OCURRIDOS

DESPUÉS DE LA ACCION

DE

SAN JACINTO,

Por D. Ramon Martinez Caro.

———◉———

MÉXICO: 1837.
——●●——
IMPRENTA DE SANTIAGO PEREZ.
A CARGO DE AGUSTIN SOJO,
Calle de Tiburcio núm 14.

Facsimile of the Spanish title page

The evident artfulness of the communications addressed to the supreme government by His Excellency, Antonio López de Santa Anna, on the 20th of February and the 11th of March of the present year, is in keeping with his well-known character of duplicity. It confirms the opinion in which he is generally held as a result of the many deceits he has practiced upon the nation.

The daring boldness with which he claims, before the whole world, that he obtained his liberty unconditionally; that he did not compromise either the honor, the independence, or the integrity of the territory of the nation in the agreements signed; that he has made no promises either to individuals or to any government in the treaties he concluded; and that he would have endured a thousand deaths before consenting to any such terms, either deliberately or by force, is an insult to the good judgment of the generous people whom he addresses. Such an insult deserves to be exemplarily punished in order to satisfy, as justice demands, national honor so basely sacrificed and outraged.

Many of the acts that must be investigated are still enveloped by a mysterious veil. When this is removed, we shall see if the loan negotiated in San Luis was a slanderous invention. We shall see whether the misappropriation of national funds in various ways; the so-called armistice that has been the source of untold misfortunes; the massacres of Refugio, Goliad, and the Alamo; the shameful treaties—one secret and one public—so eagerly agreed to, and as a result of which the cabinet of Texas placed His Excellency on board the *Invincible;* his promise to lend his support to obtain the recognition of Texas independence and the admission of the two commissioners that were to accompany him—Zavala being one of them—; and the official letter of July 4th to the President of the United States that

93

reveals the degrading depths to which he descended in his desire to obtain his freedom, forgetting his honor and tarnishing that of his country, were slanderous inventions or facts. In several of his confidential meetings with the Texas cabinet he made protestations of good faith and asserted that he was convinced of the necessity of recognizing the independence of Texas. In the above mentioned letter he repeated these protestations. He made numerous other proposals in his own handwriting, and affirmed them by his words and his promises. When informed that the object of the trip of Santa Anna to the United States was no other than to solicit the intervention of that government to carry out the terms of the treaties signed, whose principal stipulation was the recognition of the independence of Texas, Castillo, the Mexican representative in the United States, protested indignantly against the legitimacy of the powers of General Santa Anna to enter into such negotiations and questioned the rectitude of his motives. Lastly, who does not know that the formal recognition of the Republic of Texas by the Congress in Washington was not passed until after the arrival of Santa Anna in that capital? Who does not know that President Jackson did not send his threatening message to the Mexican nation, intimating war, until after his arrival? Both of these acts are public facts and occurred after his departure from that capital. Are these inventions? Are they slanders?

Public opinion, hitherto misguided concerning the true events of the Texas campaign and the subsequent occurrences up to the present time, will be correctly informed. The necessity of presenting the facts concerning both the former and the latter with absolute impartiality, out of regard for outraged national honor, imposes upon me a double duty as a result of the unjust and cruel attack upon my reputation. Since the attack was publicly made, I am forced to make my defence in a similar manner. I shall endeavor to present impartially the sacred truth concerning both to enable public opinion to render a just verdict in view of the whole truth.

When slander pursues a man, when his honor and reputation

are thus lightly attacked, and when to the seriousness of such a crime is added blackest ingratitude, it is necessary for such a man to enter the arena in self-defence. If while defending himself, he is obliged to become the accuser in turn, and if by his charges he brands the culprit with the stain of dishonor which he so well deserves, who is to blame? Certainly not the defendant who avails himself only of the legitimate weapons of self-defence.

Fortunately, the time has come when proven guilt can no longer triumph over merit and outraged honor. The good judgment exercised by the whole nation in electing to the supreme power General Anastacio Bustamante in recognition of his high character and his wisdom is the best guarantee for the establishment of justice and order, unknown among us for so long. His long and unjust exile from his mother country has given him an opportunity of bringing back to her the fruit of his observations abroad. This, added to his intimate knowledge of its vital interests and his wise selection and organization of the cabinet, will undoubtedly bring happiness to the nation, the tempestuous horizon assuming a more pleasing appearance.

Nothing is more degrading or more fatal to justice than perfidy garbed in the raiments of truth.—CICERO

General Antonio López de Santa Anna has always appeared in this garb, and to-day, robed in the same mantle of duplicity, he comes before the whole nation—that nation which has bestowed upon him so many favors, so many distinctions, so much wealth—to deceive her as he has always done. He has but recently betrayed her anew, contributing to the dismemberment of her sacred territory by agreeing to lend his support to the recognition of the independence of one of its richest and fairest departments. It is high time for the truth to speak. If it hurts, it, at least, does not give offense. Too long have force and violence prevailed, nicely veiling the injustices committed with the appearances of law and order. But let us not skip over any of the facts, let us examine from the beginning the true causes that contributed to the sad ending of the Texas campaign.

The preparations for the campaign began in October, 1835. In November, His Excellency set out from his *hacienda,* Manga de Clavo, for this capital where he took up his residence in the palace of the archbishop, located in Tacubaya, about two leagues from the city. He remained at this place until the first days in December, occupied in finishing his preparations, at which time he took command of the army. He immediately left for San Luis Potosí where he established his general headquarters and organized the troops for the expedition, with the exception of the first brigade. This unit, commanded by General Ramírez y Sesma, had previously been ordered to march to San Antonio de Béxar to help General Martín Perfecto de Cós who was threatened in that city by the enemy.

The tragedy that we now deplore had its beginning in San Luis Potosí. The first scene may be said to begin with the

97

negotiation of a loan of 400,000 *pesos* with the firm of Rubio and Erraz to meet the immediate needs of the army of operations. His Excellency had been authorized to negotiate this loan by the supreme government. Though the terms of the contract proved very disadvantageous to the nation, the transaction yielded His Excellency negotiable bonds of considerable value.[2] The settlement of the Salinas deal in favor of Erraz, in spite of the more advantageous terms offered by the former holder, Antonio Esnaurrizar, disregarded by His Excellency because it suited his convenience, increased the amount of the bonds already mentioned. As a result of the negotiations, the firm of Rubio was authorized to pay duties at the customs house of Matamoros to the amount of 40,000 *pesos* with worthless bonds which he had bought for less than half their face value, bonds that had been declared illegal tender for that purpose. By the terms of the same contract, the above-mentioned firm was authorized to import through the port of Matamoros food and supplies for the army free of duty. Among the first importations made for this purpose (supplies that never reached the unfortunate army)[3] contraband goods were introduced instead of food, according to the protest presented by the Commissary of that port. The

[2] Letter of Santa Anna to his wife, Orozimba, Texas, September 25, 1836. In order to slander me he says to her that I am on my way to Veracruz to examine his baggage where he had a considerable number of bonds that I wanted. This is an idiotic and senseless falsehood, for he should have known that I was ignorant of the existence of such bonds, since I was not an agent of the transaction as Messrs. Castrillón and Batres. The implication is idiotic because I cannot believe that he does not realize that the bonds are worthless without the proper endorsement. The bitterness of this charge is sweetened by the confession of His Excellency, admitting that he had bonds of considerable value in his baggage. This is nothing short of the admission of his theft practiced upon the nation. He has accused himself by trying to incriminate me on imaginary and groundless charges. Where did the bonds come from? They were not sent from Manga de Clavo, nor from Tacubaya. Didn't they come from San Luís Potosí? Where else could they come from? [All notes not signed "C. E. C." are the author's notes.]

[3] The officers of the various units can testify as to the provisions they received from the imported supplies.

agents of this transaction, Messrs. Castrillón and Batres, received 6,000 *pesos* as their share. The first of the above-mentioned gentlemen deposited this amount in the treasury of the Army of Operations with the consent of Santa Anna, and he was to receive the *moderate* premium of 4 percent monthly.[4]

Before our departure from San Luis, we received the sad news of the surrender of Béxar, but Santa Anna ordered that the news should not be transmitted to the supreme government.

Towards the end of December, the second and third brigades, commanded by Generals Eugenio Tolsa and Antonio Gaona, left for Saltillo, together with part of the artillery under the command of General Pedro de Ampudia. The cavalry, commanded by General Juan José Andrade, set out on the 1st of January, and His Excellency left with his staff on the 2nd, arriving in Saltillo on the 7th. The brigades arrived soon after. His Excellency remained in this place nearly a month organizing the army. On the 25th he held a review which showed the force consisted of almost 5,000 men, not counting 200 cavalry that had left a few days before under the command of General José Urrea for Bahía, nor the brigade that marched to Béxar under the command of General Ramírez y Sesma.

At this time, among other donations received from the neighboring towns, the *cabildo* of the Cathedral Church of Monterrey sent the general-in-chief 1,000 *pesos* for the expenses of the campaign. General Castrillón collected the amount. The Commissary can testify whether this amount was ever turned into the general treasury of the army of operations. If not turned into the treasury, where did it go? Let the reader judge for himself.

During the first days of February the army set out for Monclova together with His Excellency. He remained there only a few days, for on the 9th he set out with his staff and 50 mounted men for Río Grande for the purpose of joining the

---

[4] José Reyes López, Commissary of the Army of Operations at that time, who is now in the capital, can say whether the documents regarding this deposit exist in the archive under his care.

brigade of General Ramírez y Sesma which was there. Before leaving, he issued orders setting the time and the manner of the departure of the second and third brigades and of the cavalry. At the same time he ordered that the troops should be placed on half rations of hard-tack and that each man be allowed one *real* a day. The officers were to provide themselves with their necessary supplies out of their regular pay, without receiving an extra campaign allowance.

I have been unable to find out the reason for this unjust and mysterious order, unjust because it marks the beginning of the privations of the soldiers, just as they set out on their long march over deserts,[5] in the middle of the winter, which is very severe in those regions, without sufficient clothes, particularly among the wretched recruits who in the main were conscripts and were practically naked; mysterious because in San Luis Potosí the Commissary General of the Army, Colonel Ricardo Dromundo, brother-in-law of His Excellency, had been given the necessary funds for two months' provisions and supplies for 6,000 men. What became of these provisions and supplies? When we arrived in Monclova the said Commissary was already there. If he had secured the supplies that he was supposed to get, why, then, was the soldier put on half rations of hard-tack?[6] From this time dates the discontent that began to permeate all ranks and which increased notably after the desert was reached and the sad perspective of advancing farther and farther without the relief of the hospital corps that had set out from the capital became apparent. This corps was never seen by the army. During the entire campaign the army had to depend on medical students

[5] From Monclova to Río Grande is more than 80 leagues and from there to Béxar almost 100. No supplies can be secured in all this distance, for even water is scarce and found only at long intervals that have to be covered by forced marches.

[6] It should be kept in mind that before leaving Monclova His Excellency said that supplies would be found at Río Grande. No supplies were found there. The reader can imagine the horrible distress of the troops, confronted with the necessity of continuing the march over a distance of more than 100 leagues of desert to Béxar.

and a small and inadequate supply of drugs secured at Saltillo, whose cost did not exceed 300 *pesos*. Thus the munition wagons and the gun carriages had to be used to carry the numerous patients. On more than one occasion, General Ampudia and I were obliged to put in the wagons (though already filled to capacity) some of the dying wretches we found on the road. I remember particularly, the General must remember him too, a poor wretch whom we found, at the point of death, unable to move, loaded down with his gun and pack. We placed him in one of the wagons, but he expired before the day's journey was over. Of course, he, like many others, received no spiritual consolation. Such was the sad spectacle offered by the army on its march. In fact, only the heroic constancy and the unlimited endurance so often displayed by the Mexican soldier succeeded in overcoming the disheartening spectacle presented to their eyes.

His Excellency finally reached Río Grande. There he found the brigade of General Ramírez y Sesma which he ordered to proceed to San Antonio de Béxar. The general-in-chief, his staff, and the 50 mounted men of his escort followed a few days later. We overtook the brigade before it reached Béxar, about two days' journey from that place, and His Excellency took over the command in order to enter the city, which he did on the 26th of February, without encountering any resistance on the part of the Americans. According to the citizens of the place, the enemy, which numbered 156, took refuge in the so-called fortress of the Alamo[7] the moment they saw our troops approaching. On the following day, His Excellency placed a battery of two cannons and a mortar within 600 paces of the fort and began a bombardment, taking possession at the same time of several small isolated houses that were to the left. These were nearer to the enemy's position and were occupied by our troops who suffered the loss of several killed and wounded in the operation. Around the fortress there were ditches which were used by the enemy

[7] A mere corral and nothing more, built about 500 paces from the town, on the opposite side of the San Antonio River. The town is named after the river. Many of the walls of the fort are of adobe.

to fire upon our troops, while our soldiers, in order to carry out their orders to fire, were obliged to abandon the protection that the walls afforded them, and suffered the loss of one or two men, either killed or at least wounded, in each attempt to advance. During one of our charges at night, His Excellency ordered Colonel Juan Bringas to cross a small bridge with five or six men. He had no sooner started to carry out his instructions than the enemy opened fire upon this group and killed one man. In trying to recross the bridge, the colonel fell into the water and saved himself only by a stroke of good luck.

On the 29th or 30th, His Excellency sent Colonel Bringas to meet the brigade of General Gaona with instructions for him to send, by forced marches, the picked companies of his brigade. These arrived in Béxar on the 4th of March. The following day the orders for the assault which was to take place on the 6th were issued.

It has already been stated that when we entered Béxar we were assured by the citizens that there were only 156 Americans. In the time intervening between our entrance into the city and the day set for the assault, the enemy received two small reenforcements from González that succeeded in breaking through our lines and entering the fort. The first of these consisted of four men who gained the fort one night, and the second was a party of twenty-five who introduced themselves in the daytime. Two messengers succeeded in leaving the fort, one of whom was the Mexican, Seguín. The entry of these reenforcements and the departure of the messengers were witnessed by the whole army and need no particular proof.[8] At the time of the assault, therefore, the enemy's force consisted of 183 men.

Early in the morning of the 6th the four attacking columns as well as the reserve took up their respective positions as assigned by the general order of the 5th, a copy of which was transmitted to the supreme government. From this it will be

---

[8] It is to be kept in mind that the reenforcements succeeded in entering the fort and the messengers in leaving it through no lack of vigilance, for 600 men, cavalry and infantry, surrounded it.

seen that our force numbered 1400 men in all. At daybreak and at the agreed signal our whole force moved forward to the attack. The first charge was met with a deadly fire of shot and shell from the enemy, the brave colonel of the Toluca Battalion, Francisco Duque, being among the first who fell wounded. His column wavered as a result of his fall, while the other three columns were held in check on the other fronts. His Excellency, seeing the charge waver, gave orders for the reserve to advance. The brave General Juan Valentín Amador, General Pedro Ampudia, Colonel Esteban Mora, and Lieutenant-Colonel Marcial Aguirre succeeded in gaining a foothold on the north side where the strife was bitterest, which encouraged the soldiers in their advance and resulted in their capture of the enemy's artillery on that side. The enemy immediately took refuge in the inside rooms of the fortress, the walls of which had been previously bored to enable them to fire through the holes. Generals Amador and Ampudia trained the guns upon the interior of the fort to demolish it as the only means of putting an end to the strife.

On the opposite side, where there was another entrance to the enemy's stronghold, the resistance was equally stubborn, but Colonels Juan Morales and José Miñón, commanding the attacking column, succeeded in overcoming it. Though the bravery and intrepidity of the troops was general, we shall always deplore the costly sacrifice of the 400 men who fell in the attack. Three hundred were left dead on the field and more than a hundred of the wounded died afterwards as a result of the lack of proper medical attention and medical facilities in spite of the fact that their injuries were not serious. This is a well-known fact, as stated before, which made the fate of those who were instantly killed or mortally wounded enviable to those who lingered in pain and suffering without the proper comfort or relief. The enemy died to a man and its loss may be said to have been 183 men, the sum total of their force. Six women who were captured were set at liberty.[9] Among the 183 killed there were five

[9] In the report made on that date to the supreme government by His Excellency it is stated that more than 600 of the enemy were killed. I my-

who were discovered by General Castrillón hiding after the assault. He took them immediately to the presence of His Excellency who had come up by this time. When he presented the prisoners, he was severely reprimanded for not having killed them on the spot, after which he turned his back upon Castrillón while the soldiers stepped out of their ranks and set upon the prisoners until they were all killed.[10]

The official reports of General Urrea, who was operating in the Bahía and Cópano region, were received about this time. The first gave an account of the engagement at San Patricio in which he took several prisoners whom he sent to Matamoros. His Excellency reproved him for this act, reminding him of his duty in fulfilling the orders given regarding prisoners, which were that they should be executed on the spot. His second report gave an account of the engagement on the Nueces in which Doctor Grant, twenty adventurers, and three Mexicans that were with him were killed. The last of his reports refers to the action that took place at Encinal del Perdido. This episode, which after the minutest investigations still remains covered by a mysterious veil, was the chief cause of the infinite hardships and sufferings we endured as prisoners and of the dangers to which we were exposed.

General Urrea says in his report [11] that, having received information that Fannin was abandoning the fort of Goliad with all his force in an attempt to reach Victoria, he immediately set out in pursuit and succeeded in overtaking him at the Encinal del Perdido where he began an attack on him between four and five in the afternoon, the engagement lasting until dark; that on

self wrote that report and must now confess that I put down that number at the command of His Excellency. In stating the truth now, I must say that only 183 men were killed. I call upon the whole army to witness my statement.

[10] We all witnessed this outrage which humanity condemns but which was committed as described. This is a cruel truth, but I cannot omit it. More cruel falsehoods have been promulgated against my character.

[11] In speaking of official documents which I do not have at hand, I may fall into some slight error as to the literal contents of such documents, but not as to the sense.

the following morning he renewed the attack after he had received two pieces of artillery and reenforcements; that the enemy then sent him a short note, written in pencil, proposing several articles of capitulation;[12] and that he replied to this note by saying that he had no authority to enter into any terms, being able to grant only an unconditional surrender.

Lieutenant-Colonel José Holzinger, whom the Texans took as a prisoner to Velasco, gave a very different account of the incident; and the cabinet granted him his liberty, issuing to him a satisfactory release, expressing their thanks for the services he rendered to several of the prisoners. This is evidenced by the letter which he addressed to the Texan Colonel, J. A. Wharton, in which, complying with his request, he gives a detailed account of the incident.

But let us return to General Urrea. In his private letter to His Excellency regarding this action, after giving him a long detailed account of the circumstances, he concludes by recommending the unfortunate prisoners, who numbered more than 200,[13] to the clemency of His Excellency. He further states that he has sent all the prisoners to Bahía in charge of Lieutenant-Colonel José Nicolás de la Portilla, whom he appointed commandant of that place, where the prisoners are to remain and await the pleasure of His Excellency, while he [Urrea] continued on his march towards Victoria.

In replying to the recommendation of Urrea, His Excellency strongly reprimanded him, expressing his displeasure and commanding him at the same time not to soil his triumphs with a mistaken display of generosity. He ordered him to execute all the prisoners, and a copy of the order was sent also to the com-

---

[12] The short note cited above was transmitted by General Urrea with his report of the action.

[13] I cannot state the exact number, because, as I have said before, I have not the documents which I am citing. I am certain, however, that there were more than 200. These documents will be found in the private papers of His Excellency which were in his baggage, sent to Veracruz together with mine. By this time, His Excellency must have disposed of those documents as he saw fit.

mandant of Bahía. The order not having been carried out, it was repeated directly to the commandant a few days later.

The prisoners were finally executed as it is well known, that is to say, they were taken out from the fort in groups, led out of the city a certain distance, and shot down at random. Sixteen or seventeen who escaped miraculously owe their lives to this refined cruelty. Later, when we were prisoners in their camp, each one of these became a tiger in his persecution of us, particularly of His Excellency and me.[14]

The commandant of Bahía notified His Excellency at about the same time that 83 men had been taken prisoners by Colonel D. N. Bara. He sent him the original report of Colonel Bara in which it appeared that five men who were making their way to the fort, ignorant of the surrender of Fannin, declared that they had just landed at Cópano and that their companions were still on board the vessel that had brought them. The colonel informed them of Fannin's surrender and told them to ask their companions to land and surrender, promising them that they would be treated with all consideration if they surrendered without offering resistance. They acceded to his request and were all taken to the fort to await the disposition of His Excellency. When he received this information, he ordered me to write to the commandant, giving him instructions to have all the prisoners executed as provided by the circular of the supreme government, for though they had not engaged in active fighting, the fact that they had introduced themselves into the country armed, confirmed their intention of taking an active part in the war.[15]

Fortunately, when Captain D. N. Savariego, bearer of the order, learned that it extended to the eighty-three men, he asked to be allowed to speak to His Excellency, and I myself led him to the room where he was. Captain Savariego told him that the colonel who had taken these men had asked him to ask the

[14] My conduct as a prisoner will be seen later on. I pride myself in having acted nobly, only to be repaid with calumny and evil.

[15] This is a terrible interpretation of the circular in which it is expressly stated that those prisoners who are not taken fighting are not to be executed.

clemency of His Excellency for the unfortunate prisoners who had surrendered without making use of their arms. Hardly had he spoken, when for his reply he received such bitter reproof that he left the room disgusted. At the same time, His Excellency called me and ordered me to alter the order which had already been written in final form, instructing the commandant of Bahía to hold the eighty-three prisoners until a thorough investigation was concluded concerning the circumstances of the surrender, allowing them only one ration of meat a day. The investigation was immediately instituted by General Cós, who used Lieutenant-Colonel Pedro Francisco Delgado, a member of the secretarial staff of His Excellency, as his secretary. He took the declaration of Captain Savariego and sent it to Bahía from where it was to be returned as soon as possible with the additional information necessary for a final decision of the case. Those unfortunate wretches escaped a tragic end by this coincidence, for they would have been executed in spite of the fact that such an act was contrary to the spirit of the circular of the supreme government.[16]

In the meantime, the public sale of the goods and supplies taken from the enemy,[17] who had hurriedly taken refuge in the Alamo the moment we entered Béxar, continued. This sale was conducted by two members of the commissary department of the army under the supervision of the Commissary.

At the same time, before our departure from Béxar, Colonel Ricardo Dromundo and another man (I do not remember his

[16] If after I obtained my liberty, His Excellency had remained a prisoner, and if I had made the above disclosures to the Texans, after hearing the calumnies which he has promulgated concerning me, would His Excellency be free and in perfect security at Manga de Clavo to-day? I fear not. He might not even be alive to-day. But such an act would have placed me on a par with him. The best way to defend oneself is not to descend to the level of the offender. I speak to-day, only because I am addressing my native country to whom I owe a justification of my acts.

[17] A miserable prize and the only one taken. Even if it had been distributed among the troops, as it should have been, it would have hardly given each man more than one *peso* apiece, since the net proceeds did not exceed $2500. The sale took place at the corner of the house occupied by His Excellency.

name) at their own request were authorized to introduce one
shipment of *supplies and provisions* through La Bahía and
Cópano free of duty in view of the absolute scarcity of supplies.
I do not know that this shipment was introduced, but I suppose
it must have been.

General Filisola, second in command of the army of operations, in his *Representation* addressed to the supreme government
on the 19th of August of last year, has already expressed, with
his characteristic prudence and moderation, the ill-advised
measures taken by His Excellency, the general-in-chief, after the
capture of the Alamo and his misconceptions with regard to the
campaign. Since my object is not, nor should it be, to criticize
the military operations, and since not being a military man, I
could only criticize such acts as common sense without any
knowledge of military science condemns, I will limit myself to
the opinion cited. Its weight rests on the well-merited reputation
of the above mentioned general.

The general-in-chief and his staff left on the 31st, and I
accompanied the second in command in his carriage. On the
second day's journey, His Excellency ordered his carriage to
return to Béxar from where it was to proceed to San Luis. It
was to be used by some *travelers* to whom 2,000 *pesos* had been
given by His Excellency, who in turn had received this sum
from Colonel Ricardo Dromundo. From what funds this money
was taken, I do not know. Captain D. N. Badillo was to accompany the travelers on horseback.[18] His Excellency continued the
march on horseback, arriving in González the 2nd of April. He
set out again on the 3rd accompanied only by his staff, a picket
of cavalry, and myself (it was my duty to accompany him).
He left General Filisola in charge of the crossing of the
river which had to be crossed by the small brigade commanded by
Colonel Agustín Amat, the artillery, the wagons, etc. His
Excellency arrived at the Colorado on the 5th and continued on

---

[18] Decency and respect for public morals do not permit further details
to be given.

the 6th to San Felipe de Austin, after he joined the brigades of Messrs. Sesma and Tolsa.

General Castrillón and Colonel Treviño, who pushed forward in advance of the main body, captured an American who was stationed as an advanced scout. He declared that he belonged to a detachment of about sixty men, situated on the opposite side of the river and that General Sam Houston was on the left side of Groce's Crossing with only 800 men, because during the last few days more than 400 others had deserted his ranks.

His Excellency says in his report, a most original document, that when the enemy discovered our troops, it began firing upon them from a redoubt it had built for its protection; that he raised a trench and, placing two six-pounders in position, kept a constant fire in reply without suffering any losses;[19] that he immediately reconnoitered the bank of the river both to the right and to the left for a distance of two leagues in search of a crossing to surprise the enemy that night; that his efforts were fruitless [20] because the river is both deep and very wide; and that its waters were high and not even a small canoe could be found. He further states that the rivers of that country present great difficulties to an expeditionary army [21] because they are large and subject to floods in the spring as a result of the melting of the snow in the mountains [22] and the frequent rains which themselves cause numerous delays in the operations.

His Excellency continues: "On the 8th I ordered the con-

[19] Perhaps His Excellency does not consider the death of two soldiers and a mule driver a loss.

[20] All the officers and men present at the time, some of whom are in this capital now, may declare to what efforts His Excellency refers, and whether he again mounted a horse or moved from his tent until the time for our departure, after we arrived before San Felipe.

[21] Why was the necessary equipment for crossing these rivers not taken by the army? His Excellency may claim that he did not know the country, but why did he not consult with those who did? Most of the difficulties encountered were well known beforehand.

[22] When His Excellency speaks of melting snows in the mountains, has he forgotten that he was speaking of the immense plains of Texas? He alone has ever seen mountains in the deserts of Texas.

struction of two barges (flatboats), for which it was necessary to bring the lumber from the distant houses. After the work was begun, it was seen that it would require ten or twelve days for their construction because of the lack of carpenters, and that it would take three or more days to place them where they were to be used. I considered such a delay an irreparable waste of time.[23]

"General Filisola had not arrived at the Colorado, and General Gaona, who should have joined our force long since, *did not even say when he would be able to join us.* The conditions faced by the leader of the enemy were no longer unknown to me. Intimidated as he was by the successive triumphs of our army; overcome by the rapidity of our marches over a country which offers so many natural obstacles, some of them almost insurmountable to the enemy,[24] and suffering from want and desertion which impelled him to look for his salvation in the retreat he was undertaking, there was nothing more advisable than to pursue him and give him battle before he could improve his condition.

"We were unable to cross the Brazos at San Felipe.[25] In view of these circumstances, I decided to reconnoiter the right bank of the river for ten or twelve leagues, taking for granted that this flank was covered by the division of General Urrea, who, as I have stated before, was on his way to Brazoria. On the 9th, I left San Felipe for this purpose with 500 grenadiers

[23] Two American carpenters who had joined our forces, aided by two other men, finished one of the said barges in a day and a half. In three days, therefore, they could have finished the two. How does His Excellency figure out it would take ten or twelve days?

[24] "Obstacles that were almost insurmountable to the enemy" says the general, to the enemy who was acquainted with the country, who had at their disposal steamboats, barges, canoes, etc. Maybe they were no obstacles to us who lacked all these facilities.

[25] I do not see why. After the two barges were completed, a matter of three days, would the enemy, intimidated by our triumphs, terror stricken, suffering from desertion and want, and in addition, immensely inferior to our force in number, have prevented us from crossing? Our force consisted of more than 2,000 men.

and riflemen and fifty mounted men,[26] leaving General Ramírez y Sesma with the rest of his division to be reenforced at any moment by that of General Gaona.[27] Three days later, after painful marches and countermarches, during one of which I walked for five leagues, I took possession of Thompson's Crossing in spite of the efforts of a small detachment of the enemy that tried to defend it but succeeded only in wounding one grenadier and our bugler. As a result of this unexpected operation, I also succeeded in capturing a fine flatboat and two canoes from the enemy.[28] The staff, the officers, and the troops con-

[26] Why reconnoiter the right bank when it was known that the only enemy that existed was on the left? Why not reconnoitre the left bank where the enemy was? With forces vastly superior to those of the enemy, now intimidated, and with fortune still smiling upon us, as His Excellency claims, why were we not led directly to the enemy in order to destroy it? The route along the right bank was better suited to the future designs of His Excellency, who already saw himself arriving in Harrisburg, proceeding on to New Washington, thence to Nacogdoches, and as far as the Sabine, returning along the coast to Cópano, and embarking there for Matamoros. (Orders had already been issued to General Vital Fernández at Matamoros to dispatch the Mexican war schooner El Bravo to El Cópano to await there orders from His Excellency.) From there he was to go on to Tampico, continuing by land to San Luis Potosí, where he would join the travelers and descend upon the capital of the republic to be received with triumphs, ovations, offers of the presidency, etc. This was the true motive for his decision.

[27] His Excellency has already stated that General Gaona had not even communicated to him when he was likely to join him. As a matter of fact, Gaona was, at this time, lost in the desert beyond Bastrop and could not tell when he would arrive.

[28] It is worth while noticing that this brilliant measure was not decided upon prior to our departure from San Felipe, but that it was the result of an unforeseen coincidence. Soon after we left San Felipe four Americans on horseback were sighted and we left our road to follow them, but not succeeding in overtaking them, we returned to our former route. Colonel Treviño, who had gone ahead of us, found a negro and his wife in one of the houses and took them to His Excellency to whom they declared that they had come from Thompson's Crossing where there were a few Americans. His Excellency offered the mulatto 100 pesos to return to Thompson's to tell the Americans he had seen us but that we had taken a different route. The mulatto fulfilled his mission, going to Thompson's immediately and returning at once to serve as guide. It was thus that we captured the crossing, but the mulatto never received the 100 pesos.

ducted themselves with bravery and courage in this engagement.
"Through some of the colonists taken, among them a
Mexican [29] I discovered that the heads of the Texan government, Don Lorenzo de Zavala, and the other leaders of the revolution were at Harrisburg, twelve leagues distant on the right
bank of Buffalo Bayou; and that their arrest was certain if our
troops marched upon them without loss of time. More important
than the news was the rapidity of our march, which, if successful, would completely disconcert the rebellion,[30] Without
confiding in any one I decided to take advantage of the opportunity. I crossed with the grenadiers.[31]

"To intercept Houston's march and to destroy with one stroke
the armed forces and the hopes of the revolutionists was too
important a blow to allow the opportunity to escape.[32]

"In the early morning of the 19th I sent Captain Marcos
Barragán with some dragoons to the crossing at Lynchburg, three
leagues distant from New Washington, to keep a lookout and
to give me timely notice of the arrival of Houston.[33] At eight

[29] I did not know that a Mexican could be a colonist in his own country.
[30] There is no doubt that the idea was brilliant, preferring to disconcert
the rebellion rather than stamp it out as he could have done by attacking it
at San Felipe as indicated. But let us consider for a moment the state and
the ramifications of the revolution at this time. The revolutionists had been
destroyed at San Patricio, la Bahía, and Béxar, and there was no other
force left in the field except Houston's, cut off at Groce's Crossing. I do
not know why His Excellency preferred to take possession of four or six
men who made up the cabinet in order to execute them to falling upon
Houston and destroying him. He, being a military man, may know the
reason.
[31] It is a well-known fact in the army that immediately after our arrival
at Thompson's the troops were ordered to cross to the opposite side at once
in a canoe, this operation having taken place, therefore, before learning the
important news to which His Excellency refers.
[32] Why was the enemy allowed to escape at San Felipe? At that time
we had over 2,000 men, as it has been stated, and the enemy was intimidated
and terror-stricken. Why the desire of giving it battle now with the hope
of destroying it when we had only 700 men? The facts cannot be reconciled.
I suspected as much all the time.
[33] It is true that Capt. Barragán went to Lynchburg Crossing with
some dragoons on the 19th, but not to observe the arrival of Houston. He

o'clock, the morning of the 20th, Capt. Barragán came to me and told me that Houston was approaching Lynchburg. All the members of the division heard of the approach of the enemy with joy, and, in the highest spirits, continued the march already started towards that place.[34]

"When I arrived, Houston had taken possession of the woods on the banks of Buffalo Bayou, whose waters join the San Jacinto at that point and flow into those of Galveston. His position would force him to fight or take to the water. The enthusiasm of my troops was such that I immediately engaged him in battle; [35] but, although our fire was returned, I was unable to draw him from the woods. I wanted to draw him out to a place that suited me better.[36] I retired about one thousand *varas* and camped on a hill that gave me an advantageous position, with water on the rear, heavy woods to our right as far as the banks of the San Jacinto, open plains to the left, and a clear front.[37] While taking our position, the cannonade was kept up by the enemy and Capt. Fernando Urriza was wounded. About one hundred men sallied forth from the woods and daringly threw themselves upon my escort placed on our left.[38]

"At nine o'clock on the morning of the 21st, in full view of

was to prepare the barges that were to be used by our troops in crossing the river at that point.

[34] It is true that we were already on our way to that point but for the purpose of crossing the river at Lynchburg in order to continue to Anahuac, as previously arranged. It is to be noted that His Excellency ordered both Harrisburg and New Washington burned before we left. He did likewise with several houses along our route.

[35] If the situation of the enemy was so desperate, why didn't His Excellency press the engagement to a decisive termination?

[36] If the position did not suit His Excellency, could the enemy have been in such a distressing situation as to be forced to fight or take to the water? The enemy could not have exercised such poor judgment as to choose the worst location to encamp, having reached the ground long before our forces.

[37] We shall later see whether the open plains helped us to prevent our being completely surprised, and that at four in the afternoon.

[38] From the report the reader is given the impression that this engagement took place contemporaneously with the cannonade. It did not occur until about five in the afternoon, more or less.

the enemy, General Cós arrived with 400 men [39] from the battalions of Aldama, Guerrero, Toluca, and Guadalajara. He left one hundred men under the command of Colonel Mariano García to bring up the baggage that was detained at a bad crossing near Harrisburg. These men never joined us. I immediately saw that my order with respect to the 500 *chosen* infantry had been disregarded, for the greater part of the reenforcement was made up of recruits that had been distributed among our troops at San Luis Potosí and Saltillo.[40] In view of the circumstances that made me superior to the enemy, this serious disobedience instantly caused me the greatest displeasure, realizing that the reenforcement so anxiously awaited and with which I expected to inflict a decisive blow to the enemy was insufficient.[41]

[39] Later on we shall see what His Excellency says the enemy thought of this reenforcement of 400 men.

[40] Regarding these 500 *picked* men of which His Excellency speaks so much, let us see what General Filisola says in his official communication to the government, of May 14th of last year, inserted in his *Representación* made to the government about the Texas campaign, the 19th of August of the same year. He says: "His Excellency crossed to the left bank of the Brazos at Old Fort, on the 15th of the said month, and immediately marched upon Harrisburg with the Matamoros battalion, the chosen companies of Guerrero, *primero activo de México,* and Toluca, a six-pounder, and sixty picked dragoons. He left me instructions to send General Cós with 500 men and two pieces of artillery to Velasco. On the 17th I received orders from His Excellency reducing the number of troops to be taken by General Cós to 200 men, and on the 18th I received new orders instructing me to send General Cós to him with 500 infantry and 500 cases of rifle ammunition. This order was complied with on that day, the force being made up from the battalions of Guerrero, Aldama, and Guadalajara." There is nothing here to indicate that he asked for *picked* troops, and, I place more confidence in the testimony and known probity of Filisola.

[41] Three is the charm. This may be the reason for the three attempts made by His Excellency to strike the decisive blow. In San Felipe he tried it by going in search of the enemy on the right bank of the river, when he knew it was on the left bank at Groce's Crossing. At Harrisburg he marched to arrest the members of the cabinet of Texas to shoot them, but they, being aware of the fate that awaited them, fled. The last attempt was at San Jacinto, fateful and tragic day whose effects we have seen. Some fatalists may still exclaim that it was fate! There is no fate. All these evils and disasters have had their origin in the lack of foresight and mismanagement of the campaign from the beginning. The Prince of the Peace

"Fatigued as a result of having spent the morning on horseback, and not having slept the night before, I lay down under the shade of some trees while the troops ate their rations.   I sent for General Manuel Fernández Castrillón, who was acting as major general, and I ordered him to keep a close watch and to advise me of the slightest movement of the enemy.[42] I also asked him to wake me up as soon as the troops had eaten, for it was necessary to take decisive action as soon as possible.[43]

"As fatigue and long vigils provoke heavy slumber, I was sleeping soundly [44] when the din and fire of battle awoke me.   I immediately became aware that we were being attacked and that great disorder prevailed.   The enemy had surprised our advance posts. . . .[45]

has truthfully said in his memoirs recently published "The greatest evils often have their origin in a careless slip or an oversight at the beginning of our undertakings.   To this we give the name of fatality."   Would that his undertakings had ended there!   It would not have been so bad.   His weakness and fear later sacrificed the most sacred interests of our country, making her drink the cup of bitterness to its very dregs in the dismemberment of her territory.

[42] Fortunately, dead men tell no tales.   It is for this reason that the conduct of this officer is attacked here and later on, without regard for the fact that he fell in the glorious defence of his country.

[43] According to the orders issued, the attack was not to have taken place until early the next day.   What decisive action was to take place when the troops finished their meal?   If General Castrillón and many brave companions fell, death sealing their lips, fortunately some have miraculously survived them to enlighten the nation as to the facts and to honor the memory of the brave men who fell in her defence.

[44] It is well that His Excellency admits it.   If a general-in-chief, who has been confronted by the enemy for only twenty-four hours, an enemy who on the day before makes a false attack to feel our strength, is forced to lie down and rest from the hardships of one night's vigil, what can be expected from the unfortunate soldiers, really fatigued by the many hardships of the campaign?   Can they be blamed if they too, were sleeping at the time of the attack?   When the head sleeps, the rest of the body is not awake.

[45] The horrible memory of that moment makes the pen drop from my hand for a few minutes.   Imagine our being surprised at four in the afternoon, in the middle of an open plain, with nothing to obstruct the view of the enemy from our front!   They succeeded in advancing to within 200 yards from our trenches without being discovered, and from there they

"Although the evil was done, I thought for a moment that it might be repaired. I ordered the permanent battalion of Aldama to reenforce that of Matamoros which was sustaining the line of battle; and hurriedly organized an attack column under orders of Col. Manuel Céspedes, composed of the permanent battalion of Guerrero and detachments from Toluca and Guadalajara, which, simultaneously with the column of Col. Luelmo, marched forward to check the principal advance of the enemy.[46] My efforts were all in vain. The front line was abandoned by the two battalions that were holding it, notwithstanding the continuous fire of our artillery commanded by the brave Lieut. Arenal. The two newly organized columns were dispersed, Col. Céspedes [47] being wounded and Capt. Luelmo killed. General Castrillón who ran from side to side to restore order among our ranks, fell mortally wounded.[48] The recruits bunched themselves [49] and confused the tried soldiers, and neither the first nor the second made any use of their weapons. In the meantime the enemy, taking advantage of the opportunity, carried their charge forward rapidly, and shouting madly,[50] secured

spread death and terror among our ranks. This is unpardonable. Our country, our honor, humanity, the shades of the bleeding victims sacrificed by that criminal negligence call for vengeance. The shadows of those who fell, so cowardly murdered, at Refugio, Goliad, and the Alamo had called for vengeance for some time. Divine Providence, tired of so many injustices, may at last avenge them all.

[46] The principal movement of the enemy was the complete surprise which it was able to carry out. At that time, His Excellency was sleeping soundly. The rest of the engagement developed with lightning rapidity, so that by the time he reached our front line it had already been defeated and completely routed. When did he organize the two columns, then? Colonel Céspedes is here now and can testify as to the truth.

[47] He was wounded in our trenches so seriously that he is still suffering from the effects of his wound.

[48] His daring and loyalty in trying to overcome the confusion, which has no parallel or equal, cost him his life, but he died while carrying out his duty.

[49] Those who were recruits and those who were tried veterans all were completely confused by the suddenness of the unexpected surprise.

[50] Their war cry was "Remember the Alamo."

a victory in a few minutes which they did not dream was possible.[51]

"All hope lost, with everyone escaping as best he could, my despair was as great as the danger I was in. A servant of my aide-de-camp, Juan Bringas, with noble kindness offered me the horse of his master, and earnestly pleaded that I save myself. I looked about for my escort and was told by two dragoons who were hurriedly saddling their horses [52] that their companions and officers had fled. I remembered that General Filisola was at Thompson's Crossing, sixteen leagues distant, and, without hesitation, I tried to make my way to that place through the enemy's ranks.[53] They pursued me and overtook me [54] a league and a

[51] I do not see why, when their scouts had made certain of the absolute disregard that reigned in our camp, succeeding in burning the bridge on our rear at three, thus cutting off our retreat. Observers placed on the top of trees near us had watched our camp and given an account of our lack of precautions. Why then, should they not have imagined a victory over an enemy that had given itself up to sleep without even posting advance guards?

[52] It is too much to admit that even the cavalry had unsaddled their horses and turned them loose to graze, while the enemy was in sight.

[53] God forbid that His Excellency should have made his way through the enemy. I was a short distance away—not exactly among the enemy—when I saw him coming already in flight and I followed him immediately. Thank God we were not among the last who fled, for of those very few survived to tell the tale. We continued at full speed until we reached the bridge on the Brazos, eight miles away, but only to find it burned. We retraced our steps a short distance and entered a small thicket, where he dismounted and left me. I followed a path with Lieut. Col. José María Castillo Iberri, Capt. Marcos Barragán, and some others whose names I do not recall. They all succeeded in crossing a creek, but I was prevented from following them by the approach of the enemy who was already entering the woods. I turned back and hid among some thick brush. There I remained all night in constant danger of death, for to make things worse it was a full moon night. After daybreak, totally exhausted, I gave myself up to two of the enemy who were passing nearby. Fortunately, one of them was French and when I addressed him in his language he prevented his companion from firing his gun, which he was making ready. Would that I had not had this good luck, for had I been shot I would have been spared the many sufferings and agonies which I endured during the five and a half months I was a prisoner. What is still more, I would have been spared the sad and cruel disappointment with which His Excellency repaid me for my well-known

half from the battlefield, at a large creek where the bridge had
been burnt. I turned my horse loose and with difficulty took
refuge in a grove of small pine trees. The coming of night permitted me to evade their vigilance. The hope of rejoining the
army and of vindicating its honor gave me strength to cross the
creek with the water above my waist, and I continued on my
route afoot. In an abandoned house I found some clothes which
I exchanged for my wet ones. At eleven o'clock on the 22nd,
I was overtaken again by my pursuers [55] just as I was crossing
a plain, and thus I fell into their hands. Not recognizing me
because of my clothes, they asked me if I had seen General Santa
Anna.[56] I replied that he was ahead of me and this happy
thought saved me from being assassinated on the spot as I found
out later.[57]

good services as his secretary, a fact known to all the army, forgetting my
noble conduct while a prisoner with him. I shall refer to this further on.

They took me to Houston, whom I found suffering from a wound in his
foot. Hardly had I disclosed my identity as the secretary to His Excellency
when this very fact provoked such indignation among his followers (mostly
adventurers) that had I not been sitting by the side of Houston, more than
a hundred bullets would have made me their mark. The mere name of His
Excellency or of anything closely connected with him provoked the greatest
indignation.

Houston addressed several questions to me to ascertain the whereabouts
of His Excellency, to all of which I truthfully replied that I did not know
where he was. After he spoke to his followers, calming them, he sent me
with one of his aides to the place where the other officers who had been
taken prisoners were being kept.

[54] Had they done so, His Excellency would have never written the report
which I am now refuting. We were too far ahead for them to overtake us.
On the other hand, the enemy was not pursuing definite individuals, for they
knew nobody, much less, His Excellency, who wore no military insignia.

[55] Not his pursuers, but the pursuers of all of us. His Excellency insists
in believing that they were pursuing him only.

[56] I cannot understand how a person who is known, as he claims he was,
could disguise himself by merely changing his clothes. (That is all the
disguise he had.) How did he alter his face? I would like him to answer
that.

[57] A very happy and opportune thought. Had I been in the place of His
Excellency, I would have replied in the affirmative. Did he deny his identity
only when he was arrested? Let it be, lest it be said that the desire to
incriminate guides my pen.

"Your Excellency will see at once, from what I have stated, the principal causes of an event that has, with justice, astonished the nation and for which I alone have been held responsible.[58] I have been thought dead, and consequently unable to present the facts as they were.[59] But since, fortunately, I find myself alive and enjoying freedom, I am obliged to clarify the facts until the causes stand out as bright as the light of day [60] in order that justice may render its verdict.

"The sending of Capt. Miguel Bachiller with special mail that had arrived from the capital [61] dispatched to me by the supreme government, and which was intercepted by the enemy was no less a cause.[62] As a result, the enemy acquired positive information regarding our forces at a time when it was retreating, wondering what it could do, astonished by our operations and triumphs.[63] Thus it became aware that I was at New

[58] The causes are too self-evident. It need not be said that all the praise for the success of the expedition is due to His Excellency, but rather that in view of the notorious facts he must be held responsible for the mishaps just as he would have been lauded for the success. In case of failure the leader of such an expedition is subject to an investigation by a council of war that shall determine the true cause or causes of the unfortunate outcome.

[59] Judging from this report, he presented the facts, but not as they were.

[60] I doubt it, very much.

[61] His Excellency sent this officer, who was in his secretarial staff, on a special mission from Harrisburg to Thompson's Crossing where Filisola was. Having fulfilled his mission, and being ready to return, the mail that had just arrived from the capital was sent with him to His Excellency. It is a sad spectacle to see how in the report written at Manga del Clavo the facts and circumstance are woven at will by the author.

[62] The reply of Filisola to the communication of His Excellency was not carried by the courier who was taking the mail just arrived from Mexico, but by Capt. Bachiller, who regardless of the courier from the capital would have set out anyway. If the capture of the courier was prejudicial, it could not have revealed any information concerning the recent operations of His Excellency, for it was bearing only mail from the capital that, being 600 leagues away, could not contain any information concerning recent movements in Texas.

[63] The enemy knew what it was doing too well. From the Colorado it followed on our tracks so much so, that it was later generally stated that it halted and rested one night just two miles from our camp. If it was retreating, why follow the road we were taking when it had so many others it could have used in perfect tranquillity?

Washington, it learned the number that made up the division that was operating in that region and the situation of the rest of our forces, all of which cleared the confusion in which it found itself as a result of our continuous offensive and the appearance of our victorious columns [64] at the points least expected. From the dispatches it learned everything that it desired; and, coming out from the uncertainty that was making it retreat to the Trinity, it gained new courage. This could not have happened without knowing that my force was inferior to theirs. The arrival of the reenforcements under General Cós was regarded by the enemy as a ruse, believing it a party sent out during the night before, to return in the morning in full view. This was told to me by the enemy afterwards. [65]

"General Gaona, who did not join me as he should—the cause of whose delay I have not yet learned [66]—prevented me from setting out from Thompson's Crossing with twice the force I had. I took only 700 infantry in order to leave General Ramírez y Sesma the necessary force for the protection of that point. [67]

[64] "Our victorious columns were ever upon the enemy," says His Excellency. It is a proved fact that from San Felipe to San Jacinto, the opposite was true, for the enemy was constantly on our rear. The amusing thing is that His Excellency never knew it.

[65] The enemy saw a party of 400 men arrive and took it for a party sent out by His Excellency to deceive it. This is what he claims. Has he forgotten already that in the state of desperation, fear and terror in which he has painted the enemy, it could not have imagined such a reenforcement to be a ruse, but rather that its very fear would have exaggerated their number and taken it for the advance of the whole army moving to surround it?

[66] Was His Excellency ignorant of the fact that Gen. Gaona was lost in the desert near Bastrop? Did not the whole army know this? Is this the way of rewarding the services and activity of a loyal officer?

[67] There was nothing to protect at that point. If His Excellency desired to keep it, he should have remembered that the second in command of the army would arrive soon after, as he did, with the division commanded by Colonel Amat, the battalion of Aldama, and a picket of cavalry besides the artillery. The picket of cavalry had been left at Atascosito under General Woll. Why then, didn't His Excellency take the whole brigade of General Ramírez y Sesma?

"General Cós reduced his 500 men by leaving 100 near Harrisburg as an escort for the baggage he was conducting.[68]

"Lastly, the conduct of General Castrillón [69] and of the other officers to whom the vigilance of our camp, in full view of the enemy, was entrusted contributed considerably to the misfortune.

"My duties as general-in-chief did not forbid my resting, for no general is forbidden this necessity, nor can it be expected that he should not succumb to natural necessity.[70]

"They have, perhaps, tried to accuse me of being incautious because I did not march with all my troops in a body, but chose to advance with only a small division as I did.   In the first place, it is necessary to keep in mind, in order to destroy this objection, that I left Thompson's Crossing to execute an important operation whose purpose was to surprise and capture with a single blow the directors of the revolution who were but a short distance away.[71]   As soon as I discovered that the enemy was

[68] Of what use would a hundred additional worthless recruits, as His Excellency calls them, been to us?   Did he want more victims still?   On the other hand, if General Cós, after whom General Treviño was sent to make him hasten, had abandoned the baggage which he was bringing without leaving an adequate guard, and the baggage should have been lost, he would never have heard the end of it.

[69] Allow me to draw a veil over this subject on which I could speak so much at the risk of being accused of partiality.   It is enough to say that in spite of the bitter recriminations made against him, His Excellency feels forced to admit that he displayed extraordinary valor.

[70] Were the rest of the men made of iron?   If we kindly grant that His Excellency was overcome by the vigils of a single night, we will have to grant with much more justice that the soldiers, who are the ones that bear the brunt of the fatigue in a campaign, were all the more entitled to a rest.   If we admit these premises, why hold it against anyone that no watch was kept in the camp?   Why blame anybody for being asleep, when His Excellency himself, succumbing to a necessity of nature, as he says, was himself asleep?

[71] If this is true, then His Excellency did not leave Thompson's Crossing with only 700 men as a result of the failure of General Gaona to arrive on time.   Again if his departure had for its object the capture only of the cabinet, that is, the directors of the revolution as he says, who could not have been more than six or eight, but let us say 100, was not his force sufficient for the purpose?

retreating by way of Lynchburg, I asked for reenforcements in order to make my force superior to theirs.[72]

"Having demonstrated, as I have done, that the catastrophe of San Jacinto was caused purely by the faults and carelessness of some of my subordinates and the disregard of orders by others,[73] there remains nothing for me but to deplore my participation in the engagement.

"Fortune turned its back upon me at the very moment when my efforts were to be crowned with success.[74]

"Having presented these facts, I will continue the narrative of the incidents experienced during my imprisonment.[75] These

[72] When we left Harrisburg, His Excellency received information of the march of Houston to Lynchburg, whereupon Filisola, who was at Thompson's was ordered to send 500 infantry and 50* cases of ammunition with General Cós. This dangerous mission was entrusted to Lieut. Col. Castillo Iberri, aide to His Excellency. In order for Houston to reach Lynchburg, he had to pass by Harrisburg, as he did, after we left. Instead of waiting for him we continued our march to New Washington, three leagues above Lynchburg, leaving the reenforcement sent for exposed to the danger of being attacked, and what is still more important, leaving our communications cut off with the above-mentioned crossing, where the main body of the army was. This was shown by the capture of Capt. Bachiller and the courier who were coming to our camp from Thompson's Crossing. Besides, if on the 20th, the indefatigable Capt. Barragán had not arrived with news of Houston's approach to Lynchburg, just as we were leaving New Washington, we would have continued that day to Anahuac as planned, advancing further and further and cutting ourselves more completely from the rest of the army. This mystery has been sufficiently explained in the note questioning the motive for our departure from San Felipe de Austin, on the 9th of April.

[73] The opposite has been sufficiently well established, and it could still be proved further (though I do not deem it necessary) if the documents were all in my possession as they are in that of His Excellency.

[74] There were good reasons for his efforts not having been crowned with success.

[75] Were there no casualties in the battle, no men killed or wounded, no prisoners taken? Do not such essential details belong in the report of a battle? Compare the report of the enemy as translated and presented by His Excellency in his *Manifiesto* with the original, and the care with which many of its phrases have been changed and others omitted will be seen.

* There is a discrepancy here. Cf. with note 41 which says 500 cases of ammunition. [C. E. C.]

have not escaped either *malignant interpretation* nor the most bitter recriminations, without consideration for the sad plight of our country and without my being heard.[76]

His Excellency continues the narration of the events that took place during his imprisonment, but he so distorts the facts and passes over so many in silence, that I beg the reader to compare his account with the one I will now present briefly and truthfully, leaving it to the severe but just verdict of public opinion. Relying on their high principles and good faith, I call upon Colonels Juan Nepomuceno Almonte and Gabriel Núñez as eyewitnesses of the events to testify as to my veracity.

I am not acquainted with the circumstances of the first meeting that took place between His Excellency and Houston, when the former was brought in as a prisoner, that is to say, the first interview between the conqueror and the conquered, which took place, the 22nd in the afternoon, the day after the engagement. Various accounts have been given, but I will not recount any of them because I was not an eyewitness of the occasion.

I have already stated how I was conducted by one of Houston's aides to the place where the other officers who had been taken prisoners were kept. Shortly after the arrival of His

[76] His Excellency denominates as a malignant interpretation the evidence and the irrefutable contents of the many documents published, all of which bear out the just accusation which the country has presented, demanding satisfaction for many outrages, sealed by the violation of its sacred territory and the contempt and loss of its honor. Santa Anna, who himself was the motive, the cause, and the means of so many calamities, with inconceivable indifference presents to the nation the record of the most shameful and infamous acts a man can commit. All these acts, I as an eyewitness can testify, emanated from him, were urged by him with humiliating supplications, for the sole purpose of obtaining his liberty and his life. And these acts, I repeat, are confirmed here, and he even tries to make them appear meritorious. When he signed them, he signed his own shame and that of the nation, and all only to save his life. His conscience should make it an unbearable burden.

I shall present these incidents in the manner and form in which they took place, in order that they might be seen in the proper light, deducing impartially from them the true cause and the object of the negotiations which he concluded.

Excellency in camp, Mr. Thomas J. Rusk, who was acting as secretary of war for the Texans, came looking for me and took me to the presence of Houston, where His Excellency was standing by his side. A very short time elapsed between my arrival and that of Colonel Almonte, and soon after, agreeable to a decision I was informed that accompanied by one of Houston's aides I should go back to the battlefield to search for and bring back the portable *escritoire* and other belongings of the private secretarial staff of His Excellency.

We left for the purpose, taking with us one of our soldiers to bring back whatever we found. To me alone was reserved the sharp pain of beholding our battlefield after the action. The first thing that met my eye—one that has remained engraved in my mind—was the sight of General Castrillón where he fell, already stripped of his clothes. A short distance from him and in the same condition I saw the bodies of Colonels Peralta and Treviño, Lieutenant Colonel Luelmo, other officers whom I did not know, and about fifty soldiers. These were all the dead at this place which had been our battle line. We made our way to the woods, about one hundred paces away, and upon our arrival there, the soldier we had brought had already found His Excellency's *escritiore* for which we were looking. I sat down for a moment to catch my breath, as if one could breathe in that atmosphere of sorrow and mourning, and busied myself with sad reflections, asking myself while I mused "Where are our six hundred victims?"

The arrival of the aide, who had left me alone, warned me that it was time to return. As we started back, I told him that I did not believe the number of the dead was as large as it was claimed, for both on our battle line and in our immediate vicinity the dead did not exceed one hundred. Wishing to satisfy my doubts, he led me to the entrance of the road taken by our troops in their flight, and there I saw, both to the right and to the left, as far as the eye could see, a double file of corpses, all men from our force. Moved by this sad spectacle—would that it had been the last—I still had the more bitter sorrow of being conducted a short distance to the left, where there was a small creek, at the edge of the woods, where the bodies were so thickly piled upon each other that they formed a bridge across it. "At this place," said the aide, "they rushed in such confusion and in such numbers that they converted the crossing into a mud hole, obstructing the way, and our soldiers in the heat of battle massacred them." I turned my face in horror; and, noticing the effect produced on me, he repeated, "Let us go." "Yes," I replied, "take me away from this place." We made our way back to where the soldier was with the *escritoire,* and he told me that he had seen both His Excellency's and my own bed a short distance away. I asked for permission to take them back to camp, and this being granted [77] we returned to Houston's presence.

I immediately opened the *escritoire* and His Excellency dictated first an order to Filisola and then two others.

By the first of these orders, General Filisola was told that an armistice had been concluded, and that, consequently, he was to retire and see that the other divisions did likewise. But he was not apprised that the armistice favored the enemy alone, for it is a notorious fact that after this order was transmitted, the enemy continued to harass our troops, and that our dispersed fugitives were pursued for many days thereafter. General Cós was taken prisoner on the 24th, Colonel Romero on the 25th, and Lieut. Col. González on the 26th; while both during these days and afterwards several of our soldiers were taken prisoners. What was the nature then of the armistice concluded on the 22nd? [78] Let a single document or signature be presented to prove that the enemy agreed to an armistice and I will allow myself to be shot. It cannot be said, either, that a verbal agreement

[77] Thanks to this lucky thought, His Excellency slept in a bed with mattress from the first night of his imprisonment and did not have to sleep on the ground as did everybody else, including Houston.

[78] Colonels Céspedes and Almonte, Lieut. Col. Castillo Iberri, and several other individuals who were taken prisoners and who are now in this capital, can testify to this fact. Furthermore, see Houston's report, where it is stated that General Cós was not taken prisoner until the 24th.

was made by the enemy and later violated. Nothing would be
farther from the truth. The first three cited orders written at
the suggestion of Houston had no other purpose than to calm
the boundless indignation noticed on every side and to avoid the
imminent danger of the moment.

In the second communication of His Excellency to Filisola,
he was told to order the commandant at Goliad to release all
the prisoners, etc., while on the part of the enemy, they not only
did not set a single one of our prisoners at liberty but, as it has
already been stated, continued taking others. By the third order,
he was instructed to exercise all care both in his division and
those of the other generals to prevent any damage being caused
to the property or the persons of *that country* [79] by the retreating
troops.

On the following day, the 23rd, we secured permission from
Houston to erect a tent near his, which was surrounded by eight
sentinels, after His Excellency, Colonel Almonte and I were
placed in it. At the same time, through the mediation of
Wharton, who was acting as major general, I succeeded in getting back a trunk of mine, which though it had been broken into
and 180 *pesos* that I had in it had been stolen, still contained
some clothes. Of these I gave to His Excellency whatever he

[79] Note how soon His Excellency referred to that department of the
republic as a different country. On the other hand, with all the fields laid
waste and all the towns burned either by the enemy or by our troops, the
cattle all scattered in the woods, what property was to be respected? No
idea can be given of the countless evils attendant upon such an order. As
a result of it, and protected by the so-called armistice, the enemy had access
to our camps, claiming that they were looking for some of their slaves,
their true object being to ascertain the actual condition of our army. General Woll, on the other hand, who had come to the enemy's camp protected
by the same guarantees and the terms of the fateful armistice, invested with
the sacred rights of a peace agent, according to instructions given him by
Filisola, was practically reduced to a prisoner, not being allowed to return
until the month of May, after the country had been sacrificed and its honor
debased. The numerous insults and outrages offered to an honorable country
by those ungrateful sons whom she had nursed in her bosom and by four
adventurers who, with a little more care could have been totally destroyed,
cause one to blush with shame and indignation.

needed, for besides not being proper for him to continue wearing the disguise which he had assumed it was too unbecoming.[80]

General Filisola had been urgently ordered to retreat agreeable to the terms of the armistice. He took into consideration the dangerous and critical position of the general-in-chief and of the other unfortunate prisoners who were in danger of being shot to avenge the massacres of Refugio, Goliad, and the Alamo. Furthermore, he considered the difficult and dangerous situation of the army, whose condition is described in detail in the respectful and well-documented *Representación* addressed to the supreme government on the 19th of August. He replied to His Excellency, therefore, that, complying with orders, he would suspend the hostilities (which he had already begun) and would recross the Colorado.[81] He further stated that he had commissioned General Adrián Woll to proceed to the enemy's camp as his representative for the purpose of finding out the terms of the armistice. The only fruit of the commission of this officer were the repeated vexations, insults and dangers to which he was exposed during the month and a half that he was forcibly detained, with hopeful promises or evasive answers to his just and strong protests.

We have stated that the day after we were taken prisoners permission was obtained for the erection of a tent for His Excellency, Colonel Almonte and me.[82] Three days later, that is,

[80] His Excellency was changing his clothes at the side of the trunk, when he noticed the loss of one of the buttons from the front of his shirt. Six months later he has been good enough to say that he had missed this personal article shortly before. This is a cruel and infamous insinuation, characteristic of him.

In the letter which I wrote to His Excellency from New Orleans, 'the 3rd of November of last year, and which I have been told has been published in this city (in the *Cosmopolita*) this incident and several others are discussed with greater details. A misdirected vengeance and an unfounded ill-will have caused these insinuations to be made against me.

[81] At this time the order had been given in the enemy's camp for all the prisoners, without exceptions, to be shot the moment the Mexican army advanced upon them.

[82] Colonel Núñez did not join us until the third day.

on the 25th, Don Lorenzo de Zavala, who was acting as vice-president of the so-called republic came, and on the 27th, the president, David G. Burnet, and the rest of the cabinet arrived. In the first interviews with His Excellency nothing was said of the measures taken or that were to be taken because of the circumstances. Only Zavala, upon his arrival, after mutual apologies had been exchanged between them for their political disagreements, told His Excellency of the danger to which he, together with Col. Almonte, was exposed. To them the Texans attributed the origin fo the campaign. From here on it is necessary to acknowledge the just praise which is due Colonel Almonte for the dignity and the firmness of character which he always displayed, in spite of the harsh treatment and the threats to which he was subjected.

The enemy broke up camp the 1st of May, because, though it was a mile from our former camp, the stench of so many corpses as there were unburied and unburnt, serving as food for carrions, was unbearable. The enemy took a position about three leagues away, near a large establishment (ranch). We were taken to this place by water in a flatboat. The day after, Zavala, the vice-president, Bailey Hardeman, and P. H. Grayson, members of the cabinet, secretly questioned me on what I knew regarding Fannin and the rest of the prisoners who, it was claimed, had been executed by the express orders of His Excellency after they had capitulated. Zavala added, in order to intimidate me, that a member of the secretarial staff of Santa Anna had assured him that His Excellency had ordered the commandant of Goliad by three separate dispatches to execute the prisoners. They said that no one could give, better than I, his private secretary, the facts concerning a deed which was responsible for the indignation and excitement that reigned all around us. They assured me that my disclosures would be kept under the strictest secrecy, and that I would receive the corresponding reward, etc. I flatly denied everything, doing in this nothing more than my duty. But permit me, at least, to explain or make known the circumstances under which I denied it. His

Excellency had sent an order to General Filisola instructing him to send him his baggage and mine in which were all the documents of the secretaryship. If Filisola had not sent them on to Matamoros, fearing they might fall into the hands of the enemy, and if by complying with the order of His Excellency, the documents had fallen into the hands of the Texans, they would have discovered the copies of the orders in my own handwriting, which were written as stated before. What would have been my fate then? What human power could have saved me from death, or perhaps worse than death? If, on the other hand, intimidated by the horrible situation in which we were, awaiting death either by order of the enemy or as a result of the indignation of the undisciplined mob that might mutiny at any moment without recognizing any authority to appease its anger by killing us; if, I repeat, in view of these dangers and many others, I had confessed the guilt of His Excellency, would he be alive and free to-day? Certainly not. What has been my recompense? Guided by false appearances, giving free rein to his well-known first impulses of the moment and to an unpardonable levity, he has tried to malign me with no other proof or foundation than the only spring of all his actions—*Force* and *Power*. When the sensitive cords of the heart are touched, it is humanly impossible to remain indifferent. It is for this reason that I invoke the indulgence of the nation whom I am addressing, if I am forced to engage its attention now and then in defense of my honor. But let us return to the subject that holds our interest.

The gentlemen left me and went to join their companions. At about twelve, they all came to where we were and presented to His Excellency a draft of a treaty in English. After Colonel Almonte translated it and I made a copy of it, he read it and expressed to Zavala the impossibility of carrying out the terms stipulated in view of the guarantees which were demanded and the difficulty of getting them ratified. He assured him that the best guarantee was his own signature and his pledged word, and asked him to persuade the cabinet of this fact and urge upon them the importance of his immediate release and return to Mexico which was essential before anything could be done. Nothing more was said about the proposed treaty, nor was it ever mentioned again. And to think that His Excellency was to make use of this insignificant document, never again mentioned or discussed, to justify the agreements which he later signed on the 14th of May, stating that on that date he finally succeeded in reducing the pretentious claims of the Texans to the terms signed! What about the treaty he signed while on the steamboat, before the 14th? Why does he pass over this in silence? Was he unable to gloss it over as the others? I shall present the details attendant upon it.

On the 3rd, after Zavala had breakfasted with us, and after the exchange of mutual compliments with His Excellency, he left us promising to do all he could during the day to settle matters. He returned, in fact, a few hours later and after embracing His Excellency he said to him, "Everything is arranged. We will board the steamboat this afternoon, just a short distance from here, and you will be freed from the soldiers and this rabble. There, with more ease, everything will be settled." He added that it would be necessary to conclude a secret treaty in order to overcome the distrust of the cabinet, since it was unadvisable for His Excellency to sign a public agreement pledging himself to the recognition of the independence of Texas. His Excellency agreed, and, after repeated embraces, Zavala left us again until four in the afternoon at which time he returned with the whole cabinet to take us to the steamboat.

Houston expressed opposition to this measure, and even tried to prevent it from being carried out. However, one of the members of the cabinet explained to him in unmistakable terms that his interference was prejudicial to the plans of the government and this made him consent. We left for the steamboat under the custody of a heavy guard, reaching our destination almost at nightfall. Soon after, all the officers who were prisoners were taken in like manner to the steamboat, but His Excellency would not speak to any of them because he said he was indignant at all of them. Perhaps it suited him best. The first hours after our arrival were taken up with private conferences, now with one, now with another member of the cabinet. Having reached a satisfactory understanding, the final discussion and drafting of the treaties that were to be signed was begun the following morning.

The whole morning was taken up in the discussion and drafting of the articles of the public treaty. The members of the cabinet were all well disposed and General Rusk, already named to replace Houston who was wounded, also expressed his assent to and approval of the negotiations. Let us see how these favorable circumstances were dissipated like smoke. His Excellency, who instinctively felt that his position had improved, but ignoring the determined character of the persons with whom he was dealing, conceived the idea of trying a new policy. This change of mind, cost us dearly. The public treaty having been drafted,[83] we proceeded to the secret treaty (agreeable to what His Excellency had promised Zavala). But at this point he said that he had not made any such promise, that his word and good faith were sufficient for him to be trusted to carry out what he had promised. Immediately the cabinet began to disagree among themselves, each one forming his own opinion, and General Rusk left very much displeased, stating that he would leave with the army early in the morning, which he did.[84]

[83] The officers who were prisoners and who, as has already been stated, were on the steamboat, can testify whether we did not spend the whole day in the above negotiations. Many of them are at present in this capital.

[84] An employee or partner in the herds of Antonio Tayafé who was there on that day, having come in company with General Woll, communicated to me his consent to my using 130 *pesos* which he had given me for safe keeping. I told His Excellency the circumstances and he replied to me by saying, "I do not need any money." Consequently, after consulting Almonte and Núñez, we decided to accept this sum on our joint responsibility, and I gave the said gentleman the corresponding receipt. See the more detailed account of this incident in my letter to His Excellency, November 3, of last year, in which I challenge Almonte and Núñez to deny the facts.

After my arrival in this city I have seen Tayafé for the purpose of taking up the receipt given to his partner but he has told me that the man is in Matamoros. He stated that he had seen the receipt and that he would

We were left in the same situation as before, if not worse, because the slight goodwill we had gained after so many agonies was lost by this incident. The day after the departure of Rusk, we were taken to Galveston, where we were placed in the Texan schooner *Independence*. We remained on board this vessel three days, at the end of which we were moved into another steamboat and taken to Velasco where we were lodged in a small room which was surrounded by sentinels. There we were left to our own fate. Imagine our situation! It is humanly impossible to describe. Three or four days passed, after which time, after endless pleadings and complaints, the cabinet again convened, not in its full number but a majority of its members and new conferences were begun which lasted six or eight days. After a thousand difficulties, increased by the greater distrust inspired by the conduct of His Excellency in the first steamboat, the public and secret treaties were finally drawn up. Agreeable to the last article of the secret agreement, I closed and sealed it in duplicate, delivering a copy to His Excellency and another to the Texan president, David G. Burnet.

As great dissatisfaction was observed among the troops that guarded us, who were not in sympathy with the release of His Excellency as agreed in the treaties, the cabinet expressed the advisability of delaying the execution of this dangerous measure until the excitement subsided. In the interim, Zavala, who after the incident of the steamboat already recounted had left and gone to his home which was nearby, came to see us again. The protestations of friendship between himself and Santa Anna were renewed to the extent that His Excellency insisted that he should accompany us to this capital as one of the *Commissioners of the Republic of Texas*. As a result of this renewed friendship and interest, he was a daily guest at our table together with various members of the cabinet.

write to the man to send him the receipt in order that it might be settled by me, the only party responsible for the sum. Compare these facts with the light and slanderous manner in which His Excellency asserts that I stole 130 *pesos* from him, and draw your own impartial conclusion.

Finally the first of June was decided upon as the date on which we were to board the Texan schooner *Invincible,* but on that day several malcontents from among the troops stirred up the majority of the guards. It was necessary for the members of the cabinet and others to spend the whole morning making speeches using their influence to persuade the populace of the necessity of permitting His Excellency to leave in order to put an end to the war and secure the recognition of independence. With this, some were persuaded, while others making a virtue of necessity, submitted. It was at this time that His Excellency had the happy thought of writing his famous tender farewell, which needs only to be read carefully to judge it in the proper light.

At four o'clock, on the same day, we were taken aboard, after a terrific storm which came up suddenly, a prelude to the one that awaited us. Lorenzo de Zavala and Bailey Hardeman, appointed by the *Republic of Texas Commissioners near the government of the Republic of Mexico,* who were to be presented by His Excellency to further the ratification of the treaties concluded, were also to board the schooner on the day immediately following, the 2nd. We impatiently waited for the arrival of these gentlemen to set sail, but the day passed without their making their appearance. The steamboat *Occeano* [sic], from New Orleans entered the port just about this time. There were 130 volunteers, commanded by Thomas J. Green, aboard this steamboat and they, joining the malcontents in Velasco, forced the cabinet to order the captain of the vessel to put us ashore. The order was communicated to His Excellency and caused him to write an official protest which was carried ashore by the above-mentioned captain, who, accompanied by several other gentlemen, returned at about three and brought back the reply.

This truly exasperating incident had its effects, and caused us to feel the greatest fear for our lives, particularly on the part of His Excellency, who in a state difficult to describe asked the captain in writing if he was disposed to use force to carry out the order. To this he replied verbally that he was. In the meantime, the gentlemen who had come aboard used their influence and persuasion to convince His Excellency of the advisability of obeying the order, and he finally acceded. As a result, we were again taken ashore, but we were landed on the opposite side of Velasco, at a place called Quintana, in order to avoid the danger of any disorder or attack from the mob. We remained there three days, at the end of which Captain Patton arrived with his company from Goliad, specially detailed to guard us, and we were turned over to him. In his party were four desperate characters who had escaped from the execution of Fannin and his companions and had sworn to kill His Excellency. This is enough to give an idea of our painful situation. After we were turned over to Captain Patton, as stated, he took us to Velasco and lodged us in the second story of a house whose first floor was a restaurant. We were never in greater danger, nor were we ever exposed to so many vexations and insults. I was unable to stand the horror of our situation; and, overcome by the sad and pitiful condition in which we were, knowing that my spirit was becoming more depressed and saddened every minute, I tried to rise, but I had hardly taken a step before I fell unconscious to the floor, where Colonel Núñez assisted me with the aid of His Excellency and Colonel Almonte.

The following day, a certain Bartolomé Pagés, a young Spaniard who had a wine shop in the place, came and expressed a desire of speaking with His Excellency. This he succeeded in doing during one of the moments the guard was not watching. He explained his plan of going to New Orleans and, if he were given the necessary funds there, of arranging for our escape upon his return. In view of this fact, letters were written, after he had left, to the Mexican consul in that city. These were sent to Pagés by one of our servants. Although in these letters no specific orders were given for money to be delivered to him, for fear that they might fall in the hands of the enemy, the spirit of the recommendations clearly indicated the object of his mission. We did not see this young man again, nor hear about him, until later as expressed in this account.

After four days, that is, on the 11th of June, Captain Patton took us to a small board house, a mile from Columbia, which had only two rooms. He placed us in one of these and he and his company occupied the other. Early in the morning, on the 27th, a drunken American appeared, asking for General Santa Anna. His condition caused our guard to disregard his inquiry. He, however, disrespectfully approached a small window in our room. Through this he addressed the same question to Colonels Almonte and Núñez who were seated about six paces from the window. As neither one of them replied to him, he fired a pistol which he had concealed; but luckily the bullet passed between the two colonels and naturally did not harm them. His Excellency was still in bed, and I had gone out to take the air, being about twenty paces from the house at the time.

In spite of this incident, and several others of little consequence occasioned by our proximity to Columbia, we enjoyed, nevertheless, a few hours of peace, especially at night. Soon our past anxieties returned, for we heard that General Rusk had issued orders for our removal to Victoria, where he was with his army. The soldiers were clamoring for His Excellency to be tried by a court-martial and executed in the spot where Fannin and his companions had been shot.

Happily, at this juncture Stephen F. Austin arrived from the United States, paying a visit to His Excellency on the 1st of July. As a result, after several conferences, it was decided to write to the president of the United States, General Andrew Jackson. This letter was signed by His Excellency on the 4th of the same month and Austin himself took charge of it. This measure, which was purposely made public, counteracted the desire of having us sent to the army and we never heard a word about the matter again.

The owner of the house we were occupying claimed that

he was obliged to use it, and, as a consequence, we were moved further into the interior to a house of Dr. Phelps, located about six leagues away. It was the only house in Orozimba. It was at this place that we enjoyed the only peace we had during our imprisonment, due mainly to the distance we were from the general lines of communication. This prevented our frequent contact with the people which had previously given the malcontents and the trouble makers an opportunity to add to our sufferings.

During that time (August 14) the letters that were given to the young Spaniard, Pagés, had a disastrous effect. The incident has been variously related by the different parties, each one coloring his account to suit his desire, some with insufficient information, and others in the belief that I would not be able to retell it. I will proceed, therefore, to narrate the incident, just as it happened and as I would relate it if I were on the brink of eternity.

One evening Colonels Almonte, Núñez and I were in our rooms. His Excellency was lying down in his own room. The sergeant of our guard came in just then and told us that several ladies and gentlemen wished to see us. Looking out of the window, we saw several persons, but due to the distance we were unable to recognize any of them. We all made excuses for not appearing, His Excellency excusing himself likewise. As our visitors had already dismounted from their horses and entered the hall, Dr. Phelps, the owner of the house, invited us to come out and we were obliged to accede. Imagine our surprise upon seeing Pagés among our visitors! We took a seat, Colonel Almonte sitting down by the ladies, while I found a place next to Pagés.

Although while there we were prohibited from speaking any other language except English, nevertheless, the lively desire of learning the outcome of the mission made me disregard the order. Speaking between my teeth, I asked Pagés what news he had. Turning his face slightly towards me, he replied saying, "I was unable to do anything because they took away the crew

I had secured for the schooner which I bought for 5,000 *pesos* given to me in New Orleans. Furthermore, the distance at which you now are from the seashore would preclude any hope of an escape even if I had the means for the attempt." He then said that he could send me supplies from those he bought if we needed them. He was unable to say anymore for at this moment, the sergeant, noticing our conversation, made his way past the company present and rudely dragged Pagés from his seat and began abusing him with a thousand epithets, scolding me for having disregarded orders. Fortunately, I justified my act by saying that I was ordering supplies, for we had absolutely none. This incident put an end to the visit, and soon after, I told His Excellency what Pagés had said. Without regard for the danger we were in, His Excellency broke out in a loud voice, "Those are all inventions of that man. They are going to try to collect every penny from me in New Orleans, but I will refuse to pay a single cent." He concluded by saying that he did not wish for any of the provisions that were going to be received; that he preferred not to eat. Almonte, Núñez and I were not of the same opinion and in view of our great need of them we decided to accept the provisions on our own responsibility.

I request the attention of the reader to this incident, imploring his indulgence for the minuteness with which my honor, my self-esteem, and my reputation have obliged me to recount it.

Captain Patton who had been away during the day arrived late that night and was immediately informed by the sergeant of what had happened. He called me aside to ask me the details, and I satisfied him by assuring him that next morning he would see the provisions that I had ordered. Early next morning I was told that Pagés wanted to see me. Accompanied by the captain, I went out to see him, and this very fact caused Pagés to show some alarm. He told me that he had come to ask me for the list of supplies I wanted. This was sufficient to make the captain suspicious. He asked him on what ship he had come. He had scarcely replied, saying the American schooner *Pasaic,* when Patton left him. He took me to a nearby wood and said, "Look at the troops that arrived last night to reenforce the guard (There were about forty men there.). We had already received news concerning that schooner from New Orleans. Five days ago, I received orders from General Rusk, by Major Smith whom you saw here the other day, instructing me to place a ball and chain on Santa Anna and Almonte (He showed me the order).[85] It is necessary that I find out to-day what brought that man here. I will take you to the Landing (at Columbia), there we will talk with him, and we shall find out what passed between you two yesterday." He then told me to return to the house, and as soon as I was a few paces away, I observed that he gave instructions to the sergeant to watch me closely.

I immediately saw that we were all in a compromising situation, and that personally I was already in very bad. Consequently, as a precaution in case they should search our belongings, I at once took out from His Excellency's writing desk the copies of the two letters addressed to New Orleans, both written in my own handwriting. Although, as it has already been stated, nothing was definitely said in them with regard to funds, the fact that Pagés was recommended was sufficient to incriminate His Excellency in particular. A little later, the captain came in, and, showing Almonte an order he had for my removal to Columbia (Almonte said later that it had been written by Dr. Phelps) he told me to get ready to leave. During one of the moments when the captain was out of the room, His Excellency said to me, "Perhaps they will set you at liberty as I have told you before, taking into consideration that you are not a military man. If such is the case, as soon as you reach New Orleans,

---

[85] Keep in mind that one of our orderlies said to Colonel Núñez, two days before Pagés had been to see us, "Capt. Patton has a ball and chain which he is going to put on the president." At that time we were ignorant of the return of Pagés. This fact will show the criminal shamelessness with which it has been asserted by certain degraded men that the ball and chain were placed on him on my account. It is not strange. Society never lacks depraved men. They find their chief delight in the misfortunes of their fellow-men and are the natural tools of inhuman and corrupt individuals. Like sores of the body politic, they contaminate the whole social structure.

you will present yourself to the consul and protest in my name against any funds that may have been paid out for me." [86]

The lack of time and the fear of being caught just then, by people who were suspicious even of a glance, talking with any one in private prevented me from saying anything concerning what had happened. We left soon after. When we arrived where the schooner was, we boarded it, and found Pagés already there. After a few questions, the answers to which showed the alarm he felt, the captain said to him, "Very well, look at these letters which came by this same schooner. In them we are informed that the government in New Orleans took away the crew because it considered them suspicious. We are warned to be on guard."

"To whom does this schooner belong?"

"To me," replied Pagés.

"To whom does the cargo belong?"

"To me also, excepting a part which belongs to a passenger." [87]

"What was the purpose of your visit to General Santa Anna yesterday?"

"I went for a ride, in order to accompany the ladies who wished to meet him."

"What did you say to this gentleman?" (turning his eyes towards me).

"When I told him I had arrived from New Orleans, he said that he was without provisions and I promised to send him some to-day by a cart." [88]

[86] See my letter to His Excellency previously mentioned in which I say to him, "At the very moment I was busy trying to present a protest in your name, consulting the consul on the subject, you wrote a letter defaming me." The consul told me at the time that I could assure His Excellency that the protest was unnecessary and that his mind could be at ease on the subject for no one would claim a dollar from him.

[87] A man like Pagés, who was well known in the country and who two months before had no capital, was there anything else needed to convict him on the spot?

[88] Had he revealed the impossibility of realizing the plan, (which I had

While inspecting some papers which Pagés had in his hat, the captain took those which were in English and read them, passing those in Spanish to me to read, though he understood this language to some extent. Among them was a safe conduct issued by the Mexican consul to protect Pagés during the voyage against any war vessels he might encounter. This was a document of little importance, considering that the schooner was flying the American flag and could not be molested. Nevertheless, this insignificant document caused him much harm.

In view of the facts, the captain decided to carry his investigations further and consequently ordered the arrest of Pagés, the captain of the schooner, a passenger, and the whole crew. The following day, a judge from Colombia came, and after three more days spent in taking declarations, making investigations, and inspecting all the papers of the ship's captain, exhausting every imaginable means for bringing out testimony to reveal the accomplices of Pagés, they were all set at liberty, except the latter who was detained as a prisoner because of the aforesaid safe conduct.

Now, then, where is the plan he had for effecting the escape of His Excellency? Was it not necessary, at least, that he should have taken the captain of the vessel into the secret? But this is not all. Even if he had not found out while he was in New Orleans that we were twenty or thirty miles inland, he would have needed forty or fifty trusty men, who would necessarily have been in the secret, and he could not have brought any passengers.[89] Again (supposing we had still been in the port) he would have had to slip into the harbor at night. It was impossible for an American schooner with forty or fifty men to come in unnoticed in the day time. Besides, after landing his force, he would have had to surprise our guard to overcome it

not revealed to Capt. Patton) how could I have explained the circumstances? How was I repaid for constantly exposing my life for His Excellency?

[89] How could he have left New Orleans for Texas, in an American schooner with forty or fifty sailors when the ordinary crew is six men, including the captain and the pilot?

without attracting attention, to take us aboard, and to weigh anchor. And having performed this miracle, would we then have been out of all danger? The schooners *Independence, Invincible,* and *Brutus,* when not in this port were in Galveston Bay, near Velasco, or cruising in the Gulf. Was it not more than likely that we would have been captured? What then?

Having demonstrated that there was no such project, and the difficulty of carrying it out even if it had been contemplated, granting that we had not been removed from the port, let us now consider the utter human impossibility of realizing such a plan after we were removed twenty-five miles inland from the port.

Let us lay down as a principle that the schooner could not enter through Velasco with a crew of forty or fifty men except at night for the reasons already expressed. It would then have had to make its way up the river for a distance of twenty-five or thirty leagues to the landing. Let us grant that this obstacle could be overcome. From the landing to the place where we were it was more than six leagues by land. How could the crew get to us through a country infested by the enemy with two intervening towns between us? Let us grant that this second obstacle could be overcome, that the guard was overpowered, that we were able to cover the said distance, and that we were safe in the schooner (all these miracles taking place during the night). What would we have gained then?

No one ignores the fact that there are always at least two steamboats on the river continually cruising between the towns located on its banks, specially Brazoria, midway between Velasco and the above-mentioned landing. This being the fact, the general alarm which our escape would have occasioned on the following day, the need of a whole day for the schooner to make its way down the river to Velasco, being forced to overpower the steamboats and being dependant upon favorable winds to cross the bar, would have made the success of the venture extremely doubtful. What human power could have overcome all these obstacles?

From all these it is to be concluded: 1st, that there was no plan to escape; 2nd, that even if any had been entertained, it was absolutely impracticable from every point of view; 3rd, that it is an incredible falsehood to claim the denunciation of an imaginary plot, for there can be no effect without a cause; and lastly, that it is perfectly evident that, when he asked for the above-mentioned letters from General Santa Anna, Pagés had no other idea in mind save the acquisition of money by this means, his plan being to go to New Orleans, secure 5,000 *pesos*, buy a schooner and a small cargo and, without any plan for the liberation of the prisoners, return as he did to a country where no one could ask him to give an account, and to enjoy there the fruit of the lack of foresight and caution on the part of those who gave him the documents with which he acquired the capital he desired.   This is all there was to the matter, and nothing more.

Captain Patton returned to Orozimba, leaving me in Columbia guarded by two soldiers.   As the incident of the schooner had brought some of the members of the cabinet to that city, I decided to take advantage of the opportunity to plead for my liberty.   I could very likely have obtained this as early as the month of May, for Messrs. Hardeman and Grayson had urged me to request it when we were in Velasco, basing my claim on the fact that not being a military man, I should be released as was done in the case of others in similar circumstances.[90]   I did not do it at that time because I did not want to appear selfish.   The reward I received for my self-denial has been seen.   My pleadings were seconded by those of other persons, Captain Patton himself contributing in no small way to my release after he returned from Orozimba.   Finally, on the 13th of September my petition was granted, and I was given passage on the schooner *Fannin* which was sailing on the following day. While suffering from malaria, a common malady in that region, I boarded the vessel and, as a result, I reached New Orleans in such a condition that two persons had to help me ashore.   The

[90] The chaplain of the army, several customs officials, and other persons taken prisoners from vessels of the Mexican merchant marine.

worst is that I was without pecuniary resources and even without baggage. Behold the reward for all the hardships endured in the Texas campaign, for the many dangers, vexations, sorrows and sufferings experienced after its termination at the battle of San Jacinto! Supported by perfect justice, impelled thereby to answer the falsehoods circulated against me, feeling duty bound, since I have been pitilessly attacked, to defend my honor before the public and the whole world, and, above all, dominated by a desire for the happiness of my generous country, I have spoken truthfully, both regarding those incidents concerning it and those that touch my own person, without making use of those despicable means which my heart abhors. On the contrary, had I not been compelled by the false accusations brought against me to speak, I would not have appeared before the public, because, not having occupied a public post, I did not have to speak. Having been challenged to speak, I have but fulfilled a duty.[91]

MEXICO, May 20, 1837.

[91] The following documents are appended: No. 1 Juan José Holzinger to Colonel John A. Wharton, Velasco, June 3, 1836; No. 2 Santa Anna to the Minister of War and Marine, Manga de Clavo, March 11, 1827; Santa Anna to the Minister of War and Marine, Manga de Clavo, March 11, 1837 [to this is appended Houston's report of the battle of San Jacinto, April 25. 1836 in translation]; No. 3 Santa Anna to Filisola, San Jacinto, April 22, 1836; No. 4 Santa Anna to Filisola, San Jacinto, April 22, 1836; No. 5 Santa Anna to Filisola, San Jacinto, April 22, 1836; No. 6 Filisola to Santa Anna, Camp on the St. Bernard, April 23, 1836; No. 7 Articles of Agreement proposed by the Texas Government, no date; No. 8 Public Treaty of Velasco, May 14, 1836; No. 9 Secret Treaty of Velasco, May 14, 1836; No. 10 Santa Anna's Farewell to the Texans, Velasco, June 1, 1836; No. 11 Santa Anna to Captain H. Brown, Commandant of the *Invincible,* on board the *Invincible,* June 4, 1836; No. 12 Santa Anna to Burnet, Velasco, June 4, 1836; No. 13 Burnet to Santa Anna, [Velasco, June 4, 1836]; No. 14 Santa Anna to Gen. Andrew Jackson, Columbia, July 4 1836 [to this is attached Houston's report of the battle of San Jacinto].

POSTSCRIPT [92]

AFTER finishing the present account, it was necessary for me to leave my home in order to attend to its publication. On Sunday, the 21st of May last [1837], while attending to this matter, I was unexpectedly set upon by Col. Almonte and D. N. Legof at about four o'clock in the afternoon. They made me a prisoner and took me to the military headquarters of this city where the above-mentioned colonel turned me over to Bernardino Santa Cruz, of the second active battalion, and sergeant of the guard, giving him a small piece of paper on which he wrote with pencil, in my presence as well as that of several other soldiers, an order providing for my imprisonment.

Almonte and Legof, self-constituted deputies, left me in charge of the guard and returned half an hour later to take me to the jail of the Deputation where I remained until the following day, the 22nd. I was then removed to that of the Ex-Acordada.

I am ignorant of the authority which those two individuals had over my person, for even granting that an order for my arrest had been issued, it is certainly degrading for a colonel to constitute himself a deputy to carry out its execution. On the other hand, if such an order did exist, which I do not believe possible, for it was not shown to me nor to the above-mentioned sergeant of the guard, how can an individual be arrested on the mere accusation of another without first being heard, without a previous verbal judgment, and without practicing the corre-

92 The author adds the following explanations after the appended documents. There is no heading given in the text, and without a careful perusal of the documents, the reader might pass over this section without noticing it. These explanations are followed by one additional document: Letter A, José Reyes López to Santa Anna, Mexico, April 5, 1837. This letter will be found translated in Santa Anna's *Manifesto Doc. 4*. [C. E. C.]

sponding investigation as provided by Article 43 of the fifth constitutional law? If it is true that there was no order, with what authority did Col. Almonte and Legof proceed to reduce me to a prisoner? Article 2, paragraph 1, of the first constitutional law clearly states that "No citizen may be imprisoned without an order from a competent judge, given in writing and duly signed, nor may he be arrested without orders from the authorities designated by law." Let them not claim now that there was an order from a judge, for had there been any such, they would have exercised good care to have shown it to me, both when they took me to the principal jail and when, half an hour later, they removed me to that of the Deputation. Of course, they may have tried to cover their tracks since, providing themselves with such an order to answer any criminal charge that may result as a consequence of this infamous act in violation of the laws. This has very likely been done, for it has always been thus in the struggles between might and right, favoritism and discrimination. But let us kindly suppose that some judge was induced to issue the order in opposition to Article 43 of the fifth law just cited. Are Almonte and Legof less guilty on this account? Who authorized them to become the ministers of justice? Has not every tribunal its own officers to carry out its orders? Useless protests! The truth of the matter is that I am a prisoner, that I have been insulted, outraged; and the law . . . the law . . . what does it matter? Those that have no influence need not invoke it. The law is but the plaything and exclusive property of the powerful whose tool it is.

Having been taken, as I said before, to the Ex-Acordada, they took a would-be declaration on that same day in the presence of Col. Almonte and of Lieut. Col. Ignacio Sierra y Rosso, practicing attorney and clerk of the general revenue office, who appeared as my prosecutor, acting as the representative of General Santa Anna. The cause of the proceedings was not made known to me nor was the name of the accuser disclosed as is provided by Article 47, of the fifth law, thus violating at the same time Article 2, paragraph 4 of the aforementioned first constitutional law. Having concluded the above-mentioned declaration, I was deprived of my papers over my protest that they constituted my defence and justification. The judge ordered me to turn them over to the acting secretary, José Andrade, which I did. They did not even take an inventory of them, so unjustly and illegally was I deprived of my papers. Afterwards, by dint of repeated requests and demands, both on my part and on that of my representative, they were returned to me on the 9th of the present month, that is to say, 19 days after the secretary took them into his keeping. Before this took place the examination of them was begun by my opponent, Sierra y Rosso, in my presence and that of the judge. Although the judge and the clerk of the court had to leave their office to attend to the visit of the jail which the supreme court of justice makes weekly, he continued the examination, taking out those he wished and returning the rest to me. And would it be thought that the already cited Article 2, paragraph 4, of the first law did not suffer any other violation than the taking of my papers? This was but the least of them. It was also violated by the search which was carried out in my room situated on the street of the Coliseo, my residence being in the Gran Hotel de Mexico. It is true that I was previously asked to name a person of my confidence to witness it. But it is likewise true, that, although I named such an individual of my acquaintance, one who lived in the said hotel, he was not present at the time the search was carried out because the secretary did not give him due notice, nor did he request his presence to witness the act. In spite of this fact the search was carried out, and my room was opened and ransacked as much as was thought proper. He failed, however, to find anything to gratify his anxiety as is shown by his hasty proceedings and inquisitorial impatience.

Up to here I have given a faithful account of the vexations, insults and scandalous procedure to which I have been subjected from the moment in which my arch enemies, Almonte and Legof, violating the rights of society, its laws, and all individual guarantees, pounced upon me like carnivorous beasts and reduced me to prison on their own authority. I suppose I should congratulate myself that such an outrage did not go beyond these limits, thanks to its having taken place in the middle of the day. They might have gone much further, prompted by the motives that inspired them, but since my life has been spared, permit me to make the following observations, or rather to draw a comparative analogy, to show the immense difference that exists between the acts of those gentlemen and my conduct, regardless of the point of view from which they may be considered.

Col. Almonte, because of his position as aide to the general-in-chief, was always in the most intimate contact with me and we were joined by the closest friendship from the beginning of the first ill-fated Texas campaign. On various occasions he helped out in the work of the secretaryship of His Excellency which was under my care. For these reasons, we had a mutual regard for each other and our friendship grew apace. After the unfortunate engagement of San Jacinto, fate willed that we should continue in the same intimacy, for we were excluded from the rest of the prisoners and put together with the general-in-chief who was also a prisoner. Thus we were exposed to the same dangers, the same privations, insults, hunger, misery, and want; and we shared equally all sufferings. Our opinion as to the fundamental origin of so painful a disaster as that in which we found ourselves being identical, he disclosed to me a thousand and a thousand times his immutable determination of severing all relations with General Santa Anna after we were set at liberty, convinced, as he was, of his inconsistencies and as a result of other circumstances which I am not free to explain. For a space of almost six months, we shared the same bed. During many confidential conversations, we always agreed upon our disapproval of the greater part of the measures adopted by General Santa Anna in regard to the Texans. Finally, as proof and testimony of our intimate friendship, he revealed to me in July of last year the plan which the said general had confided to him, by which the two were to escape, abandoning Col. Núñez and myself to our fate. To this he would not consent. And yet, it is that same Col. Almonte, let me repeat it a thousand times, who to-day is still the friend of General Santa Anna. It is he who has outraged me, insulted me, and imprisoned me. How miserable is human kind! How gladly I now ask that his present acts be compared with the praiseworthy conduct observed during our imprisonment as described in the paragraph which I dedicated to him in my previous account of the Texas campaign! Let it not be thought on this account that I am trying to justify myself. I have left the cited paragraph just as I wrote it because its contents are true and were not inspired by flattery, a weakness which is absolutely foreign to my character and my principles. Yea, contrary to all my principles, I repeat, which were indelibly engraved upon my heart from infancy and cannot, therefore, admit of any variation as is the case when such principles are studied and learned after adolescence.

Now let us talk of Legof. This man after having rebelled against the supreme government in Zacatecas, was taken prisoner to this capital where he was kept as such in the building of the Ex-Inquisition until he was sentenced and banished from the republic. He remained in New Orleans until Col. Núñez went to that city in December of last year. It was he who brought him back to this country, removing from him, on his own authority, the sentence that exiled him. They both embarked from Tampico on the American schooner *Louis Jones*. From there they proceeded to Vera Cruz, doubtlessly counting upon the friendship and protection of General Santa Anna for the toleration of his return to the republic. This assumption has proven correct.

If he had but been content with remaining in those regions, well and good, but he dared to come to this capital with a commission which perhaps was not the most honorable. He has spied upon me day and night until the perpetration of the criminal attempt to arrest me. He insulted me by word of mouth, continually threatening me with death and using improper expressions, characteristic of his class and low breeding. He went so far as to tear brutally the front of my shirt. Such an insult and vexation have been infinitely more painful and distressing to me than the unjust and illegal imprisonment to which I have been subjected. Such an act is all the more punishable when perpetuated by an obscure man, a declared enemy of the supreme government, by whom, as I have said before, he had been exiled. For such a man to insult and offend so atrociously an individual who has just sacrificed himself in the service of that supreme government, undergoing the hardships of the entire first Texas campaign; who succeeded miraculously in overcoming unheard of dangers, after having been sentenced to be shot like the rest of the prisoners; and, in a word, one who suffered the greatest misery, exposed to the harshest and most ferocious treatment that one can imagine, is a crime all the more punishable. Should a citizen with such a record be thus unjustly offended by a paid ruffian? Alas, it is but the sad truth! And while the criminal Legof calmly walks the streets of the capital, I am deprived of my liberty. Astounding inconsequence of human life!

While waiting the final outcome of the plot whose only purpose has been to prevent me from publishing my account and dispelling the mysterious veil that still envelops the facts of the first Texas campaign, I will not fail to avail myself of every means possible to attain my end, the publication of my account. If, alone as I am, I succeed in doing it, I desire no further gratification for all my past sufferings, my present vexations, and the hardships that fate may still hold in store for me. I must now request the indulgence of the reader for using some expressions which escaped me, weighed down by the sorrow that overpowers my heart. It was impossible for me to repress such expressions in trying to justify myself, I have, however, spoken but the truth.

At the Ex-Acordada, Mexico, June 20th, 1837.

In spite of my resolution not to occupy myself again with anything related to the Texas campaign, I have been forced by hard necessity to answer the charges of might in its perfidious attempts to soil my honor with impunity. I have already recounted the most notable events, both during the campaign and after the disastrous engagement of San Jacinto. But in spite of the fact that anyone who reads the *Manifesto* just published by Antonio López de Santa Anna, late commander-in-chief of the army of operations in Texas, regarding the campaign, cannot but see in it only a repetition, though more elaborate, of the report made by that same officer to the government on March 11th of last year, I still find myself obliged to take exception to some of the statements made therein and to various explanations which are advanced. By means of these, he tries to disguise the truth and goes so far as to try to justify the inhuman actions by which history will ever point to the year 1836 in Texas. On the other hand, he tries to justify the misfortune of San Jacinto, and lastly, what is still more astonishing, he tries to justify the shameful transactions into which he entered after that misfortune, ignoring the prodigious number of complications which as an inevitable consequence must follow the forced attempt to weave a maze of subtle excuses which themselves weaken the ill-woven fabric and make more evident the futile defence.

"Never has the ambitious thought of obtaining universal approval for my actions entered my mind." These are the words of the introduction of the *Manifesto* we are discussing. In truth, one is forced to admit the toleration of the principle as stated here, but one must absolutely reject the favorable interpretation to which it lends itself in the mysterious and figurative sense in which it is used. I, personally, cannot pass judgment on events that transpired before my time except by following the opinion of those who witnessed them. But, according to this same principle, I do not find in the *Manifesto* any acts that deserve universal approval. I, who was an eyewitness to an infinite number of acts, many of which sensibly affected me and about which I have written, limiting myself always, however, to those that were necessary for my defence and national welfare, will not be the only one to censure them without danger of being mistaken. How, then, can I agree, even remotely, to a criminal approval of his actions? How can I help but be justly persuaded

of their universal disapproval? There is a chasm that cannot be bridged between the strong and manly voice of truth and the artificial and feigned voice of falsehood raised to drown the former. Only one side of the picture has been shown, and for this reason it has been necessary to make use of the most unjust, inhuman, and illegal procedure, putting me in prison, only to keep me from presenting the other side. (They have succeeded, in fact, up to the present.) It is easy enough to color such a picture to suit one's taste under such conditions. But now that one may see it from any point of view, the first picture will not appear so rosy. But let us return to our subject.

The sad condition of the treasury, an unavoidable consequence of the administration of that time [93] forced Congress ,on the 23rd of November of that year, to authorize the supreme government to negotiate a loan. Not being able to secure the loan in this capital, it empowered the general-in-chief of the army that was to engage in the campaign that was being planned to negotiate the loan. Congress was forced to take this action in view of the critical situation that confronted it. National honor demanded the prompt chastisement of the ungrateful conduct of the Texas colonists who had shamelessly rebelled against the supreme government of the nation, that nation that had taken them to her bosom and had showered them with favors. Agreeable to instructions, Santa Anna, who was the general-in-chief and also the president of the republic at that time, negotiated a loan in San Luis Potosí with the firm of Messrs. Rubio and Errazu, of that city, for the sum of 400,000 *pesos,* half in silver and half in bonds. Furthermore, the amount in bonds was to be used for the food supplies necessary for the army, which were to be imported free of duty, the entire sum to be repaid with the proceeds from the forced loans of the departments of San Luis, Guanajuato, Guadalajara, and Zacatecas. In default of these, the sum was to be repaid by drafts against the maritime customs houses of Tampico and Matamoros. It

---

[93] The administration of 1835.

was also granted the lenders that bonds previously issued by the last mentioned customs house were to be admitted them to the amount of 47,000 *pesos*.[94]

It is only necessary to keep in mind that the government had forbidden the acceptance of any bonds as payment of duties at that time, to realize immediately the immense advantage which such a contract gave to the firm making the loan. This was most lucrative to them but ruinous to the nation. Although the above-mentioned firm previously turned over almost the whole of the 200,000 *pesos,* in cash, agreeable to the contract,[95] Congress refused to approve it. As a result, a short while after our departure from San Luis, Mr. Errazu overtook us post haste. He immediately communicated the news to His Excellency, which, in all truth, was indeed sad news for them as well as for others. His Excellency dispatched a note to Barragán, president *ad interim,* not in the friendly terms to which he refers in his *Manifesto,* but in positive and urgent terms. This guarantee could not fail to dispel the uneasiness of the agent that had negotiated the contract with the government, who was not ignorant of the fact that the writer was the government itself.

Let us pass rapidly over the *Manifesto* until we reach the time of our stop in Béxar to which I have previously referred. The events of this period though transcendental and numerous, are made still more important by what he says in his *Manifesto* regarding them. "Having occupied Béxar, etc., the enemy retired to the fort of the Alamo, which dominates the city. With a siege

[94] It was a condition of the negotiation that the contracts were to be approved by the government. I was asked to make the authorized copies which were sent to the government. This was the only knowledge and intervention which I had in the transaction.

[95] General Castrillón deposited at this time 1,000 *pesos* in the treasury of the army of operations, which were to earn 4 per cent monthly. Mr. Errazu, a member of the firm with which the contract was negotiated, deposited 6,000 which were to earn the same interest. Both deposits were made with the knowledge of His Excellency. The last amount turned out to belong to General Castrillón also. The trick was original, to say the least. See the letter with regard to this transaction, published in the *Manifesto* of His Excellency, document 4.

of a few days, it would have been forced to surrender." Our entry into Béxar took place on the 23rd of February, and the assault was made on the 6th of the following March. Was not the fort besieged for twelve days by more than 600 men under General Sesma? If the siege had been prolonged a few more days, it would likely have surrendered. Why didn't we wait? Did we not stay in that city until the end of the said month after the assault was made? What advantage was gained by the brigades of Gaona and Sesma as a result of their having set out a few days before that of His Excellency? The first of these, whose objective was Anahuac, was detained at the Colorado by the enemy, while the second whose goal was Nacogdoches lost its way in the desert just beyond Bastrop. Such were the advantages of the so much praised triumph of the Alamo! One hundred and eighty-three unfortunate wretches who were sacrificed there cost us the lives of over 400 Mexicans! He [General Santa Anna] would have us believe that "life was guaranteed to the enemy on condition that they surrender their arms and take an oath never to take them up again against Mexico." There never was such a promise made. From the moment we entered Béxar, the enemy was asked to surrender at discretion to which the enemy never consented. Let them deny this fact if they dare; let them deny the fact that a red flag was raised on the steeple of the cathedral of that city as a sign that no quarter would be granted and that everything would be carried by fire and sword.

"The enemy," continues the *Manifesto,* "discouraged by this blow which left mournful memories (fateful, I should say) fled before us; but our flanks were constantly harassed by guerrilla bands." Only a few days after the assault, our whole army, except the brigade of General Urrea which was operating in the Bahía region, was assembled in Béxar. What flanks, therefore, and where, were being harassed constantly by guerrilla bands? We did not even know where the enemy was to be found until after the departure of General Sesma who advised us of its position on the Colorado. Already, at that time, His

Excellency believed the campaign ended. As proof of this, read what General Filisola says regarding this matter in his *Representación* to the supreme government, previously cited. "After the capture of the Alamo, which took place on the 9th of March, and the insignificant victory over Dr. Grant in which twenty adventurers were killed, together with three Mexicans who were in his company, on the 2nd of the said month, the news of which was received in Béxar on the 7th, the general-in-chief conceived the idea that the enemy would not show its face again, and that consequently the war was ended. From this false idea, and the utter contempt which was felt for the enemy from this time on, have arisen all the misfortunes that have befallen us subsequently, and unless more caution and prudence is exercised in the future in the prosecution of an enterprise which demands great firmness, much circumspection, and the greatest judgment, many more reverses may be justly expected." A little further on, Filisola says: "If the capture of the Alamo and the insignificant victory of General Urrea over Dr. Grant made the general-in-chief conceive the idea that the war was over, the later victory [96] of the same general persuaded him that his presence there was no longer necessary and that he should return to the capital of Mexico immediately by sea, going from Cópano or Matagorda to Tampico, thence by land to San Luis, etc. [97] and leaving me in charge of the campaign which was to be continued according to his instructions until matters in Texas were settled. Agreeable to this idea he ordered Urrea, on the 25th, to occupy all the places along the coast from Guadalupe Victoria to Galveston, taking for granted that the left flank was covered by Sesma. He was strictly instructed *to execute all prisoners taken* in accordance with the orders of the supreme government concerning this matter. Similar orders were given the commandant of Goliad, and the same were repeated to Gaona and Sesma, all of whom were urged to execute all prisoners taken under arms

[96] The victory of Encinal del Perdido, of General Urrea.

[97] With regard to this point, read my note [27] about the departure of the general-in-chief from San Felipe.

and to expel from the country those who had not taken an active part in the campaign. The general-in-chief likewise ordered, by the same general order of the day, that the cavalry brigade under orders of General Andrade, the pickets from the permanent battalions of Guerrero, Matamoros, and Jiménez, as well as those of the active battalions of Querétaro and First of Mexico, all the pieces of artillery then at general headquarters brought from Mexico, and the 32 wagons used for their transportation, furnished by José Lombardo and Company, be held in readiness to set out for San Luís Potosí the 1st of April. The reason given for this order was the heavy expense which their upkeep occasioned."

Let us return to Béxar and take up the *Manifesto* again. "The prisoners of Goliad were put to death in accordance with law. . . . They did not surrender under a capitulation, as shown by the official report of General Urrea." I have already given the details at length regarding this point which they still try to envelop in mystery. But the seriousness of this incident and the grave consequences that arose from it, for it was the cause of our misfortunes and sufferings while prisoners of the Texans, imperiously demand new explanations. Let us kindly suppose that the prisoners at Goliad were justly executed, agreeable to the instructions circulated by the supreme government, under date of December 30, 1835—we cannot say according to law, for the executive has no power to dictate laws—in what article of the said circular is such a penalty prescribed for the colonists of Texas? If Fannin and many of his companions were old and well-known colonists, why were they not spared from the frightful penalty of death? Santa Anna cites the official report of General Urrea, which he appends as document 6. Why did he not reproduce the private letter of this general in which he recommends His Excellency to exercise clemency in deciding the fate of those unfortunate wretches? If the letter which Lieut. Col. Holzinger addressed to the Texan Colonel Wharton is read over, it will be seen that though there was no formal capitulation, the prisoners were nevertheless promised that General Urrea would use his influence with the supreme government to obtain clemency. This promise should have been sufficient to secure a stay of execution until the supreme government could render a final decision. No doubt the government would not have failed to heed the recommendation of the victorious general on the one hand, nor, on the other, would it have passed up the opportunity of exercising its sweetest prerogative, that of granting a pardon. Far from this, however, General Urrea was bitterly reprimanded by the general-in-chief who ordered, in triplicate, the consummation of the cruel and bloody sacrifice of the innocent victims. In view of the repeated orders and the evident determination of having the prisoners executed, it is truly too much to claim now that he " would have been willing to pardon the unfortunate victims. . . ." On the contrary, one needs to have a heart of wax to advance such claims. We should not, therefore, be surprised at the statements which follow in his *Manifesto,* now occupying our attention, concerning the eighty-six men taken prisoners at Cópano who were saved by the series of coincidences already pointed out in my account of the campaign. His Excellency claims they were saved thanks to the summary investigation which he ordered to be instituted to determine their status. It is to be kept in mind that the said investigation was not ordered until after the final order for their execution had been written to the commandant of Bahia.[98]

No less surprising or absurd is the attempt of His Excellency to justify himself by the insertion in his *Manifesto* of document 8, which itself presents so many evident contradictions. This inquiry in which His Excellency asks what policy he is to observe in regard to prisoners, Mexicans or Americans, taken either by force, or as a result of capitulations, or of surrender at discretion was addressed to the supreme government from Rio Grande, or rather Villa de Guerrero, a point over 400 leagues distant. The date of the consultation was February 16, 1836, and it was addressed to the supreme government from a

[98] For the details of this incident, see the general account of the campaign, p. 107 and following.

point 400 leagues distant, as already stated. Still the humane butchery of Texans was begun on March 6th with the massacre of the defenders of the Alamo, followed by that of Goliad, etc. If His Excellency was prompted by the "desire of ameliorating, if possible, the most rigorous aspects of that Law,[99] why did he make this inquiry when he had no intention of awaiting the resolution of the supreme government in regard to it? It is with a series of such ridiculous contradictions that the sacred name of *Humanity* is desecrated! Have we sunk so low that the good judgment of the people and the common sense of the honorable nation to which His Excellency addresses such a *Manifesto* can be thus insulted?

Let us turn, though momentarily, to the passage that refers to the imprisonment of His Excellency where he exclaims: "In the palace of Mexico as in this humble hut, in the midst of the applause of a free people the same as amidst the insolent hisses of the Texans, I have always acted the same." Such words cannot be reconciled with his never-to-be-forgotten farewell address to the Texans.[100] After he negotiated treaties with their cabinet—one secret and one public—after he was placed aboard a vessel, a free man as a result of the already mentioned treaties; after he agreed to have two commissioners, former members of the cabinet, accompany him to this capital and offered to present them to the sovereign Congress of the Mexican nation, promising to use his influence with this body to foster the successful accomplishment of their mission which was no other than the recognition of the independence of Texas as the Convention desired; after he recognized their government by treating with it as an equal; after he requested and even pleaded for a meeting of the cabinet to draw up the said treaties; after all this, I repeat, he

[99] Reference is made here to the already cited circular of the supreme government which was drawn up in Tacubaya, at the residence of His Excellency, before he set out for San Luis Potosí, the occasion for it being the landing of ex-general Mejía at Tampico. The circular was later transmitted, on December 30th, 1835, to the commandant generals, etc.

[100] I have already referred to this document issued at Velasco on June 1st, 1836.

calls them outlaws and pirates. What name must we give to such conduct.[101]

The war against the Texas colonists, undeniably just and under all concepts unavoidable on the part of the Mexican republic, has been, nevertheless, the source of the most painful attacks upon our national honor as a result of the shifting and shameful scenes enacted there, the notorious agent of which is well-known. The honor of the country to which, as His Excellency says, his own belongs cannot shield, in truth, the numberless incidents that have taken place since the misfortune of San Jacinto, all of which are generally known. Much less can it be a justification for the publication of the documents that have been attached to the *Manifesto* all of which, in spite of the strenuous efforts to disguise them, can never hope to deceive by their evidence the dullest intellect. After the many and repeated assurances and guarantees pledged by His Excellency to the Texans, whom he addressed as *his friends, brave in action and generous in peace,* whom he called *his companions in arms,* horror of horrors; he now calls them his enemies, the enemies of his country! He now swears before the world that he never soiled the fair name of Mexican while in Texas! He now offers to lead his compatriots by the hand to the margins of the San Jacinto, to the very ruins where they wish to bury his glory . . . to take them to the port of Velasco that they may hear from the enemy themselves the testimony of his *firmness!* There, where he can only show them the sad resting place, the horrible spectacle of the lifeless forms of the victims that were sacrificed on that fatal 21st of April! There, the hateful field where —with absolute lack of firmness—the already mentioned treaties were signed on the 14th of May, where the proclamation of June 1st was issued, where so many other similar acts took

[101] Although the return of His Excellency was impeded at that time, this incident can in no manner invalidate the force of the signed treaties, for they were put into effect by our embarkation. If an unforeseen coincidence prevented their being fully carried out at that time, there is no doubt that had not this circumstance arisen, we would have sailed for this capital with the commissioners that were to accompany us in the same vessel.

place, all of which show everything but firmness, that firmness which he tries to prove! Great God, pardon this outburst to which justice and self-defence have forced me, violating the silence I have observed.

I wish I were not suffering from an absolute lack of means that I might be as explicit as I would like. The unjust imprisonment to which I have been subjected by some wretches who, unable to refute the eternal truths I have set down, have openly had recourse to the most scandalous arbitrariness to deprive me of my liberty in the hope of preventing me from publishing my account has reduced me to penury. I say openly, because up to the present, after three months have elapsed, and in spite of my just remonstrances, the paid minions of this outrage, safely and peacefully walk the streets.

Whenever an individual is made to suffer without being guilty, whoever is not deprived of intelligence and common sense believes himself endangered. This is but natural, for personal guarantees are destroyed. All personal rights are endangered by such an act, and then all become fearful and no one can take a step without apprehension.

"I believe that a country thus stained by an arbitrary act, is in need of being purified by the exemplary punishment of the guilty. Therefore, whenever I see a citizen arbitrarily imprisoned in any country where prompt retaliation for such a violation of the established order does not follow, I shall be forced to exclaim: This people may desire to be free, they may deserve their freedom, but they have not yet learned the first principles of liberty. [102]

RAMÓN MARTÍNEZ CARO

Mexico, August 31, 1837.

[102] Benjamin Constant, *Course in Political Rights,* II.

REPRESENTATION

Addressed to the Supreme Government

BY

GENERAL VICENTE FILISOLA

IN DEFENSE OF HIS HONOR

With Notes on His Operations as General-in-Chief
of the Army of Texas

MEXICO

1836

REPRESENTACION

DIRIGIDA

AL SUPREMO GOBIERNO

POR

EL GENERAL

VICENTE FILISOLA,

EN

DEFENSA DE SU HONOR

Y

ACLARACION DE SUS OPERACIONES

COMO

GENERAL EN GEFE

DEL EJÉRCITO SOBRE TEJAS.

MÉXICO.

Impreso por Ignacio Cumplido, calle de los Rebeldes, casa N. 2

1836.

Facsimile of the Spanish title page

MOST EXCELLENT SIR

Vicente Filisola, general of division, has the honor of addressing Your Excellency with all the respect due the supreme government, to render a true and frank account of his military and political conduct as general-in-chief of the army of operations in Texas.

Sir, the surprise and mortification which I have experienced as a result of the slanderous accusations propagated against me, framed with but little reflection and great levity, entirely erroneous in the main, and inspired by a false and malicious intent, utterly without foundation, are only commensurate with the purity and sincerity of my intentions. These slanders and false accusations have appeared in official communications and in the official *Diario* of the supreme government, the official article of the 15th of last July being particularly offensive.

If such slanders did but wound my personal pride, if I alone were accused of ignorance or of weakness, carried perhaps to an excess out of regard for the life of the first general of the republic, a prisoner among his enemies, and for the safety of 600 Mexicans, I would sacrifice my feelings in silence and esteem the sacrifice but a small matter. But there is nothing, however great, that can demand the sacrifice of one's honor, particularly when, as in this case, the honor involved is not exclusively my own but that of the army with which I am inseparably identified. It cannot be said that the army adjudged me unworthy of its command, nor that it has thought its well-earned reputation stained by the retreat undertaken under my orders.

Consequently, I come before Your Excellency and before the nation not only to vindicate myself but to demand justice against the low and petty intrigues by which personal animosity has tried to defame me, I come, also, to ask for an explanation of the depreciating words with which my conduct has been condemned while threatening to bring me to a formal trial. If such a trial is to take place, as I desire and believe advisable, the penalty should not be imposed before the trial. No greater penalty can be inflicted upon me now, however, than that to which I have already been subjected by the manner in which my acts have been presented to the public in the official communications and circulars of the government, bent on placing upon me the whole responsibility for all our misfortunes, though they are the result of various causes. The idea that I alone could have repaired the great losses attendant upon an unfortunate defeat, had I been willing, has been made popular.

To remain silent under such circumstances would be an injustice to myself, an equally unjust offense to the army, and an admission of the small esteem in which my character as commander has been held.

It is not, therefore, a spirit of vengeance that guides my pen, I will restrict myself to that which is strictly necessary for my justification. The bitterness of the attacks made upon me will not be a weapon in my defense. The truth which the government has a right to expect, that truth with which Your Excellency should be acquainted, shall not be sacrificed to considerations of the moment, for time alters conditions but truth endures forever and belongs to private and public morality.

Now is the opportune moment for the truth to be told, while men who can testify or impugn it are still living. Later it might not have the same force nor the same merit. In the future this truth might be an enigma which if presented today might be explained.

Your Excellency will permit me, therefore, to ask that this truth be not attributed to any criminal designs, much less to passion, or to political inadvertence, for it is necessary that I now speak out. Though I tried to make myself understood before, my dispatches of the 28th of April and the 14th and 31st of May [1] were misunderstood because I was unable to give the painful details which I now present. The danger that my communications might fall into the hands of the enemy made it imperative that I should not go into details.

After giving these details, I shall plead my cause as I may deem convenient and shall list the accusations piled against me, refuting them in due time.

In the official communication referred to it is assumed: First, that the unexpected defeat of the vanguard commanded by the general-in-chief and his unfortunate imprisonment produced such discouragement in the army that a retreat was undertaken as a result, and that during the march, the army lost successively all the advantages gained, though the enemy never showed its face, considering our force superior and fearing that a new engagement might prove disastrous to them. Second, that I gave blind obedience to the orders of the general-in-chief obtained under duress. Third, that it will always be considered strange and reprehensible that I should have thought of nothing else after the occurrence than a retreat which was mistaken by the enemy for a flight. Fourth, that my acceptance of terms exacted from the general-in-chief by threats of death cannot be contemplated without the deepest indignation. Fifth, that it is a shame for me to have retreated without risking a new engagement; and still a greater shame to have been the first to recognize the usurpers and rebels of Texas as an organized government.

From the note of the Minister of War to General Urrea of May 31st, it is clear that the latter informed the said minister in his secret report of the 11th of that same month of the following services rendered by him. First, that he covered the rear-guard of the army during its retreat from the right bank of the Brazos to the Colorado. Second, that by placing himself in

---

[1] Filisola to the Secretary of War, Arroyo de San Bernardo, April 28, 1836; Filisola to Secretary of War, Guadalupe Victoria, May 14, 1836; and Filisola to Secretary of War, May 31, 1836. All documents cited are appended to the original edition.

the vanguard and by his successful operations he enabled the army to cross the said river. Third, that he saved the artillery. Fourth, that he opposed the retreat of the army. Fifth, that he was confident that as a result of the measures taken by him His Excellency, the president and general-in-chief, might obtain his liberty soon and embark in Galveston for Vera Cruz. Sixth, that he had been opposed to my determination to retreat from the beginning. In the note which that same general addressed to me, a copy of which he transmitted to the said minister on the 1st of last June, he adds the following considerations. First, that before starting on his march to Matamoros from Guadalupe Victoria he spoke to me at length and believed he had convinced me of the urgency of not abandoning the line of Béxar, Goliad, and Cópano until the receipt of new orders from the supreme government. Second, that the enemy, defeated in every engagement which it had dared to sustain and having lost the greater part of its strongholds, had been obliged to abandon their homes, etc., and now saw their only hope in a suspension of hostilities. Third, that the army of operations, after mustering a force of 4,000 men and while occupying a secure position, gave an exhibition of cowardice by failing to undertake any operation to attract fortune to its standards or to try to ascertain at least the fate of its commander-in-chief, furnishing a rallying point for deserters. Instead of all this it is claimed that it began a retreat which Urrea, speaking with the frankness of a soldier, cannot but characterize as a shameful flight, from which emanated the general discouragement that spread throughout the army, excepting the division which he had the honor to command. Fourth, that in my relations with the rebellious Texans I recognized their government as legitimate, and that I granted them privileges which have always been repugnant to the nation. Fifth, that he disapproved the retreat of the army while still on the right bank of the Brazos, being obliged to acquiesce in it only because my orders, transmitted to a detachment of his division which was in Columbia, instructing it to join me without awaiting orders from him, left him with only

400 men in Brazoria and with his rear guard unprotected. Sixth, that His Excellency, the president, is today a prisoner much to our shame. That he had expected, of course, for us to do the opposite of what he commanded. Urrea continues listing a multitude of considerations with no other object than to make me appear ridiculous before the nation, while expressing his indignation and disdain. At the same time he makes himself appear as the only defender of our national honor and our national rights. In the letter of General Vital Fernández of June 2nd, it is stated that I approved a treaty of His Excellency, the President, and the Texan rebels by which the territory of the republic is dismembered. In the letter of the Minister of Foreign Relations, it is asserted that in all these transactions I have been unmindful of my duty and my honor. The official article concludes by saying that the supreme government will doubtless hold me accountable for my acts before the law as prescribed therein, leaving my vindication or punishment in the hands of justice.

Never in my life, Your Excellency, have I undertaken a military campaign with greater goodwill and enthusiasm than when I offered my services for the Texas campaign. Let all those who witnessed my efforts to improve the service from San Luis to Laredo, from there to Monclova, from Monclova to the Brazos and thence back from its banks to the Chilquipín, where I found the orders to turn over the command to Urrea, testify. Not only did I more than fulfill those duties incumbent upon my office, but I even performed the duties of the lowest member of the army, enduring every fatigue and giving an example of sobriety, endurance, resignation, simplicity, and unselfishness. These circumstances, Your Excellency, made me believe that I would deserve better treatment than has been accorded to me. Nevertheless, I had determined, out of regard for the service, to be the only victim, taking upon myself whatever blame for the ill-fate of the undertaking that might be imputed to lack of foresight or care on the part of the supreme government, or that might reflect upon our national honor, I

informed the government of my determination in the communication of the 31st of last May, but I had no idea that more
serious and aggravating slanders would be propagated afterwards, nor was I aware of the low, debasing, and immoral intrigues to which some of my aspiring subordinates have resorted since, nor did I expect the hasty and unmerited rebukes
of the Minister of Foreign Relations and the Secretary of War.
I have been placed, therefore, in the indispensable necessity of
subordinating all considerations to the vindication of my honor.
My duty to myself, to my country, to my family, and to my
friends demand it. Were I to keep silent any longer, it would
amount to a tacit admission of the slanders which cast a blot
upon them all. I take it for granted that the government is
now fully convinced, in view of my communications of the 14th
and 31st of May last and of the 10th of June ² of the imperative
necessity in which the army found itself of retreating, aware
of the true causes that prompted the operation. But it is no
longer sufficient for my vindication before the country, which
has become acquainted with all the recriminations imputed to
me, that the supreme government alone should be fully satisfied
upon this point. It is necessary that my communications be
made public and that I be heard, for no one should be condemned without first being given an opportunity to defend himself. I am a Mexican by adoption. I have attained the highest
rank of my career and consequently no personal interest could
have moved me to enter the Texas campaign other than love
for my adopted country and my honor, so lightly attacked since.
But I shall defend it at all costs, for without it I care not for
life itself, or anything in this world. I am well aware that I
can count on no influential support, for I have always relied
on my personal honesty and my services, both of which will
avail me but little under the present circumstances. But I must
try every resource out of regard for my honor, and, should
I fail in my attempt, I shall have at least the consolation of

² Filisola to the Secretary of War and Marine, Motas de Doña Clara,
June 10, 1836.

having exhausted all means as demanded by honor. Allow me, therefore, Your Excellency, to refute each and every one of the imputations in the order in which they have been presented, proving these charges false by exposing the feigned services which others claim to have rendered.

First, the defeat of the 21st of last April and the imprisonment of the president, cannot be said to have destroyed the morale of the army, for you cannot destroy that which does not exist. I will, however, relate what was done at this time and not what could or should have been done.

After the capture of the Alamo on the 6th of March and the insignificant advantage gained on the 2nd of that same month by the death of Dr. Grant, 20 adventurers and 3 Mexicans who accompanied him, news of which reached Béxar on the 7th, the president and general-in-chief supposed that the enemy would not dare to show its face again and thought that the war was over.

It is from this false conception and the disdain conceived for the enemy that the misfortunes which we have since suffered have emanated and from which we may still expect many others if we persist in displaying the same carelessness which has been exhibited in considering a question which demands the greatest firmness, circumspection, and judgment.

With this false idea in mind, the president decided that there was nothing else to do but to detail the various generals and divisions to occupy the different parts of Texas. Consequently, on the 11th, he ordered Generals Sesma and Woll to march to San Felipe de Austin, continuing afterwards to Harrisburg and Anáhuac. The battalions of Aldama, Matamoros, and Toluca, 50 men from the mounted regiment of Dolores, and 2 six-pounders, altogether a total of 725 men, were assigned to this division to which rations for 8 days were issued. It should be constantly kept in mind that in speaking of rations, His Excellency, after we left Monclova, gave orders that these should consist of a half pound of hard-tack and not a pound as provided by the ordinance. Each soldier was allowed a *real* a day, while the officers were to look after their their own needs as best they could, with no other allowance than their regular salary, giving them the right to claim their additional campaign allowance at a future time whenever it could be satisfied.

Col. Juan Morales was ordered to proceed to Goliad that same day, taking the battalions of San Luis and Jiménez with rations for one month and a twelve-pounder, an eight-pounder, and a mortar. In view of the news received from General Sesma, stating that the enemy with 1,200 men seemed to be preparing to defend the crossing of the Colorado, and in view of the communication of General Urrea from San Patricio, advising us that he was leaving that place for Goliad where it was said that the enemy was fortified with 500 infantry and 14 pieces of artillery of various calibers and would probably offer resistance, His Excellency ordered General Tolsa to reenforce the first with the battalions of Guerrero and Primero Activo de Mexico and 40 cavalry from Tampico; while Col. Cayetano Montoya with the battalions of Tres Villas and Querétaro and a twelve-pounder was to reenforce Urrea. One month's rations were issued to both of these reenforcements.

His Excellency had already decided by this time that General Gaona should march to Nacogdoches with the battalions of Morelos and Auxiliaries of Guanajuato. He was further convinced of the advisability of this measure by the report of General Urrea concerning the abandonment of Goliad by the enemy and their subsequent capture at Encinal del Perdido on the road to Guadalupe Victoria, where the force had surrendered with all its artillery. General Gaona, therefore, set out for Nacogdoches with the two battalions above-mentioned, two four-pounders, twenty presidial troops, and fifty convicts, to all of whom rations for forty days were issued on the 24th. The total number of men in this division was 725.

If the capture of the Alamo and the unimportant victory of Urrea over Dr. Grant made the general-in-chief think that the war was over, the triumph of Perdido persuaded him that his presence was no longer necessary in Texas and that he should

return to the capital of Mexico, going from Cópano or Matagorda to Tampico and thence overland to San Luis, etc., leaving
under my care whatever remained to be done in Texas subject to
his instructions.   With this idea in mind, he instructed Urrea
on the 25th to explore the entire coast from Guadalupe Victoria
to Galveston, with the understanding that his left was covered
by Sesma.   He charged him under the strictest responsibility to
comply with the orders of the government in having all prisoners
executed.   Similar orders were transmitted to the commandant
of Goliad for the execution of the prisoners there, while the
same instructions were given to Gaona and Sesma with regard
to all those taken with arms.   These commanders were to drive
out of the country all those not actively engaged in the war.
By the general order of the day, the cavalry brigade commanded
by General Juan José de Andrade, the pickets and detachments
of the permanent battalions of Guerrero, Matamoros, and
Jiménez, and the active battalions of Querétaro and Primero de
Mexico, all the pieces of artillery at general headquarters, and
the thirty-two transport wagons belonging to José Lobardero
and Company were instructed to make preparations to leave on
the 1st of April for San Luis Potosí.   The reason given for
this measure was the excessive expense which their presence
entailed.

It is very opportune, Your Excellency, to state at this point
that those of the enemy who were killed at the Alamo and in
the various engagements of Urrea were all adventurers who
had come from New Orleans after the colonists took Béxar,
with the exception of thirty citizens of Gonzales who succeeded
in reenforcing Travis the day before the assault, and a few
of the leaders.   Consequently, the forces of the colonists or inhabitants of Texas remained as yet untouched.

None of the measures adopted up to that time had been
in accord with my idea of things.   On various occasions I
tried to speak to His Excellency upon the matter, but all to
no avail, because he would listen to nothing which was not in
accord with his ideas, which I regarded as dangerous in the

extreme. As His Excellency had, or seemed to have, confidence in the counsel of Col. Almonte, I approached him, suggested that we should go to his house, and asked that he show me a map of Texas, which he did. With this before us, I pointed out to him all the reasons I could think of for my disapproval of what had been done up to that time by His Excellency, and I entreated him, with the greatest earnestness, to communicate these reasons to him, for I wished this remonstrance to be taken as a formal protest to safeguard my responsibility to the country for any adverse consequences in our military operations resulting from the measures taken. It was my opinion that, leaving garrisons in Béxar, Goliad, and Cópano, the army should march in a body until the main force of the enemy was defeated, forcing it to abandon the country or take refuge on the island of Galveston, without leaving the crossings on our rear unprotected on this account. This remonstrance, reenforced by a report carefully and judiciously prepared by General Sesma, on the 15th, while on the right bank of the Colorado, resulted in the suspension of the departure of the cavalry pickets, detachments, etc., which had been ordered, as already stated, to set out for San Luis. On the 25th orders were sent by an express to General Gaona instructing him to converge on San Felipe de Austin after he crossed the Colorado. Similar instructions were sent to Urrea who was to cross the Colorado by way of Matagorda on his route to Brazoria. The general-in-chief decided to undertake the few remaining military operations in person. Because of his maxim of not subjecting military operations to discussion and confiding in his own inspiration which on other occasions had given him such happy results, His Excellency could not suffer an adverse criticism with patience. Consequently, on the 29th the battalions of sappers and Guadalajara with two eight-pounders, two four-pounders, and one mortar left for Gonzáles, under the command of Augustín Amat, with rations for one month. His Excellency, his staff, and I set out for the same place on the 31st. On our second day's journey communications from General Sesma were received stating that he had already crossed the Colorado with part of his division, but that as the river was swollen by the rains and he had scarcely any means for crossing it, he was experiencing untold difficulties in transporting the troops, artillery, munitions, etc., to the opposite bank. He added, however, that he was leaving nothing undone to expedite this perilous operation. We reached Gonzáles on April 2nd, and, as the river was high, it was necessary to construct a barge to cross it. As the impatience of His Excellency could bear no delay, he decided to continue on the 3rd with his staff and a picket of cavalry to the Colorado to join Sesma, leaving me in charge of the crossing. He reached the Colorado on the 5th, at the crossing known as the Atascosito, continuing on the 6th with the division of Sesma and Tolsa to San Felipe, where he arrived on the 7th. He left Woll at Atascosito with a battalion and a cavalry picket for the purpose of constructing a barge to enable the artillery to be taken across the river, together with the twelve transport wagons, the baggage and the other equipment I was bringing up.

Unable to cross the Brazos at San Felipe because the enemy, though in small numbers, held the opposite side, His Excellency took all the picked companies and marched down the river on the 9th, in search of a crossing which he found on the 11th at Old Fort, sixteen leagues distant from San Felipe. On that same date he issued orders from that place to Sesma and to myself to join him there. Sesma effected a juncture with him on the 13th, and on the 14th he continued without waiting for me. With but a few men over 700 and a six-pounder, he made his way to Harrisburg, where he arrived the afternoon of the 16th. I arrived at Atascosito on the 10th and succeeded in crossing my entire force by the 13th, setting out for San Felipe the following day, where I arrived on the 15th. From there I took the road to Old Fort. General Urrea was in Matagorda on that same day. The position of the army was, therefore, on that day as follows: The general-in-chief on the road to Harrisburg about twenty leagues distant from Sesma; my force sixteen leagues from the latter; General Gaona lost in the desert between

Bastrop and San Felipe, without news of him; General Urrea in Matagorda, thirty leagues distant from Sesma, more than forty from me, and fifty from the president. Urrea himself was more than thirty leagues from Goliad, while the detachments of Victoria, Cópano, and Goliad were forty and fifty leagues from Béxar, where Andrade was. Four days after the defeat of the president, Generals Tolsa, Woll, Gaona, Sesma, Urrea, and I were concentrated at Mrs. Powell's with the whole force of the army betwen the Brazos and the Colorado. It was after this that the army began its retreat in the best order. At what time, then, was the army in better order, before or after the misfortune that overtook the president? I think that the reasons for deciding upon a retreat have been clearly outlined in my communication of the 14th of last May, which I hope Your Excellency has seen fit to read.

It is claimed *that the enemy did not dare show its face.* After the first defeats, the enemy adopted the plan of laying waste the country and retreating upon our approach in order that we should find no resources as we advanced and for the purpose of being in position to take advantage of the first error we might commit. As a matter of fact, this was the policy followed throughout the campaign. When Houston abandoned the left bank of the Colorado, he took a position ten leagues above San Felipe at Groce's Crossing on the Brazos, where he had a steamboat to facilitate his crossing. His object was to observe the forces under the immediate command of the President and General Gaona. On the 15th, he was in position to have attacked Gaona, the President, or myself, either at San Felipe or on the way to Old Fort. He decided to attack the President because he was on the opposite side of the river, cut off from all communication with the other forces. He sent the steamboat downstream to attract our attention and made his way towards His Excellency. After the 21st of April, the Texans took good care to keep the Brazos, the Colorado, or the Guadalupe between their forces and ours. Consequently, if we had decided to attack them, it would have been useless, for they would have imme-

diately executed our prisoners and would have had time enough
to retreat and choose the most convenient ground for an engagement, for they were in position to keep three or four jour-
neys ahead of us. Who is foolish enough to expose himself to
failure when he is certain of success?

Second. It is claimed that *I gave blind obedience to the
commands of the general-in-chief after he became a prisoner.*
It seems to me that I have clearly expressed the true motive
for the retreat of the army in all my communications. Furthermore, in the correspondence exchanged between the President
and myself it was necessary to keep up appearances for the
means of communication were no other than the enemy itself
who saw and read it at will. It was advisable to use phrases
calculated to produce the desired effect. If it was my purpose
to retreat under any circumstances, why not take advantage of
the opportunity offered, letting it appear as a favor in order
to save the life of the President and the many other brave Mexicans, while making our retreat safer? I cannot see, Your Excellency, that I committed any crime by adopting such a plan. But
should my action be thus considered and should it become necessary that I forfeit my life, I shall deem myself more than fully
repaid by having been instrumental in saving the lives of 600
unfortunate prisoners and perhaps that of 2,500 other com-
panions-in-arms who would very likely have perished, if not
at the hands of the enemy, as a result of the rigors of the climate,
the season, and hunger.

Third. It is claimed that *it will always be strange and reprehensible that I should have thought of nothing but a retreat
which was mistaken by the enemy for a flight.* I believe, Your
Excellency, that I have sufficiently dispelled this erroneous conception in my communication of the 10th of last June, and I am
satisfied that the government has become convinced that the
enemy did not take my retreat for a flight, for I see in the
official *Diario* of the government that the text of my communication has been quoted as a reply to the accusations made by
other public papers to discredit the army and consequently the

nation. I conclude, therefore, that if a disfavorable opinion was at first formed with regard to my conduct, this judgment has been modified upon more mature reflection and in view of the above-mentioned communication. Were it not thus, it would be impossible for the official *Diario* to reply with my own words to an accusation of an opposing publication which advanced a charge almost identical to that which previously appeared in the *Diario* itself. If my dispatch of the 10th of June had not been given full credit by the cabinet, they would not have cited it in defending the fair name of the army, which, through its long march over marshy wastes made impassable by the rains, hungry, and in rags, always maintained a consciousness of its valor. The army retired because of the inclemency of the season in a country totally unpopulated and barren, made still more unattractive by the rigor of the climate and the character of the land which threatened to engulf the men, unaccustomed as they were to such surroundings.

Fourth. It is claimed that *what cannot fail to arouse indignation is that General Filisola should have accorded the enemy the recognition of a government.* As Your Excellency has doubtless seen by now the treaties concluded by the general-in-chief to which this charge refers, you will realize that nothing is stipulated in them with regard to the army then under my command which, on account of the circumstances, I was unauthorized to approve. As acting general-in-chief, engaged in operations at a distance so far removed from the supreme government, I was free to use discretion. The orders transmitted to me by the Secretary of War in his two notes of the 15th of May last,[3] gave me any additional powers not previously conferred upon me by the supreme government. It is inconceivable that a general-in-chief should not have the power to decide upon a retreat without previous consultation and an expressed order from the government, covering each particular case, nor that its only duty should be to march in one direction, towards

[3] Tornel to Filisola, Mexico, May 15, 1836; Tornel to Filisola, same date.

the enemy. The exchange of prisoners is not prohibited except in a war without quarter or by strict and specific orders to that effect. By recognizing the agreement did I do more than agree to retreat and to exchange prisoners? Were not these the specific instructions given me by the Secretary of War in the previously cited note of the 15th? The rest of the charge concerns itself with a personal agreement made by the president, that is, with his promise not to wage war against the colonists nor to use his influence to encourage it. It may be alleged that I admitted and pledged myself to the restitution of property to the colonists, promising to pay for whatever supplies the army used in its retreat. Were not this agreement mere words it might constitute a charge against me. Those who know the condition in which Texas was left as a result of the march of our forces over the burned and abandoned territory will admit that the promise was no more than an empty gesture. The agreement stipulated that personal property would be restored, but not everything that had been destroyed, nor did the president pledge himself to an indemnization of all the losses occasioned by the war. The same may be said with regard to the payment for food and equipment. Had there been any available, the army would have had to pay for them without the need of its being stipulated in a treaty. But in a country where there was nothing, in a territory totally devastated, as stated before, one cannot take by force nor buy that which does not exist.

From the San Antonio to the Rio Bravo the country is unpopulated, and neither cattle nor grain is to be found. Whatever supplies there were had either been taken by Urrea or the Mexican settlers themselves, from whom we were obliged to buy them, for they were neither our enemies nor did they have any communication with them. I shall always regret that the exchange of prisoners was not put into effect. Was ever a nation or an army dishonored or disgraced by waging war according to the usage of civilized people? Does the law of nations and the standards of our civilization accept war without quarter? Is not the exchange of prisoners of reciprocal advantage? Your Excellency will bear in mind that in our case the advantages of an exchange of prisoners was all in our favor, because in view of the previous circumstances, the lives of the Mexican prisoners were constantly endangered. The reprisal which we could carry out with the 100 unimportant prisoners in our possession could not equal the loss of a single Mexican. When General Fernández disobeyed my order for the exchange, whom did he disobey, the government, who had issued the instructions, or me? Nevertheless he has been praised for this act instead of being held accountable for disregarding the orders of the government. This, Your Excellency, is almost inconceivable, and its example will forever reflect upon the nation. It seems to me that in this matter I showed greater regard for our men by obeying orders as I was duty bound. I also think that even if the nation disapproved the carrying out of this part of the agreement, all interests could have been reconciled by accepting the exchange, for such military agreements may be and are concluded by belligerents, a conclusive treaty of peace only being beyond the faculties of a general-in-chief without special authorization.

While discussing this point, my self-esteem demands that I explain the mistaken interpretation placed upon my simple reply which I did not think required a detailed statement with regard to the powers and faculties of our constituted authorities. As a matter of fact, I stated the importance which I attached to a treaty negotiated by the President of the republic, then general-in-chief, particularly under the trying circumstances in which I found myself; but it never entered my mind that I would be grossly insulted by believing that I was ignorant of the fact that when the president of the republic assumes the command of the army he cannot exercise the executive power, nor that when such a commander is made a prisoner his command ceases. The first is an accepted truth, while the second is a self-evident fact, and I will not deny that, finding myself in the necessity of retreating for the reasons explained in detail in my communications of the 14th and 31st of May, the request of the President had a decided bearing upon my plan, but not in determining me to adopt the policy which I followed, for necessity had already made it inevitable, but rather because I saw in the agreement the opposite of what has been attributed. In other words, I determined to abide by the agreement in the hope that the enemy, who was ignorant of what was well-known to the President, that is, the condition in which he had left the army, might allow a retreat which was inevitable in order to save, by this means, both the army and the prisoners. It was in view of this that I also stated, and this much to the credit of the first chief of the nation, that in his agreement he had not considered his person but the importance of his position, by which I meant that the interests of the nation demanded the salvation of the army upon which the lives of the prisoners depended. If this additional cause for my retreat was not understood, it was no fault of mine, nor can it be said on that account that I was ignorant of the attributes inherent upon the supreme government, or of the fact that no matter how illustrious a prisoner may be, all his authority ceases upon his imprisonment. The opinion of a man who has so often held the destiny of the republic in his hand, either as the chief executive or as commander of its forces on the battlefield, particularly when this opinion concerned itself with the operations of an army from which he had just been removed by a misfortune and with whose condition he was thoroughly familiar, is entitled to serious consideration, especially since he had never communicated his plan of operations to his second in command. If the government itself instead of instructing him was instructed by him, I who had learned of his plan by the results, could do nothing more than to take his recommendations as a confirmation of my judgment. Since the supreme government in its communication of the 15th of May recommended me to safeguard the life of the president at all costs, imposing no other limitation than the recognition of the independence of Texas, though I might even go that far under certain conditions as seen by the said instructions, how can my conduct be imputed unless it be due to the false conception that I could have engaged and defeated the enemy after the unfortunate battle of the 21st of April? With regard to this point, allow me, Sir, to state that the necessary data to form a judgment with regard to my political and military conduct was not available at the time that both were so bitterly disapproved in the official replies published by the *Diario* of the government.

Fifth. It is claimed that *I should be ashamed.* I have already stated in reply to the first imputation what might be said here. With regard to the *greater shame* it may perhaps appear little in me to take up the time of Your Excellency to refute the implications to which this expression, hastily uttered, or set down in a moment of exaltation, has given occasion. Let my ratification or assent to the agreement concluded by the President be examined to see if there is any expression of mine in this document by which I recognized in the rebellious colonists of Texas an established or constituted *nation* or *government.* Even had I called the organization of the colonists a government, I do not think that I would have cast disgrace upon our republic by the failure to state *the so-called government* or to have used those adjectives which have become so common and have been repeated so often since 1810, such as *revolutionary government, rebellious government, bandit hordes,* or *parties led by chieftains.* All these which look well in a printed paper, a proclamation, or a manifesto have lost much of their original force, so that their repetition no longer offends or shames those who rebel against constituted authority. All this, I repeat, does not detract from the actual truth, that is, that a party of bandits is governed by their chief; that a people in open rebellion though it be without a legitimate cause and though their aim may not be recognized nor their status admitted by other nations or by the mother country itself, which may be in anarchy and turmoil, still have some sort of government, for men be they what they may, when they form a social group, whether large or small, inevitably have some form of government. Of all persons I should be the last to advocate the recognition of Texas as an independent nation, for I have just seen its immense unpopulated areas, its sandy wastes, its muddy fields, and its barren lands where there is not, nor can there be, any considerable population. The few who lived there before the land was devastated could scarcely be distinguished from the native nomads. When I heard that the recognition of such a territory as an independent nation had been proposed in the Senate of the United States, I could not believe that it was done seriously, nor that any ulterior motives could move them to such action, because Texas does not possess, nor will it possess for a long time, the necessary resources to constitute itself either an independent entity under a federal government or an organized province of our republic under the present political system. To take this country for a new land of *El Dorado,* as the romantic and exaggerated interested accounts would have us believe, will lead us into serious and ominous consequences. Our neighboring country might covet this land which, in comparison to its own barren wastes, may be a garden; but it can never truthfully say that Texas has the necessary elements to constitute itself an independent and self-governing member of the family of nations. This is my opinion. I cannot believe that I was obliged to set forth fundamental principles or to give definitions in each one of my official communications, making out of them a new patriotic grammar or dictionary, for I did not have the time while on the field or on the march for such things. General F. V. Fernández may, perhaps, realize from my present explanation that I have neither compromised nor disgraced our country by using the word *government* in referring to the Texan colonists in one of my official communication to him, no more than the Minister of War in his note of the 15th of May when he refers to the Texan leader as *general.* Doubtless, sir, it is a *greater shame* to stop to haggle over words when we should give our undivided attention to the serious problem confronting us.

Let us turn now, Your Excellency, to the services which General Urrea claims to have rendered, casting a reflection upon my honor and that of the rest of the army. Likewise, let us examine the charges which he formulated against me in his secret report of the 11th of May [4] to determine whether they have any better foundation than those previously enumerated.

First. He claims that *he protected the rear guard* of the *entire army,* saving the artillery, etc. That part of the army of operations which after the unfortunate event of the 21st of April was between the Brazos and the Colorado was distributed, on the 24th, upon the right bank of the Brazos at Old Fort, Columbia, and Brazoria. The first of these points was occupied by Generals Sesma, Gaona, Tolsa, Woll, and myself; the second by Colonel Salas; and the third by Urrea. The first of these points is about twelve leagues distant from the second, and the third four leagues from the second, down the river. The home of Mrs. Powell, where I ordered the concentration to take place, is situated on the plain, five leagues from the river, and almost half way between Old Fort and Columbia. The first division to arrive, on the afternoon of the 25th, was that of Salas which had occupied Columbia. The force under my immediate command arrived soon after, and a little later that of Urrea with the force that had been stationed at Brazoria. The three divisions mentioned, approached from three different directions, covering in their march upon the said point of reunion. Consequently no one of them could have protected the rear guard of all three, for they all arrived almost at the same time at the appointed place of reunion. The rear of my division was protected by the experienced and brave General Gaona, who remained at Old Fort until noon with the battalion of Guadalajara. The 26th we rested and reorganized the army at which time the reserve was assigned to Urrea, while the first infantry brigade was placed under Gaona and the second under Tolsa. General Sesma was made second in command and General Woll chief of staff. On the 27th, we resumed the march along the right bank since no enemy had appeared to the left of the Brazos, according to

---

[4] In the original *Representación* it reads "11 de Abril," evidently an error, for before the end of the next paragraph, he refers to the same communication as dated May 11, which is the correct date.

the report rendered by the presidial lieutenant, Pedro Rodríguez, commanding a detachment composed of pickets from Dolores, Tampico, and presidio troops sent out in the morning of the previous day to the crossing at Old Fort where they remained until the early morning of the 27th. That night we encamped at a small house, Gaona and Tolsa being assigned to the two most exposed approaches to our camp, while Urrea occupied the safest position. On the 28th we camped on an extended line along the left bank of the principal branch of the St. Bernard, General Urrea forming our left with his brigade, which was the least exposed in case of a surprise. The march for this day was uneventful, since there was no enemy in sight and the creek which we crossed the day before was by now impassable as a result of the rains. Not finding a crossing on the creek where we were encamped, we countermarched on the 29th to the right, following the same route over which we travelled the day before. We pitched camp upon the right bank of the second branch of the St. Bernard, which we had crossed as before stated on the 27th, and which was still impassable. I gave instructions that night for General Urrea to march early the next morning to Atascosito crossing on the Colorado that he might either repair a barge which I had left there or construct a new one in case the other had been destroyed by the weather, the flood, or any other accident. Accordingly, Urrea went ahead the next day, leaving behind his baggage and artillery in order to be free of all embarrassment. He began the construction of a barge which I finished after my arrival. He and his division crossed the Colorado and encamped a league beyond the right bank of the river while the rest of us remained on the left and had to cross his artillery and his baggage. Where, then, Your Excellency, are the skillful operations of Señor Urrea which protected the retreat of the army and facilitated the crossing of the Colorado, reflecting honor upon his military talent? Was there a general or an officer in the army who did not work and contribute more decidedly than he did to the amelioration of our sufferings?

He claims that *He saved the artillery*. This branch of the

army, Your Excellency, was never exposed during the entire campaign to any greater danger than the mud holes encountered for a stretch of two leagues along the banks of the second branch of the St. Bernard to which I have already referred. We encamped there on the 29th and it required nine days of the most painful work, as well as the imponderable constancy and perseverance of General Pedro Ampudia to take it out. During this entire time Urrea rested on the opposite side of the Colorado; more than a league beyond its right bank, and nine from where the artillery, munitions, and baggage were stuck in the mud. *His Lordship* busied himself, we might say, looking after his personal interests and other tasks totally foreign to the interests of the service. It is inconceivable that these facts should have failed to deter him from making such a claim. It is unquestionable that to claim credit for saving the artillery is equivalent to casting a reflection upon Generals Gaona, Tolsa, Sesma, and Ampudia, as well as upon all the other officers and members of the army not belonging to the division of Urrea, all of whom worked incessantly, night and day. All these toiled constantly, now pulling out the artillery and munitions by hand, and again transporting the baggage to the other side of the river, together with that portion which belonged to the division of Urrea himself. The only piece of artillery lost during the entire campaign, a twelve-pounder, was abandoned by one of the units stationed at Matagorda, under orders of Urrea. Though I ordered that a thorough investigation be instituted in regard to this incident, it was not done, at least while I was in command, disregarding the fact that this occurrence compromised the honor of the nation and left the right and rear of the army without protection.

Fourth. At the council of war which I held on the 25th of April in the house of Mrs. Powell I opened the discussion by stating that I was impelled to ask that, out of regard for my nationality and the lack of confidence in my ability, a native son of the country be made general-in-chief, assuring them that I was ready to turn over the command which had accidentally devolved upon me and to place myself blindly under the orders of whomever was chosen, be he who he may. All replied unanimously in the negative, expressing complete confidence in my honesty and patriotism. They were all of the opinion (and this was before I spoke on the subject) that it was an imperative necessity for us to recross the Colorado in order to reorganize the army, establish a base, build hospitals and warehouses, open a line of communication, and establish shops for the reconditioning of arms, etc., while we could secure positive information regarding the life or death of the President and his companions in misfortune. It is true that Urrea, who was the second to speak, explained that he regretted that the army should have to retreat but that in view of his *inexperience* he placed full confidence in the capacity and skill of the second commander-in-chief of the army. Was there a single individual throughout the whole army who did not *regret* both the necessity of retreating and the circumstances which made that operation indispensable?

The fifth accusation does not need, Your Excellency, to be refuted, for subsequent events have shown its falsity.

As to the sixth imputation, which claims that I had decided, even at that time, to retreat, I can prove the contrary by the whole army and the steps which I took at the time, as well as by my report of the 14th of the said month. Even after all this, I tried to appease the inhabitants who I found had remained at Goliad, where I established my general headquarters, and began to repair the fortifications, to reorganize the army, to drill it, to establish a general hospital, and to make this town the base for my future operations by building a shop for the reconditioning of our armament, etc. When, on the other hand, Urrea passed through this town, he alarmed the people exceedingly by stating that the army was retreating to Matamoros and by advising them to do likewise. He did the same thing at Refugio and San Patricio. In order to haul his own personal belongings, he deprived individuals of their oxen and carts—as they told me afterwards—leaving the poor wretches without the means of carrying out his own advice.

What I have stated so far is all there was with regard to the facts recounted in Urrea's secret note of the 11th of May to His Excellency, the secretary of war. It now remains, Your Excellency, to call your attention to the unfounded statements contained in the note which he addressed to me on the 1st of last June, and which he inserted in his communication to the secretary, as previously mentioned at the beginning of this representation.

First. He claims that *before setting out on his march to Matamoros from Guadalupe Victoria he made certain observations, etc.*

That this general should, in addressing me, claim to have discussed certain matters which we did not take up is astounding! I have no recollection of having spoken to Señor Urrea on that occasion concerning anything other than his march to Matamoros. With regard to the insecurity of that place and the necessity of sending some force there, it was he who made me become suspicious of its security, as may be seen from his note of May 12th,[5] which I herewith attach with all due respect. It was he who pointed out to me the maladversion of some of the inhabitants of Tamaulipas, particularly of that city, to the present order of things, claiming, as he said, that only by his timely, prudent, and energetic measures of last February, had their plans been defeated. In a word, he asked me, though indirectly, to detail him to that city and the port of Brazos de Santiago. How can Urrea flatter himself that he could convince me of the importance of any military measure in view of his limited experience? On the contrary, he gave me to understand that he wished to go to Durango because the present order of things, as he saw it, was uncertain and a frightful crisis was imminent. All of his efforts were directed to make me adopt a policy in keeping with the plot he had devised for my undoing and about which he had secretly informed the government. It was his desire to make me speed up the march by all means possible, as I have

[5] Urrea to Filisola, Victoria, May 12, 1836.

since learned from subsequent events. Therefore, he saw to it that I should find no supplies when I reached Guadalupe Victoria, distributing those at Goliad and Refugio as well as the cattle without system or order, though they had been gathered for the army by General Sesma, agreeable to my instructions. He took with him the officers who had charge of them, against my express command, in order that I might not find anyone against whom charges might be made. The twelve-pounder assigned to the defence of Cópano was removed without my being notified of it, under the pretext that it would be more useful at Brazo de Santiago. He did not officially advise me of this incident until it was too late for me to remedy the situation, making it impossible for my disapproval to reach him before he had advanced to the Nueces or beyond when, very likely, he would have disregarded my orders anyway. He drove whatever stock he was able to find before him and induced the citizens of Goliad, Refugio, and San Patricio to abandon their homes. If he did feign to advise me from Refugio that he thought I should wait for instructions from the supreme government while holding Béxar, Goliad, and Cópano, it was after he had already executed the operations above described and made certain of his march to Matamoros, having first secured all the booty he desired from Brazoria, Matagorda, La Vaca, and other points. This had been his first consideration and the constant aim in his desire to take charge of the vanguard ever since we left the house of Mrs. Powell, from where he sent practically his whole regiment to Guadalupe, together with various confidential agents, all of whom I never saw again. He instituted a sort of inquisition in his division by means of which he prohibited his guides from giving me any information and from having anything to do with me, to the extent of reprimanding one of them because he replied to the question which I addressed to him concerning the roads on the San Bernard. Finally, when he became well aware of the impossibility in which I was left of holding the line which he pretended I should maintain, he urged me to await instructions from the government. Why, then, did he not emphasize this supposed conviction in his communication written while at Refugio? Why did he take with him Lieut. Col. Luis Tola, of the engineers, from San Patricio to Matamoros when this officer had been assigned to the army to erect the necessary fortifications at Béxar, Goliad, Cópano, and other points where they might be deemed advisable? With regard to this matter I beg Your Excellency to read the note of Lieut. Col. Tola of May 30th, herewith attached.[6] Such facts are not in accord with the apparent conviction of Urrea regarding the importance of not abandoning our line. This is further confirmed by the fact that Tola was not needed in Matamoros where there was an engineer expressly assigned by the government for that purpose.

Second. He claims that *the enemy was defeated in every engagement.* Such a boastful assertion and arrogant petulance, devoid of all reason, denotes the lack of reflection or the temerity of him who thus addresses a superior with no other purpose that to wound his self-esteem by boasting before the supreme government and the public of his acts and of his lack of respect. Such boasts transmitted in a communication and given to the press arouse feelings of pity, indignation, and contempt. Pity because they reveal the ignorance of military science in him who promulgates them, indignation because, addressed to a superior, there are but three deductions to be drawn, each worse than the other, that is, either that he believes his superior as irresponsible as himself, or that he thinks he has grounds to insult him in the disrespectful manner which he does, or that he does not realize that such unfounded slanders, when transmitted to a government far removed from the theater of operations, may be responsible for the adoption of erroneous measures of little avail or even prejudicial to the cause which he pretends to uphold; and contempt because they reveal the absolute lack of character in a public functionary who, through his lack of judgment, may, while endangering the life and security of thousands of men and the ultimate fate of the greater part of a nation, subject the

---

[6] Luis Tola to Filisola, Matamoros, May 30, 1836.

government to ridicule. What does Urrea mean by his assertion that *the enemy was defeated in every engagement and deprived of its principal strongholds?* Does he mean the skirmishes of San Patricio, Refugio, and El Perdido which I will not describe in detail out of consideration for Señor Urrea himself? Does he call the battered and crumbling walls of the mission of Refugio, the fort of Goliad, and the defences of the Alamo fortresses? For each one of these skirmishes Urrea deserves to be tried by a council of war and be punished accordingly for having sacrificed the lives of innumerable brave soldiers when he could have obtained the same results without such a loss. With regard to the third of the strongholds mentioned, I will merely state that he was not present when it was attacked and that I do not care to speak about it at this time because it is not to the point. I wonder where Señor Urrea saw a fortress! I wonder if he has even seen a redoubt! I do not care to express myself at this time with regard as to who was benefited the most by the cessation of hostilities, nor do I believe it is pertinent. I cannot but feel deeply concerned for the absolute lack of military judgment of Señor Urrea, now in charge of a difficult and trying operation in which the reputation of the government and of the nation is truly at stake. *The enemy was forced to abandon their homes and property, to hide their families in the woods, while their force was reduced to an insignificant number, without military instruction or discipline, without leaders capable of directing them. It is unexplainable to this day that . . .*

This jumble of false ideas and erroneous conceptions is but a mass of words which convey nothing of that which was intended, or which were put together without any clear idea as to what they were meant to express. Who was the enemy, the colonists or the volunteers who came from New Orleans and other points? If the first were the enemy, they were not obliged to abandon their homes because the proclamation issued by the President at Béxar, after the capture of the Alamo, offered them every guarantee. Therefore, if they abandoned their homes and hid their families in the woods, they did it out of their own free will and agreeable to a preconceived plan. If the second were the enemy, they did not have either homes or families in Texas. If their number was insignificant, the misfortune of San Jacinto proved the contrary, and the number engaged in that battle did not include a thousand additional men who were scattered at that time in Anáhuac, Galveston, Velasco, Culebra Island, and aboard the steamboats. With regard to their discipline and military instruction, I must say that comparisons are always odious. I will content myself with noting that it is only too well known that the kind of people which made up the rebel forces of the Texans lived by their rifles, that is, by hunting; and that a common danger obliged them to practice discipline and cooperation. What instruction did our conscripts, recruited on the eve of the expedition, have? Had the majority of the recruits that made up our army fired a rifle before in their lives? Consequently, they had less instruction than the enemy in the use of firearms, though the traditional courage and endurance of the Mexican soldier made up for the disparity. With regard to the ability of the officers, there is no doubt that our own were superior. Nevertheless, the enemy forces were well directed. Were it not inadvisable, I would demonstrate, by the events of Refugio, Goliad, and El Perdido, their skill in unmistakable terms. I can do no less than to suggest to Señor Urrea to study his own operations and those of the enemy a little better before undertaking another campaign, in order that he may be better able to judge the results. Perhaps an event such as that of San Jacinto, which he so bitterly laments now, will not be so incomprehensible to him then.

Third. He claims that *the army of operations gave an example of cowardice when, gathered with a strength of more than 4000 men, it decided to retreat.*

I will refer to what General Andrade says on this point in his communication of the 30th of July which has been printed. If there were examples of cowardice in the army, I am forced to say that the following may be so interpreted. First, that Señor

Urrea, having been assigned to form the right wing of the army with a considerable force of cavalry and infantry and with instructions to follow the coast to Goliad, the most important point for our war operations, since it covered the port of entry of Cópano through which we were to receive the supplies sent from Matamoros, he failed to reach the said point until the 21st of March, by which time the vanguard of the army, commanded by Generals Sesma and Tolsa, was already on the Colorado, fifty leagues beyond, after having cut off whatever enemies there were between that river and the San Antonio, leaving them with no other escape than that of the sea. Second, when the President reached Harrisburg, Urrea had not yet advanced beyond Matagorda, for which reason Sesma was left without support, and later the right wing of the army was left uncovered. Third, having decided, at the council of war held at Mrs. Powell's on the 25th of April, to send a party of cavalry to Old Fort to gather the fugitives of the battle of the 21st and to find out, if possible, the fate of the President, General Adrian Woll assigned this duty to a party from Urrea's regiment, who refused to consent to it, making it necessary to make up the party from the pickets of Dolores and Tampico and presidial troops which had not accompanied the President because of the tired condition of their horses. Fourth, while all the army stayed on the left bank of the Colorado for nine days to help pull the artillery, munitions, and baggage out of the mud, he not only crossed over to the right side, but encamped more than a league beyond. Fifth, while in command of the reserve and of the only cavalry available, the most useful means to cover a retreat in an open country, he, nevertheless, asked to be allowed to advance to Guadalupe three days before the army undertook the march. Instead of taking two six-pounders, as ordered, he took two four-pounders in order to travel lighter and give an example of *obedience* and prove his determined opposition to a retreat. Sixth, a part of the division under his command abandoned a twelve-pounder and left behind a lieutenant-colonel and the artillerymen, though there was no enemy in sight. And seventh, he asked to be allowed to proceed to protect Matamoros, undertaking this operation with such haste that he even left his wounded at Goliad where I found them and sent them on later.

He claims that *the army was concentrated to the strength of 4,000 men.* After we left Béxar the army never, at any *time,* numbered even 3,000, its total strength having been 2,563 when concentrated at Mrs. Powell's, where all the divisions occupying the territory between the Brazos and the Colorado were gathered. The rest of the army was scattered in Matagorda, Victoria, Goliad, Cópano, and Béxar, any one of these places being no less than fifty leagues from Mrs. Powell's as a result of the impassable condition of the rivers.

He claims that *our conquests were adequately protected.* There is no doubt that, if all had been as well protected as Matagorda, as shown above, we could have lived in perfect tranquillity.

He claims that *no effort was made to attract fortune to our side.* How indiscreet, Your Excellency! From Mrs. Powell's to San Jacinto there are about 50 leagues and one must cross the Brazos to reach that point. A force of 1,000 men, fully equipped, cannot accomplish such an operation in less than 4 days, and the 50 leagues would require 6 more days, making a total of 10. Five days had already elapsed since the battle of the 21st. Consequently, the enemy would have had 15 days to improve their position. If it suited them to fight, they would have waited, and if not, they would have shot our prisoners, embarked on the steamboats and other vessels available, gone around Galveston Bay to the mouth of the Brazos, and then, taking a position on our rear guard, they would have attacked the force which we would have necessarily left at Old Fort with the wounded, the sick, the baggage, the ammunition, etc. leaving us in a sack to perish of hunger. Furthermore, could we have taken the offensive within less than 15 days after the heavy rains of the 27th? What would we have eaten in the meantime? At Old Fort not even a cracker could be bought, at any price, to make a little white porridge for our sick, who were suffering with dysentery;

while all the supplies between our position and that of the enemy had been burnt or destroyed. The greater part of our armament was in sad need of repair, and we did not even have a gunsmith. Our powder for the cannons and small arms was nothing but a soggy mass. We had no medicine kit, and were without lint, bandages, or surgeons. An officer acted in that capacity, out of pity for the wounded, there being no one else to do it. But suppose that the enemy had not undertaken the operation described. Who could have prevented its taking refuge in Galveston, making us march and countermarch without any other result than the destruction of our forces, granting that we had supplies?

He claims that *we should have ascertained the fate of our first chief and gathered the fugitives.* What a lack of memory or of good will! Why did he refuse to go when ordered, instead of objecting and making other troops perform an act which he now so much deplores? Furthermore, Señor Urrea forgets that, before there was time to undertake any of the military operations which he now suggests, it was learned on the 28th of April, while on the banks of the San Bernard, that the first chief was alive and that an armistice had been concluded with Houston. To celebrate this news he and other officers asked me to sound bugles and drums, all of which I refused, replying that even though His Excellency might be alive, it did not make his painful defeat any less a misfortune to the nation, and that I could not permit that it be celebrated. He also forgets that he pleadingly asked me to allow him to go and see His Excellency to find out his condition and that I replied to him that I thought the undertaking was dangerous and that I was of the opinion that it would be better to send General Woll, for he understood English. Does this show indifference on my part to the fate of the President? Does this show a desire to injure him? Why his different attitude afterwards? Because the exigency of the moment is passed and the feelings of that first moment have given place to others. Such is life.

He claims that *I abandoned our position and began a retreat*

*which, speaking with the frankness of a soldier, he cannot but
call a shameful flight.* As a matter of fact, the marches undertaken by that *soldier* and his division from the Colorado to
Victoria, from there to Goliad, and from Goliad to Matamoros
may, with more correctness, be said to have resembled nothing
but a flight. This cannot be said of the retreat of the army
which, in addition to having been carried out in all possible comfort, it allowed a rest of ten days on the Colorado, twelve at
Goliad, and twelve on the Nueces. The force under General
Andrade, stationed in Béxar, did likewise, and performed its
march with that circumspection, firmness, and order which has
always characterized that distinguished general.

Urrea claims that *the result was the discouragement of the
army.* This imputation is made in too light and careless a spirit.
Although I could successfully refute it, I do not wish to do so,
in order not to fall into the same fault. I might take the liberty
of explaining with facts to Señor Urrea how and by what means
an armed force can be discouraged, but this might be too harsh
and perhaps useless. I will content myself with saying only that
the whole army was made up of determined Mexicans who never,
during the entire campaign, knew what it was to be afraid, and
who retreated only because the lack of all resources, the weather,
the season of the year, and the circumstances of the moment
made it inevitable, but who bore the greatest hardships with a
resignation that bordered upon stoicism and the highest heroism.

Fourth. He claims *that I recognized in the Texans a
legitimate government.*

This is to speak without a knowledge of the facts. I challenge
Urrea to cite a single proof in support of what he so lightly
affirms. With regard to this subject, I refer him to what I have
already stated.

Fifth. He claims that *he disapproved the retreat of the army
while still on the banks of the Brazos.* Let Generals Gaona,
Sesma, Tolsa, Woll, and the Commandant-General of Artillery,
Pedro Ampudia, all of whom were present at the council held
in the house of Mrs. Powell on the 25th, speak. If the en-

thusiasm of Urrea was so great as he claims in his note of June
1st, addressed to me, what was the reason for its not having been
delivered until the 11th at Santa Gertrudis, which is only forty
leagues from Matamoros, a journey that can be made in comfort
by any courier? And bear in mind that it was sent by one of
his most trusted officers. In eleven days, a special messenger can,
with ease, go from Mexico, to Goliad, as shown by the superior
order in which I was instructed to deliver the command to Señor
Urrea, and which though bearing the date of the 31st of May,
was received on the 12th of June at Los Jaboncillos, just a day's
journey from Santa Gertrudis. This in spite of the fact that
the messenger was delayed two days in Matamoros, while Urrea
issued his corresponding orders to Gaona and Andrade.

He claims *that he was obliged to retreat only because my
order to the part of his division stationed at Columbia to join me
without awaiting instructions from him left him with only 400
men and with his rear guard unprotected.* This, Your Excellency, is unexplainable. When I instructed Señor Urrea to join
me, nothing had been said regarding a retreat beyond the
Colorado, for this matter was taken up at the council of generals.
Consequently, while he was at the Brazos, so pleasantly engaged,
he could not have opposed a determination of which I, myself,
was as yet ignorant and which was not reached until after the
army was assembled. Therefore, his statement that he was
obliged to follow the retreat of the army because I left him with
only 400 men at that place is false. There is something else. As
Señor Urrea has pretended in this expedition that he was
ignorant of everything, he also pretended not to know the number of men he had at Brazoria, that is, unless his other occupa-
tions, purely of a personal character, did not permit him to find
out the actual strength of the various units that were operating
under his command. Please, Your Excellency, examine the following extract made from the totals of the forces at that time,
keeping in mind that the numbers regarding the division commanded by Urrea were approved by him.

AT OLD FORT, THE 24TH OF APRIL

Units	Strength
Artillery	50
Infantry { Zapadores	144
Morelos	382
Primero activo de México	206
Guadalajara	254
Guanajuato	285
Cavalry { Dolores	46
Tampico	21
Presidiales	20
Total	1,408

UNDER THE ORDER OF SR. URREA IN COLUMBIA AND BRAZORIA

	Strength
Artillery	20
Infantry { Ximenez	273
San Luis	394
Querétaro	258
Cavalry { Cuautla	102
Tampico	97
Ausiliares de Guanajuato	21
Total	1,165

TOTALS

First Division	1,408	} 2,573
Second Division	1,165	

DETACHMENTS

Miscellaneous		1,001
Yucatán { At Cópano		60
At the Mission of Refugio		5
At Goliad		174
Tres-Villas At Matagorda		189
Cuautla At Victoria		40
Activos de Durango		21
Presidiales		15
Total strength of the army		4,078

According to what the aide who took the order told me and what I found out later, Salas had in Columbia only 200 men.

Matagorda, Tres Villas, Goliad, and Cópano were held by the active battalion of Yucatán, while Victoria had only a detachment of sixty-one cavalry according to the table cited. How then could Señor Urrea have been left in Brazoria with only 400 men as he claims? Where were the other 565 men which are wanting to make up the 1,165 men of his division?

He claims that *His Excellency, the President, is a prisoner to-day.* . . . His Excellency knew better than Señor Urrea the precarious condition in which the army had been left, the small resources upon which it could count, and the difficulty of continuing the campaign without the necessary supplies to hold the country. These considerations, rather than regard for his life and the pitiable condition of his companions in misfortune, made him enter, with his characteristic penetration, into an agreement in which nothing is stipulated with regard to the operations of the army which it would not have had to undertake as a result of circumstances, and without being stipulated. The supreme government practically authorized me to act accordingly almost on the same date, through the respectful notes of the Secretary of War of the 15th of May. With regard to his plea that I should have shown greater pity and compassion for the inhabitants of San Antonio, Bahía, San Patricio, etc., I wish, Your Excellency, that you might hear the praises which they make of Señor Urrea for the good treatment which he accorded them. Not only are the inhabitants of those places unanimous in their opinion, but all of those from Matamoros to Leona Vicario and a great part of Tamaulipas express themselves in the same manner. Of course, it must be that they did not understand his kind intentions, or that they are naturally ungrateful.

This, then, is all there is, Your Excellency, with regard to the secret report of Señor Urrea *who claims that he caused the arms of his division to be respected everywhere; that he covered the rear guard of the army, and that by placing himself in the vanguard, he facilitated the crossing of the Colorado; that his military skill deserves praise; that he rendered distinguished service in saving the artillery of the army; that his subordination was unquestioned; that he attempted to prevent the retreat; that he wished to secure the liberty of the President; that he acted with nobility and loyalty; and that he was opposed to the shame that threatened the army and the country.* Because of his unselfishness and the great merit which he won by his secret note, I was deprived of the command without being heard, without my explanations being read. Thus the betrayer was rewarded by the command, and my last days were filled with sorrow and bitterness after forty odd years of honest service without a stain. My only consolation is found in public opinion which, without violence in its judgment, is always just. This was his zeal for the service, the honor of the army, and the glory of the government and the nation. It is because of this, that he has been promoted and eulogized to the detriment of others more deserving. I must, therefore, Your Excellency, conclude by accusing General Urrea before you as guilty of the crime described in Article 10, Title 12, Treaties 2 of the general ordinance of the army, demanding that he be brought to trial agreeable to the said ordinance. What I have stated sufficiently proves his questionable conduct, as well as the fact that though there were generals in the army whose experience and patriotism Señor Urrea cannot expect to equal, it was he alone who found fault with my conduct, while the rest were in accord with my operations, concerning which I always consulted them, not excepting Colonels Morales and Montoya of the division of Señor Urrea, who agreed with me as to the advisability of the retreat which the army was forced to undertake to Matamoros.

Permit me, likewise, Your Excellency, out of regard for the position which I held, and out of consideration for the service, to make a few statements regarding the tortuous conduct of General Vital Fernandez who, in a very direct manner, has contributed to the mortifications and displeasures to which I have been subjected, influencing the government to adopt measures which perhaps have not been very favorable to the good name of the nation, to the improvement of the service, or to justice.

This general wrote to His Excellency, the President and

Commander-in-chief of the Army of Operations, on the 29th of last April,[7] ignorant of the misfortune that had befallen him, and communicated to him that, under guard of 30 cavalry and 60 infantry in charge of Lieutenant-Colonel Tola, he was sending 140,000 *pesos* out of the 173,810 *pesos* and 2 *reales* which were deposited in the commissary at that place for the army. This remittance should have reached Goliad on May 12th; but, as soon as the said general heard of the occurrences of the 21st of April, he sent a special messenger to overtake the officer in charge of the escort with instructions for him to return to Matamoros, though he had already reached Santa Gertrudis, (this point is nearer to Goliad than to Matamoros), bringing back 110,000 *pesos* and sending the remaining 30,000 only to the army. The frivolous pretext for this act was that the Indians were in revolt, although, as a matter of fact, they are always in that condition, and the money had already advanced beyond the places which they frequent. They have never been known to attack even a party of fifteen armed men. Furthermore, the 110,000 *pesos* which were sent back escorted by the 50 infantry and the 30,000 that were sent on with no other guard than the 30 cavalry were both more exposed to being lost than if the whole amount had continued to its first destination, guarded by the original escort undivided. This act caused no little surprise to the officers of the army and to myself and gave rise to much speculation as to its motive, considering the circumstances in which we found ourselves. The antecedents of this general should be kept in mind in view of the rumors of his connivance with the plans of the colonists in February, while we were in Monclova. Señor Urrea claims to have defeated these activities by his presence. All of this made me become strongly suspicious as to the security of our rear guard and our line of communications with the supreme government. I, at least, suspected that the army would not again receive a cent out of that money. My suspicion was almost borne out, for though I immediately sent General Sesma and my aide, Lieutenant-Colonel Juan Cuevas, post haste to that place,

[7] Francisco V. Fernández to Santa Anna, Matamoros, April 29, 1836.

the army received only 140,000 out of the 170,000 and some odd *pesos* deposited there in spite of all my efforts. Out of this sum, Urrea took 55,875 *pesos*, 7 *reales* and 5 grains, as Your Excellency may see from the copies of the accounts which I enclose with all due respect, and this for only 800 and some odd men which constituted the total of the division with which he marched for that city.[8]

Another anxiety which worried us was the delay of the government's replies. I should have received an answer to my communications of the 25th and 28th of April no later than the 22nd of May, while at Goliad; but when I left that place on the 25th, no answer had, as yet, arrived. This delay furnished new grounds for our suspicions, especially when it is remembered that I bought, through Señor Urrea, a horse for the messenger, for which I paid 100 *pesos*. Our suspicions were further strengthened by the certified copies of the orders received by the postmaster,[9] which he transmitted to me and I in turn take the liberty of enclosing to Your Excellency, further corroborated by the failure to receive a reply to my communication of the 14th of last May, which, unlike all my other dispatches has not been published. It is evident that this communication was not permitted to go on until my letter of the 30th to General Fernández, in which I referred to Article 9 of the agreement, was received in Matamoros, because they wished to force me by all means possible to continue the retreat or to commit some blunder which might serve their purpose in order that Urrea might have an occasion to display his great zeal and military accomplishments, as he did in his communication of the 1st of June to secure the desired results. My communication to the Secretary of War could have reached the said dignitary on the 28th or the 29th at the latest, in which case I should have received a reply either the 7th or 8th of June, while I was still at the Nueces. But more

[8] Fernández to Filisola, Matamoros, May 7, 1836; Pedro J. de la Garza to Filisola, Matamoros, May 28, 1836.

[9] Fernández to the Administrador de correos, Matamoros, May 25, 1836; Fernández to the Administrador de correos, Matamoros, May 30, 1836.

surprising still, Your Excellency, is the following, that is, that an order of such importance as that which was transmitted to me by the Secretary of War on the 19th of May [10] should not have reached me until the 10th of June at Motas de Doña Clara, twenty-two days after it was sent, which is sufficient time for it to have been taken to and from Goliad. In a word, I received it almost the same day on which I was relieved of the command of the army agreeable to the respectful order of Your Excellency, dated the 31st of May, by which I was instructed to turn over the command to Urrea, twelve days after the first orders, and this not taking into account that the second order was detained in Matamoros for two days. But this was doubtless due to a desire to make certain that the command of the army had been given to Señor Urrea. Therefore, if the last order had been delayed longer in being issued, the first would have likewise been held longer. There was also a desire to make the army continue its retreat in order to find a pretext later for something else. Why did I not receive the order of the 19th of May, Your Excellency, on the 30th of the same month before I crossed the Nueces, while I was in position to countermarch as instructed, joining General Andrade at Mugerero Creek on the 2nd of June, to reach Goliad on the 3rd? But this did not suit the ulterior views of Urrea and Fernández. Isn't it likewise strange that my communication of the 31st of May should not have been received until the 25th of June, by which time it could have gone as far as Nacogdoches?

Do not all the facts presented, Your Excellency, amply prove the low and debasing intrigues (as I stated at the beginning of this humble representation) by which they have attempted against my honor and the better service of the army? Why the desire to delay my communications to the government and its orders to me? It is, indeed, Your Excellency, a *shame, yea, a greater shame* that by such degrading means they should have attained promotion and won the confidence and the praise of the supreme government.

[10] Tornel to Filisola, Mexico, May 19, 1836.

I have presented sufficient evidence to destroy the calumnies advanced against me and to prove the rectitude of my intentions. I shall add one more proof to show that necessity and not cowardice or fear was the true motive for my retreat. Ever since my arrival in Goliad, the commanders of the various units manifested to me that the troops could not remain exposed, without food, to the inclemency of the weather during the rainy season in that territory. Nevertheless, since my desire was to await the orders of the supreme government, I began to recondition our headquarters and make the preparations described. While there, an agent of Señor Urrea came and told me that the enemy was approaching with 1800 men to attack me.[11]   I immediately ordered General Andrade to demolish the fortifications of the Alamo, useless at all times and under any circumstances, and to spike the guns captured from the enemy, sending everything that he had in Béxar by way of San Patricio, escorted by the cavalry pickets in his command; while he, with the 400 picked cavalry and two pieces of artillery was to march along the left bank of the San Antonio to Goliad, covering that distance in four marches. I set out for the Aranzazu, which is two days' journey, intending that, by countermarching, we should meet on the same day and hour, effecting a juncture with his forces to fall upon the enemy, who, counting upon my retreat, would have in turn been surprised and would have been surrounded by our forces on all sides. But since after this operation was begun the commissioners of the enemy, bearing the terms of the armistice, came to me, the report of Escalera and Sánchez was proved groundless. Seeing, furthermore, that the enemy had the Guadalupe between their forces and ours, I pretended that my march was in accord with the request of the President and continued to the Nueces to meet Andrade. Had it not been for this incident, the enemy would have been defeated; but even then, I would have continued the retreat, just as before, for victory does not feed troops without supplies. When I reached the Nueces, I again tried to stop

[11] Información tomada en Goliad, May 25, 1836—signed Mariano Rodriguez and Manuel Sánchez.

and wait for the orders of the supreme government (which would not have reached me, for it has been shown that they would have been delayed as long as necessary for my betrayers to carry out their intentions) and I wrote General Fernández to send me supplies. His reply [12] shows that I had no hope of getting any, for even those which he says the schooner *Watchman* was taking were sufficient only for five days. What recourse was left to me, therefore, but retreat? I could not expect that any efforts would be made in Matamoros to supply me, for, besides the statement in the communication just cited that there were none, General Fernández took out from the commissary by force some of those collected for the army by Cayetano Rubio and sold them in the public square. Consequently, I ordered the troops to continue their march to that place, and I think that in doing so I did right, for otherwise some would have perished of hunger and others would have deserted. It may be said, therefore, that to this measure was due the conservation of the army, and I for one shall never regret having issued the order regardless of the comments which others may make.

Generals Urrea and Fernández at last obtained, Your Excellency, the most complete success, discrediting me, obtaining the command, and being promoted, all of which I hope will, in the end, reflect honor to the republic and credit to the service. In the meanwhile, while time decides who has acted with greater rectitude, and while finding consolation in my conscience and the integrity of those who shall pass judgment upon me, I remain perfectly tranquil. I think I have the right to ask, Your Excellency, that, if what I have thus far declared deserves any consideration, those generals should likewise be subjected to a judicial trial, agreeable to the article of the Ordinance which I have cited with reference to Señor Urrea, and as to Señor Fernández, for his participation therein.

In view of all of which, Your Excellency, I beg that you comply with my request as justice dictates.

Mexico, August 19, 1836.   VICENTE FILISOLA.

[12] Fernández to Filisola, Matamoros, May 31, 1836.

DIARY OF
THE MILITARY OPERATIONS

OF THE DIVISION WHICH
UNDER THE COMMAND OF

GENERAL JOSÉ URREA

CAMPAIGNED IN TEXAS

VICTORIA DE DURANGO, 1838.

DIARIO

DE LAS

OPERACIONES MILITARES

DE LA DIVISION

QUE AL MANDO DEL GENERAL

JOSE URREA

HIZO LA CAMPANA DE TEJAS.

PUBLICALO SU AUTOR

CON ALGUNAS OBSERVACIONES PARA VINDICARSE AN-
TE SUS CONCIUDADANOS.

———————

VICTORIA DE DURANGO 1838.

IMPRENTA DEL GOBIERNO A CARGO DE MANUEL GONZALEZ.

Facsimile of the Spanish title page

THIS is the first time in my life that I appear before the public to engage its attention. I have always prided myself upon making my action speak rather than my pen. I am ignorant of the art of weaving personal eulogies, and I am not acquainted with those fine tactics that convert faults into traits of consummate skill, that clothe mistakes with the mantle of virtue and give gigantic proportions to deeds that hardly rise above vulgar mediocrity, adorning them with assumed splendor. Nor am I accustomed to impute faults to others, reserving to myself their glory and casting upon them my own guilt. This is a favorite practice which, happily or unhappily, I have always ignored.

I tried the means prescribed by law and dictated by honor, addressing to the government a protest.[1] In this I asked that my acts be judiciously examined in order that I might be exonerated or punished as deserved if found guilty. I waited for a long time provided with the principal proofs for my defense; but, in spite of my repeated and urgent demands, I have not succeeded in getting even an acknowledgment to my communication. The case of General Filisola was being tried at the time and a principle of decorum and consideration, which he did not deserve, made me keep silence that it might not be said I was trying to injure his cause in order to avenge personal insults by his ruin. The said general was exonerated as foreseen by all those who were aware of the influences that were put into play. He first issued a *Representation* to the supreme government in which he insults me, abuses me, satirizes me, and belittles me, forgetting the respect due to authority, to the public, and to himself. He was moved by those principles that once

[1] José Urrea to the Secretary of War and Marine, Mexico, November 25, 1836. All documents listed in the notes are found in the appendix of the original *Diary*.

characterized his country [2] and made of its name a synonym for falsehood and calumny. In his military operations he conducted himself in a way that has covered the country with opprobrium and submerged us in untold misfortunes. The remainder of this century will not suffice to repair them. If to-day the republic is vilified and threatened by the ambition of a neighboring nation, if she has sacrificed her sons in vain, if her most beautiful province is lost, if a handful of rebellious foreigners insults her, if her campaign has been unavailing, if part of the army has become demoralized, if the treasury is exhausted, if the public money has been wasted in useless expense, if the people groan overcome by the weight of unbearable economic laws, if the enemy has gained new courage and obtained reenforcements, if it is necessary to undertake a new campaign and to multiply our victims and our sacrifices, if national independence finds itself endangered, if our flag has been insulted, if every branch of society finds itself in turmoil as the result of the lack of means to defray the most insignificant expenses, if internal peace is disturbed and the customs, the morals, and the century itself seem to slip back in our unhappy country, all will be due to General Filisola. The people will point to him as the cruel instrument of their misfortune, not because as Attila or Omar he raised the standard of devastation, but because, by his inaptitude or lack of courage, he opened the flood gates to the torrent of calamities that has swept over us. To have checked it, to have turned defeat into victory and glory, it would have been sufficient for him to have taken the one step that honor and duty prescribed, but he shamelessly disregarded both of them. The precipitate and disgraceful flight which he undertook in Texas while facing a vanquished enemy, a flight he has tried to disguise with the honorable title of a retreat, is the fountain of all our present calamities. It is the seal of national disgrace, a seal impressed upon us by an act of General Filisola that has brought untold misfortunes.

[2] General Filisola was an Italian by blood.

I should have said all this for my vindication at the time he was being tried, but I feared to add to the disgrace that weighed upon him and which will now pursue him to his grave. I thought, furthermore, that my offenses being very recent, the efforts to clear my name might be interpreted as inspired by vengeance, depriving my charges of their weight and robbing the verdict of its dignity. Looking at the matter from another angle I feared that if General Filisola was to be absolved anyway, as everything seemed to point out, I would arouse heated discussions in which, while disputing the pro and con, party spirit would be fanned and made to overleap the bounds of reason and public interest.

Faced by such cruel alternatives, I decided to be the only victim and kept silence before the public, making every effort possible to induce the government to institute trial against me. I have already stated that I did not succeed in getting any action, and after a useless residence of five months in the capital—during which time I was constantly petitioned to make a public declaration—I left for this capital [8] where I was to recover some very valuable documents that I had lost, and where I would have the time and tranquillity necessary to coordinate those that I will use in my justification.

Since my arrival in this capital, I have received frequent and even importune requests from many persons who urge me to write my vindication, appealing to the most powerful incentives of my soul. Some urge me as a citizen who is duty bound to defend his reputation, others as a Mexican who, out of regard for the public interests involved, should make a statement. I had refused because, as I have already said, I do not like to engage the attention of the public with my words. The interest of the country, the writings that have been published, and lastly, my own honor, however, demand that I speak and I shall do so, telling the truth by presenting the faithful diary of my operations. This will answer all invectives, refute the calumnies,

[8] Urrea prepared his *Diary* for publication in Durango, capital of the state bearing the same name.

and supply the omissions in the declarations made by a general of fateful memory. I shall speak in order that the inevitable end of the campaign intrusted to his skill may be forecast,[4] and the new blow which he is about to give to the nation by leading her sons to shameful gallows may not come as a surprise. I trust that I am deceived in my supposition, for I desire our welfare regardless of the hand that brings it. I wish to see the deep wounds of my country healed even if my hand does not apply the health balm.

Difficulties of a different nature had prevented me from previously publishing my vindication. The chief of these arose from the necessity of having to reveal serious errors that were committed, the effects of which are still felt. Thus, in speaking of them, I would be forced to raise the veil that ought to cover the policy of our cabinet. Unfortunately it never adhered to any policy nor did it ever decide upon any plan, for often its ambition or desire of ostentation, of making it appear that great things were being accomplished, when nothing worthwhile was being done, compromised our military operations. I wished to avoid this embarrassment by sacrificing my own defense, but seeing that everybody writes, that all make revelations in their own defense, that some criminally alter truth, falsifying it, that the facts are distorted, that public opinion is misled, and that I alone keep silence while unjust incriminations are piled against me, allowing despicable animosity to find expression, I have decided to speak and I will speak without consideration for any person, since none has been shown to me. Neither power nor rank shall check my pen in its course, nor shall I say anything except the truth, taking care not to fall into the noticeable fault of Señor Filisola who claims "To say strictly what is necessary for his vindication without using bitterness as a weapon of defense." Whoever has read his *Representation* to the government will see at once that his pen is guided by personal animosity, undisguised petulance, and baseness, while he who

---

[4] Filisola had just been appointed commander of a new expedition against Texas.

reads the present writing will not fail to realize the unpardonable error that has been committed by entrusting to that inefficient general the command of the army of Texas. The soldier can have no confidence in him, nor can the enemy respect him, for both saw his retreat while in command of forces that could have ended the war and freed the nation of the many evils that have befallen it and those that will yet follow by advancing a single step. Señor Filisola is not the man who will remove from the nation the disgraceful stamp that he himself placed upon it.

The said general, in his *Representation* to the government, has tried to vindicate himself from the serious charges that his military conduct merited. At the same time, he has bitterly censured me, without sparing my private life in his desire to slander me in every way. He has taken ignoble liberties to make me appear ridiculous. The diary of my military operations, which follows, will vindicate me, while the explanations which I have added will confirm the justice of the charges made against the above-mentioned general, particularly with regard to his notorious retreat. Let my diary begin to speak.

JANUARY 1836 [5]

9. I arrived at Saltillo with my regiment and part of a squadron of Durango. This force was incorporated with the greater part of the army already gathered in the city by his Excellency, General Don Antonio López de Santa Anna. I remained there until the 14th.

15. His Excellency received information regarding a party of colonists that was making its way to Matamoros for the purpose of taking possession of that port. In view of this, he immediately ordered me to set out for the said port with my cavalry and two additional pickets of mounted troops from the regiment of Tampico and the auxiliary troops from Guana-

---

[5] In the original edition of 1838, the diary is dated "Enero de 1835," which is evidently a misprint.

juato. Three hundred infantry from Yucatán were to join me
at Matamoros. With this force I was ordered to begin the
operations of our campaign along the coast as far as Lipantitlán, a fort situated on the right bank of the Nueces.

21. The days intervening were occupied in the march. Nothing worth while took place. When our division arrived at a
place called Zacate, I received a letter from the alcalde of Mier
advising me that ex-colonel José María González, with a party
of rebels, was threatening the town. I countermarched by way
of Villa Aldamas, where I left our baggage and the greater
part of our force, and pressed forward with 140 men during the
night. A violent norther accompanied by rain, and the thick
woods along the route prevented me from reaching my objective
that night.

22. I arrived with my party in Mier at eight o'clock in
the morning; and, although precautions had been taken, we did
not succeed in surprising the enemy, because the people of the
town gave them notice of our approach. The enemy fled towards
Guerrero to which place I pursued them. I had some correspondence with the city council there who favored the rebels
to the extent of permitting the flight of González and the greater
part of his party. I succeeded in capturing, nevertheless, twenty-
four prisoners, including sergeants, corporals and soldiers. They
were all Mexicans who belonged to the presidial companies. I
took them back under guard and incorporated them with our
division. They subsequently rendered very good service during
the campaign as guides and scouts. In the towns of the north,
from Matamoros to Guerrero, great adherence to the constitution of 1824 was noticed, and the people, believing that the
colonists were upholding it, kept in touch with them, being disposed to take up arms and join their cause.[6] I took advantage
of every opportunity to make them keep the peace, disclosing to

[6] Most of our Texas histories ignore completely the fact that many of the
Mexican settlers supported the revolution and served in the Texan army.
Frequent references are made in this *Diary* to the capture of Mexicans in
the Texan forces.

them the true views of the colonists, thus succeeding in keeping them quiet.

31. Our division arrived in Matamoros, having spent the time intervening in marching through the towns of the north. We remained in the city until the 16th of February.

FEBRUARY

16. Lieutenant Nicolás Rodríguez set out with six men to explore the road as far as the Nueces.

17. From twelve o'clock until ten o'clock at night the division was occupied in crossing the Río Bravo for the purpose of fighting a party of about 300 colonists whom the commandant-general of those departments and I were notified were on their way to invade the city of Matamoros.

18. I set out to join the division. At Rancho Viejo, three good leagues from Matamoros, I was informed that the enemy was retreating precipitately to San Patricio. I spent the night at this place where two foreigners, accused of being spies detailed by the enemy to get information regarding the movements of my troops, were arrested.

19. Although we still lacked practically all the necessary means to continue our march, I decided to push forward with only 500 *pesos'* worth of bread and hardtack which General Francisco Vital Fernández furnished me the night before. I spent the night at Anacuitas Ranch.

The following troops composed the division: 320 infantry from Yucatán and other places, 230 dragoons from Cuautla, Tampico, Durango, and Guanajuato, and one four-pounder. Of these I left about 200 men in Matamoros which were to follow later.

20. We moved on and crossed Colorado Creek. We spent the night on the left bank because, its waters being high, we experienced great difficulty in crossing the baggage and trains without the necessary equipment. The officer in charge of the advance guard rendered a report of no news.

21. We continued the march as far as Carricitos Ranch without mishap.

22. We marched to Chilquipín Ranch. That night I ordered a party of 120 mounted men, under the command of Colonel Rafael de la Vara, to advance as far as Santa Rosa before dawn in order to protect the scouting outpost, for I had been informed that a party of the enemy threatened it. My object was, also, to have them march a day's journey in advance to reconnoiter the Nueces.

23. I set out at three in the morning with fifteen dragoons and arrived at ten in Jaboncillos where I busied myself in sinking wells in order that the infantry might find water upon its arrival. The intervening country is made up of sand dunes for seven leagues and there is only brackish water to be found. This operation occupied us until five in the afternoon when the division arrived, at which time I pressed forward with my escort to overtake the party that I had sent ahead, for I wished to reconnoiter the Nueces personally.

24. At three o'clock in the morning I joined the party of Colonel la Vara and the scouting officer at Santa Rosa. The latter and his men set out immediately with orders to hide in the woods along the Nueces and reconnoiter the crossings, advancing, if possible, as far as San Patricio. The rest of the division continued its march from Jaboncillos and joined me at Santa Rosa where it encamped.

25. We resumed our march at four in the afternoon and I went ahead with 100 infantry and 100 dragoons. At seven o'clock that night a cold and penetrating norther began to blow. At ten I was informed by the scouting party that the enemy was occupying San Patricio. In view of this, I ordered the infantry to continue its march. Six soldiers of the battalion of Yucatán died from exposure to the cold.[7] I moved forward with our cavalry until I joined the observation party that awaited

---

[7] Throughout the *Diary* it is to be noted how the troops from Yucatán suffered from the cold. These men were practically all Maya Indians, accustomed to the tropical climate of their native peninsula.

me in a woods, two leagues on this side of Santa Gertrudis, where I arrived at half past eleven that night. I immediately wrote to Don Salvador Cuéllar, who lived in that town and from whom I expected exact information as to the enemy, asking him to come out immediately and meet me on the march.

26. The infantry arrived at the above-mentioned place at dawn, led by the guides which I had sent for the purpose. It began to rain at three in the morning and it looked like snow. I immediately gave orders to Lieutenant Colonel Nicolás de la Portilla for the infantry and the mounted cavalry to encamp in the woods, with instructions not to break up camp until the following day, provided the rain ceased. Taking advantage of the bad weather, I moved forward immediately. Leaving the road to our right we made our way through woods and across creeks until eleven that night when we came upon the Nueces, a league above Lipantitlán. Not being able to cross at this point I had to retrace my steps to the said town where I succeeded in crossing with much difficulty. I took a position on its left bank. Cuéllar, with two companions, came to inform me that there were seventy Americans at San Patricio, waiting to be reenforced by Dr. Grant and his sixty men who had gone to the Río Bravo to round up horses. The night was very raw and excessively cold. The rain continued and the dragoons, who were barely able to dismount, were so numbed by the cold that they could hardly speak. Nevertheless, being as brave as they were faithful, they showed no discouragement and we continued our march.

27. I arrived in San Patricio at three in the morning and immediately ordered a party of thirty men headed by Capt. Rafael Pretalia to proceed to the ranch of Don Julián de la Garza (a league distant) to attack twelve or fifteen men who were guarding 150 horses there. I ordered forty dragoons of the remaining force to dismount; and, dividing them into three groups under good officers, I gave instructions for them to charge the position of the enemy, protected by the rest of our mounted troops. The enemy was attacked at half past three in the morning in the midst

of the rain, and although forty men within the fort defended themselves resolutely, the door was forced at dawn, sixteen being killed and twenty-four being taken prisoners. The town and the rest of the inhabitants did not suffer the least damage. I captured a flag and all kinds of arms and ammunitions. Captain Pretalia reported at six o'clock that he had surprised the guard in charge of the horses, had captured all of these, killed four men, and taken eight prisoners. In these operations one dragoon was killed and one sergeant and three soldiers wounded. I ordered the horses of my division that were in poor condition to be replaced with fresh mounts. Having been informed that Dr. Grant was about to arrive, I sent some Mexicans to watch the roads by which he was expected. I ordered two parties of twenty men each to reconnoiter the vicinity of Goliad. Colonel Fannin with 600 men and 19 pieces of artillery was in the fort there. I detailed, also, two men of the town to observe the enemy.

28 and 29. In San Patricio and no news. According to our lists I had on this day 199 infantry and 183 cavalry.

MARCH

1. Still in San Patricio. Received news that Dr. Grant was returning from the Río Bravo with a party of forty or fifty picked riflemen and I marched that night, with eighty dragoons, to meet him. The north wind was very strong and the cold was extreme for which reason I decided to wait for the enemy ten leagues from San Patricio, at the port of Los Cuates de Agua Dulce where he would have to pass. I divided my force into six groups and hid them in the woods.

2. Between ten and eleven in the morning Dr. Grant arrived. He was attacked and vanquished by the parties under my command and that of Colonel Francisco Garay. Dr. Grant and forty of the riflemen were left dead on the field and we took six prisoners besides their arms, munitions, and horses. I countermarched to San Patricio and sent out new scouts to Goliad.

3-6. In San Patricio. Received news from Goliad. The troops drilled daily and received military instruction.

7. In San Patricio. The troops I had left in Matamoros joined me.

8. I was informed that the enemy was taking steps to attack me in San Patricio. I marched during the night to meet them, taking 300 men and the four-pounder in our division. Ten leagues from Goliad I ambushed my troops on the road to await the enemy.

9. In ambush on the Ratas Creek.[8]

10. I received news that the enemy had changed its plan and was making ready to march, with 400 men, to the aid of those who were besieged by our army in the fortress of the Alamo. I countermarched to San Patricio and ordered the cavalry to make ready to fight the enemy on the march.

11. In San Patricio.

[8] "On the night of the 7th, Jesus Cuéllar, known as *el Comanche,* presented himself in San Patricio claiming that he had abandoned Fannin's force to throw himself upon the clemency of the Mexican government. He was very likely sent by Fannin to observe our force and position. He told General Urrea that Fannin had decided to attack him and that by this time he had probably effected a juncture with the force at the mission. Consequently he promised to take us to a spot where we could lay in ambush while he went and brought the enemy into our hands. . . . His brother, Salvador, who had accompanied our forces ever since we left Matamoros, pledged himself for his brother's loyalty. General Urrea, confiding in his sincerity, ordered 200 men, 1 cannon, and 150 cavalry to set out early in the morning of the 8th of March for Las Ratas, 8 leagues away, on the San Refugio road. When our destination was reached, Cuéllar left us and Gen. Urrea proceeded to arrange the small force to carry out his plan. The surprise would have been difficult in the location chosen, for the woods where we were to hide was extremely sparse and all the trees were dry and devoid of foliage. The enemy would have detected us long before its approach. Our front, left, and rear were immense plains with not even a blade of grass, while the creek was dry and so shallow that it did not cover the infantry placed in it. General Urrea must have realized our disadvantageous position for at midnight he ordered us to return to our camp. We all were glad to hear this command, no one having felt easy while in that place."
Diary of Col. Garay as quoted in Filisola, *Memorias para la historia de la guerra de Tejas,* II, 405-407.

12.   Our whole division set out, leaving a small detachment there.   I received the reply of the general-in-chief to my report of the capture of this place and the defeat of Dr. Grant.   His Excellency thanked me and praised me highly for my services, authorizing me to provide for my troops by *taking cattle and supplies from the colonists as well as all their belongings.*[9]

13.   I marched towards Goliad and was informed enroute that the enemy had dispatched a strong detachment to occupy the port of Cópano and that they would halt at Refugio Mission. I dispatched a picket commanded by Captain Pretalia and thirty civilians headed by Don Guadalupe de los Santos with instructions for the first group to hold the enemy at the mission until I arrived with my division.   I selected 100 mounted men and 180 infantry; and, with our four-pounder, continued the march during the night, leaving the rest of our troops encamped on the Aranzazu Creek.

14.   I arrived at the said mission at daybreak where I found Capt. Pretalia holding the enemy in the church where they had taken refuge.   The moment they saw me they set the houses in their immediate vicinity on fire.   I reconnoitered their position to my satisfaction; and, convinced that it afforded means for a good defense, I realized that in order to take it I would be obliged to suffer heavy losses.   I at once decided to lay siege to it and to fatigue the enemy all that day and night in order to surprise them at dawn the following day.   But the pitiful stories which the civilians of the place related about the thefts and abuses they had suffered at the hands of the enemy, excited the indignation of the officers and troops of my division, and decided me to take advantage of the opportunity afforded by the coming out of a party of eighty men to get water at a creek situated about a gunshot from their fortification to order a group of infantry and another of cavalry to start a skirmish, hoping to draw out the rest of the enemy from their intrenchment.   The

[9] Antonio López de Santa Anna to José Urrea, Béxar, March 3, 1836; also Santa Anna to Urrea, Béxar, March 23, 1836; and Santa Anna to Urrea, Camp on San Bernard Creek, April 6, 1836.

eighty men retreated immediately to the fort. The officers and troops manifested a great desire to attack the enemy; and, wishing to take advantage of their enthusiasm, I immediately ordered a column of infantry to make the charge, protected by the fire of our cannon which had been moved forward sufficiently to destroy the door of the church. With our cavalry covering our flanks, our advance was so successful that the infantry arrived within ten paces of the cemetery without a single man being wounded. The enemy, coming out of its lethargy, opened up a lively fire upon our men. The troops, being mostly recruits from Yucatán, stopped spellbound the moment their first impetus was spent, and all efforts to force them to advance were unavailing, for the greater part of their native officers who a moment before had been so eager disappeared at the critical moment. These men were, as a rule, unable to understand Spanish, except in a few cases, and the other officers, not being able to speak their language, were handicapped in giving the commands. The infantry took refuge in a house and corral situated about fifteen paces from the church. I ordered a part of the cavalry to dismount in order to encourage the former by their example. Not succeeding in making them advance, and the dismounted cavalry being insufficient to take the position of the enemy, the moments were becoming precious, for at that very moment another party, coming from Cópano, was threatening my rear guard. I, therefore, ordered a retreat. This operation was not carried out with the order that might have been expected from better disciplined troops. In the meantime our cannon had been moved forward to within twenty paces of the cemetery, but my brave dragoons removed it in order to continue harassing the enemy from a distance, where the enemy fire could cause us no damage. Not one of the enemy dared show his face.

I ordered Col. Gabriel Núñez, with a part of the cavalry in our reserve, to go out to meet the enemy that was approaching in our rear. The enemy had taken refuge in a woods which a large creek made inaccessible. I ordered sixty infantry, commanded by Col. Garay, to dislodge them. They killed eleven and took seven prisoners, but the thickness of the woods did not permit a more decisive victory before darkness enabled the enemy to escape.

According to all the information I secured, the number of the enemy that had shut themselves in the church was 200 and they lacked water and supplies. This would make it imperative, unless they succeeded in escaping during the night, for them either to come out and fight us the following day or surrender. In order to prevent their escape, I placed several lookouts at the points through which they might effect it, but the necessary vigilance was not exercised by all of them and the enemy escaped, favored by the darkness of the night which a strong norther and the rain made more impenetrable and unbearable. On the other hand, our troops were very much fatigued as a result of having marched all the day and the night before and of having spent the 14th in constant fighting without taking food. On this day I had the misfortune of losing six infantry and five dragoons who were killed, while twenty-seven infantry were wounded, three officers among them; also ten dragoons among which one of the first was Lieut. Juan Pérez Arze of the Jiménez battalion who had commanded the pickets.

15. This day at dawn, as I approached the church, I noticed the absence of the enemy and ordered the place to be occupied. Six wounded men, four others, some colonist families and several Mexicans who had been commandeered were found. Having re-enforced the detachments that I had on the road to Goliad and El Cópano, I ordered all the available cavalry to pursue the enemy. We killed sixteen and took thirty-one prisoners.

Envy and calumny have united in trying to denounce me for the engagement of the 14th. Those who have criticized my conduct were ignorant of my position and of the intentions of the enemy. But I who divined them, as I later found out,[10] had no time to lose, for it was essential to destroy a force with which the enemy intended to make itself formidable. This had to be

[10] W. Fannin to A. C. Horton, Fort Defiance, March 14, 1836; also Fannin to Samuel A. White, Fort Defiance, March 14, 1836.

done with about 200 horsemen and a very poor body of infantry, not knowing when the reenforcement sent from general headquarters would reach me.

16. Leaving the wounded and the baggage under the care of Col. Rafael de la Vara, and instructing him to keep a watch on the port of Cópano, for which purpose I left the necessary guard, I marched with 200 men, infantry and cavalry, to Goliad, sending out scouts to reconnoiter the road to the town. The parties dispatched to pursue the enemy captured fourteen. A messenger of Fannin was intercepted and we learned beyond all doubt that the enemy intended to abandon the fort at Goliad and concentrate its force at Victoria; that they only awaited the 200 men that had been sent to Refugio to execute this operation. On the 14th and 15th I had fought and dispersed the latter force. In order to observe the enemy and cut off its communication with Victoria, I ordered Capt. Mariano Iraeta and sixty men to take a position on the road between this place and Goliad to watch it. I halted that night at San Nicolás.

The many hardships endured by my division, and the rigor of the climate that was felt particularly by the troops accustomed to one more mild, made my position extremely difficult because of the necessity of properly guarding the adventurers that I had taken prisoners. I constantly heard complaints, and I perceived the vexation of my troops. I received petitions from the officers asking me to comply with the orders of the general-in-chief and those of the supreme government regarding prisoners. These complaints were more loud on this day, because, as our position was not improved, I found myself threatened from El Cópano, Goliad, and Victoria. I was obliged to move with rapidity in order to save my division and destroy the forces that threatened us. Ward had escaped with 200 men; the infantry was very poor and found itself much affected by the climate. I was unable, therefore, to carry out the good intentions dictated by my feelings, and I was overcome by the difficult circumstances that surrounded me. I authorized the execution, after my departure from camp, of thirty adventurers taken prisoners during the previous engagements, setting free those who were colonists or Mexicans.

17. Very early on this day I found myself on the right bank of the San Antonio. I halted at San José Ranch from where I could keep a watch on Goliad. I sent scouts to Guadalupe Victoria, situated nine leagues distant. During the night Capt. Pedro Pablo Ferino and two scouts came to me. Under orders of Don Juan Antonio de los Santos, they had been on the road to Béxar watching for the force that was to join me from that point. Ferino told me that Col. Juan Morales was approaching with 3 cannon and 500 men from the battalions of Jiménez and San Luis. I repeated the order previously given to this officer to take a position a league from Goliad, on the Manahuilla Creek, north of the fort. I broke up camp early in order to march to join the division that was coming from Béxar, which I did at the appointed place. I passed near Goliad and reconnoitered it from as close a point as possible. In the afternoon my advance guards notified me that the enemy was approaching and shortly after, a body of cavalry was seen advancing along the edge of a woods. I ordered Col. Morales with the picked companies of Jiménez and San Luís to go out and meet them. This operation was sufficient to make the enemy retreat. They were pursued by a large detachment which forced them to get back into the fort from where they opened a fire with their artillery, keeping it up until nightfall. After having again carefully reconnoitered this place and its vicinity, I returned to my camp with my force. I took all the precautions prescribed by the art of war and demanded by circumstances. I had plenty of warnings that made me fear the flight of the enemy, so I reenforced the advanced cavalry pickets which I had placed along the river to keep watch. Our troops were obliged to bivouac all night, exposed to a continuous rain and a strong north wind which made the cold unbearable. No rest was possible during the entire night.

19. Our advance guards turned in a report of no news. I was making ready to place our artillery on a high slope on

the left bank of the river, within a rifleshot of the fort, and was about to cross with the cavalry for the purpose of inspecting the points by which the enemy could be approached, when I received notice that they had abandoned their position and were on the way to Guadalupe Victoria. I immediately ordered 360 infantry and 80 cavalry to be ready to march, and at eleven o'clock, having confirmed my information, I set out to overtake them, leaving the rest of our force and the artillery and baggage under the care of Col. Francisco Garay, with instructions to explore the fort and take possession of it if it was really abandoned. I did not think it proper to take personal charge of this operation, fearing that the enemy might escape. I desired to obtain a triumph for our nation on this day to celebrate my birthday—pardon my personal pride. After marching two leagues, I was informed by my spies, whose activity is truly marvelous, that we were near the enemy, and that it seemed that they were not taking all the force that had garrisoned Goliad. I ordered 100 infantry to return, therefore, to protect the artillery and ammunitions which were being brought up, and redoubled the vigilance of the rest of my forces. At half past one in the afternoon, I overtook the enemy and succeeded in cutting off their retreat with our cavalry, just as they were going to enter a heavy woods from where it would have been difficult, if not impossible, to dislodge them. They were marching in column formation and carried nine pieces of artillery. Seeing themselves forced to fight, they decided to make the best of it and awaited our advance with firmness, arranging their force in battle formation with the artillery in the center. My troops, though fatigued by the rapidity of the march, were filled with enthusiasm at seeing the enemy, for they thought that to overtake them and defeat them was all one. Although our force was inferior and we had no artillery, the determination of our troops made up the disparity. Expecting the artillery and our munitions to reach us soon, agreeable to instructions given, I decided to engage the enemy at once. Our fire was immediately returned by their rifles and cannons. I ordered the brave Col.

Morales to charge the left with the rifle companies; the grenadiers and the first regiment of San Luis, under my immediate
command, to charge the right; the remainder of the battalion
of Jiménez, under the command of Col. Salas, to form itself
into a column and charge the front; while the cavalry, commanded by Col. Gabriel Núñez, was to surprise the enemy's rear.
These instructions having been issued, the orders were immediately carried out and a determined charge was made on the
right and left flanks.   In order to obtain a quick victory, I
ordered my troops to charge with their bayonets, at the same
time that Col. Morales did likewise on the opposite flank; and,
according to previous instructions, the central column advanced
in battle formation, sustaining a steady fire in order to detract
the attention of the enemy while we surprised the flanks. Though
our soldiers showed resolution, the enemy was likewise un-
flinching.   Thus, without being intimidated by our impetuous
charge, it manoeuvred in order to meet it; and, assuming a
hammer formation on the right, they quickly placed three pieces
of artillery on this side, pouring a deadly shower of shot upon my
reduced column.   A similar movement was executed on the left,
while our front attack was met with the same courage and cool-
ness.   Our column was obliged to operate in guerrillas in order
to avoid, as far as possible, the withering fire of the enemy,
who kept up a most lively fire, for each one of their soldiers
had three and even four loaded guns which they could use at the
most critical moment.   The fire of the nine cannons, itself lively
and well directed, was imposing enough; but our soldiers were
brave to rashness and seemed to court death.   The enemy put
into play all its activity and all the means at its command to
repel the charge.   While defending themselves from our determined attack, they built up defences with their baggage and
wagons, forming a square.   It was necessary, therefore, for the
officers, who vied with each other in daring, to display all their
courage and the utmost firmness to maintain the soldiers at their
posts—less than half a rifle shot from the enemy, in the middle
of an immense plain, and with no other parapet than their bare

breasts. In order to protect our soldiers as far as possible, we
ordered them to throw themselves on the ground while loading,
raising up only to fire. In this way the distance between our
force and the enemy was further decreased. Realizing the importance of preventing the enemy from finishing its fortifications,
especially in the form in which they were doing it, I tried to disconcert them with a cavalry charge on their rear, and placed
myself at the head, convinced that the most eloquent language
and the most imperious order is personal example. I found the
enemy prepared to meet us. Although disposing of very little
time, they had foreseen my operation and received me with a
scorching fire from their cannons and rifles. Our horses were in
very poor condition and ill-suited for the purpose, but the circumstances were urgent and extraordinary measures were necessary. My efforts, however, were all in vain, for after repeatedly
trying to make the dragoons effect an opening in the enemy's
ranks, I was forced to retire—not without indignation. I placed
the cavalry in a position where it could continuously threaten
the enemy, avoiding, as far as possible, their fire. Seeing that
our artillery and munitions did not arrive, my anxiety was great.
In the midst of our trials and in proportion as they increased
I cast furtive glances towards the point by which they were
to come. But I saw no signs to ease my anxiety, for not even
those that I had sent to rush our munitions returned. The sun
was going down and our munitions would soon give out. They
were exhausted sooner than I expected. Though I had given
instructions for the infantry to be provided with four rounds
to the man, this order had been neglected in part under the
frivolous pretext of lightening their load. They had counted
on the early arrival of what was coming up on our rear, for
when we left the camp at Manahuilla our ammunition was being
loaded. The party conducting it, however, lost its way and did
not arrive until the following day. I decided to make a new and
simultaneous charge on all fronts to see if I could disconcert
the enemy before the sad moment arrived when we would be
entirely without munitions. I gave the necessary orders and,

as the bugler gave the signal agreed upon, all our forces advanced with firm step and in the best order. I placed myself again at the head of the cavalry and led the charge on one of the fronts. All our troops advanced to within fifty and even forty paces from the square. So brave an effort on the part of our courageous soldiers deserved to have been crowned with victory; but fortune refused to favor us. The enemy redoubled its resistance with new vigor. They placed their artillery on the corners, flanking, in this way, our weakened columns. The fire from the cannons, as well as from the rifles, was very lively, making itself all the more noticeable in proportion as ours died out for lack of ammunition. In these circumstances, I ordered all our infantry to fix bayonets and to maintain a slow fire with whatever powder remained. For almost an hour, this unequal contest was kept up, then I finally gave the order to retire, menacing the enemy with our cavalry, divided in two wings, in order to allow the infantry to execute the movement. Our forces gathered in orderly fashion at the designated point of reunion. I joined them there and addressed them in terms suited to the occasion, but the troops needed no exhortations, for far from being discouraged at seeing their efforts frustrated, they were burning with desire to undertake a new bayonet charge. After so many hardships, a new attempt, besides being dangerous, was unadvisable. I concluded by saying to the soldiers just as the day closed, "Let us gather our forces, let us wait for our ammunition and artillery, let us watch the enemy during the night, and tomorrow I shall lead you to victory. You do not need your cartridges, for you have your bayonets, and your courage is boundless. The enemy is terrified and will not be able to resist any longer the charge of such brave Mexicans. I promise you a complete victory."

The soldiers were satisfied and filled with pride. I placed the infantry a little more than 200 paces from the enemy, protected from their rifles by a gentle slope. I detailed cavalry and infantry pickets to points from which they could observe the enemy. I moved the wounded to the woods which the enemy had tried to take possession of when I overtook it, and which was situated to the rear of our infantry. During the night I closed the circle formed by our advance guards and moved our scouts forward until they could observe the slightest movement in the other camp. The enemy spent the night digging a ditch all around the square. My aides: Lieut. Cols. Ángel Miramón and Pedro Pablo Ferino, Capt. Mariano Odriosola, and the militia captain, José de la Luz González were with me, all harassing the enemy and keeping it awake with false bugle calls. I also visited our outposts. The enemy's cavalry, which was small in number, had escaped the moment we overtook them, thanks to their good horses. Some there were who, choosing the fate of their brave companions, dismounted and abandoned their horses. I took advantage of this to replace the worst mounts of our dragoons.

20. At daybreak I inspected the position of the enemy which I found to be the same as that of the day before, with the exception of the trenches formed by their baggage and wagons, now reenforced by the piling up of the dead horses and oxen and by the digging of a ditch.

I issued orders for the battalion of Jiménez to take its position in battle formation; the rifle companies were to advance along the open country; and the cavalry, in two wings, was to charge both flanks.

The troops having taken up their respective positions, rations were issued consisting of hard-tack and roast meat. The latter was furnished by the teams of oxen that had been taken from the enemy the night before. Those that remained to the enemy were killed by sharpshooters detailed for the purpose. The day before, some of the infantry had taken cartridges belonging to the cavalry and as a result some of the rifles were loaded, but they were fixed on this day.

At half past six in the morning the ammunition arrived, which, as stated before, had been lost the day before; and although more had been ordered from Col. Garay, this had not arrived up to this time. One hundred infantry, two four-pounders (not a twelve-pounder), and a howitzer were added to my force. I placed these as a battery about 160 paces from the enemy protected by the rifle companies. I ordered the rest of the infantry to form a column that was to advance along the left of our battery when it opened fire. As soon as we did this and began our movement as planned, the enemy, without answering our fire, raised a white flag. I immediately ordered my battery to cease firing and instructed Lieut. Col. Morales, Captain Juan José Holzinger, and my aide, José de la Luz González to approach the enemy and ascertain their purpose. The first of these returned soon after, stating that they wished to capitulate. My reply restricted itself to stating that I could not accept any terms except an unconditional surrender. Messrs. Morales and Salas proceeded to tell this to the commissioners of the enemy who had already come out from their trenches. Several communications passed between us; and, desirous of putting an end to the negotiations, I went over to the enemy's camp and explained to their leader the impossibility in which I found myself of granting other terms than an unconditional surrender as proposed, in view of which fact I refused to subscribe to the capitulation submitted consisting of three articles.[11] Addressing myself to Fannin and his companions in the presence of Messrs. Morales, Salas, Holzinger and others I said conclusively, "If you gentlemen wish to surrender at discretion, the matter is ended, otherwise I shall return to my camp and renew the attack." In spite of the regret I felt in making such a reply, and in spite of my great desire of offering them guarantees as humanity dictated, this was beyond my authority. Had I been in a position to do so, I would have at least guaranteed them their life. Fannin was a gentleman, a man of courage, a quality which makes us soldiers esteem each other mutually. His manners captivated my affection, and if it had been in my hand to save him, together with his companions, I would have gladly

[11] B. C. Wallace, J. M. Chadwich, J. W. Fannin, Terms of Capitulation, Camp on Coleto Creek, March 20, 1836. Also see Document No. 6, Santa Anna's *Manifesto*, p. 57.

done so. All I could do was to offer him to use my influence with the general-in-chief, which I did from the Guadalupe.

After my ultimatum, the leaders of the enemy had a conference among themselves and the result of the conference was their surrender according to the terms I proposed. They immediately ordered their troops to come out of their intrenchments and to assume parade formation. Nine pieces of artillery, three flags, more than a thousand rifles, many good pistols, guns, daggers, lots of ammunition, several wagons, and about 400 prisoners fell into the hands of our troops. There were ninety-seven wounded, Fannin and several other leaders among them. I gave orders for all the baggage to be taken up, the prisoners to be escorted to Goliad by 200 infantry, and the wounded who were unable to walk to be carried in the carts or wagons taken from the enemy. They had lost twenty-seven killed the day before. I lost eleven killed, and forty-nine soldiers and five officers were wounded. Capt. José María Ballesteros was seriously injured.

Right on the battlefield, I wrote a note to Col. Garay telling him of the outcome and asking him to make a report to the general-in-chief, for it was impossible for me to do it at the time because I was marching to Guadalupe Victoria without stopping to rest.

Through a dispatch from Col. Garay, I learned that he had taken possession of Goliad where he had found eight pieces of artillery which the enemy had been unable to take with them. When he took possession, the houses of the city were still burning, having been set on fire by the enemy before it retreated. Combustible materials were left to prolong the fire, and very few houses were saved.

According to papers taken from Fannin he had called for reenforcements to come to his help and there were good reasons to believe that the forces dispersed at Refugio might make their way to Victoria. I left my instructions for Col. Morales to conduct all the armament and war materials taken from the enemy to Goliad. With the greater part of the infantry, one cannon, and all the cavalry available, I started for Victoria in order to occupy it and the Guadalupe before the enemy did so. I spent the night in the ranch of Coleto, ten miles distant from that place.

Señor Filisola has referred to this engagement, that of San Patricio, and the one of Refugio as mere *skirmishes* because he could not think of a more derogatory term. He has added, on page 29 of his second pamphlet, *that I deserve to be tried by a council of war and to be punished accordingly for each one of these, because I sacrificed hundreds of brave soldiers when similar results could have been obtained without such a sacrifice.* The sincere narration I have made of the facts, and the effect which these so-called *skirmishes* had upon the success of the campaign—preventing the besieged at the Alamo from receiving reenforcements of men and munitions, and clearing completely almost the whole territory of Texas so that Señor Filisola might be saved the horror of seeing the enemy a single time—prove the injustice of the accusation and show his character of duplicity and perfidy that reviles and debases him. Señor Filosola forgets that in his letter of the 20th of April, dated at Old Fort, he says to me in a *post data,* referring to these skirmishes, *"I congratulate you for the brilliancy of your glorious operations, which, in my opinion, leave nothing to be desired."* Is one who deserves to be tried by a council of war addressed thus? Has the opinion of the writer radically changed concerning the glory of my actions as a result of personal feeling? How despicable and false does this man who talks so much of honor appear! I received from General Santa Anna flattering praise beyond my expectations for the importance of my services, while the series of *skirmishes* which I sustained during my march reduced the force of the enemy practically to nothing. Thus, the army was enabled to advance without firing a shot, while I had no rest, working continuously every hour of the day, always in pursuit or in search of new forces to combat.

21.   Continued our march at daybreak, taking my place with our advance guard formed by the company of Jiménez. I took possession of Guadalupe Victoria at half-past seven in the morn-

ing. The inhabitants—Mexicans, French and Irish—had been in communication with me, and when I arrived they had arrested six of the enemy who were in the town. Two hours after our arrival a party of twenty was seen down the river making their way towards Victoria. I issued orders to cut them off from the woods along the banks of the Guadalupe, and these having been carried out, they were all killed or taken prisoners. On this day a sergeant, who was coming from Goliad, took seven others which were executed by Capt. Pretalia before he reached Victoria when the shooting sustained against the first group was heard.

At eleven of the same day an enemy force of about 100 men was discovered up the river. They were making their way to Victoria also, doubtlessly acting in combination with the party of twenty that had just been destroyed. As they had good guides with them, they succeeded in evading my vigilance and hid themselves in the woods after having exchanged a few shots with our cavalry, detailed to keep them from getting into the woods. But having found out the point to which they would likely make their way, I managed to cut off their retreat by way of Lavaca Lake.

On this day I sent an order to Col. Morales to join me with the rest of the troops, consisting of the battalions of Jiménez and San Luis. I issued instructions for the safeguarding of Cópano and the prisoners who were in Goliad.

22. With 200 infantry, 50 horses and 1 cannon I marched towards the port known as Linn's House. At two in the afternoon I arrived at a place called the Juntas where four creeks come together, ten leagues from Victoria. The enemy force that I was looking for had just arrived. Four members of their force, who were looking for food, were captured and they declared that the enemy was hiding in the nearby woods. I instantly took possession of all the avenues leading to and from the woods; and, having made certain that they could not escape without coming upon our soldiers, I sent one of the prisoners to inform their leader, warning him that if he and his force did not

surrender immediately at discretion they would all perish shortly.
Mr. Ward, the so-called colonel and leader of the force, solicited
an interview with me, and five minutes of conversation were
sufficient for him to agree to surrender with the 100 men under
his command among whom were ten ranking officers. I decided
to spend the night at this point (Las Juntas) ordering the
cavalry to reconnoiter the port of Linn, where flour, sugar, rice
and potatoes were found. These supplies were carried to Victoria and were distributed, without charge, to the troops, agreeable to the orders of the general-in-chief.[12]

General Filisola, making use of those indefinite terms which
he handles so skillfully to make vile suspicion fall upon those
whom he wishes to defame, has represented me as a man who
busied himself generally during the campaign in looking after
his own private interests, who pillaged the towns to enrich himself with the booty. This is but one of the many despicable
calumnies and falsehoods which he distributes so prodigally.
According to the already mentioned order and the one of March
23, and agreeable to others received, I was authorized by the
general-in-chief *to take from the colonists their cattle and everything that belonged to them, using it for the support of my
troops.* I made use of this authorization, but there is not a man
who can say that I charged the troops anything for the supplies
received, much less that I took from the soldiers whatever they
selected or chose, bartering with their misery. Another general
who also made haste to write a *Representation* to sustain that of
Señor Filisola, repeats these accusations, these falsehoods, and
these exaggerations. This is not strange; but that he should
have had the daring and temerity to call on me to point out
a single case of demoralization, of excesses, of lack of discipline, of indolence, or of neglect on the part of other officers
is incredible. To make such a challenge one must not know
what honor is, or be so accustomed to such vices as to attach
no importance to them. I will state, therefore, in order to

[12] Santa Anna to Urrea, Béxar, March 26, 1836.

satisfy the general who thus challenges me, that it was he himself who in the main furnished the occasion for that horrible picture of misery which General Filisola depicts in his official note of the 14th of May when he complains that he had to buy corn at 90 *pesos* a *carga,* bread at 3 *pesos* a loaf, cornbread at 2 *reales* a piece, brown sugar at 20 *reales,* and firewater at 8 *pesos.* General Gaona, who is the one I am referring to, engaged in that infamous trade with the supplies brought for the army, monopolizing them as it approached Matamoros, and selling them to his brigade at a profit of more than a hundred per cent. He it was who pillaged the town of Bastrop and delayed the march of his division for eight days in order to transport the booty, violating the order which the general-in-chief sent to him by special messenger, commanding him to join his division in Austin. And yet I am accused of levity because I complained of the corruption and abuses of a part of the army. The said general, however, has deserved undue praise from General Filisola, notwithstanding that during the campaign he complained so loudly against his scandalous conduct. It is necessary to admit that General Filisola adds to his many failings the unpardonable one of inconsistency. I beg to be allowed these digressions, because, if I were to take a special section to answer the personal recriminations brought against me, I would have to repeat many facts frequently. Therefore, I prefer to place my explanations where they fit into the text of my narrative. I will proceed with my diary. The active battalions of Querétaro and Tres Villas arrived in Goliad to-day and brought a twelve-pounder.

23. I returned to Victoria with the prisoners taken with Ward and received news at this place that eighty-two men had surrendered at Cópano with all their arms and munitions. I sent scouts to Lavaca Lake and the stream bearing the same name, as well as to that of La Navidad. I dictated ten orders for the security of Cópano and the prisoners at Goliad, the establishment of hospitals, and the rebuilding of the fort there by the prisoners, excusing from this work only those who were officers. I gave instructions also for all the forces with which I was to continue

the campaign to join me, bringing the artillery and the corresponding ammunition. Among the instructions given on this day I ordered that a thorough investigation be undertaken to determine the views and principal aims that moved the officers who are our prisoners to take up arms. The findings of this investigation are among my papers.

I spent the 24th, 25th, 26th, and 27th in organizing my forces, equipment, and ammunition, and in drawing up many instructions for the security of the military posts that I was leaving on our rear, as well as for the better care of the wounded who have been up to now in the hands of a bad surgeon. As among the prisoners there were men skilled in all trades, I secured surgeons from among them who were very useful to us as well as to the sick in the hospital at Béxar, where I sent those that were needed.

On the 25th I sent Ward and his companions to Goliad. The active battalion of Querétaro joined me on the 26th. On the 27th, between nine and ten in the morning, I received a communication from Lieut. Col. Portilla, military commandant of that point, telling me that he had received orders from His Excellency, the general-in-chief, to shoot all the prisoners and that he was making preparations to fulfill the order.

This order was received by Portilla at seven in the evening of the 26th, and although he notified me of the fact on that same date, his communication did not reach me until after the execution had been carried out. All the members of my division were distressed to hear this news, and I no less, being as sensitive as my companions who will bear testimony of my excessive grief. Let a single one of them deny this fact! More than 150 prisoners who were with me escaped this terrible fate; also those who surrendered at Cópano and the surgeons and hospital attendants were spared. Those which I kept, were very useful to me as sappers.

I have come to an incident that has attracted the attention of foreigners and nationals more than any other and for which there have not been lacking those who would hold me responsible, although my conduct in the affair was straightforward and unequivocal. The orders of the general-in-chief with regard to the fate decreed for prisoners were very emphatic.[13] These orders always seemed to me harsh, but they were the inevitable result of the barbarous and inhuman decree which declared outlaws those whom it wished to convert into citizens of the republic. Strange inconsistency in keeping with the confusion that characterized the times!

I wished to elude these orders as far as possible without compromising my personal responsibility; and, with this object in view, I issued several orders to Lieut. Col. Portilla, instructing him to use the prisoners for the rebuilding of Goliad. From this time on, I decided to increase the number of the prisoners there in the hope that their very number would save them, for I never thought that the horrible spectacle of that massacre could take place in cold blood and without immediate urgency, a deed proscribed by the laws of war and condemned by the civilization of our country. It was painful to me, also, that so many brave men should thus be sacrificed, particularly the much esteemed and fearless Fannin. They doubtlessly surrendered confident that Mexican generosity would not make their surrender useless, for under any other circumstances they would have sold their lives dearly, fighting to the last. I had due regard for the motives that induced them to surrender, and for this reason I used my influence with the general-in-chief to save them, if possible, from being butchered, particularly Fannin. I obtained from His Excellency only a severe reply, repeating his previous order,[14] doubtlessly dictated by cruel necessity. Fearing, no doubt, that I might compromise him with my disobedience and expose him to the accusations of his enemies, he transmitted his instructions directly to the commandant at Goliad, inserting a copy [15] of the order to me. What was done by the commandant is told in his

[13] Santa Anna to Urrea, Béxar, March 3, 1836; also Santa Anna to Urrea, March 23, 1836; and Santa Anna to Urrea on the same date.

[14] Santa Anna to Urrea, Béxar, March 24, 1836; also Santa Anna to Urrea, Béxar, March 3, 1836.

[15] Santa Anna to Urrea, Béxar, March 23, 1836.

diary. Here, as well as in his communications,[16] are seen the motives that made him act and the anguish which the situation caused him. Even after this lamentable event, I still received a letter of the general-in-chief, dated on the 26th, saying: *"I say nothing regarding the prisoners, for I have already stated what their fate shall be when taken with arms in their hands."*

In view of the facts presented, and keeping in mind that while that tragic scene was being enacted in Goliad I was in Guadalupe Victoria, where I received news of it several hours after the execution, what could I do to prevent it, especially if the orders were transmitted directly to that place? This is to demand the impossible, and had I been in a position to disregard the order it would have been a violent act of insubordination.

If they wish to argue that it was in my hand to have guaranteed the lives of those unfortunates by granting them a capitula-

[16] *Diary of Col. Nicolás de la Portilla.* This interesting extract is given in full here because of its bearing on the Goliad Massacre.

March 26. At seven in the evening I received orders from General Santa Anna by special messenger, instructing me to execute at once all prisoners taken by force of arms agreeable to the general orders on the subject. (I have the original order in my possession.) I kept the matter secret and no one knew of it except Col. Garay, to whom I communicated the order. At eight o'clock, on the same night, I received a communication from Gen. Urrea by special messenger in which among other things he says, 'Treat the prisoners well, especially Fannin. Keep them busy rebuilding the town and erecting a fort. Feed them with the cattle you will receive from Refugio.' What a cruel contrast in these opposite instructions! I spent a restless night.

March 27. At daybreak, *I decided to carry out the orders of the general-in-chief because I considered them superior.* I assembled the whole garrison and ordered the prisoners, who were still sleeping, to be awaked. There were 445. (The eighty that had just been taken at Cópano and had, consequently, not borne arms against the government, were set aside.) The prisoners were divided into three groups and each was placed in charge of an adequate guard, the first under Agustin Alcerrica, the second under Capt. Luis Balderas, and the third under Capt. Antonio Ramírez. I gave instructions to these officers to carry out the orders of the supreme government and the general-in-chief. This was immediately done. There was a great contrast in the feelings of the officers and the men. Silence prevailed.

Portilla to Urrea, Goliad, March 26, 1836; also, Portilla to Urrea, Goliad, March 27, 1836.

tion when they surrendered at Perdido, I will reply that it was not in my power to do it, that it was not honorable, either to the arms of the nation or to myself, to have done so. Had I granted them terms, I would then have laid myself open to a trial by a council of war, for my force being superior to that of the enemy on the 20th and my position more advantageous, I could not admit any proposals except a surrender at discretion, my duty being to continue fighting, leaving the outcome to fate. I believe that I acted in accordance with my duty and I could not do otherwise. Those who assert that I offered guarantees to those who surrendered, speak without knowledge of the facts.[17]

28. I began to comply with the orders of the general-in-chief in which he outlined the plan of operations that was to be observed for the continuation of the campaign.[18] My division, composed of infantry, cavalry, and artillery, was divided into two infantry brigades. The first under the command of Col. J. Mariano Salas, consisting of the battalions of Jiménez and Querétaro, set out on this day to reconnoiter the ports on Lavaca Lake, carrying with it a twelve-pounder and the corresponding artillerymen and munitions for both the cannon and the infantry.

29. The cavalry set out for the purpose of reconnoitering the banks of Lavaca and La Navidad Creeks.

30. The second brigade, composed of the active battalions of San Luis and Tres Villas under orders of Col. Juan Morales, marched towards the Villa of Santa Anna, taking two pieces of artillery and the corresponding train.

31. I left Victoria with my escort, leaving at this place a detachment commanded by Capt. Telésforo Alavez. I spent the night on the banks of the Arenoso.

[17] Urrea has a note in the original *Diary* calling attention to the statement of Santa Anna in his *Manifesto* with regard to the terms of surrender. See Santa Anna's *Manifesto*.

[18] Santa Anna to Urrea, Béxar, March 23, 1836; Santa Anna to Urrea, same date; Urrea to Eugenio Tolsa, Victoria, March 27, 1836; Urrea to Joaquín Ramírez y Sesma, Victoria, March 27, 1836.

APRIL

1. On this day I joined the infantry brigades at Santa Anna and ordered eight dragoons to proceed to the inspection of Cox's Point, gathering all the supplies and war material found at that place as well as along their route.

2. I remained in Santa Anna and gave instructions for the temporary commandant of Tres Villas, Augustín Alcerrica, to march to the left bank of La Navidad with 200 men from his division and the part of the active troops of Yucatán that were attached to his command. He was to occupy the houses located near the main crossing of the said creek.

3. I marched with the rest of the infantry to join Señor Alcerrica at the place to which he had been sent on the previous day and spent the night there, having first detailed a party of cavalry to reconnoiter all the places in the immediate vicinity of Santa Anna. Fourteen negro slaves with their families came to me on this day and I sent them free to Victoria.

4. The cavalry that had been sent to Cox's Point joined us bringing several barrels of flour, beans, sugar, and lard. I ordered the infantry to continue their march.

5. I pressed forward with the cavalry and joined the infantry at Tres Palacios Creek where I spent the night and from where I sent out scouts to the Colorado.

6. I occupied Cayce's Crossing on the said river, exploring both banks, and placed sixty men on the left bank to make the crossing safe.

The 7th, 8th, 9th, 10th, and 11th I transported the division to the left bank of the said river and explored the banks both upstream and downstream. The flood rising and the stream increasing in volume during these days as a result of the heavy rains, it was necessary to construct barges and overcome many difficulties in order to cross the river. Those who have seen it know that it is wide and deep and that it is not easy to carry out such an operation with the rapidity that military operations demand and the art of war prescribes.

On the 9th, I wrote to the general-in-chief and to General Sesma, who were detained on the banks of the Colorado, notifying them that the principal difficulties had been overcome and that I now would be able to continue my march. On the same day I sent young Dr. Harrison, my prisoner, (the son of a general of the United States) to the colonies with the special mission of speaking to the colonists who had not taken up arms, offering them guarantees and the protection of the army. It will later be seen that this measure was not fruitless.

12. As I have explained, I was not able to renew our march until the 12th. I set out with the whole division towards Matagorda agreeable to instructions from the general-in-chief and encamped on its left bank, five leagues from Cayce's.

13. I continued the march early in the morning and took possession of Matagorda at ten o'clock. This had been abandoned by the enemy and only a single sailboat was found there in which six or eight men who were on the pier made their escape with extraordinary speed, it being impossible to prevent it. We came near enough to speak to them and we tried to persuade them not to flee, but it was useless, though they did promise to return. Inhabitants were noticed on Culebra island, situated to the south, in sight of Matagorda. There were three ships in sight, one anchored at the said island and two on Caballo Crossing. I inspected the mouth of the river and ordered that the roads leading to the San Bernard be likewise reconnoitred. In the warehouses were found many cotton goods, abundant dry-goods, fine crockery and crystal ware, a great number of bales of cotton, tobacco, and abundant supplies of all kinds. The enemy had had no time to take away all of these goods. I gave instructions for all of them to be gathered and for an inventory to be made, the goods to be placed at the disposal of the general-in-chief. I also ordered some brown domestic and other goods and supplies to be distributed among the troops that needed them. A flag and two three-pounders were also found.

On the 14th I selected a point on the pier to be fortified and gave instructions to Capt. Juan José Holzinger, of the engineers, to carry out my orders, acting in accordance with the principles of his profession.

On the 15th I arranged for the division to continue its march to Columbia, leaving 230 infantry and a twelve-pounder with ten artillerymen to garrison Matagorda and to defend the point that was to be fortified. I appointed Col. Augustín Alcerrica commandant and left him four presidial soldiers with which to send me news, for these men being well acquainted with the country are the best suited for the purpose. I received orders from the general-in-chief which showed that he was preparing to undertake his unfortunate expedition to Harrisburg.[19] I counter-marched to Matagorda and joined my division that afternoon at Cayce Crossing and spent the night there. In compliance with the orders of His Excellency, of the 13th, I notified him that I had given instructions for the supplies that were coming from Matamoros to be placed at Guadalupe Victoria, intrusting their care to the commandant of that point. On the same date, I notified His Excellency of the encounter sustained by a part of my division against the Tarancahuaces who had appeared at the house of Dimmit and demanded the delivery of the supplies that were kept there, claiming that they belonged to the Americans. Capt. Balderas refused their demand and when they attacked him he routed them completely. Their brave chief Antoñito and other braves were left on the battlefield, while the remainder fled.

17. The march was continued, and we encamped on the outskirts of a spacious woods along the San Bernard.

18. The march was continued and we halted in some houses located in the said woods.

19. We encamped on the San Bernard. The cavalry outposts met some mule drivers of Don Antonio Tallafé who were out looking for supplies. They belonged to the part of the army that was at that time on the Brazos. Two Americans and a Pole, who protested that they did not belong to the enemy forces, were

[19] Santa Anna to Urrea, Thompson's Crossing, April 13, 1836.

arrested. A group of cavalry scouted the banks of the said creek and found the houses located there uninhabited.

20. I continued the march, leaving on our rear fifty dragoons and Tallafé's mules to be loaded with corn and beans which were found in abundance in the houses situated along the banks of the San Bernard. I encamped in the house of Mrs. Powell. Señor Filisola acknowledged receipt of my letters and referred to my operations as *very effective*.[20]

21. The march was continued at four o'clock in the morning and by pressing forward with the chosen companies, some troops from Jiménez, and sixty horses, I occupied, at four o'clock, the town of Columbia and its port which is two miles distant on the Brazos, called La Puerta. Two Americans were found who asserted that their families and others were hiding in the immediate woods. I sent one of them to go and allay their fears and assure them, on my part, that they could return to their homes without the least fear. Both in the port and in Columbia we found goods, food supplies, and liquors in abundance. I ordered an inventory of all of them to be made and provided for their safety. I appointed Col. Mariano Salas military commandant of the place.

22. I left Salas the battalion of Jiménez, all the cavalry, and some pickets from San Luís and Guerrero. With the remainder of the troops, one mortar, and one four-pounder I marched to Brazoria which I occupied at ten in the morning of the same day. Many English, American, and German colonists awaited me at this place with their families as a result of the commission I had given to Dr. Harrison on the Colorado to allay their fears. They expressed satisfaction with the treatment accorded them, which was no other than that which should be accorded to peaceful and industrious citizens who had refused to take up arms against their adopted country at the instigation of the rebels.

Having a horrible idea regarding us as a consequence of the war without quarter which was being waged, they considered it a very particular favor to be treated as, in justice, they should

[20] Vicente Filisola to Urrea, Old Fort, April 20, 1836.

be; and as proof of their gratitude, they gave me information that was very important for our war operations, offering to contribute to its termination by persuading those colonists who had taken up arms to lay them down. They felt confident that they would, as soon as they were assured that their lives and property would be respected. They offered, among other things, to turn over to me Galveston Island, asking me first to guarantee the lives of the many families that had taken refuge there and in the port of Velasco. I reassured them on this point and offered to grant them all the privileges that were within my power, because I was intimately convinced that a conciliatory policy and a philanthropic and humane attitude would do as much, if not more, than our arms in putting an early end to the campaign. Sad experience has proved this, but that blind fatality which seems to pursue our destiny, blinded our government at the time.

Many advantages could have been secured from the good disposition of the colonists of Brazoria, and I had intended to avail myself of it, ignorant that the unfortunate event of the previous day was to sweep away my most flattering hopes, making all our trials and the many victims that had fallen up to this time a useless sacrifice, with no other fruit than the eternal shame and disgrace of an unnecessary retreat.

It is a homage due to justice to confess that Dr. Harrison had contributed very decisively to the good disposition that was noticeable among the colonists. He thought, on his part, that he owed me his life and he omitted no means to express his gratitude, even going to the extent of risking it a second time because he thought he owed it to me. I was assured at Brazoria that Houston did not have more than seven or eight hundred men, for although there were three or four hundred others under arms, part of these were garrisoning Velasco, while the rest were scattered and unable to offer any resistance.

Through several declarations which confirmed each other, I found out that the intentions of this leader at that time were to take possession of Galveston and defend it long enough to permit the families to embark with their negroes and the property gathered there. But circumstances forced him to make a stand; fortune favored him at San Jacinto; and he who in the course of unfavorable circumstances could have obtained no glory as a soldier and might have perhaps disappeared from the scene, presented himself now as the conqueror and the hero.

Men were not lacking, of those who had served under him, who now offered to lead me to that formidable Houston. There were even those who voluntarily offered to contribute to his defeat, for they desired it because the greater part of the men under his command were adventurers who were worse enemies of the colonists than we ourselves, practicing a thousand extortions and being the cause of their ruin and that of their property while protesting to sacrifice themselves for their happiness.

Many goods, liquors, and food supplies were found in Brazoria also, which, according to the colonists themselves, belonged to the enemy. They voluntarily offered to gather these supplies and take them to the three points I designated for their deposit and safe keeping.

In the afternoon I occupied the left bank of the Brazos with the chosen companies of San Luís and Querétaro.

23. I was about to start for Velasco in order to continue afterwards to Galveston, when I received the mysterious executive order of General Vicente Filisola, instructing me to march to Old Fort with all the troops under my command and without making a single halt. This order was dated on the 23rd at three in the afternoon [21] and I received it between nine and ten in the morning of that same day, which shows an unpardonable error. The same order had been transmitted directly to Col. Salas, who, without waiting for orders from me, immediately complied with it. [22] As a result of this operation my rear guard was left unprotected, since I was four leagues ahead in a very thick and marshy woods where not even the rays of the sun penetrated. Velasco is almost as far from Brazoria as this

[21] Filisola to Urrea, Old Fort, April 23, 1836, at 3 in the afternoon.
[22] Jose Mariano Salas to Urrea, Columbia, April 27, 1836.

point is from Columbia and, had I undertaken the operation that I had planned a few hours before the receipt of the said order, attacking the enemy in their stronghold, I would have found myself in dire distress without the support of a force upon which I depended for my operations. It never occurred to me that this force would be removed without my knowledge. There are many instances where superior orders must be obeyed regardless of the manner in which they are transmitted, but there are others in which exception must be taken and this, in my judgment, was one of them.

I was ignorant, at that time, of the circumstances that dictated this precipitate movement, since Señor Filisola only said to me, on a small piece of paper, without date: *"The President has suffered a misfortune according to a dispatch sent to me by a colonel who says that he will be here tonight. It is necessary, therefore, for you to do everything you can to reach this place with all your force as soon as possible."*

My division at that time was in the finest condition. Each soldier could hold his head up proudly, for up to then they had met only victory in every encounter with the enemy. When ordered to countermarch, the disappointment was modified only by the hope that the enemy was to be met on some other front. It could not be thought otherwise, since everyone, even to the last soldier, was convinced of our superiority and of the worthlessness of the enemy. It is true that the force that had attacked the president, as well as its location were unknown; but it is also true that it could be no other than Houston's and we knew the strength of his force. Everything seemed to point, therefore, to a concentration of our forces in order to march upon him and repair the defeat suffered by our vanguard, now that the enemy was weaker than before its triumph as a result of the engagement. In virtue of this, I ordered my aide, José de la Luz González, to take the two large boats that were in Brazoria up the river to Columbia in case they were needed there to cross the Brazos. Having received the order for my march between nine and ten in the morning of the said day, I set out at eleven, having first ordered all the goods and supplies belonging to the enemy to be placed at the disposal of the troops in order that they might take whatever they needed and could carry it without embarrassment in the march. As there were food supplies in Columbia, and we were to pass by that point, it was not necessary to overburden the soldiers nor the commissary department.

While on the march, I sent Capt. Pretalia with a cavalry escort to see Señor Filisola and to inform him of the high spirit of my division, showing him how advantageous it would be to advance upon the enemy before it could receive reenforcements. It was impossible for me while on the march to set down the great many ideas that rushed to my mind at the time. I instructed Pretalia not to lose a singe moment in fulfilling the important commission intrusted to him, and to use all possible means to influence Señor Filisola to advance upon the enemy without the loss of a single moment. Among the instructions given to this officer, I charged him to explain the means that I had for crossing the Brazos quickly at Columbia, if the enemy was between this point and general headquarters, and that if I was being called in order to advance from there upon the former I could undertake this operation from where I was, before wearing out my soldiers and without losing precious time, since I had the means with which to do it. I could cross the Brazos at the same time that the main body of the army, or any part of it, did so at another point, and, acting in combination, surprise the left flank of the enemy while its right or front was being attacked. Once this operation was decided upon, it was impossible for the enemy to escape unless it fled. If it waited, it was more than likely that we would repair our misfortune, rescuing our prisoners and saving the honor of the nation. But it is not yet time to make observations on this point which I will reserve for another place.

At five in the afternoon (of the 23rd) I arrived at Columbia, where I found my escort and Lieut. Col. Angel Miramón awaiting me, this being the entire force left by Salas. At this place I found out some of the details given to Miramón by Capt. Ruíz, aide to General Filisola and the courier who brought the orders for Col. Salas and myself. When I learned that the place to which our dispersed soldiers would naturally make their way was to be abandoned and that a retreat was to be undertaken, a thousand contending sentiments rushed over me and my displeasure was shared by the part of the army under my command. A few hours before, we thought only of flying to avenge our companions and our general-in-chief, and now the first rumors of turning our back upon them in their misfortune began to be heard. Such a sudden change could not but arouse extreme feelings of despair and dismay, of shame and indignation. I decided, however, to resume my march immediately, without stopping any longer than was necessary to load the available mules of the commissary department with whatever supplies they could carry, leaving all the rest there, for I did not dare to destroy them, being still uncertain as to the final decision of the second general-in-chief. Nevertheless, I ordered several barrels of powder and more than 200 rifles that were found at Columbia and which I could not take with me to be thrown in the river. When I departed from Brazoria, I left Col. Garay in ambush with two picked companies to observe the movements of the colonists, giving him instructions to follow me that afternoon. In Columbia I left my escort with orders to burn the boats which were coming as soon as they arrived, and to follow Garay, covering his rear. This night I encamped a league from the last mentioned place, for although the march had been short it had been difficult because of the muddy condition of the woods, and it was impossible for the soldiers to advance further without undue fatigue.

24. I renewed the march early and, after traveling eight leagues, halted in order to wait for the troops that had been left as a rear guard in order that they might join me. While halted, I received a dispatch from Señor Filisola in which he asked me to march to the place to which the guide that he had sent should lead me.[23] His Excellency, at this time, was undetermined as to where to go. He wrote me under date of the 24th, from camp,

[23] Filisola to Urrea, In Camp, April 24, 1836.

which he had reached the night before. He has officially asserted,
however, that he was at Old Fort the afternoon of the 23rd.[24]
Col. Garay and all the force which I had left as a rear guard
joined me in the afternoon, and, in keeping with the urgency with
which I was called, I resumed the march at nightfall, reaching
Mrs. Powell's place the 24th at midnight. Here I found
Señor Filisola and all the forces that had left Old Fort on the
23rd. The part of my division left at Columbia was there also.

A spirited proclamation issued on the 24th [25] promised the
army an advance to avenge national honor and the blood of our
companions. Enthusiasm filled all hearts and no one could
doubt that such solemn promises would be kept. Imagine my
surprise at hearing from the very lips of General Filisola his
determination to abandon the scene of war! I expressed my
opinion that now was the opportune time to advance upon the
enemy; I offered to do so with my division, emphasizing the
probabilities of our triumph; but although I did everything I
could to have my opinion accepted, my advice was not heeded.

25. A council of war, composed of all the generals and ranking officers of the various units, was attempted, but when it was
learned that the greater part of the latter were opposed to a retreat—in my own division there was not a single man who
favored it—it was decided that the council be composed only of
generals, ordering all other officers to their respective camps and
telling them that they had been assembled only to recommend to
them the care of their respective commands while the council
was being held.

No one could know the attitude that prevailed among the
troops better than their immediate officers. Because of this fact,
their opinion should have been more important than that of
the generals who could judge of the spirit of the army only
by their own feelings.[26] It is true that there were cowardly men,

[24] Vicente Filisola to the Secretary of War and Marine, Victoria, May
14, 1836.
[25] Filisola to the Army, April 24, 1836.
[26] Filisola to the Secretary of War and Marine, Guadalupe Victoria, May
14, 1836.

as it is always the case, but they were by no means in the majority. I was certain of the morale of my division because I knew how my troops felt, and I surmised the general attitude that prevailed among the rest of the army because it was made known to me by several of the officers who were opposed to a retreat. I, also, was opposed to this measure and expressed myself publicly, though always ready to abide by the decisions of the general-in-chief, as I was duty bound to do. Even before joining the main body of the army, I had manifested my opposition to a retreat as shown by my private communication of the 24th to Señor Filisola and Senor Sesma.[27] This same day, the 25th, the army was reorganized and I was placed in charge of the reserve, composed of a brigade made up of the battalions of Jiménez and San Luís which had formerly belonged to my division and the cavalry regiment of Cuahuila and other unassigned pickets. A retreat having been determined upon, it was decided to cross the Colorado at Cayce's Crossing. Col. Garay was sent that same day to prepare the means of effecting the passage. In order to enable him to march with greater celerity, he was allowed to take the greater part of the Cuahuila troops. Señor Filisola reviles me bitterly for this action on page 27 of his *Representation*. If he did not see this body of troops again it was because the army having countermarched to Atascosito. I instructed Garay, agreeable to orders of Señor Filisola, to go to Guadalupe Victoria, where he rejoined the army.

26. The march was started and I covered the rear guard. On this day it began to rain at eleven o'clock in the morning, and seeing that the vanguard made no progress, I went ahead to learn the cause, and I found out that many difficulties were being encountered in crossing the first fork of the San Bernard. I did not reach camp until two or three hours after the other brigades arrived. It was dark and raining. The cause for my delay had been the greater obstacles I had had to overcome in

---

[27] Urrea to Filisola, In Camp, 4 leagues from Columbia, April 24, 1836; Urrea to Ramirez y Sesma, April 25, 1836.

effecting the crossings after the other divisions had made them impassable with their wagons and herds.

When Señor Filisola narrates the events of this day (which he designates as the 27th) he does me a great injustice and makes such a ridiculous statement, permit me this remark, that, like all his other statements which depend for their faith upon his word, it has no value. He says on page 23: "We camped that night in a small house and Messrs. Gaona and Tolsa covered *the most exposed* posts with their brigades, while Señor Urrea took care of *the best protected* location. On the 28th (It should be 27th) we camped in a single row on the left bank of the principal branch of the San Bernard. Señor Urrea and his brigade occupied the left which was *the least exposed position in case of an engagement.*"

This base insult not only to my person but to the brave men under my orders, who covered themselves with laurels and on whom victory never turned her back, proclaims a heart possessed of all the ignoble passions, incapable of justice, and unwilling to admit its own errors. When did Señor Filisola see me show signs of cowardice? When was I ever known to turn my back upon, or to fear danger? If my presence was so unimportant, why was I called with such haste only to be given a worthless position in the army? Was it because during my operations I always went in search of the enemy, pursuing it to its last hiding place, or was it because of the fear that possessed General Filisola? Let those who saw me campaign in Texas, and those who read the diary of my operations decide the question. As for the rest, I do not believe that I owe His Excellency any thanks, for on that night there was no danger, the general having exercised his usual prudence to avoid it.

27. It was still raining in the morning when I set out and, as I left, I ordered two good scouts to return and reconnoiter the roads by which the enemy might advance, with orders to go as far as the Brazos for the purpose of crossing that river and bringing, if possible, those that had been dispersed in the battle of San Jacinto. Between three and four in the afternoon

the scouts overtook my brigade while on the march, bringing with them a presidial soldier with papers for Señor Filisola from His Excellency, General Santa Anna. This soldier informed me that he had set out from Béxar with mail for His Excellency, the general-in-chief, and that when he arrived at the Brazos in search of the army he met a certain Smith and two other Anglo-Americans who, by orders of Houston, were looking for Señor Filisola to deliver to him the dispatches of His Excellency, General Santa Anna; that the said men had taken the correspondence for General Santa Anna and had given him the one for Señor Filisola.

Both from this information and from the passport (signed by General Santa Anna) given to the said soldier, I learned that His Excellency was a prisoner. All the members of the brigade under my command were overjoyed to hear this news for we had been told that he had been killed in the battle.

I assembled the brigade and communicated the news to the men, urging them to turn upon the enemy as they desired. Bugles were sounded immediately, and the whole brigade broke out into loud acclamations and hurrahs which demonstrated very clearly the sincere enthusiasm that reigned among all classes,

As soon as the soldier who was bearing the said papers gave me the information recorded, I sent him with one of my aides to overtake Señor Filisola, who was already encamped upon the second branch of the San Bernard.

Late that evening I was called by order of General Filisola to appear at his tent.

All the generals of the army having gathered there, Señor Filisola read to us the letter and dispatch which Santa Anna, now a prisoner, had sent him with instructions for the army to retreat agreeable to an armistice entered into with Houston.

I perceived some confusion among several of my companions, but I cannot say what it was. The retreat had already been undertaken by orders of General Filisola and the dispatch of General Santa Anna was taken to be only a safe conduct so that the army should not be disturbed by the enemy. It was decided to reply to General Santa Anna, giving him the impression that our movement was being executed agreeable to his orders.

I called the attention of General Filisola to the fact that it was indispensable to explain why the Brazos had been abandoned before the receipt of his communication. This was done by telling the general, now a prisoner, that our first movement had had for its purpose the abandonment of useless posts to concentrate our forces and then turn upon the enemy. No other excuse could be thought of, for in fact, we had sufficient forces to have kept our position upon the Brazos, holding all the *useless* posts, and to have organized an excellent division which, by advancing upon the enemy, could have obtained victory and vindicated the honor of the army and of the nation.

In the above-mentioned council, I insisted on turning back upon the enemy, and not succeeding in having my proposal accepted, because the enemy was thought to be very numerous, I proposed to Señor Filisola that I be permitted to go to Houston on pretext of taking to His Excellency his mail and bringing back the armistice. The army could await the result of my mission in the vicinity, from where, once information as to the weakness and impotency of the enemy was obtained after my return, it could march upon it. Many objections were offered to my plan though its importance was recognized, and it was decided finally that General Adrián Woll should undertake the commission, but that the army should continue its retrograde movement, although with assurances, at the time, that a position would be taken on the Colorado.

28. General Woll went to the enemy's camp. I petitioned Señor Filisola to be allowed to remain two or three days' journey in the rear of the army, assuring him that we would not be molested by the enemy, for I could block any possible advance. My object in presenting this petition was to make the march less embarrassing and to afford some comfort to the brigade under my command, for in the two previous marches, having to cover the rear guard, we had been delayed on the road the

whole day without time for the troops to eat or to clean their guns to keep them in that good condition in which they ought to be kept by troops in a campaign. Señor Filisola agreed to allow me to stay all day in camp, but when he set out with the rest of the army he shortened his permission to only half a day, instructing me, and even begging me, to join him before dark.

This morning Señor Filisola explained to me how cumbersome he considered the wagons and even the artillery, and told me that he had decided to abandon everything that might tend to hinder the speed of the march which he believed essential until the Colorado was reached, adding that in view of the armistice arranged with Houston, whatever was left by the army was safe, since the Texans would take care of it. I was surprised to hear such an opinion from the general in command of the army, and I exerted myself to disabuse his mind with reasoning, repeating what I had already expressed. I said that, "the armistice and the retreat of the army, as stipulated in the dispatches of General Santa Anna, are nothing but the orders of the Texans to save themselves from the blow which they expect, since they have no other way out of the danger; and General Santa Anna has merely availed himself of the opportunity offered to resume communication with us." This was my opinion, and General Gaona suported me in combatting the idea of abandoning the artillery.

At seven o'clock in the morning Señor Filisola set out with the first and second brigades, while that of the reserve which was under my orders remained in camp occupied in cleaning their arms, washing their clothes, etc.

At three that afternoon I held an inspection of arms and munitions and immediately after started our march following on the tracks of the army. We had traveled about two leagues when we came upon all the wagons and smithing equipment of the army stuck in the mud. I called the manager of our transportation division in order to find out the cause of his plight. He told me that he did not know why he had been left in this

abandoned condition, that he was ignorant of the route followed
by the army, and that no escort nor guide had been provided.
He added that he did not think that he could carry the carts
and wagons any further without help, for in addition to the
load of arms, munitions, food, dirt, sacks, and other utensils
of the army loaded on the wagons, there were a great number of
sick men, Col. D. N. Infante among the latter. I immediately
ordered one of my aides to overtake Señor Filisola and to inform
him for me of the condition in which I found the said carts
and wagons, telling him that my brigade could not leave this
point until it was able to take the carts also. I asked him, therefore, for any unloaded mules that he might have to lighten the
cargo of the others. I also ordered my brigade to take up whatever they could carry, and, in fact, the troops and the officers,
without excepting Cols. Juan Morales and Mariano Salas, gladly
took up the greater part of the sacks and carried them to firm
ground. By this means, and by dint of great efforts, the carts
were put in motion again. The mules which we asked Señor
Filisola to send arrived and the load was lightened. The carts
and wagons having been started, I ordered the picked companies of Jiménez and San Luis to escort them. I arrived at
Señor Filisola's camp at nightfall, and at about ten that same
night the carts and wagons together with the escort that I had
left came in. Thus, for the time being, the sick were saved, who
otherwise would have perished, partly as a result of the raw night
and partly because the rest would, perhaps, have fallen into the
hands of the enemy, had they been left in such shameful abandonment.

As soon as I appeared before Señor Filisola, he informed
me of the great anxiety he felt regarding the difficulty of quickly
occupying the crossing at Atascosito on the Colorado. The
general feared the enemy might resume an offensive against
us, and he knew that they could reach the said crossing in one
day's journey from San Felipe de Austin. The army had left the
main road and was now in a mud hole where the men were
hardly able to stand up. The mind of Señor Filisola conceived

only alarming and terrifying ideas, imagining what was not and could not be possible under the circumstances. I had a long discussion with him, and in spite of all my efforts to make him see reason, it was impossible for me to free him from the apprehensions that had him beside himself, restless and fearful. I promised him to comply with the orders which he entreated and begged that I carry out. These were that on the following day I should take the vanguard of the army and occupy the crossing at Atascosito, thus securing for him the means of crossing the Colorado.

29. A little before seven in the morning the march was resumed and I took the vanguard with my brigade in order to put into effect the previous orders, by which I was instructed, if possible, to take possession of the above-mentioned crossing on that day. For this purpose I was ordered to leave the artillery of my division in the care of the first brigade commanded by General Gaona.

The march was extremely painful. The road lay along a muddy lake that threatened to engulf the men and the beasts; and we had no signs to guide us other than the general direction in which we were traveling, imitating sailors in a way. In spite of the great difficulties that had to be overcome, a party of cavalry reached Atascosito at five in the afternoon, at six a part of the infantry arrived, and by seven the whole brigade was encamped at that place.

30. I sent a messenger to General Filisola at daybreak, advising him that the crossing of the river was safe. I ordered groups of cavalry and infantry to scout the left bank in an effort to find means to cross over to the other side. Two small canoes were found which were used to place an advance guard on the other side and to transport a party of cavalry to scout the opposite bank.

On this day a good deal of lumber suitable for the construction of barges was gathered and we began to construct one capable of transporting the artillery and trains of the army.

MAY

1. We remained on the Colorado scouting its banks and constructing the barge that was used by the army in crossing. My brigade crossed that same day in the canoes, and remained on the right bank until the seventh of May.

8. After the whole army had occupied the right bank of the Colorado, I marched with my brigade to Guadalupe Victoria.

In preparing for this march, Señor Filisola gave me instructions to reorganize the detachments at Victoria, Goliad, and Cópano, which were composed of troops belonging to the brigade under my command. He also instructed me to send him food as quickly as possible in order that the army might suffer no want.

9. On the road.

10. My brigade arrived at Guadalupe Victoria and I occupied myself with the fulfillment of the orders of General Filisola.

11, 12, and 13. We remained at Victoria. Señor Filisola arrived with the whole army on the last mentioned day.

14. Agreeable to orders of Señor Filisola, I marched to Matamoros with my brigade, but before leaving, I had an interview with His Excellency and, with the greatest earnestness, I tried to convince him of the wisdom of not retreating any further and of staying where we were until new instructions were received from the government. I believe that the general wished me away in order to act more freely.

15 and 16. On the road to Refugio Mission.

17. We found a deposit of food supplies there. Rations for 12 days were issued to the troops. These consisted of hardtack, rice, and lard. The cavalry received rations of the last two articles only.

From the 18 to the 27th we were on the road to Matamoros.

28. We arrived at Matamoros. News was received that the port of Brazos de Santiago was threatened by hostile ships. I marched with 250 infantry to that point and proceeded as far as the mouth of the river. I took steps to insure their safety

and ordered a fort to be constructed in the first place mentioned, at the entrance to the bar.

31. I received communications from General Francisco Vital Fernández telling me that Señor Filisola was continuing his retreat to Matamoros; that he had ordered the prisoners taken at San Patricio and Agua Dulce that were held in Matamoros to be sent to Galveston; and that he had approved the treaty made by General Santa Anna while a prisoner, recognizing thereby the independence of Texas. Immediately upon receipt of this news, I returned to Matamoros.

JUNE

1. Having traveled all night, I reached Matamoros at dawn. With regard to the orders of Señor Filisola to set the prisoners free, I gave instructions that they be disregarded, and addressed a communication to him protesting against the retreat, etc., etc. At the same time, I sent an account of everything to the supreme government by special messenger.

I have traced the course of all my military operations during the Texas campaign to this point in order to answer with facts the accusations, recriminations, and personal insinuations which Señor Filisola has so freely used against me in order to revile my person and my conduct. In the following observations I propose to vindicate my honor from these accusations, and to prove that the charges I made against him, later adopted by the Ministry of War, were as just as they were true.

Señor Filisola, in trying to defend himself from the serious charges brought against him, has summarized the various accusations in his *Representation* to the government. The prime object of all his efforts and endeavors seems to be his desire to justify the necessity and advisability of a retreat, emphasizing the skill with which this operation was accomplished. The move, however, will always justly be looked upon as a treasonable and shameful flight. By examining all the facts presented in the notes addressed to the government between the 14th and the

31st of May,[28] it is seen that he claims to have undertaken the retreat: first, in order to save the lives of the president and the prisoners which an advance of the army would have endangered; second, because of the discouragement experienced throughout the army as a result of the misfortune of San Jacinto; third, because the general-in-chief had not made his plan of operations known, nor outlined any that could be followed; and fourth as a result of the absolute lack of food and supplies of all kinds which could not be secured and of the many obstacles presented by the country for an advance. In addition to these he presents, both in his official communications to the government and in his *Representation,* other ridiculous and extravagant reasons that do not deserve to be examined closely because they are based on circumstances that were the direct outcome of his first mistake.

It is absolutely false that Señor Filisola undertook the retreat in order to save the lives of the president and the prisoners, for he says, on page 48 of his *Representation* that when the news of the reverse of San Jacinto became known in the army "the alarm and discouragement was general among all classes, being generally believed that *all the prisoners, including the president, had been executed."* On page 51, he says that on the evening of the 28th he received reliable information indicating that the latter was alive, but in his note of June 10th, to the Minister of War, he asserts that he has good reasons to believe that the general and all the prisoners had been executed. There is another document, purposely suppressed by Señor Filisola from his second public utterance which corroborates my statement. It is a dispatch addressed to the Minister of War, dated the 25th of April, in which he says, "On the 18th the president asked me to send him immediately 500 men with General Cós,

---

[28] Filisola to the Secretary of War and Marine, Guadalupe Victoria, May 14, 1836; Urrea to Filisola, In camp, 4 leagues from Columbia, April 24, 1836; Urrea to Ramírez y Sesma, April 25, 1836; Filisola, *Representation to the Government;* Filisola to the Secretary of War, In camp, on the right bank of the Nueves, May 31, 1836.

which I did. But his entire command was completely defeated in the immediate vicinity of New Washington, just a little beyond Harrisburg, on the 21st. Only three officers and six men were saved" (Doc. No. 1 as published by the said gentleman in Leona Vicario). The authentic documents to which I have referred prove conclusively that Señor Filisola failed to tell the truth when he asserted that he undertook the retreat in order not to jeopardize the lives of the prisoners; and that he lacked that sincerity which is expected of a person of his rank when he made this statement, for it was generally believed by everybody in the army, according to him, that all were dead. Amidst the confusion of his ideas and the impossibility of explaining his conduct, he has made himself most ridiculous by trying to justify his acts by the communication addressed to him by the Ministry, on May 15th, recommending that the life of the president be saved. How could Señor Filisola have foreseen on the 22nd of April the order of the 15th of May which was to serve him as an excuse for his conduct? Well might I use here certain of his phrases, exclaiming *"It is a shame that by such means the praise and the trust of the government should be obtained."* The said general, has repeated in several of his writings that *even without the orders of the general-in-chief, he would have attempted a retreat,* it being impossible for him to maintain his position, since the condition of the army would not have been greatly improved even by victory at San Jacinto. I shall later have an occasion to call attention to the serious inconsistency of the said gentleman on this point. At present I merely wish the reader to notice particularly the comical contrast between the pompous proclamation issued on the 24th of April and his subsequent conduct. That monument of petulance and boastfulness was published on the 24th, and on the 25th he was already notifying the government of his determination to establish his base of operations on the right bank of the Colorado, placing the river between himself and the riflemen whom he feared so much. This official note is suppressed in the published documents appended to his *Representation.* Not deeming it safe

even at this point to establish a base, he recrossed the Guadalupe
and the Nueces, writing from the right bank of the latter to the
government, on May 31st, that there was nothing to do but
to continue the retreat until the Rio Bravo was crossed and
Matamoros was reached. Had not the government put a stop
to this continuous necessary retreat, he would have continued his
retrograde movement until he reached the main plaza of Mexico
City in order calmly to establish his base of operations there.

The general has tried to find a justification for his conduct
in the general discouragement which he claims prevailed throughout the army as a result of the defeat of San Jacinto. This
statement cannot be reconciled with what he says in his own
Representation where he asserts, that *resolute Mexicans composed the entire army, men who never knew fear throughout,
the entire campaign in Texas, but who were compelled to retreat
by the circumstances of the moment, the weather, the coming
of the rainy season and the absolute want of all the necessary
resources.* These pronounced contradictions prove that Señor
Filisola had no real motive for the retreat, and that in his
flounderings he has grabbed at the first straw to save himself.
Could the weather or the season be made more propitious by retreating? Was the dire necessity of the army remedied by such
a movement? Was not the army obliged to destroy, before
leaving, a great amount of supplies which it could not take?
Was not the greater part of the artillery and the numerous arms
and munitions taken from the enemy likewise destroyed? Was
not part of the equipment of the army itself destroyed? Is it
not a fact that the greater part of the supplies stored in Matagorda, Columbia, Brazoria, and Béxar were abandoned? Was
not the greater part of those deposited at Laredo and Rio Grande
lost because they were not removed in time? Was not the cargo
of the schooner *Watchman,* which arrived at Cópano just as
Señor Filisola was abandoning this line of defence, lost? Was
not the commandant of the said port, John Davis Bradburn,
left to the mercy of the enemy, forcing him to go in a rowboat
to the island of Padre Ballí from where he had to make his way

on foot and while in bad health, to Brazo Santiago?[29]   Is it
not true also, that had we advanced, the supplies stored by the
enemy, as well as numerous cattle, would have fallen into our
hands?   That he would have been enabled to hold our conquest
and to save us the shame and the suffering of a retreat which
its candid author dares to assert was made in comfort, declaring
that by it we saved what was already lost?   His reply to all
this is that it was impossible to advance because of the prevailing discouragement of the troops.   The whole army will deny
this assertion with the exception, perhaps, of those timid men
who advised and influenced him.   Such a statement is further
refuted by the facts related in my diary of April 25th; by the
precautions which he took to have his opinion prevail in the
council of war; by his refusal to admit to the said council the
officers of the various units who unanimously opposed the retreat; and finally, by his declaration to the assembled generals
that it was not a council of war, that he had merely called them
together to hear their opinion, reserving the right to act as he
saw fit, since he and he alone was responsible for whatever took
place.   He made this declaration in reply to my persistent opposition to a retreat.   In view of my determination and resolution
to sustain my opinion against all objection, he decided on this
measure. He doubtlessly feared that I might influence the opinion
of those present, and still more, that if the council was formal, its
minutes might be published some day, furnishing the evidence
for the indictment brought against him by the nation for having
cowardly abandoned a campaign that could have been terminated
victoriously.   The events just narrated destroy the second contention of Señor Filisola.

His third point rests on another evident falsehood.   His
own argument reflects but little honor upon its author.   The
president had, from the beginning, a definite plan of operations
which he had communicated to his generals and which, if put

---

[29] John Davis Bradburn to the Commandant General of the Army of
Operations in Texas, Brazo de Santiago, July 18, 1836.

into practice, would have accomplished all that was desired.[30] I carried out my part, occupying the points that had been assigned to me. General Gaona claims that he was lost in the desert at Bastrop, but he made good use of his time to stain the honor of the army with his shameful conduct. General Ramírez y Sesma, on the other hand, took twenty days to travel fifty leagues—the distance from Béxar to the left bank of the Colorado—because he was afraid of Houston who was retreating at his approach. Nevertheless, it is undeniable that on the 22nd of April the army was in a position to advance advantageously, for General Gaona was on the left bank of the Brazos, at Old Fort, with 1,000 men; while Filisola was on the right with almost 600 men, both of them only 16 leagues distant from San Jacinto. I, with part of my division on the left bank and the means of transporting the rest across in one day, was twenty-five leagues distant. Therefore, if General Filisola, had abandoned his policy of retreating, and had crossed the river the same afternoon that he received the news; if instead of making the 1,000 men under Gaona recross the river, he had ordered me to advance upon San Jacinto immediately, it is beyond all doubt that by the 25th or 26th we could have fallen upon the enemy with almost 3,000 men, our rear guard being protected by more than 1,500 men distributed in Béxar, Goliad, Matagorda, and other points. Can the success of such a combination be doubted? Is it not self-evident? Does not the position of the army show that a plan had been previously followed? Señor Santa Anna has reached the same conclusion as I have upon this point, as seen by his *Manifesto*.

General Filisola tried to justify himself at the time by exaggerating the number and the quality of the forces of the enemy. He imagined hundred of soldiers which did not exist, and believed that Houston's men were tried and seasoned veterans. Previously, in order to belittle my actions, he had referred to those whom I had defeated and overcome in all my encounters,

[30] Santa Anna to Urrea, Béxar, March 23, 1836.

as mere adventurers, made up of insignificant and independent bands. Thus fear makes mountains out of ant hills.

From all the information obtained since, and it is confirmed by General Santa Anna as well as by the official reports of Señor Filisola to the government, it seems certain that Houston had only 720 men. Of these, two were killed and twenty-three were wounded, Houston being among the last, leaving a force that was barely sufficient to guard an equal number of prisoners. Under such circumstances, it is impossible to believe that nearly 3,000 men, all in fighting trim, could not have obtained a complete victory, being superior to the enemy in every respect.

Let it not be said that I am speaking in the light of subsequent information that could not have been ascertained at that time. General Filisola, who mocks me because I said that the enemy was defeated in every engagement and its best troops destroyed, confirms this very assertion by one of those grave inconsistencies so characteristic of His Excellency. In one of his official communications he says, "The President intended to put the finishing touch to his handiwork, for the complete occupation of Texas seemed already to be fully accomplished. The army had taken the fort of the Alamo, *it had fought and destroyed the greater part of the troops which the enemy called regulars,* taking a considerable amount of artillery, guns and ammunition; it had crossed three large rivers; *and, amidst hunger and privations, it was actuated by an ardent zeal inspired by the defense of the integrity of its native land.* A little more caution would, no doubt, have crowned his heroic efforts and exertions with success." Speaking of himself, Señor Filisola should have added "and a little more courage," for the total absence of it was the cause of the horrors endured by the army on its shameful retreat and the reason for plunging the nation into a sea of endless misfortunes. According to the words of the general himself, then, the force of the enemy was too weak and insignificant to withstand the army that was advancing to give it battle. He admits that only the last touch was lacking to the handiwork of Santa Anna. Certainly, he could not have been blind to the catastrophe that would overtake him if he retreated, nor to the great sacrifices that the nation would be forced to undergo in order to reconquer Texas. If the guns were out of condition, it was his own fault, and one needs have very little self-respect to advance such an argument. To claim that the lives of the prisoners would have been endangered by an advance is madness, *because they were all thought to be dead already.* To allege the lack of supplies is a positive falsehood, for those on hand had to be destroyed. To say, likewise, that the soldiers were without clothes and shoes to undertake a three days' journey is as much as to say that by retreating, these necessities would be obtained. In reality, only misery, hunger, and hardships without end awaited them. What was lacking then? Determination, patriotism, military vigor, all qualities that he who unfortunately commanded—and to-day commands—the army of Texas did not possess. Granting as true that the general-in-chief did not acquaint him with his plan of operations, which is false, military usage left him in position to decide whatever he wished, a fact that makes all his excuses very poor indeed. Therefore, when he immediately decided upon a retreat and the abandonment of Texas, sending an urgent request to General Andrade to evacuate Béxar and to spike his guns, burning all the equipment he was unable to transport, we are forced to admit that these measures were the norm for his plan of operations. The man in whose hands national honor was deposited could conceive of no other plan.

General Filisola frequently forgets the heroic rôle which he is supposed to play in the comic farce which he has written. We have seen the sad and pathetic picture so touchingly presented by him of the physical and moral condition of the army, which he considers was unable to fight a band of adventurers. Suddenly, believing that he sees an opportunity of excusing himself and of incriminating me, he changes his opinion and describes it as an army full of life and vigor, fired by enthusiasm, and capable of everything. Referring to the order of the government instructing him to hold all the places occupied in Texas, he says that he should have received this order while he was near the Nueces, and hints that it was maliciously delayed. Had it reached him then, he could have countermarched, he says, and, joining Andrade, they would have together occupied Goliad. He affirms also that when he was near the Nueces one of my messengers told him that the enemy, with 1,800 men, was contemplating an attack upon him, whereupon he immediately issued orders to Señor Andrade to spike the artillery and to evacuate Béxar with his 400 mounted troops in order that he might countermarch, and, agreeable to a plan which he had decided upon, surround and destroy the enemy. Recalling his first description of the army, all these assertions are empty boasts. Why didn't he undertake the three days' journey that was necessary to attack the enemy before, when he was in a better position? He had not, then, experienced the want and penury which later afflicted him. Furthermore, there is a positive falsehood with regard to the orders sent to Señor Andrade. In the official communication of the 18th of May, Filisola merely instructed him to evacute Béxar, first spiking the artillery.[31]

The fourth reason for the retreat is based on the alleged lack of food and supplies of all kinds necessary for an advance. The peculiar situation and condition of the army presented additional difficulties he claims. But I have already shown that we had provisions in abundance and that there were more supplies ahead of us. As to the second claim, the observations already presented prove beyond a doubt that the success of the campaign would have been complete in every sense of the word had we given the last blow that was needed. In order for Señor Filisola to justify his conduct, it will be necessary for him to present a concrete statement of the probable results of an advance and of the advantages of a retreat in order that by comparison it might be seen whether he chose the least of two evils. I have outlined the advantages of the first move. Let us see what the said general claims for the second.

---

[31] Filisola to Juan Andrade, Goliad, May 18, 1836.

According to his official dispatches and to what he says in his *Representation,* the army was in a most lamentable state, without clothing, food, hospitals, warehouses, or supplies in its rear after its long march. It was faced with the necessity of retracing its steps over a distance of more than 200 leagues, just as the hot season approached and the rain threatened to make the crossing of the large rivers more difficult. It was exposed to the constant menace of the enemy on its rear, and its march had perforce, to be slow, encumbered by its many trains and the lack of adequate transportation facilities. Señor Filisola should have also taken into account the moral effect of such a move upon the morale of the soldiers, who were intimidated in no small manner by the precipitate retreat. He should have thought of the encouragement which the enemy would derive and the effect upon its pride. He should have kept in mind the immense sacrifices that would be necessary to reconquer the abandoned territory and to repair the losses suffered during the retreat. Add all these facts together, leaving aside the consideration of the material effects of such an operation, and let it be said impartially to which alternative, retreat or advance, would the balance of justice incline?

Señor Filisola has the courage to say, even after witnessing the horror and desolation experienced by the army during its march back to the Rio Grande, that it was conducted *in the best order, with all possible comfort, and without losing a single article from its immense trains and baggage, out of all proportion to the army; that not a single patient or wounded soldier was abandoned either;* and that he evacuated all those points which, because of their nature, were of no intrinsic or strategic importance, judged from a military point of view. It is here that the words of Señor Filisola, used in speaking of the victories of my division, may be properly applied, exclaiming as he does, "For each of the actions he praises he deserves to be tried by a council of war and to be punished accordingly." Let his own reports of the retreat be read [32] and let the reader judge for him-

[32] See note 24.

self whether an army marching under such conditions can do it in order and comfort, keeping in mind particularly that the sad plight of the army, in the middle of marshes, was due entirely to the fear and inefficiency of its general, who in his anxiety to get as far away from the enemy as possible, decided to make his way through the lowlands, leaving the good road of San Felipe de Austin to his right. He could have followed this road without difficulty by undertaking an extra march of a little more than two leagues, avoiding all the trouble and inconvenience of the long march through the marshes. General Filisola has openly failed to tell the truth in all his statements. He has recounted acts which he never performed, he has omitted those details that reflect upon him, and he has denied those that may reflect credit upon me. He abandoned the sick,[33] destroyed trains and munitions; and evacuated points which he claimed were insignificant such as Goliad but which later he informed the government were essential to the establishment of a line of operations.[34] Regarding all these facts, I refer the reader to the diary written by an officer who was an eyewitness of the events as they happened.[35] See also my Diary for the 23rd of April.

[33] *The Texas Telegraph,* September 21, 1836. Ampudia to Juan Nepomuceno Seguin, Arroyo de San Bernardo, May 4, 1836.

[34] Manuel Micheltorena to the General-in-chief of the Army of the North, General Headquarters, Matamoros, June 8, 1836.

[35] Extract from an anonymous *Diary.*

"April 29. On this day our misfortunes reached the limit. The wagons had stayed behind since the day before and several of our sick, who were looked upon with the greatest disregard, died. It made one indignant to see them insulted even by the generals, particularly Gaona, as if the men were of bronze not to get sick under such hardships and suffering. Our vanguard left at eight but the rear guard had not been able to leave by ten. Before starting on the march, we abandoned part of our armament, some munitions, several bales of canvas and miscellaneous camp utensils—some of these were utilized by the troops,—artillery tackle, nails, and other things in order to lighten the wagons. While we were forced to do this, some of the officers had three and four mules each and many of the generals more than four times the number allowed them, using these to transport personal booty. The cost of the equipment which was finally abandoned will be told in due time. I traveled on foot, wading through the mud which was knee deep and falling

The general who manifested such pity for the fate of the prisoners and the plight of the soldiers, who gave such a beautiful definition of what constitutes love of country, affirming that it was our love for those with whom we live, violated the principles of humanity and ignored his own definition the moment he heard the news of the defeat of San Jacinto. Impelled by fear, thinking only of retreat, he ordered a flat boat burned that might have been very useful to some of our fugitives to save themselves. In his panicky terror, he went so far as not to permit any bales of cotton to be left, fearing, no doubt, that the enemy might use them to obstruct his retreat.[36]

This general has stoutly defended himself from the serious charge of obeying the orders of a general-in-chief who was a prisoner. To justify his conduct and sustain his contention that he acted from a conviction of the advisability of retreating

down at every step until I lost my boots. I continued barefooted. We barely advanced thirty or forty paces without having to call on the soldiers to help pull the artillery out of the mud, where it sank to the hub. After traveling five or six miles, we encamped at about six in the afternoon, every unit stopping wherever it was and the generals and officers were obliged to do likewise. Scattered groups could be seen on every hand. The artillery was left stuck in the mud after it had traveled two or three miles. The ammunition, food supplies, and baggage were strewn all along the road and that part of them which by dint of great sacrifices reached camp was practically useless. Much equipment was lost, many mules were disabled, and the troops were unable to take their rations because these did not arrive and there was nothing to eat. In a word, it is difficult to give a picture of our condition on this day. It was a complete defeat. Gen. Urrea was ordered to march with his brigade to secure the transportation of the army across the river. Despair reigned among the officers and the men. Bitter recriminations were heard everywhere because the roads were not first reconnoitered, plunging us into untold hardships and privations. The main highway to San Felipe de Austin is on high ground and we had traveled over it in the middle of heavy rains without difficulty. Why was not that road followed if it was not known whether the one followed was traversible during the rainy season?"

The *Diary* of this unknown officer continues for two pages, but the above will suffice to give an idea of the hardships endured by the army during the retreat.

[36] Portilla, *Diario*, April 22 and 27.

and not out of regard for the orders of Santa Anna, he has gone to the extreme of claiming that he would have acted as he did even without such orders. Seeing that his own documents,[37] purposely omitted from his *Representation,* denied his statements, he has advanced a number of ridiculous theories to prove that Santa Anna acted of his own free will in spite of the fact that he was in the hands of the enemy. He has further tried to prove that Santa Anna signed the treaties, convinced of the inability of the army to undertake new war operations. Santa Anna himself has denied this assertion in his official note to the Minister of War.[38]

If we look about to determine some of the causes that were, perhaps, responsible for the misfortune of San Jacinto, we will find that the inefficiency, or lack of foresight of Señor Filisola was one of the most important. I will let Santa Anna speak of this matter. In his *Manifesto* he says:

"Limiting myself to those faults committed by some of my subordinates that were, directly or indirectly, the cause of the lamentable catastrophe I am discussing, I will ask your excellency to keep in mind that General Filisola sent me a reenforcement made up of recruits when he could have sent me seasoned soldiers. He had with him the battalion of sappers, made up of veteran troops in its entirety, but he did not send me a single man out of it. Being able to have selected the best men from the regular battalions of Guerrero, Aldama, Activos de México, Toluca, and Guadalajara, he failed to do so. Thus, he disregarded the very spirit of my instructions, for, if I distinctly ordered him to send me 500 picked men, it was because I wanted no recruits to be sent, aware as I was that there were many

[37] Filisola to the Secretary of War and Marine, Mrs. Powell's place, 5 leagues from the Brazos, April 22, 1836; Santa Anna to Filisola, San Jacinto, April 23, 1836; Filisola to Santa Anna, San Bernard Creek, April 28, 1836; Filisola to Santa Anna, San Bernard, April 28, 1836; Filisola to the Secretary of War and Marine, San Bernard Creek, April 28, 1836; Santa Anna to Filisola, San Jacinto, April 30, 1836; Filisola to Santa Anna, Rio Colorado, May 5, 1836.

[38] See Santa Anna's *Manifesto.*

among our troops. Had not this been clearly my purpose, I would have used some other phrase.

The sending of Captain Miguel Bachiller with special mail that had arrived from the capital, dispatched to me by the Supreme Government, and which was intercepted, was no less a cause. As a result, the enemy acquired positive information regarding our forces at a time when it was retreating, wondering what it could do, astonished by our operations and triumphs. Thus it became aware that I was at New Washington, it learned the number that made up the division that was operating in that region and the situation of the rest of our forces, all of which cleared the confusion in which it found itself as a result of our continuous offensive and the appearance of our victorious columns at the points least expected. From the dispatches, it learned everything that it desired; and, coming out from the uncertainty that was making it retreat to the Trinity, it gained new courage. This could not have happened without knowing that my force was inferior to theirs. The arrival of the reenforcement under General Cós was regarded by the enemy as a ruse, believing it a party sent out during the night before, to return in the morning in full view. All this was told to me by the enemy afterwards."

Can Señor Filisola still say that in deciding upon his course of action he was mindful only of what is prescribed by military usage, where he found nothing applicable to his situation?

Continuing in his attempt to vindicate himself he says that in acknowledging the armistice, or better said, the terms dictated by the enemy, he did nothing more than to promise to retreat and agree to an exchange of prisoners in conformity with the accepted rights of civilized peoples which prescribe war without quarter. This is the cloak with which he wishes to cover the shameful conduct he pursued. But let us grant his argument and then ask where are the prisoners that were returned to us in exchange for all those released by Señor Filisola? How will he explain the evident infraction of the law in delivering the slaves that were claimed in violation of the laws of the republic which prohibit slavery and declare free any one who sets foot upon its territory?

Not content with having signed his own infamy, Señor Filisola debased himself to the point of using cringing and servile language in addressing the commissioners who took back the ratification of the treaty. To give an unequivocal proof of his subservience and servility he agreed to release a negro who was his coachman, and issued orders for his conduct to be imitated throughout the army, giving the commissioners of the enemy a safe-conduct authorizing them to recover whatever they thought belonged to the colonists. General Andrade did not permit them to inspect his camp. When they presented themselves in Matamoros with their permit [39] I told them that I did not recognize their authority, nor the government they represented, nor the agreements that had been concluded, and that I could not obey such orders. As I had previously told them that if they came to me with such demands I would treat them as they deserved, I ordered them to be taken prisoners and I sent a full report to the government, justifying my action as a reprisal for the unbecoming treatment accorded to General Woll. By this means I hoped to obtain the liberty of some of our prisoners. All the slaves within my jurisdiction continued to enjoy their liberty, and all the goods taken from the enemy were distributed among the various units of my command. The order of Señor Filisola for the delivery of the supplies taken from the enemy at Matagorda was appended to the safe-conduct.

The observations presented up to this point have had as their object to prove the justness of the charges made against Señor Filisola by the War Department and by me. He has in vain tried to vindicate himself from these accusations. It now remains for me to answer those which he made against me, but I formally declare that I will answer only those directed against my military conduct or my reputation, for I am duty bound to ignore those indecent and ridiculous remarks whose main object

[39] Passport issued by Filisola to Henry W. Kearnes, Henry Teal, and Victor Loupy, Rio de las Nueces, June 3, 1836.

is to irritate me by wounding my pride. They find their inspiration in his wounded self-esteem or in boundless self-conceit. It is also my desire to engage the attention of the public as little as possible. The military charges he presents against me are: 1st, that I was responsible for the only cannon lost by the army; 2nd, that I kept the army from getting supplies from Victoria, Goliad and Refugio; 3rd, that I misled some of the officers; 4th, that the slowness of my march prevented the execution of military plans; 5th, that I refused to allow a picket to gather dispersed fugitives; 6th, that remaining idle, I refused to help while the army was struggling to pull the artillery out of the mud; 7th, that I asked to be permitted to proceed to Guadalupe Victoria and to Matamoros ahead of the main army, abandoning even the sick; 8th, that I left the army without sufficient funds by taking more than my share for my division; 9th, that I terrorized the people of the towns. The personal charges which he makes against me are: 1st, that I tried to discredit him, becoming involved in low and debasing intrigues; 2nd, that I took what he calls "my booty," making it my principal thought; 3rd, that I practically instituted an inquisition in my division; 4th, that I failed to take the oath in June; 5th, that I maliciously weakened the force under my command.

General Gaona, to avoid being himself accused for his shameful conduct, has chosen to make common cause with Señor Filisola, by charging. 1st, that I voted in favor of a retreat and was the first to reach Matamoros; 2nd, that I took charge of the vanguard as the least dangerous command, abandoning the army, and not helping even in the construction of barges; 3rd, he challenges me to cite a single case of demoralization in the army, or of excesses committed by the troops. In this charge, he is seconded by Señor Andrade.

The *Representation* of Señor Filisola is replete with innumerable sarcastic and derisive remarks whose main object is evidently to humble and belittle me. Such is his aim when, referring to the events of the 26th of April, he says purposely that he ordered me to the most secure and the least exposed

post, placing the brave and experienced General Gaona in charge
of the most dangerous position. As a matter of fact there was
no danger at any point. When did His Excellency know me to
tremble before the enemy, or to try to avoid danger? (Turn to
what I say in my diary on this date.) Likewise, and with
ignoble bad faith, he says that instead of taking two six-
pounders as ordered from Guadalupe Victoria I took two four-
pounders *in order to travel lighter and give an example of
obedience and a proof of my opposition to a retreat.* One needs
a large dose of bravado to make use of such sarcasm! He
merely confirms the exactness of a statement made by an officer
who said "His Excellency, while in Texas, was alternately too
bold or too shy." The event to which he refers occurred on
the Colorado as follows. Señor Filisola ordered me to go to
Guadalupe Victoria to secure supplies for the army, because
Señor Sesma, who had been sent to that place for the purpose,
had marched, by mistake or as a result of the poor instructions
of Señor Filisola, to Refugio Mission, situated in an opposite
direction from the Colorado, where we were. When I set out
on my march, leaving the main body of the army, I asked for the
artillery belonging to my brigade and Señor Filisola gave orders
for the two six-pounders to be delivered to me. The artillery
was still at the river crossing, about a league distant from the
point occupied by Señor Filisola and me. I do not know why
two four-pounders were sent instead of the six-pounders ordered.
I immediately notified His Excellency who gave me the following reply: "Take the ones sent which will be easier to transport,
since in carrying out your commission for securing supplies
you will have to reconnoiter the country and clear the way of
whatever obstacles may be found between here and Victoria."
Señor Filisola will remember that it was necessary to unload
the ammunition for the six-pounders which had already been
placed on the mule packs and change it for one more suitable
for the four-pounders which I took with his consent. What
charge, I ask, can he bring against me then? That which
results from the bad faith, the lack of conscience, and the evil

passions of the accuser. All his other charges are similar and I must not engage the attention of the public with tiresome and totally unnecessary refutations. I will proceed, therefore, to answer the military and personal charges which I have already enumerated.

1st charge. The post of Matagorda was garrisoned by 240 men under the command of Col. Agustín Alcerrica. After the misfortune of San Jacinto, I ordered them to suspend the work on the fortifications that were being constructed, and to send all the materials that might be useful for the construction of flatboats to Cacey's, agreeable to Señor Filisola's orders, in order to facilitate the crossing of the main army and to enable it to secure the food supplies stored in Matagorda. Alcerrica received my orders, as evidenced by his acknowledgment,[40] but, notwithstanding the fact, he abandoned the place as a result of the false information which he received and later transmitted to me.[41] The actual circumstances, as well as the reason for the abandonment of the twelve-pounder, are set forth in the summary investigation which I ordered. The details are given in the declaration made by the temporary commander of the battalion of Tres Villas.[42] In addition to the above-mentioned orders sent to Col. Alcerrica, I sent new instructions, with the approval of Gen. Filisola, for him to join Col. Garay, when the army countermarched from the San Bernard to Atascosito Crossing on the Colorado. He was later ordered to march to Guadalupe Victoria in his company. Alcerrica, however, had already placed himself in safety. All the foregoing facts prove that I was not responsible for the loss of this piece of artillery. Furthermore, Filisola himself vindicates me from the charge in the last paragraph of his communication to the government.[43] Why this strange inconsistency?

[40] Agustin Alcerrica to Urrea, Matagorda, April 29, 1836.

[41] Alcerrica to Urrea, Cacey's Crossing on the Colorado, May 3, 1836.

[42] Testimony given by Lorenzo Carrillo, Matamoros, June 8, 1836.

[43] Filisola to Secretary of War and Marine, Guadalupe Victoria, May 14, 1836.

2nd charge. Señor Filisola has deceived both the government and the public. If a part of the food deposited at Guadalupe Victoria was missing, it was because Señor Sesma sent it to Refugio by mistake, as before stated and as told to me by Señor Filisola himself. Another reason for their not being intact is that a portion was sent to him, by my orders, while he was on the road. I afterwards sent him the supplies that were in Refugio to Goliad, letting him have some of my own as long as they lasted. I also gave him a good deal of cattle which served to maintain the army at Guadalupe Victoria and Goliad.

3rd. The officers who left Guadalupe Victoria with their respective units did so by virtue of an order from Señor Filisola and without my knowledge as to whether they had any accounts in arrears. Regarding the countermarch of Luis Tola, Lieutenant Colonel of Engineers, it is evident, from his own statement,[44] that he did not execute this movement by my orders.

4th charge. The diary of my operations refutes this charge, showing that I was never idle, not even when I was supposed to rest, forced to pursue the enemy in every direction and to abandon the direct course I was following. Comparisons are odious but since Señor Filisola forces me to make them I will say that when he arraigns me for not occupying Goliad until the 21st of March, by which time Señor Sesma was already on the Colorado, he should have taken into account the immense difference there is between marching along a straight line, clear of obstacles, without meeting the enemy along the entire course, provided with supplies, and able to encamp without fear of attack; and marching without supplies, with unseasoned infantry. spiritless on account of the weather such as the Yucatán troops, without reasonable security during the hours of rest, following a zigzag course, and fighting and pursuing those who defended the country. Nevertheless, Señor Sesma and I crossed the Colorado on the same day, and I left behind a well-established line

[44] Luis Tola to Urrea, Matamoros, October 3, 1836.

of communication from Matamoros to the Colorado itself, after having cleared the country to facilitate the march of the main army.

5th charge. I regret to have to repeat so frequently that Señor Filisola fails to tell the truth, but it is a fact that he never asked me to cooperate in gathering our dispersed fugitives, though he did refuse to permit me to go in person to search for them. When I offered to advance with only my cavalry to reconnoiter the enemy's camp, since he would not allow me to engage it with my whole division, he refused my demand. On the day before my arrival, General Woll asked for permission to take a battalion to Old Fort to protect our dispersed fugitives, but his petition was not granted. I refused the use of my cavalry, but not for that purpose, for just as I marched into the camp of Señor Filisola at Mrs. Powell's, an officer, detailed for the purpose, was leaving. I later refused the use of my cavalry to make of it a flying squadron to protect the rear of the whole army, because I considered the measure useless and destructive for the horses. I finally convinced His Excellency of this fact.[45]

6th charge. If I encamped on the opposite side of the Colorado, it was in obedience to orders of Señor Filisola, who had expressly instructed me to make the crossing safe *to avoid a real shameful and dangerous engagement,* as stated in his official note of May 14th. The troops crossed in two canoes which I found at that place. His Excellency will remember that when he disclosed to me his intention of abandoning the artillery and everything that embarrassed his march I strongly opposed his decision, offering to turn back with my brigade to bring up whatever was left behind. As witnesses of this assertion, I cite Cols. Juan Morales and Mariano Salas who were determined to second me in this proposal.

7th charge. I do not believe that I incurred in any guilt by asking to be allowed to push forward in advance to Guadalupe

---

[45] Adrian Woll to Urrea, Matamoros, October 4, 1836.

Victoria or to Matamoros. If any fault, it would be on the part of he who granted such a petition. Nevertheless, as I have already stated before, when I marched to the first mentioned place, it was by express orders of Señor Filisola to secure supplies for the army, and I proceeded to Matamoros for similar reasons. Señor Filisola's letter of the 14th of May [46] vindicates me from this charge. A reading of this document reveals the inconsistency and the perfidy of the man who has alternately heaped upon me recriminations and insults, praise and flattery, as passion moved him. With regard to the abandonment of the wounded and sick, His Excellency deceived the government and the public, because though he first instructed a party of cavalry to protect them, later, not wishing to subject the wounded to a rapid march, he ordered that they be left. They were later taken to Brazo de Santiago in the schooner "Second Courier" at my request, having remained in the meantime in the hospital at Goliad.

8th charge. On this point I did nothing but insert the communication contained in his letter of the 14th to the commissary general of Tamaulipas. I sent him the expense accounts of the various units and he made the distribution of the funds without any intervention on my part. He sent Señor Filisola the balance of the funds before my arrival in Matamoros. When I took charge, there were 20,000 *pesos* still in the commissary of the army.

9th charge. The testimony of the colonists of Santa Rita, given on October 6, and that of the Irish colonists given in Matamoros [47] answer this charge. I will proceed to answer the personal charges.

The first one made by Señor Filisola is that I discredited him by taking part in low and debasing intrigues. As to his loss of reputation he has no one to blame but his own conduct. As to the intrigues, the public shall decide, after reading the corresponding documents, what their nature was, and whether there

[46] Filisola to Urrea, Guadalupe Victoria, May 14, 1836.
[47] Henry Wall Shannon to Urrea, Matamoros, September 29, 1836.

were any. I did nothing more than address the supreme government, explaining in detail the shameful acts with which our national honor was being stained. The severe reply given by the government to that general is self-explanatory.[48]

2nd. I hope that Señor Filisola will make public a list of the goods that belonged to me and which he calls my "booty." I likewise hope that he will show the list of supplies given by other officers to their troops without charge out of those taken from the enemy. In short, I want some evidence to be presented to prove whether I monopolized the food supplies or not, whether I charged the troops for such goods or placed them at their disposal, agreeable to the orders of the President.

3rd. I am ignorant of the circumstances that made Señor Filisola assert that I had established an inquisition in my brigade. He claims that I reprimanded a guide who replied to his inquiries regarding the direction of several roads. I must reply that His Excellency again fails to tell the truth in this instance, for he constantly made use of my best guides, to such an extent that he left me without any. This charge can be traced only to his extremely bad faith, for what could be my interest in hindering or obstructing the military operations of the army, engaged as it was in defending a cause which I embraced with my whole heart? His Excellency will remember, though he will not confess it, that on several occasions he said to me that *I was the only general on whom he could rely*, that on the morning of the 27th of April he came, sorely tried, to my tent, bemoaning his inability to make the army break up camp because they refused to obey him any longer, and that he begged me to use my influence to make the army obey him, which I did. Since we are speaking of inquisitorial methods, if any one can be accused of having used them, it is Señor Filisola himself. When I sent two agents with horses, money, and instructions to enter the enemy's camp and take a letter and a secret note to General Santa Anna disclosing a plan for his escape, Señor Filisola took the documents away from them without even giving me an explanation of his mysterious conduct.

[48] José María Tornel to Urrea, Mexico, June 25, 1836.

4th. I sent in my oath on the 1st of June, as many officers who saw me do it can testify. If because of the circumstances which delayed the messenger, he did not receive it on time it is not my fault. His Excellency also deplores that I did not express my opinion at the time of the council held at Mrs. Powell's, or later before I arrived in Matamoros. In reply I will say that at the said council, before it, and afterwards, I expressed my constant objections to a retreat. At the time we reached Refugio Mission I persuaded His Excellency of the need of maintaining the line of defence on the San Antonio. If I failed to address a formal protest to him at this time it was because His Excellency either deceived me or disarmed my purpose by assuring me, in a conversation we had at Guadalupe Victoria, that he would hold the said line. Afterwards, he has had the great temerity to deny this fact, which if not true as he maintains he could have denied in his reply to my protest, a thing he failed to do. The documents relative to the subject [49] confirm the truth of my statements on this point as well as my continual opposition to the retreat.

5th. In this accusation, His Excellency displays his habitual disregard for accuracy, and his characteristic bad faith, for the whole battalion of Jiménez and all the cavalry, as well as some pickets from the battalions of San Luis and Querétaro remained in Columbia, and His Excellency cannot claim, therefore, that only 200 men marched with Señor Salas, for the said force adds up to almost 500 men by his own figures, cited in his charge to prove my guilt. I should state also that the said figures, though acknowledged by me, were calculated after Señor Filisola ordered my brigade to be reenforced by the cavalry troops of the other brigades. It should be also kept in mind that the parts of the Jiménez, San Luis, and Querétaro battalions stationed in Béxar and Goliad, are likewise included.

The General complains bitterly that his official correspondence

---

[49] Urrea to Filisola, Refugio Mission, May 17, 1836; Filisola to Urrea, Goliad, May 17, 1836; Filisola to Urrea, Santa Rosa, June 14, 1836; Urrea to Garay, Atascosito, May 6, 1836; Juan Jose Andrade to Filisola, Béxar, May 16, 1836; Francisco Duque to Urrea, Béxar, May 18, 1836.

was delayed, and although he does not dare accuse me directly, he does cause suspicion to fall upon me by making use of those indefinite expressions so well suited for calumny, which His Excellency wields with unexcelled skill. The letter of the postmaster of Matamoros [50] clears me from this charge, and I feel confident that nothing to the contrary can ever be brought against me.

The first three accusations which General Gaona dares to make against me are answered by what I have already stated, and, regarding the fourth, I will say, in order to satisfy Señor Andrade in particular and to confound Señor Gaona, that I never asserted that the whole army had been demoralized, but that corruption had found its way into a part of it, the most scandalous example of this having been given by the last mentioned general and the agents of his shameful speculations as proved by the general opinion and clamor of the army. All these facts have been published, but he has not dared to refute them.

The army conducted itself with unfailing heroism. To all the adversities to which it was subjected by the incompetence and even inhumanity of its commander, it offered a stoic endurance. The greatest proof that can be given of its worth and true character is that, in spite of the discouragement which the disclosures and frequent complaints of Señor Filisola and his companions who longed for the pleasures and ease of Mexico tended to spread, it has chosen to remain in the theatre of war where it is to this day. I could not have said anything derogatory concerning the division of Señor Andrade, because I did not come in contact with it until I reached Matamoros. Much less could I have spoken ill of this division when in its ranks there are officers and leaders more than worthy of their rank. I have had the misfortune of having this unjust charge brought against me, but no attention has been given to the opinion expressed by Señor Filisola in his note to the government of June 10th, in which he says that among the things that were wanting for the success

[50] Francisco Garcia to Urrea, Matamoros, August 1, 1836.

of the army were "activity, military instruction, *and a better morale among all classes of the army.*" Here is another fact to increase the immense catalogue of inconsistencies of His Excellency.

I have concluded the enumeration of the principal charges brought against me, and, as I have said before, I ought not to go into that turbid stream of irate expressions and ridiculous invectives with which Señor Filisola aims to wound my pride, for it would be a long and painful task. I will only state, however, in answer to Filisola's denial, that I did cover the retreat of the whole army as every man in the army can testify and as corroborated by his own orders.[51] It is likewise a fact that, by taking charge of the vanguard of the army, I enabled it to cross the Colorado, a fact which the general himself admits in the eighth paragraph of his official note to the government of May 14th. The summary of the orders just cited is a link that should be added to the chain of evidence *regarding the good order observed in the retreat.*

As a consequence of my communications to the government, giving a report of the state of things in Texas; and as a result of the information received through Señor Filisola himself; the abandonment of the points which the government recommended should be held; and the other considerations expressed by the War Department in its communication,[52] Filisola was removed from the command and ordered to turn it over to me. When I was informed of this disposition I privately expressed to the President and the Secretary of War the reasons why I thought someone else more deserving than myself should be placed in command, exerting myself as far as possible to make them see my point of view, and even suggesting the general who, under the circumstances, was better fitted to carry out the designs of the government, offering to continue to lend my services in the campaign. I officially reiterated my request to be relieved as soon as possible, repeating that I had accepted the command only out

[51] General Orders of the Army, April 24, 25, 26, 1836.
[52] Tornel to Filisola, México City, June 25, 1836.

of regard for the utter disorganization and despair of the army, then in absolute want of everything and without the necessary resources to meet its most essential needs. I owe the pecuniary assistance that relieved the extreme needs of the army to the generous hospitality of the inhabitants of Matamoros and of General Francisco Vital Fernández. It was on one of these occasions of penury that, irritated by the inefficient and corrupt manager of the customs house of the port, who denied me every sort of help, and who was an obstacle to the acquisition of supplies from the merchants because his conduct gave them no guarantees; that I removed three employees, fearful also of the consequence of our needs reaching a point beyond endurance. I replaced them with honest, well-to-do men, who were known throughout the department. I decided upon this measure in view of the unlimited powers conferred on me by the government to meet the situation. The stupid and dishonest district judge was also involved in my act of removal, because he made common cause with the manager of the customs house. Like a certain judge in a melodrama, as soon as he learned of my decision, he tried to institute an investigation. The measures taken produced the desired effect and kept the army from perishing, since up to that time I had received only promises from the government. The document appended [53] safeguards me against any charge of arbitrariness that may be brought against me.

It has been seen by the orders of the government of June 25th, that Béxar, Victoria, Goliad, and Cópano were to be held and a line of fortifications to be established, extending it as far as possible. These orders were repeated to me with instructions that in case these points had been abandoned they should be reoccupied.[54] They arrived too late, for the army was already in the vicinity of Matamoros. Nevertheless, I addressed General Andrade, who was my second, transmitting to him the orders of the government and inserting instructions for him to turn back.[55]

[53] Tornel to Urrea, México, June 10, 1836.
[54] Tornel to Urrea, México, June 7, 1836.
[55] Urrea to Andrade, Matamoros, June 8, 1836.

He replied by painting a sad picture of the state of the army.[56] But before I received his reply I had repeated my orders in a still more emphatic manner.[57] To these, Señor Andrade replied by explaining his absolute inability to observe my orders and by notifying me of his determination to continue the retreat.[58] In such a trying situation there was no recourse left to me but to report the case to the government who, in turn, was forced to accept the actual state of affairs, giving instructions for the army to remain in Matamoros where it could be reorganized and its needs provided for.[59] I have the satisfaction of being able to say that its destitute condition was improved; that the artillery, the ammunitions, and the equipment were repaired; that the troops were provided with clothes; that the sick and wounded were treated; that military instruction was given; and that it may be safely said that everything was made ready to renew the campaign. I transmitted to the government the plan that I intended to follow. I can flatter myself with the opinion that if a small fleet had been sent and one half the resources and funds that have been provided for the preparation of the second expedition, had been placed at my disposal, the Mexican flag would now wave over Texas. I constantly told the government that not a single additional man was needed beyond those under my command. I was called to Mexico ostensibly for the purposes expressed in the order of the 26th of August,[60] but not a word was spoken about it after my arrival. This closed my career in Texas, but to save the honor of those involved in the machinations used for my removal I shall let a veil drop over the matter.

I have finished my vindication and I only regret the impossibility of having been more laconic. This exposition lacks the oratorical flourishes and forethought that are evident in that of Señor Filisola, because I speak the simple language of truth and

[56] Andrade to Urrea, Animas, June 13, 1836.
[57] Urrea to Andrade, Matamoros, June 12, 1836.
[58] Andrade to Urrea, Carrisitos, June 14, 1836.
[59] Tornel to Urrea, México, July 2, 1836; also Tornel to Urrea, México, July 4, 1836.
[60] Tornel to Urrea, México, August 26, 1836.

base my whole defense upon it. If with its help I succeed in convincing my fellow-citizens that I am not as that general pictures me, and that His Excellency is in no way like the portrait which he paints of himself, I may well say: what else can I wish? Firm in this conviction I will end, leaving the readers to decide in their judgment what hopes can be entertained for the reconquest of Texas while things continue as they are. The principal motive that has prompted me in this undertaking has been my desire to prevent the loss of that precious territory and to avoid a repetition of the gross errors committed.[61]

Durango, August 19, 1837.

[61] A *Postscript* is added after the documents which follow this *Diary*. In the *Postscript* the author quotes at length from Don Ramón Martínez Caro's "A True Account of the First Campaign in Texas." Since we have translated this writing, the *Postscript* has been omitted.

RELATIONS BETWEEN TEXAS
THE UNITED STATES OF AMERICA

AND

THE MEXICAN REPUBLIC

BY

JOSÉ MARÍA TORNEL Y MENDÍVIL [1]

MEXICO
1837

---

[1] José María Tornel y Mendívil was Secretary of War during the Texas campaign. He had held a number of prominent positions before coming to this post, chief among them being the governorship of the Federal District. He was a great orator and exercised a great deal of influence among certain classes until his death in 1853.

TEJAS

Y LOS

ESTADOS-UNIDOS DE AMÉRICA,

EN

SUS RELACIONES

CON LA

REPUBLICA MEXICANA.

—•❀•—

ESCRITO

POR EL GENERAL JOSE MARIA TORNEL.

———

MÉXICO.

Impreso por Ignacio Cumplido, calle de los Rebeldes N. 9.

1837.

Facsimile of the Spanish title page

For more than fifty years, that is, from the very period of their political infancy, the prevailing thought in the United States of America has been the acquisition of the greater part of the territory that formerly belonged to Spain, particularly that part which to-day belongs to the Mexican nation. Democrats and Federalists, all their political parties, whatever their old or new designations, have been in perfect accord upon one point, their desire to extend the limits of the republic to the north, to the south, and to the west, using for the purpose all the means at their command, guided by cunning, deceit, and bad faith. It has been neither an Alexander nor a Napoleon, desirous of conquest in order to extend his dominions or add to his glory, who has inspired the proud Anglo-Saxon race in its desire, its frenzy to usurp and gain control of that which rightfully belongs to its neighbors; rather it has been the nation itself which, possessed of that roving spirit that moved the barbarous hordes of a former age in a far remote north, has swept away whatever has stood in the way of its aggrandizement.

Jefferson, the embodiment of the most exaggerated democratic principles, the philosopher who exercised the greatest influence upon the government and laws of his country, the statesman who stamped upon it its singular and national character, who voiced the aspirations of its thousands of settlers and adventurers, used to flatter his fellow-citizens with the future possession of the Isthmus of Panama, while promising the Colossus of the North to gain a foothold upon the banks of the Saint Laurence. The atheist of Monticello thoroughly understood the desires and ambitions of his countrymen. In order to win universal popularity, he used to encourage their ambitious dreams of expansion, founded on no other right than the ominous one of might. It will, therefore, be strange indeed to find a single

American who does not revere Jefferson as a semi-god, because everyone considers him the prophet of his country's destiny, the man to whom Providence confided its secrets.

Other Americans who aspire to be called moderates, would content themselves with the extension of the boundary to the Pánuco, as claimed by some writer who stated that this formed the western limits of Florida. Still others who are accused of lacking spirit and of being timid in their aspirations would content themselves with the acquisition of the lands watered by the Rio Bravo del Norte. The treaty of limits of February 22nd, 1819, which gave to the United States title to a *contested territory*, had no other purpose than to pave the way for and bring closer the acquisition of the two Floridas, leaving for a better and more propitious occasion the deletion of the imaginary boundary line then traced. Although in 1832, after more than four years of delays, the same terms of that treaty were accepted by the Mexican republic, it was foreseen with all certainty that they would never be observed by the United States. Our continuous revolts made that country conceive the hope that we would neglect or abandon our national and sacred charge, while the ill-advised colonization laws and our still more imprudent and scandalous mismanagement of the public lands, so coveted and yet so freely and generously distributed and given away, clearly showed that we knew neither how to appreciate nor how to keep the precious heritage of the Spaniards. Unfortunately they were not mistaken in their assumption, for at every step we have displayed that candor, weakness, and inexperience so characteristic of infant nations. Too late have we come to know the restless and enterprising neighbor who set himself up as our mentor, holding up his institutions for us to copy them, institutions whch transplanted to our soil could not but produce constant anarchy, and which, by draining our resources, perverting our character, and weakening our vigor, have left us powerless against the attacks and the invasions of this modern Rome. The example of an *ever increasing* prosperity was treacherously pointed out to us, and, attributing to the written law the influence of habit and

custom, we adopted the first without the steadying influence of
the second.   Thus we have chosen to live in perpetual contradiction, in an anomalous state.   How costly have been to us
the gifts of these new Greeks!

As a native of America I cannot regret the triumph of the
Revolution of 1776, nor can I condemn the vast experiment in
social welfare that has been undertaken upon our continent.   But
that same Revolution which bore such happy results for the
American people,—even though they may not be as extensive,
as perfect, and as complete as its partisans would have us believe
—brought many misfortunes to the human race when considered
from other points of view.   The greatest of these, the French
Revolution, was the direct outcome of the American principles
indiscreetly adopted with ardor by the young French soldiers
who, by order of their sovereign, came to America in search of
battlefields where the pride of England might be humbled.   While
the Anglo-American provinces were taking their place among the
nations of the world, enjoying the advantages of English civilization, their prosperity multiplied and established now on a firmer
basis by their independent existence, France was paying with
the blood of her sons and the head of her king for the services
which both rendered to democracy.   But not only France, all
Europe, the entire world, has suffered a profound shock which
has shaken the stability of nations.   It is undeniably true that the
condition of man has been improved to a certain point, but it is
doubtful whether this improvement is sufficient recompense for
so many and such cruel sacrifices.   If happiness were now secure
beyond all doubt, France, the whole universe, would find consolation at the tomb of the millions of fallen victims.   But the
struggle between absolutism and liberalism still rages, and each has
advanced its claim for domination and power.   England may well
say that she has secured ample and bloody vengeance for the help
which her continental rival gave to her rebellious colonies.

Spain, also, effectively contributed to their emancipation without foreseeing the consequences which such a seductive example
would have later.   It was the cause undoubtedly, of her losing

all her possessions upon the American continent. It is strange, indeed, that the Spanish cabinet should have shown such ignorance and lack of foresight as to prepare the downfall of the nation merely for the purpose of doing at the time whatever harm it could to its enemy. It is not strange, however, that it should have flattered itself with the expectation of the gratitude of the people for whose liberty Spain labored so effectively and with so much zeal, nor that Spain should have considered the nation just born *like Venus out of the foam of the sea* as her friend and natural ally. If gratitude were measured by the value of the benefit received, Spain had the right to expect the Americans to treat her with unswerving justice and with boundless consideration. Has the conduct of the United States and its people towards Spain been in keeping with the services received? Not exactly. Upon her, they have practiced their ruthless policy of expansion; their first usurpations were attempted against her territory. It is thus that parasite plants are brought into being, live, and grow at the expense and detriment of the vigorous tree that gives them shelter.

The treaty of alliance signed by France and Spain on August 18th, 1796, completely subordinated the will of the latter to that of the Directorate of the French Republic. This peace and this alliance were the shameful outcome of the precarious condition to which the Peninsula was reduced as a result of the defeat of its armies in the northern provinces. From that instant, the country was reduced to a merely passive attitude, obliged willy-nilly to follow the path marked out by the interests of France. That government, taking advantage of the desire expressed by Charles IV to advance the Duke of Parma—who for family reasons he wished to raise to the dignity of king—offered for His Highness an increase of territory to consist of Tuscany, or the three Roman legations, or any other continental provinces in Italy, in exchange for Louisiana *with the same boundary and limits as now possessed by Spain and which were the same it had when in possession of France*. It was thus stipulated in the preliminary, secret treaty of October 1st, 1800, signed by Alexander

Berthier for France and by Mariano Luis Urquijo, Spanish Minister for Spain. France, on its part, risked nothing, for none of the provinces offered belonged to her. It gained, however, possession of a territory which she had discovered and settled and whose dominion it had not given up until 1764. France could use this territory to reestablish her influence in America, and, although wedged in between the United States and Spain, it gave her an important position on the Gulf of Mexico, closed to her by the English cruisers. Bonaparte, who was already contemplating his reconciliation with monarchies and hoped soon to assume the regal purple himself, was pleased with the prospects of the erection of a new monarchy near France, whose republicanism was no longer anything more than an empty and pompous name. It was later seen how, embarrassed by the situation of Europe and realizing, perhaps, that it was impossible for him to keep Lousiana against the attacks and expeditions of England, he sold it to the United States for seven million *pesos*. Some of those who claim to have known the secrets of Napoleon's cabinet, assert that this transaction was bitterly opposed by the celebrated Talleyrand, but that the strong will of the Emperor finally predominated as usual. Ever since the conclusion of the treaty of San Ildefonso, Spain had feared that France might see proper to dispose of Lousiana. Since in spite of the instructions given to the plenipotentiary, Urquijo, nothing was said on this point in the treaty, she requested and succeeded in obtaining a formal agreement by which France pledged herself not to dispose of this territory without the prior consent of Spain. In view of the fact that no such consent was sought in 1803 and that the interests of His Most Catholic Majesty were not considered, the cabinet of Madrid presented a useless protest which was not even acknowledged. The United States, realizing the immense value of the territory acquired, the aim of all their efforts for so long a time, took care, through their skillful diplomats, to draw up the treaty of sale in such elastic and obscure terms as would permit territory that had never belonged to France to be included as part of the purchase. As the latter was more vitally interested in the prompt payment of the stipulated sum in order to meet the expenses of the war in which it was engaged, and since she risked nothing of her own in the transaction, France readily acceded to the treaty without manifesting any scruples concerning the ambiguity of its terms with regard to the territory involved.

The United States rejoiced over the acquisition, for the paltry sum of thirty-five million francs, of a territory whose boundaries covered more than sixteen hundred leagues. This was the extent of the ideal and imaginary boundaries assigned to Louisiana. The real limits to which they aspired were the Perdido on the east and the Rio Bravo del Norte on the west, chosing to bide their time for the realization of this ambitious dream. The American ministers, Pinckney and Monroe, presented these claims to the cabinet of Madrid which indignantly rejected them, claiming that neither West Florida nor the Provincias Internas of Mexico had ever been part of the territory of Lousiana, and that France never received these vast domains by virtue of the so-called treaty of *retrocession*. The cabinet of Madrid, alarmed by so daring a pretension to which force might give added weight in the future, asked the government of the Emperor of the French to declare in clear and unequivocal terms that should remove all doubts and make impossible all unjust claims of the United States, whether the limits which they now wished to assign to Louisiana were those agreed upon by the treaty of sale, intimating that these could be no others than those of the treaty of *retrocession* of 1800. Prince Talleyrand replied to the Ambassador of Spain in Paris on the 12th Fructidor, in the year 12, in the following terms: "The eastern limits of Louisiana are marked by the stream of the Mississippi, the Iberville River, Ponchartrain Lake, and Lake Maurepas. This line of demarcation marks the extent of the territory ceded by Spain to France by virtue of the treaty of the 30th Ventuous, in the year 9. France would not have demanded of Spain anything beyond these limits, and, since France has done nothing more than to transfer to the United States the rights acquired, the latter cannot demand a cession of greater territory from Spain, unless such an additional grant is agreed upon by some subsequent treaty between the said country and Spain." This same Minister wrote to the Spanish Ambassador in Paris on the 27th of July, 1804, stating that he had just informed the United States that *Louisiana had been ceded to them in a similar manner and with the same boundaries as it had been ceded to France by Spain. He added that this statement would be repeated to them in the most positive manner as often as His Most Catholic Majesty desired.* It is obvious that since the contracting powers in the treaty of San Ildefonso were France and Spain, these two powers alone could interpret the terms of that treaty, being the only two who knew with accuracy the extent of the territory which had been the subject of their negotiations. It little matters whether France, in a period more remote occupied a greater territory, even granting that it was all designated as Louisiana, if she did not cede it to Spain in 1764. For this very reason the latter could not have given back to the former in 1800 any more than it had received, for obviously one cannot restore that which one did not receive. Now then, France officially declares in the treaty of San Ildefonso that she does not claim to have acquired other territory than that which she herself ceded to Spain freely when she gave her the island and city of New Orleans and all other territory belonging to France west of the Mississippi. Ever since the final treaty of peace, known as the treaty of Paris of 1763, the eastern limits of Louisiana had been fixed by a line running along the center of the Mississippi from its source to the Iberville River and from the lakes of Ponchartrain and Maurepas to the sea. At that time the port of Mobile, with all the possessions of His Most Christian Majesty to the left of the Mississippi, except that portion which had been granted to the king of Spain, were ceded to the king of England. In order to regain the port of Havana and that part of the Island of Cuba occupied by the English, the King of Spain gave to the English, as compensation, all his possessions east and southeast of the Mississippi. It was thus that the former French and Spanish territory was reorganized under the name of West

Florida. During the Revolutionary War, in 1779, the English were driven out of this interesting territory by the arms of the king of Spain who continued to enjoy peaceful and undisturbed possession of it after the retrocession of Louisiana. It never occurred to France to claim it as part of her former dominions in the treaty of San Ildefonso. During the three years following, and after the terms of the treaty had been put into effect, Spain continued, similarly, to hold Texas, and she exercised unequivocal rights of sovereignty without the least objection or dispute on the part of France. It was left for the cabinet of Washington to interpret the treaty of 1800 in a manner as daring as it was arbitrary.

To wish, to wait, and to act describe the distinctive character of the government and the people of the United States. No nation in the civilized world can equal them in their boundless ambition. The object of their heart's desire having been determined, they lie in wait for the propitious moment, assuming a disinterested and indifferent attitude in the meanwhile which is foreign to their true feelings, until circumstances favor their designs, when they ruthlessly trample everything in the way of their desire. This is a historical truth as clear as the light of day. Let us now turn to the facts.

As long as Spain kept a semblance of power and was the ally of the Emperor of the French, her rights were respected. During this time the Americans contented themselves with informing the cabinet of Madrid from time to time, with shocking petulance, that they understood the letter and the spirit of the treaty of San Ildefonso better than the two contracting parties. The negotiations were reduced to the exchange of a few diplomatic notes, without the government of Spain becoming aware of the warning voice that foretold the impending doom. She could have settled this matter before her days of misfortune arrived, but she let the opportunity pass and she lost everything.

The events of Madrid and Bayone in 1808, the subsequent uprising of the Spanish people against the hordes of Napoleon, the disordered state of the administration which naturally followed, the weakness of her revolutionary governments, barely able to maintain a precarious existence, all these circumstances united to favor the ambitious plans of the United States who now, ill-concealing their joy, threw off the hypocritical mask with which, for a time, they covered their true designs. The thinking men of the United States had clearly foreseen that their emancipation would be but the prelude to the emancipation of all the New World. They realized that sooner or later the important revelation that resistance to a remote and tyrannical power could be crowned with complete victory would not be disregarded by the Spanish colonies. Nor were they ignorant of the fact that their early independent existence, their progress in civilization, and the experience gained through their own administration would assure them a preeminent position of power and influence in determining the fate of the new nations when they became established. To cooperate in this great enterprise was to safeguard their own existence by the most effective means. In spite of the advantageous position of the United States, of their growing maritime power, of the war-like disposition of their inhabitants, of the determination displayed in their struggles, of the abundant resources of their soil and the bright prospects of their industry, they could not aspire to a superior rank among the nations of the world, as long as they had to compete with the old and powerful countries of Europe. The setting changed, however, with the appearance of other independent nations in the New World. It was, therefore, to the essential interest of the United States to encourage by their example, their counsel, and their material help the insurrection of Spanish America. Here they saw the realization of their ulterior motives enhanced by the sympathy created for themselves and the inherent weakness of the ephemeral governments of the new nations. Egoism is an inseparable vice of the genius of the Anglo-Saxon race. If they proclaim or sustain the august rights of liberty and independence, it is not because of the noble sympathy felt for a just and sacred cause; rather it is out of regard for their interests, it is their own improvement which they seek with indefatigable zeal. The time that has elapsed since our fortunate emancipation, a time so rich in disappointments, has removed the band that inexperience placed over our eyes. Who is ignorant to-day of the real cause, the prime motive behind the decision taken by the United States in favor of the independence of the Spanish colonies? This general assertion does not preclude the existence of a few philosophers, in whose number I am glad to include the earnest John Quincy Adams, the Demosthenes of the west, Mr. Clay, the Cicero of New England, Mr. Webster; the ill-fated congressman from Louisiana, Livingston, and a few other sincere friends of the liberty of mankind, who worked for the independence of America out of pure, philanthropic, and disinterested motives. But it cannot be denied that the immense majority of the American people participated in our melancholic tragedies for the purpose of weakening the power of Spain and out of a desire to exercise a direct influence, inevitable as a result of the vigor of a people full of life and dynamic activity, upon the fate of poorly educated peoples who would in the end destroy themselves by their excesses and the horrors of continuous civil war. Nothing could withstand the popularity of the Anglo-American system of government. The influence of Spain seemed to end at the Pillars of Hercules. The newborn star of the nations that rose upon the ruins of a decrepit monarchy shined fitfully and with a reddish glow.

The Americans decided to fan the spirit of insurrection in the Spanish colonies during the darkest hour of the conflict for their former ally and benefactor, taking advantage of the critical situation, and aware of the ultimate success which they foresaw. Companies which rendered direct services to the rebels were organized in Baltimore, expeditions were outfitted in New York; money, munitions, and armament were liberally furnished in New Orleans to carry on the struggle against Spain, to destroy and banish her commerce. It was thus that the plans to weaken more and more the power of a friendly nation were put into execution in order to snatch from her, immediately after, her most valuable possessions.

They began by fomenting an insurrection against the Spanish authorities in Baton Rouge; after this took place, they skillfully guided public opinion in their favor so as to create a political party who asked for annexation to the republic. The authors of the tumult, claiming to fear the spread of lawlessness, used the incident as a pretext to send in troops to occupy the territory in revolt. Soon after, they had the audacity of adding it to the United States by a solemn act of Congress. Similar tactics were followed to gain possession of Amalia Island, Mobile, and West Florida as far as the Perdido. The results not having been entirely satisfactory, the government of the United States then threw off its mask and took possession by force, agreeable to a previous and scandalous authorization of Congress, of all the territory which they had been unable to gain by deceit. Having carried the limits of the republic to the Perdido and rounded them out to the south, they assumed their longed-for supremacy in the Mexican Gulf region. To the protests raised against so monstrous and Machiavelian a policy, the Americans replied that the territory thus occupied was merely being held in trust until a satisfactory settlement could be reached. Without waiting for this negotiation, however they immediately annexed these territories to the republic by another act of Congress. They had fully foreseen the impotency of Spain to regain the lost territory. To distract attention and gain their ultimate aim, they employed their old and unfailing policy of alleging grievances, of advancing claims for redress, and of demanding indemnization for supposed injuries received. No one ignores the fact that Spain, overcome by the host of misfortunes that weighed down upon her, at last ceded, after holding out as long as she could, the two Floridas to the United States on condition that the claims for damages caused by French Corsairs—not Spanish—to American commerce in the ports of the Peninsula as a result of the famous Berlin and Milan decrees be given up by the United States. It is worthy of notice to keep in mind that the cabinet of Washington did not gain this territory by insisting upon its former claims regarding the boundaries of Louisiana, but that they gained their desire by pressing Spain for the settlement of indemnization claims, thus obtaining by these means what they had failed to get by their former contentions. The subject of the two Floridas is a closed incident. Let us turn to the subject of Texas and see how the same ends are sought by similar means.

Nothing can be proved as clearly as the exclusive possession of Texas, always enjoyed by the Spaniards and acknowledged and respected by the French during their whole occupation of Louisiana. It is very appropriate to cite here what Don Luis de Onís, extraordinary envoy and minister plenipotentiary of His Most Catholic Majesty in the United States, wrote in support of the rights of his country questioned with such impunity.

"The province of Texas," says Onís, "where Spain has maintained establishments ever since the sixteenth century is limited on the east by Louisiana and comprises the extensive country that lies between the Medina, where the government of Coahuila ends, and the presidio of Nuestra Señora del Pilar de los Adaes, now abandoned. The presidio is only a few leagues distant from the fort of Natchitoches, 20 leagues from the mission of Adaes, 40 from Nacogdoches, 150 from the abandoned presidio of Orcoquisac, 200 from Bahía del Espíritu Santo and 40 from the presidio of San Antonio de Béxar. It is beyond all doubt that by order of the viceroy of Mexico, Marqués de Monclova, given in 1689, Captain Don Alonzo de León, governor of the province of Coahuila, proceeded to the exploration of the territory as far as Bahía del Espíritu Santo and the San Marcos which empties into it. The chief of the Tejas Indians received him in the most friendly manner. In 1690 he took possession of the territory and founded the mission of San Francisco de los Tejas. By the royal order of November 12, 1692, issued by His Most Catholic Majesty, new explorations were ordered to be made in the said province by sea and by land. As a result, an expedition was outfitted and the Cadodachos River was explored. Twenty-two years later, in 1715, while the Duque de Linares was viceroy of Mexico, Louis de Saint Denis and three other Frenchmen penetrated into the province as far as the Spanish presidio of San Juan Bautista.

They came from Louisiana and were commissioned by that government to buy cattle in the Spanish missions of Texas. These Frenchmen were arrested and taken to Mexico City. The fourth expedition into Texas was then decided upon and Alférez Don Domingo Ramón was appointed leader of the undertaking. This expedition was received with the greatest rejoicings on the part of the Indians, and Captain Ramón appointed a son of the chief of the Tejas as governor of all those Indian nations. He established the four missions and Spanish settlements of San Francisco, la Purísima Concepción, San José, and María Santísima de Guadalupe, the last being situated seven leagues from Natchitoches. By the royal *cédula* of 1719 several changes were made in the jurisdiction of the Spanish officers in the province of Texas. Captain Ramón died soon after at the presidio of San Juan Bautista del Río Grande. War having broken out between Spain and France during the regency of the Duke of Orleans, the French attacked the Spanish mission of los Adaes. As a result, the mission and its settlers were removed for the time being to the presidio of San Antonio de Béxar. The viceroy of New Spain, Marqués de Valero, accepted the generous proposal made by Marqués de San Miguel de Aguayo, who offered his person and his wealth to drive the French out of the territory they had so unjustly invaded and occupied by waging war against them. Marqués de Aguayo, having been appointed Governor General of Nuevas Filipinas, that is, the provinces of Texas and Nueva Estremadura, raised 500 dragoons and two companies of cavalry with which he set out for the province of Texas in 1719, penetrating as far as Los Adaes without opposition, for the French had retired to the presidio of Nachitoches. When the king of Spain heard of this expedition, he gave orders for the province of Texas to be fortified as soon as the hostilities against the French had ceased and the province had been reoccupied. Marqués de Aguayo reestablished the old missions and founded other establishments, among them the presidios of Nuestra Señora del Pilar de los Adaes, Loreto or Bahía del Espíritu Santo, and Dolores which to-day is known as Orcoquisac. He improved the condition of San Antonio de Béxar, removing the settlement to a location between the San Antonio and the San Pedro. The province of Texas having been reoccupied, reenforced and pacified, the Marqués de Aguayo asked for 200 Tlaxcalteca families and an equal number of families from Galicia, or from the Canary Islands, to be settled in the province. The king ordered that the 400 families be recruited in the Canary Islands, and it was with some of these that the Villa de San Fernando was established in the vicinity of the presidio of Béxar. Towards the close of 1730,[2] the Spaniards residing in the presidio of Béxar undertook several expeditions to the north of the province as a result of the hostility of the Indians against the presidio of San Sabá where several soldiers and missionaries were killed. A campaign was organized against the Indians under the command of Colonel Diego Ortiz de Parrilla. Soon afterwards, an attempt was made to establish a general and uniform line of presidios to protect the Interior Provinces of New Spain. Later, the Marqués de Rubí was commissioned to proceed to an inspection of these presidios to determine their present condition. As a result of this commission which seems to have taken years for its execution, the *Regulations for Presidios* were issued on the 10th of September, 1772. By these, a line of presidios was to be established from the coast of Sonora to the Mexican Gulf, terminating with the one on Bahía del Espíritu Santo. In the province of Texas those of San Antonio de Béxar and Bahía del Espíritu Santo have been maintained to the present, while the one at Orcoquisac and that of Nuestra Señora de los Adaes have been abandoned in view of their uselessness, since Spain came into possession of Louisiana."

In spite of these facts of which the Anglo-Americans are perfectly well aware, they claim that the western boundary of Louisiana extends as far as our Rio Bravo, insisting that all the territory which it drains belonged to France. On what grounds, on what proof, do they base their claims? On none more specific

[2] Evidently an error as to date. The San Sabá mission was not founded until after 1758.

than the voyage of Robert Cavelier, commonly known as Mon-
sieur La Salle, made in 1684 for the exclusive purpose of finding
the mouth of the Mississippi which he had previously discovered
in April, 1682. The accounts of this voyage are so confusing
that it has been impossible, up to the present, to determine
whether La Salle, during his wanderings in the Mexican Gulf in
search of his river landed in the Bahía del Espíritu Santo, or San
José, or Matagorda. Joutel, the inseparable companion of La
Salle during his second voyage, from the time that he embarked
at La Rochelle, and the chronicler of the history of his misfortunes, asserts that they landed in Bahía del Espíritu Santo
between 28° and 29° north latitude. "The plan of La Salle,"
says Joutel in his diary, "was to look for the bay of Espíritu
Santo and, having discovered this, to send thirty men by land to
explore the coast to the right and to the left which doubtless would
have resulted in the discovery of the fateful river, avoiding many
misfortunes. But Heaven refused to grant this favor and La
Salle, abandoning his first plan and forgetful of the care which
so important a matter required, contented himself with sending
the pilot and one of the mates of the *Belle* to make the exploration. They returned without having seen anything as a result of
a heavy fog that came up. The only information gained was
that given by the mate of the vessel who said that he thought that
the bay was a river that ran parallel to the shore, which was a
likely conclusion. No importance was attached to this information. The wind having changed on the 12th, we raised anchor
and continued our course to the southeast in order to get away
from the shore. When an observation was taken at midday, we
found our latitude to be 28° 50′ north. As the wind changed
just then, the current, which flowed from the south, led us
towards land again and we were obliged to anchor in five or six
fathoms of water. Here we spent the night." Joutel makes it
clear that while wandering aimlessly in this expedition they
anchored here and there wherever appearances gave any indica-
tion of being near the Mississippi. In other words, he makes it
clear that it was not their intention to occupy any other territory,

much less to acquire possession of new lands, for they had not received any such commission from the king of France. It is true that Joutel tells how, having landed with his companions, La Salle was obliged to build a fort in order to defend himself against the savages, but he does not tell where this fort was constructed. For this reason, it might just as well be inferred that it was built in the country of the Illinois. But be this as it may, the account of Joutel gives us all the evidence needed to annul all the claims which, as a result of La Salle's voyage and exploration, the Americans have presented to advance their interests. I will copy the part of his diary which best serves my purpose, stating that this work was published 149 years ago. "According to what everybody says with regard to this enterprise, it is concluded that its success was frustrated by the death of La Salle. What really prevented its being snuffed out immediately was the fact that his death remained unknown for two years. At the end of this time, when the *Spaniards in Mexico were informed of the whole affair, they immediately sent troops to destroy the weak garrison which La Salle had left in the fort he had constructed where he landed before setting out overland in search of the Mississippi.* They destroyed the fort so completely that seven or eighty years elapsed before Iberville, a Canadian nobleman, a man of spirit and courage, famous for his magnificent expeditions to Hudson Bay and other parts, decided to renew or revive the enterprise. He came to France in 1698 and equipped a fleet with which he set out for the Gulf of Mexico. As he was a good sailor, he scouted along the coast with such good fortune that he found the fatal mouth of the Mississippi where he constructed a fort and left a well-supplied garrison. He returned to France to secure new supplies, and having done this, he again embarked and succeeded in penetrating into the interior. Here he became acquainted with many savage nations with whom he made friendly alliances. He constructed another fort which he also garrisoned well and then returned to France. When he attempted another voyage, he died on the way. The lack of supplies and reenforcements made this magnificent enterprise fail once more."

This proves that the permanence of the French in Spanish territory cannot be advanced as an argument to establish a title of
possession because, just as soon as news was received by the
Spanish of this occupation, they immediately took steps to re-
assert their rights and went so far as to drive out by force those
who, in their misfortune, had been left to occupy the territory.

Granting that discovery has always been an argument for
dominion and overlordship, this itself would establish the claims
of the Spaniards, who preceded all the other nations as discoverers of that part of the Americas. Among the first explorers
of this region are Juan Ponce, in 1512; Lúcas Vásquez de Ayllón,
in 1525; Pánfilo de Narváes, in 1527; Hernando de Soto, in
1538; and Luis Moscoso, in 1542. In 1545 Pedro Meléndez
discovered the bays of Santa Rosa and San Bernardo, together
with others, landing in all of them. The provinces of Hirrihigua,
Moscoso, Umbarracuxi, Acuera, Ocali, Apalache, Altapalia, Cafa,
Movila, Chasquin, Guigate, Uhanque and Guachoya, were also
visited, Hernando de Soto having died in the last of these in 1642
after he crossed the Mississippi and visited Río Negro. In some
of the above-mentioned places, the Spanish conquerors and explorers erected establishments. No one has doubted that the
Spaniards were the discoverers of Florida, nor is the fact unknown that the vast expanse from the Pánuco to 48° north latitude, covering over 600 leagues through which flowed the Mississippi, was designated by this name. Why should exception be
taken now to the discovery of the coast of the territory to-day
known as Texas? The Spaniards occupied the principal points
along the Gulf Coast and thus controlled the entire coastline of
the Mexican Gulf, never permitting foreigners to approach it. It
was thus that they acquired an undisputed title to this region.
As early as 1693 the province of Texas was inseparably united
to the Spanish crown by the expedition of Don Gregorio Salinas,
the French being confined to Mobile and the immediate vicinity.
In 1719, Philip V ordered it fortified. At that time the French
did not extend beyond Natchitoches, where they remained until
1742. In that year Governor Sandovál permitted them to ad-

vance their fort a gunshot's distance and for this incident he was tried and deposed. France herself never attached any great importance to the discoveries of La Salle. In the treaty of Aix-la-Chapelle alone did she refer to him and then in very general terms with reference to the Mississippi and the Illinois, both of which La Salle visited in his first voyage. After La Salle's and Iberville's expeditions came to an unhappy end, the king of France on September 14, 1712, issued a patent to Crozat, his secretary, granting to him exclusive commercial privileges and the sole right of colonizing the region about the Mississippi for a period of fifteen years. This grant was very vague and although it attacked Spain's sovereignty over several of her dominions, it was never carried out and remained a mere project, or an ambitious dream. Spain never recognized the rights granted by this patent, while France consistently respected Spanish sovereignty in Texas, at least as far as Nacogdoches and ten leagues beyond. Spain, on her part, maintained and exercised her power without taking into account the incursions of La Salle or the arbitrary patents granted to the secretary of Louis XIV. France never extended the limits of Louisiana to the points claimed by the Americans in any of her diplomatic negotiations. The real or supposed voyages, the legally or illegally granted patents, the true or imaginary accounts, the dreams or the realities of the cases in hand, all are given credit by the Americans in so far as these support their claims, *because they recognize no other right than their own desire and no other justice save their own convenience.* How their fortunate acquisition of Louisiana has been utilized and is now being used to further their covetous ambitions! It has meant nothing to them that France recognized certain limits as indisputable. They persist in their incredible pretension of understanding the rights of that power better than herself, exhibiting greater zeal in claiming them. It is very much to the point to cite here what General Wilkenson, whom we all knew in Mexico, writes in his memoirs. "The claims of the United States to the still undetermined western frontier induced the Spanish government to move forward one of its divisions, in the spring of 1806, to occupy all the territory to the east of the Sabine as far as Arroyo Hondo, a small rivulet six miles from Nachitoches, which was, according to the Spanish commandant, Herrera, the old boundary of the province of Texas. To repel the invasion, the President of the United States ordered a small number of troops to be gathered at Nachitoches and it was there that I joined them. They were ill-equipped and ill-prepared, but as soon as the detachment received the necessary equipment, I proceeded with it to attack the invaders who, with foresight, avoided the conflict by the timely recrossing of the Sabine. This was followed by the negotiation of a peaceful agreement in which it was stipulated that while the final arrangements were pending between the two governments, the subjects of neither one could occupy or invade any part of the territory that lies between the Sabine and Arroyo Hondo. This agreement was religiously observed by the Spaniards from that time on, but very little respect was paid to it by the citizens of the United States who subsequently undertook several expeditions against the province of Texas. If these did not have the open approval of the government they, at least, were carried on with its connivance, if we are to judge by subsequent events." This Anglo-American, so distinguished in the service of his country, so well-versed in the tangles of its policies, recognizes the Sabine as the limits universally attributed to Texas and refers *to the territory that lies between the Sabine and Arroyo Hondo* as disputed territory. He admits the aggressions of the citizens of the United States against the province of Texas, adding in unmistakable terms with the frankness that characterized him that they relied, if not on the open approval of their government, at least upon its connivance. Can anyone doubt it? Wilkenson could not doubt it because, as he asserts, the fact was proved by *subsequent developments*. The Americans who at times extended their claims to the banks of the Pánuco, while at others, they contented themselves with those of the Rio Bravo and even with the Guadalupe, finally agreed to confine their frontier to the left bank of the Sabine. By the treaty of limits of February 22, 1819, they acquired the *contested territory* although they tried to claim still more, supporting their claims with inaccurate maps. They even went so far as to forge and place in their files certain others which they brazenly included in their records.

The reason that moved them to reopen the question of limits with the Mexican nation, which, upon acquiring its independence, had unquestionably fallen heir to the obligations as well as the rights of Spain concerning its neighboring powers, has not been as yet determined. Perhaps their intention was to annul the former negotiations in the hope of securing better terms in the new treaty. This was a natural expectation, considering our inexperience and the embarrassing condition of our internal affairs. They encountered, however, sufficient patriotism and the necessary foresight on the part of our administrators to block their desire, for our government demanded as the basis of all negotiations, even in regard to commerce and navigation, the admission of the treaty of limits of 1819. Thanks to this conduct, which will always reflect honor upon the Mexicans who observed it, whatever their party, we were saved from the net they had spread out for us with the flattering hope of encountering in our statesmen less dignity and firmness than characterized the agents of the Spanish Government.

In the acquisition of the Floridas, as in their constant desire to carry the American flag to the banks of the Rio Bravo, the same identical policy has been followed, the same violent attacks have been made, and the same bad faith has been most brazenly displayed. Have not the ancient republics, including the ambitious Rome, been left far behind when compared with this tumultuous democracy that with its gigantic arms reaches out from the Atlantic to the Pacific and threatens to seize a whole continent? Sometimes she advances peacefully, drawn on by the lure of imaginary rights which pave the way for her diplomatic intrigues. At others, she does not disdain to use force or resort to conquest. Let us agree that the vicinity of a republic which intervenes in all the transactions of the Americas is very detrimental; that her school of politics stands as a new, complete, and unique phenomenon, exacting as its own whatever adds to its aggrandisement and to its strength, ignoring ancient and established rights and the tranquil and peaceful possession through centuries. Tocqueville, who has studied so carefully the characteristic psychology of the people of the United States says, "It is undeniable that the English race has acquired an astonishing preponderance over all the other European races that have migrated to the New World. As long as the republic remains bound only by uninhabited territories and thinly populated countries, as long as she does not encounter a powerful nation to check her in her course, she will continue to extend beyond the present limits. *The established boundaries agreed upon by treaties will not hold her, on the contrary, she will trespass these imaginary barriers on every side.*" This is not an acrid recrimination. The French philosopher writes from the evidence presented by facts, and as a result of his observations of a policy that has never been altered nor modified. Has the treaty of limits signed in 1819, and later renewed in 1832, restrained that race in its forward advance to which the deserts are no longer an obstacle? Has the renunciation made by the United States of all their rights and claims to the territory situated to the west and to the south of the line described had any value? Has it not been but a vain promise which they never expected to fulfill? Far from restraining their impulses, this treaty has stimulated them all the more keenly. The government of the United States never considered the obligations contracted by that treaty as a serious impediment to its policy of expansion. The passion of the Anglo-American people, their pronounced desire to acquire new lands, is a dynamic power which is enhanced and nourished by their own industry. An ill-defined line, the source of a yet unknown river, scientific explorations with the pretext of establishing *monuments that shall mark with perfect accuracy* the limits of both nations, all these have given a golden opportunity to the combined efforts of the people and the government to promote their plans to acquire what belongs to their neighbors. Do not believe that as a result the march of aggression can be easily followed. What the cunning of the

United States lacked was made up by our unexplainable candor.
Though the plan of operations was conceived in Washington,
Mexico contributed directly to its execution. The colonization
of Texas, thrown open to adventurers from the United States,
afforded them the best means for gaining that territory *without
the disregard, the violation, or the infringement of existing
treaties.* Who does not sense the devious spirit of a policy which,
in this ruthless manner rendered the most solemn and sacred
efforts to maintain the rights of our nation useless? Let us look
at the circumstances and we will be forced to admit the facts.

As one of the clauses of the treaty by which Louisiana was
returned to France stipulated that its inhabitants could move to
any portion of the dominions of His Most Catholic Majesty they
might desire, the Anglo-Americans skillfully took advantage of
this provision to introduce themselves into Texas. As former
inhabitants of Louisiana, they pretended to feel an absurd attach-
ment for the Spanish Government. This happened toward the
end of 1820. Early in 1821 the Americans had already succeeded
in securing permission to introduce 300 families, all of these were
to be Catholics, and were to take an oath of obedience and loyalty
to the sovereign of Spain. The grant was made as a free gift
and it did not carry a single one of those precautionary measures
which the circumstances and the character of the new settlers so
imperiously demanded. Moses Austin headed the enterprise.
His prophetic name was considered a good omen for the proposed migration through deserts into the promised land. Such
forethought on the part of the leader of the new *chosen people*
is astonishing, but the ignorance and carelessness displayed by
the Spanish authorities is even more so. They should have
realized that the United States plan and carry out their conquests
quietly, without endangering the peace with the nation whose
territory they intend to take. They should have remembered
that, instead of resorting to open and hostile preparations, they
make use of hidden ways and means which, though slow and
apparently inefficient, lead to an unfailing success. By a similar
policy they had just deprived two powerful European nations

of dominions located in their vicinity. Why didn't we take this lesson to heart when we had it so near at hand? To open the door to Americans was a grave mistake, but it was continued until its consequences could no longer be ignored. Not long ago, in order to justify their rebellion, the colonists alleged that they incorporated themselves with the Mexican nation on condition that it should continue to be governed by a federal republican system and since this condition had remained unfulfilled the contract was broken insofar as they were concerned, leaving them at liberty to govern themselves as they saw fit. Where can we find greater shamelessness? In the humblest terms, Austin petitioned the Spanish authorities for permission to settle a few families in the vicinity of Nacogdoches, pledging himself to defend with his arms and his person the Spanish Government. The government was then a monarchy and there was no stipulation in regard to the form of government of the nation which so indiscreetly, yet so generously, gave shelter to her neighbors. Such a demand was impossible, for it would have been absurd. Moses Austin died in June, 1821, and his son, Stephen, with whom we all became acquainted in Mexico, took up the colonization scheme. He addressed the authorities of the Internal Provinces, petitioning them for new favors and a greater grant of territory. These authorities referred the matter to the supreme government of Mexico, stating that the families already introduced numbered more than 500, while adventurers came in daily without any of the qualifications stipulated by the grant. As independence had been proclaimed in that year and the struggle to secure it continued until the end of it, it was natural that the nation, with its attention occupied by an enterprise of greater importance, should have left the empresarios of colonization schemes to do almost as they pleased. They took advantage of the circumstances to establish themselves—as is their wont— without attracting attention or creating a stir. Nearly two years elapsed without a definite solution of this grave matter being reached, and naturally enough, those who were interested in gaining time did not stand idle. In February, 1823, the imperial government ratified the grants under the absolutely inadequate colonization law of January of that year. As a result of the new political outbreak which brought about corresponding changes in administration another year elapsed and it was not until August, 1824, that a new colonization law was passed. This, though inadequate, at least contained some restrictions; but, as fate would have it, they were never observed. How we have contributed to our own ruin and shame!

Policy and national interest demanded that both the regulations concerning colonization and the supervision of their strict enforcement should be in the hands of the national government and not of the state of Coahuila and Texas. The former was in a position to know the designs of our open enemy better and could, with more judgment, dictate preventive measures to forestall or avoid altogether the imminent danger that threatened us.

It was much easier to seduce and surprise men who had just entered upon a political career, who had no personal experience, who could not be acquainted with the subtle machinations of international diplomacy, and who, in a word, could be won over by the promise of a large and unexpected fortune. Our lawmakers did not even think of this possibility because we were all lulled by the most perfect confidence. The power of making colonization contracts was delegated to the state government of Coahuila and Texas. Such contracts were in fact made with a truly astounding prodigality. We made a present of Texas to the Americans of the North, sometimes freely granting them our territory and sometimes giving it to Mexicans without resources or wealth for the ostensible purpose of colonizing it. With a few honorable exceptions the real object of the Mexicans in obtaining these grants was to sell at the lowest price and to the citizens of the United States the land thus acquired. The soul of Alexander VI seemed to have descended and have been reincarnated in the persons who exercised the government of Coahuila and Texas. With the liberality of that renowned Pope, they distributed the rich, precious, and coveted lands of Texas. Let us review these grants. Although I may appear profuse in enumerating them, I cannot fail to do so in order that the whole nation may realize the extent of the spoliation, and in order that the world may see the ingratitude of the greedy land speculators. They were like the asps of the fable. *After we took them to our bosom, they destroyed us.* The following account of the contracts granted is taken literally from the report made by Coahuila to the supreme government, June 23, 1834.

"On December 23, 1824, the congress of the state granted the Sewane Indians permission to establish themselves on the banks of the Colorado.

"Stephen F. Austin was granted permission, April 27, 1825, to colonize 300 foreign families in the territory still unoccupied within the limits of his former grant, with the exception of the ten litoral leagues. On March 7, 1827, the following lands were surveyed for him that he might settle 500 additional families. Beginning at the San Jacinto, where the line of the ten litoral leagues of the Mexican Gulf terminates, the line shall run along the right bank of the river to its source, thence a straight line shall be drawn directly north to the point of intersection with the road that goes from there to Nacogdoches, thence continuing to the west to a point north of the headwaters of the La Vaca, thence a line shall be drawn southward to the headwaters of the said river, and thence proceeding down the eastern bank to the ten litoral leagues of the Mexican Gulf, continuing east to the point of departure."

"On October 6, 1825, Empresario Martín de Leon was granted permission to establish a town on the Guadalupe, said town to be known as Victoria, leaving the demarcation of the grant to the commissioner appointed by the government.

"The contract of Juan Lucio Woodbury to colonize 200 foreign families was made November 14, 1826, and the following limits were assigned. Beginning at the point of intersection of the 31st parallel north latitude and the western boundary of the colony of Robert Leftwitch situated between the Colorado and the Brazos, the line shall ascend in a northeasterly direction to the point of intersection with the 32nd parallel north latitude and the aforesaid grant, thence the line shall continue to the west along the southern limits of the colony of Stephen Wilson to the 104th meridian where a cornerstone shall be placed. From here the line shall descend along the said meridian to the point of intersection with the old road between Río Grande and Béxar, thence it shall continue along the said road to the Medina, thence upstream along the right bank for a distance of ten leagues, thence a straight line shall be drawn to the east until the Guadalupe is reached, thence upstream along the right bank of the said river to the point where the lands of the colony of Col. Milam end, thence following along the boundary of the said grant it shall continue, crossing the Colorado to the western limits of the colony of Leftwitch, thence to the point of departure. Although this grant was annulled because its terms were not fulfilled by November 14, 1832, as stipulated, it continued in force by virtue of decree No. 72 issued by the legislature, February 12, 1829, allowing him two more years for its fulfillment. The time expires November 14, 1834.

"Joseph Vehlein and Company contracted with the government of the state, December 21, 1826, to colonize 300 families within the territory hereinafter stipulated. Beginning at Nacogdoches the line shall proceed south to a point outside of the twenty leagues from the frontier which run parallel to the Sabine, and of the ten litoral leagues of the Mexican Gulf. From here it shall turn west to the San Jacinto, then upstream along the left bank to its source, thence proceeding along a straight line drawn due north to the road between Béxar and Nacogdoches, thence along the said road and towards the said town, thence following the road generally designated as Toro beginning at a point just before reaching the Trinity, thence up until it meets the first road, and thence along this road to Nacogdoches, the point of departure. The time allowed for the fulfillment of this contract terminated December 21, 1832, but Congress, by decree No. 192 of April 27, 1832, having extended the time for three years, it will terminate December 21, 1835.

"On December 22, 1826, David G. Burnet contracted to colonize 300 families within the following grant. Beginning on a line drawn due north from Nacogdoches and running for a distance of fifteen leagues parallel to the Sabine, the dividing line of the United States to a point outside of the twenty leagues adjoining the boundary where a monument will be placed, thence the line shall proceed to the Navasoto, hence downstream along the left bank of the creek following the main bed to the point of intersection of the said creek with the Béxar-Nacogdoches road, thence the line shall follow the left side of the road to the Toro hill just before reaching the Trinity, thence it shall follow the upper road to Nacogdoches and the point of departure. This line shall leave to the right all the lands granted to Woodbury. This contract should have expired December 22, 1832, but it was continued in effect until December 22, 1835 by virtue of decree No. 192 issued April 27, 1832.

"On May 21, 1827, John Cameron contracted to colonize 100 families in the following grant. Beginning at the point of intersection of parallel 32 north latitude with the western boundary line of the colony of Robert Leftwitch, situated between the Colorado and the Brazos, the boundary shall follow a straight line westward to the point of intersection of parallel 32 north latitude with the 101st meridian, thence proceeding north along the said meridian, it shall run for 21 leagues, thence a straight diagonal line shall be drawn to the southeast to the western boundary of the colony of Robert Leftwitch, thence along the said line to the point of departure. This contract expires May 21, 1836, its time having been prorogued by decree No. 185 issued April 4, 1832, by which three years' grace was allowed.

On November 20, 1827, the Empresario, Stephen F. Austin, contracted to colonize 100 families in the following grant. Beginning at the point of intersection of the Béxar-Nacogdoches road and the Colorado, the line shall follow the eastern bank of the said river upstream for a distance of 15 leagues, thence the line shall run due west parallel to the said road to the dividing line of the watershed of the Colorado and the Brazos which

is the dividing line between this colony and the grant made to the
Nashville Company, thence the line shall follow the boundary
of the said company to the road that goes from Béxar to Nacogdoches, thence along the said road to the point of departure.
The said Austin contracted, July 9, 1828, to colonize with an
unspecified number of families the litoral lands that lie along
the coast of the Mexican Gulf between the La Vaca and the San
Jacinto, this subject to the approval of the federal government
which was given April 22, 1828, when the following boundaries
were assigned. Beginning on the left bank of the La Vaca at
the point where it empties into the sea, the line shall run along
the coast of the Mexican Gulf to the point where the San Jacinto
empties into Galveston Bay, thence upstream along the left bank
of the said river for a distance of ten leagues, thence a line
shall be drawn to the west, running parallel to the coast to a
point on the La Vaca, ten leagues from the coast, thence the line
shall follow the left bank of the said river downstream for a
distance of ten leagues to the point of departure.

"The foreigners James Powers and James Hewetson contracted with the government, September 29, 1826, to colonize
200 families with the required consent of the federal government, in the following grant. Beginning on the left bank of
the Guadalupe at the point where it enters the sea the line shall
follow the coast east to the point where the La Vaca empties
into the sea, thence it shall follow the right bank of this river
upstream for a distance of ten leagues, thence a line shall be
drawn to the west running parallel to the coast to the Guadalupe.
Thence it shall follow the left bank of this river downstream
to the point of departure. On March 13, 1821, they asked for
an additional grant of land which was made to them as follows.
Beginning on the bank of the Guadalupe, at a point ten leagues
from the coast at a corner of the former grant, the line shall run
parallel to the coast to the Nueces which is recognized as the
boundary between this state and Tamaulipas, thence down the
left bank of the said river to the point where it empties into
the sea, thence along the coast to the said river and to the point

of departure, including in this grant the ten litoral leagues only. Agreeable to decree No. 184, issued February 23, 1831, the grantees were permitted to introduce 200 additional families, the time limit being extended three years. The decree, however, was annulled April 24, 1832.

"John McMullen and James McGloin contracted to colonize 200 Irish families, August 14, 1828, in the land granted to John G. Purnell and Benjamin Drake Lovell with the boundaries assigned to the grant made to the latter. Leaving the ten litoral leagues along the coast of the Mexican Gulf as provided by the law of August 18, 1824, the grant shall begin at a point on the left bank of the Nueces, ten leagues from the coast, thence the line shall follow the said river to a point ten leagues from the presidio of Bahía del Espiritu Santo, thence a straight line shall be drawn to the mouth of the Medina where it enters the San Antonio, thence the line shall follow the right bank of the said river to its point of intersection with the old road between Béxar and Presidio del Río Grande, thence along the said road to the Nueces, thence down the said river along the left bank to the point of departure.

"John Cameron contracted with this government, August 18, 1828, to colonize the land formerly granted to Col. Reuben Ross deceased, now granted to the said Cameron with the approval of the federal government and with the following boundaries. Beginning at the western terminus of the colony of General Arthur G. Wavell, on Red River, the line shall follow the said river, which is the dividing line between this republic and the United States of the North, to the point of intersection with the 102nd meridian west longitude from London thence due south along the said meridian for a distance of twenty leagues, thence east along a line parallel to Red River and twenty leagues from it, to the western limits of the colony of General Wavell, the point of departure. By decree No. 195 the time limit was extended for three years.

"The foreigners, Stephen Julian Wilson and Richard Exter, contracted with this government, April 20, 1828, to colonize

100 Mexican and foreign families in the following grant. Beginning on the right bank of the Arkansas at the point that marks the boundary between this state and the territory of New Mexico, the line shall run along the said river downstream to its point of intersection with the 102nd meridian west of London, thence south for a distance of twenty leagues along the said meridian, thence west along a line parallel to the Arkansas to the western limits of the territory of New Mexico, thence along the said boundary to the right bank of the Arkansas, the point of departure.

Miguel Ramos Arizpe contracted with this government, November 12, 1828, to colonize 200 families in the following grant. Beginning at the presidio of San Fernando, now the town of Rosas, the line shall run northwest to the point of juncture of the San Antonio and the Escondido, thence by way of Laja's Crossing as far as the Río Grande or Bravo del Norte, thence leaving to the left the former location of the presidio of Monclova, the line shall follow along the bank upstream for a distance of thirty leagues, considering as part of this grant the lands that lie between the stated line and the banks of the river to the point where the thirty leagues terminate, a line will be drawn to the southwest continuing to the highest point of the Sierra in the direction of the place called Las Ventanas, thence it shall follow along the highest ground west to the water spring del Poso y los Horcados which is the source of the San Antonio, thence from this point, including within the boundary the pasture lands of los Aparejos, San Casimiro, San Rodrigo, San Diego and the former location of the presidio of Agua-Verde, along the La Vaca to the source of the Escondido, thence along this river to where it joins the San Antonio, the point of departure.

"John L. Woodbury, acting for D. J. Vehlein contracted with this government, September 11, 1828, for the following grant. Beginning on the coast of the Mexican Gulf at a point twenty leagues distant from Sabine Bay, measured along the coast and to the west, the line shall ascend to the north, parallel to the Sabine and at a distance of twenty leagues therefrom, for a

distance of ten leagues, thence the line shall run northwest for
ten leagues parallel to the coast and along the line that marks
the boundary of the grants made to the said party, December
21, 1826, across the Trinity to the left bank of the San Jacinto
at a point ten leagues from the coast or Galveston Bay, thence
the line shall run downstream along the left bank of the San
Jacinto to its mouth in Galveston Bay, thence the line shall follow the coast and its indentations to the open sea, thence along
the gulf coast to the point of departure. The island of San
Luis is not to be included as part of this grant, since the supreme
government excluded it by the previously cited resolution.

"From the Atoyac to the Sabine are found several foreign
families who have established themselves there with the consent of both the state and national governments. Likewise,
several foreigners have settled on the banks of the Trinity and
the San Jacinto, with the previous consent of the supreme government and of the state.

"Victor Blanco, acting for Juan Domínguez, contracted with
this government, January 28, 1829, to colonize 200 Americans
and European families in the vacant lands along the twenty league
zone of the frontier in the following grant. Beginning on the
Arkansas at its point of intersection with the 23rd meridian west
longitude from Washington, the dividing line between the Mexican Republic and the United States of the North, the line shall
run south along the said dividing line for a distance of forty
leagues, thence west for twenty leagues, the distance of the reserve
zone established by the colonization law of August 18, 1824,
thence the line shall ascend north running parallel to the 23rd
meridian west longitude from Washington to the Arkansas, which
also forms part of the dividing line between this republic and the
United States of the North, thence downstream along the right
bank of the said Arkansas for a distance of twenty leagues to the
23rd meridian west longitude from Washington, the point of
departure.

"Mariano Grande, acting for His Excellency, Lorenzo de
Zavala, Governor of the state of Mexico, contracted with this

government, March 6, 1829, with the approval of the federal government to colonize 500 Mexican and foreign families in the following grant. Beginning at the confines of the communal lands of Nacogdoches, the line shall run along the highway that goes to Natchitoches by way of Borregos and Chalán Crossing to the right bank of the river, thence west along the coast for twenty leagues, thence north along a line parallel to the Sabine to Nacogdoches, the point of departure. The ten litoral leagues on the southern edge of this grant being included as part of it, likewise the reserve twenty league zone along the United States boundary, the lands of the town of Nacogdoches on the north side, and the others belonging to the state on the west.

"Rafael Antonio Menchola acting for Martín de Leon contracted, April 22, 1829, for an additional grant of land to the contract made April 13, 1824, to settle 41 families which he agreed to introduce, offering to increase their number by 150 more. In view of this, the following additional grant was made. Beginning on the La Vaca at the point where the middle road to Nacogdoches crosses it, the line shall run upstream along the said river for one league, thence along a line parallel to the said road across the Guadalupe by Lego's Crossing to the Coleto, thence down the Coleto to the Guadalupe.

"Juan Antonio Padilla and Thomas J. Chambers contracted with this government, September 28, 1829, to introduce 800 foreign families to be settled within the bounds of the following grant. Beginning at a point where the line marking the twenty league zone along the international boundary of this republic, opposite the 23rd meridian west of Washington terminates on the Red River, a line will be drawn parallel to the dividing line in a northern direction as if to cross the Arkansas to a point twenty leagues from the said river, thence the line shall run west parallel to the Arkansas to its intersection with the 25th meridian west of Washington, thence along the bank of the said river eastward to the point of departure.

"Stephen F. Austin, acting for himself and Samuel M. Williams, contracted with this government, February 4, 1831, to colonize 800 foreign and Mexican families in the following grant. Beginning at a point on the La Vaca, ten leagues from the coast, the line shall run along the said river upstream to its western source, thence a straight line shall be drawn to the northwest till the Béxar-Nacogdoches road is reached, the road commonly known as the upper road, thence along the said road in a northwesterly direction to the Colorado, thence upstream along the right bank of the said river to the mouth of the Brazo Salado or Colorado which empties into this river fifteen leagues above the mouth of the Pecan or Nueves, thence a straight line shall be drawn to the northwest continuing to the divide of the Brazos and the Trinity, thence along this ridge southwest to the principal headwaters of the San Jacinto, thence down this river to the line that marks the ten litoral leagues, thence along this line east to the point of departure.

"José María de Aguirre, acting for His Excellency, General Vicente Filisola, contracted with this government, October 12, 1831, to colonize 600 foreign families in the following grant. Beginning at the point where the boundary of the grant made to General Arthur G. Wavell touches the line of the twenty league boundary reserve, the line shall follow along the limits of the said grant westward to its extremity, thence a straight line shall be drawn across several tributaries of the Trinity to the point where the grant of Stephen F. Austin adjoins the grant of David G. Burnet, thence along the limits of the latter to the Sabinas, thence leaving free the boundary reserve, the line shall ascend to the point of departure.

"Manuel Royuela and the foreigner, John C. Beales, contracted March 14, 1832, to colonize 200 foreign families in the land formerly granted to Stephen Julian Wilson, the new grant having the following limits. Beginning at a monument which shall be erected at the point of intersection of the 32nd parallel with the 102nd meridian west of London, a point which lies to the left or southwest of the grant made to Col. Reuben Ross, the line shall run west along parallel 32nd to the eastern limits of New Mexico, thence north along the dividing line of this state to a point twenty leagues south of the Arkansas, thence east to the 104th meridian, the limit of the grant petitioned by Col. Reuben Ross lying to the west, thence south to the point of departure.

"Juan Vicente Campos, attorney-at-law, as representative of the Mexican Company organized by Mariano Dominguez, Fortunato Soto, Juan Ramón Mila de la Roca, and Juan Carlos Beales, contracted March 1, 1832, to colonize 400 families in the following grant. Beginning at the head of the La Vaca the line shall run to the northwest along the boundary of the grant made to Stephen F. Austin and Samuel M. Williams to the road between Béxar and Nacogdoches, thence along this road northwest to the Colorado, thence upstream along the right bank of the said river for a distance of 15 leagues, thence a straight line shall be drawn parallel to the said road to the Guadalupe, thence downstream along the left bank of this river to a point five leagues southwest of the said road, thence a line shall be drawn to the east continuing to the point of departure.

"James Grant and John Charles Beales contracted, October 9, 1832, to colonize with 800 families the following grant. The survey shall begin by occupying the line which is reputed to be the dividing line between this state and Tamaulipas in the part traversed by the Nueces and the Bravo del Norte, thence upstream along the left bank of the said Bravo to the 24th meridian west of Washington, thence up along the said meridian to the 29th parallel, thence along this parallel to the Nueces, thence down the right bank of the said river to the point on the dividing line previously cited where the survey began. In addition to the land included within these boundaries, the empresarios were given whatever land was left over in the grant made to John L. Woodbury and Joseph Velhein after the 200 families which they contracted for had been settled. It is further understood that if Woodbury and Velhein should not settle the agreed number of families before the expiration of the time stipulated by their contract, all the land granted to them shall revert to the above-mentioned empresarios. The limits of the said grant being the following. Beginning at the point of intersection of the 31st parallel with the western limits of the colony of Robert Leftwitch which now belongs to Austin and Williams and which lies between the Colorado and the Brazos, the line shall run northwest to the point of intersection of the 32nd parallel with the limits of the said grant, thence the line shall run west adjoining the southern limits of the colony of John Cameron to the 100th meridian, thence down the said meridian to the point of intersection with the old Río Grande-Béxar road, thence along the said road to the Medina, thence up the said river along the right bank for a distance of ten leagues, thence a straight line shall be drawn east to the Guadalupe, thence up the said river along the right bank for a distance of ten leagues to the point where the lands of the colony of Col. Milan terminate, thence the line shall continue across the Colorado till it meets the western limits of the colony of Leftwitch at the point of departure.

"Fortunato Soto, Mexican citizen, and William Egerton, Englishman, contracted with the supreme government, January 10, 1834, to colonize 800 families in the grant hereinafter described. Beginning at the point of intersection of the 101st meridian with the Río Bravo del Norte, the line shall run along the said meridian south for a distance of fifteen leagues, thence west to the 102nd meridian, thence up across the Bravo and continuing for a distance of fifteen leagues, thence west to the 101st meridian, thence along this meridian down to the point of departure.

"The contracts of Green, De Witt, Frost Thorn, Robert Leftwitch, Benjamin R. Milam, and General Arthur G. Wavell, although cited in the description of the boundaries of some of the grants preceding are not given here because the time for their fulfillment having expired, they were declared null and void agreeable to article 8 of the law of March 24, 1825. The supreme government annulled these contracts March 21st, 1832, for failure to introduce the families stipulated."

If it is written in the uncertain and obscure book of destiny that we are some day to lose the department of Texas, let the fact remain buried in the inscrutable designs of fate as evidence of the unexampled perfidy displayed by the colonists and settlers and as testimony of ill-requited Mexican generosity. Our generosity knew none of the bounds which prudence dictates. It has been seen how through unwisely granted contracts one-tenth of the population of the United States could have found its way to Texas if the empresarios had had at their command adequate facilities for its transportation. As a result of this difficulty, speculators have thrown open the door to all the adventurers that can transport themselves at their own cost. They have even encouraged the very scum of the United States, those who because of debt or crimes found themselves obliged to flee from the rigor of the law in search of a more secure refuge in an unsettled country which was nominally governed by a well-regulated and organized body politic. Personal interest, therefore, demanded a complete ignorance of the moral character and actions of those who made their way to *this new sociological garden.* The grants gave rise to the scandalous practice of placing the lands on sale in the markets of the United States and, at times, of Europe. Lacking the necessary resources to carry out the proposed colonization of their grants, the speculators usually had no other recourse save the very lucrative one of selling the rights they had obtained so cheap. In proportion as the property thus acquired changed from hand to hand, the lenient terms upon which the grants had been made were lost sight of completely and the last holders, who had in no manner contracted any obligations whatsoever with the Mexican authorities, gave little or no heed to our civil laws or the moral obligations which devolve upon those who voluntarily incorporate themselves in any society. They recognized no law except that which the colonists themselves framed, never consulting the government of the state except to demand constantly more and more lands. Sovereign authority resided in the *ayuntamientos* [city councils] which were exclusively made up of the most influential members among the colonists themselves. It was these bodies who imposed taxes, distributed the land, and exercised independent and absolute authority in all matters. The most trivial duty imposed upon them by our laws was scarcely respected. The state of Coahuila from April, 1832, to August, 1834, received no other revenue from the colonists than the miserable sum of 1665 *pesos*, 1 *real* and 6 grains. It is to be particularly noticed that it was precisely during this period that over half of the territory of Texas was given to the colonists. The revenue of the public lands in the United States is one of the most valuable resources of the nation, the one that has been of greatest importance in funding their public debt. Well might we have followed their example to replenish our exhausted treasury by selling what we did not care to keep. But our blindness has been so great that we have given away lands that are a paradise. We have turned them over to our own enemies without exacting a penny or receiving anything else in exchange. We are forced to admit this truth by the facts that stare us squarely in the face. We are, today, reaping the fruit of our inadvertence.

The colonists organized their departments pretending to conform to the constitutions of the republic and of the state because these were somewhat analogous to the institutions of their own country and afforded them a basis upon which they could build a body of legislation entirely suited to and in perfect keeping with their habits and customs. Trial by jury was established for all civil and criminal cases by the law of the state of Coahuila and Texas of April 17, 1834. This only was lacking in order that nothing might be wanting to make Texas legislation identical with that of any part of the United States. I have cited this law because the Texans, in proclaiming their independence from the Mexican Republic, had the audacity to assert that we had exercised the unheard-of tyranny of not permitting them to resort to trial by jury in their legal procedure. They consider trial by jury the safeguard of the fundamental rights of man. The inhabitants of Texas are in the great majority natives of the United States, particularly of the western neighboring states. The land speculators of that country have come in great

part from among this class among which there are some who
exercise great influence in the politics of the United States because of their position and wealth. All of this has contributed
to create in Texas an Anglo-American colony rather than a
Mexican population. Neither their inclination, their manners,
their language, nor their politics tended to separate them from
their own people. All of this developed no sympathy for the
country of their adoption. The settlers planned to form an
entirely new association modeled by their customs, their habits,
and their convictions. What result could be expected? It was
natural that the colonists should organize themselves so as to
strengthen their common ties of union in order to turn their
combined strength against the country who had taken them to
her motherly bosom. Who does not discern in the simultaneous
and combined developments the working out of the ancient
policy of acquiring our territory? It is no longer necessary to
invoke the treaty by which Louisiana was purchased, it is no
longer necessary to excuse the ambitious policy of the American
government as the personal desire of Aaron Burr. It was super-
fluous for that government to subject him to the farce of a trial
from which he had the certainty of being absolved. It was not
necessary to take advantage of the enthusiasm of Bernardo Gutiérrez and of Alvarez Toledo to introduce into Texas 700 Anglo-
Americans with the pretext of supporting our independence. The
territory is now indisputably possessed by the Anglo-Americans.
Physical strength and moral prestige is now on their side. Of
what use is a vain and empty title of dominion to the Mexican
nation? Protected by our own neglect, encouraged by our frequent revolts, resistance grew and gained strength until one day
it was able to take the field openly against our nation.

In the first colonization laws, Texas settlers were granted
total exemption from duties. This privilege was extended for
two more years after the expiration of the time limit of the first
grant. Consequently, over a coastline that extended for more
than 150 leagues and all along the vast frontier, they introduced
not only what was needed for the development of the infant

colonies, but much more which was sent as contraband into the other departments of the republic. As a result, the colonists enjoyed a privilege which gradually developed in them the habit of not contributing in any way to the support of our national burdens. They went further and crippled our revenue by the ease with which they were permitted to engage in this illicit commerce. As long as matters continued thus, it was useless for the Americans residing in Texas to proclaim their independence, for they were independent in fact and it was even advantageous for them to claim that they were a part of the Mexican nation in order to enjoy the benefits conferred by the laws upon her sons. But it was evident that the moment the Mexicans awoke from their lethargy and attempted to consolidate their dominions by means of those measures to which all nations resort in similar cases, they would meet with a decided opposition which would not hesitate to resort to arms. The colonists had taken care to provide themselves with arms for their defense.

The first ten years of our independence went by without a check being placed against the concealed policy of conquest which brought the Anglo-Americans to the fertile and uninhabited fields of Texas. We may go further and say that the very movement was ominously accelerated by ourselves. The colonization laws could not have been more liberal nor could our inadvertence been greater. The belief that our powerful neighbor was our best friend unfortunately grew apace. It was thought that in order to create a system fundamentally American as opposed to European governments, the United States were called upon, because of their having been the first to gain their independence and because of their energetic character and their growing power, to lead the alliance of American republics. First, the advanced scouts, then the hidden spies, and lastly the accredited agents collaborated in rapidly promoting their ulterior motives. To Mexico they sent a skillful minister, one thoroughly familiar with the customs in the provinces that once were Spanish colonies, who knew intimately the fine art of political intrigue, who read our weaknesses and was not slow

to take advantage of them. This able diplomat did as much good
to his country as harm to ours. To-day, he never speaks of our
affairs and of our leading men without a compassionate glance
of disdain. But his services were not needed, for by the time
he came the iniquitous work was consummated.

With the astonishing increase of population in the United
States as a result of the extraordinary immigration from Europe,
the government began to feel that the permanence of the Indian
tribes in the territories they formerly occupied was an embarrassment. Their permanence was guaranteed by sacred treaties
and solemn agreements. Nowhere else on the face of the globe
is the feeling of the white race stronger against those which,
in its pride, it designates as colored. This was sufficient for the
expulsion of the men of bronze, the redmen, and for the despoli-
ation of their property. This policy was all the more advisable
because in the lands occupied by some of these tribes deposits
of the fatal and coveted metal had been discovered. Furthermore, the Indians had cleared the woods, and the lands were now
ready for cultivation. What was there to restrain Anglo-
American greed? Nothing! Might was on their side, the miserable Indians had nothing but their weakness. Treaties have
weight only as long as it suits the most powerful of the negotia-
tors to observe them. In the United States where the governments of Europe are so loudly denounced because they favor
the strong and oppress the weak, no consideration is shown for
the Indians whenever the interest and progress of the nation
is concerned. In 1830 it was definitely decided to expel the
Indian tribes from Georgia and Alabama. "The circumstance
which makes the expulsion of these unfortunate wretches from
their native haunts more lamentable," says Mrs. Trollope, "is
that they were rapidly assimilating our civilization. Their life
no longer consisted of aimless wanderings in search of game,
they had become tillers of the soil. The tyrannic hand of brutal
power has not driven them from their hunting grounds as before,
nor from their favorite streams and the sacred tombs of their
ancestors, but it has dispoiled them of their homes, which, as

they ascended the scale of our civilization, they have learned to beautify. It has driven them from the newly broken fields which were already their pride, it has deprived them of the fruit of their labor and the bread they earned by the sweat of their brow." And to what purpose? Only to add a few miles of uninhabited lands to the outskirts of the United States. It is not my purpose in relating this recent catastrophe that has just befallen the primitive dwellers of this continent to place upon the United States the curse of having exterminated an innocent people and of having driven the survivors to unknown deserts. The world has passed judgment upon this classic example of injustice and it is not for me to excite the sensibility of those who sorrow for the misfortunes of humanity. What I aim to point out clearly is that at the same time that the Indians were despoiled of their territory, it was planned to deprive the Mexican Republic of its own. All these tribes have been moved to territories along our frontier because, realizing its weak defence, it has been foreseen that the Indians will pass into our territory, freeing the United States of the redmen which they have always considered a burden. In 1834, Samuel Houston, to-day the president of the would-be republic of Texas, tried to introduce the Creeks, not a few of whom now live in the department. The Coshates settled southeast of Nacogdoches, the Chactaws to the southwest, the Caddos to the northeast, and the Cherokees, Saginaws, Creeks, and Kickapoos to the north. Colonel Almonte, who has visited that territory, affirms that these Indians live in *rancherias,* till the soil, raise cattle, and are very much advanced in civilization. If our government should try to attract them, giving them the lands they desire, instructing them in the fundamental principles of our politics, and explaining to them the equal rights which all men enjoy agreeable to our laws, regardless of color or race, they would doubtless become our friends. Thus, those who have been driven by inexorable fate in its inexplicable destiny might become our useful allies.

Greater still is the astonishment of the civilized world to see the United States maintain the institution of slavery with its cruel laws to support it and propagate it, at a time when the other nations of the world have agreed to cooperate in the philanthropic enterprise of eradicating this blot and shame of the human race. Don Lorenzo de Zavala in his *Trip to the United States,* a work which he seems to have written to laud them to the stars while depreciating his country to the lowest depths, at a time when perhaps he was already meditating his dark treason, cannot resist the natural instinct of repulsion inspired by the contrast of the humane and truly liberal policy of Mexico and the cruel and sanguinary one of the United States in regard to the slaves. "In crossing from the Mexican Republic to the states of our sister Republic," says Zavala, "the philosopher cannot help but feel the contrast presented by the two countries, nor can he fail to experience a grateful feeling for those who abolished this degrading traffic in human flesh, removing from our midst every vestige of so humiliating a spectacle of misery." As a matter of fact, without having proclaimed as pompously as the United States the rights of man, we have respected them better by abolishing all distinctions of class or race and considering as our brothers all creatures created by our common father. The land speculators of Texas have tried to convert it into a mart of human flesh where the slaves of the south might be sold and others from Africa might be introduced, since it is not possible to do it directly through the United States. "It seems," says Mrs. Trollope, "that it is a general and deep-rooted opinion throughout the United States that the black race cannot be trusted. According to the prevailing opinion of the country, fear is the only force that moves a slave. It is not strange, therefore, that these poor wretches should act in keeping with such a policy." This mutual distrust, this reciprocal fear between master and slave will some day result in the freedom of more than three million men, a fact to which the thinking men of the neighboring republic are not blind. The example furnished by the magnanimous and just policy recently adopted by England will doubtless exercise a great influence.

She has liberated her slaves taking upon herself the indemnization of their value to the masters. What will be the course followed by the United States? To maintain and encourage this institution as long as possible and when the fatal hour of destiny arrives which is to destroy this tyrannous and opprobrious system, to treat them as the Indians, *driving them into Mexican territory also.* Fortunately my opinion is confirmed by the speech of Mr. North, president of a college in New York. "It is impossible," he says, "to tolerate any longer the abuses of the institution of slavery as practised in some of our states. A domestic insurrection is not necessary, nor the intervention on the part of foreign governments to abolish a system so repugnant to our sentiments and contrary to all our institutions. Public opinion has already condemned it, and the moral forces of the nation will sooner or later bring about its total abolition. But the question that arises now is: On what conditions can liberty be restored to this oppressed class? In other countries the two races have become amalgamated and thus incorporated into a homogenous social group. Our case is not the same, however. Our slaves when free will remain to the third, fourth, and even the thousandth generation the same as they are to-day, that is, they will maintain themselves as a distinct, unfortunate, and wretched social group. Consequently, when their chains are removed, and this will doubtless take place soon, either simultaneously or gradually, it is evident that this country will find itself flooded with a population as shiftless as their condition is deplorable, a population which, as it increases, will weaken our strength, and whose very numbers will bring crime and poverty in its wake. Whether as slaves or as freemen they will always constitute a burden upon us. Why, then, should we hesitate for a single moment to encourage their deportation from our country?"

The arguments of North are so urgent in their appeal that he is not in sympathy with the establishment of a negro colony upon the African coast, a plan that has served only to distract the philosophic spirit of some of the friends of humanity but which can do no more. It is upon Texas and perhaps upon New Mexico and the two Californias that the anxious eyes of those who even now are giving their attention to the future destinies of the colored race rest. As in the United States nothing is done without a preconceived plan, and since everybody works by common accord as if by an admirable instinct for the realization of the ends pursued, it is incredible that the slow working out of the means by which some day certain difficulties whose transcendental importance has been fully realized will be solved should have been ignored in their reckoning. Thus we see the concurrence of an infinite number of interests of the United States converging for the stimulation of their policy of expansion. The party spirit that directed the bloody diatribes against our administration of 1830 cannot detract from the merit that accrues to it for having given its serious consideration to the situation in Texas and for having attempted to raise a dam to restrain the torrent that threatened to engulf us. By its resolute policy it succeeded at least in removing the mask from the face of our enemies, disclosing with incontestable and self-evident facts the true condition of affairs and opening the eyes of those who in their good faith had been deceived. The real policy of the United States, their ambitious projects, and the determination of the colonists to second such a policy was clearly revealed. The law of April 6, 1830, is an honorable distinction for those who framed it. It is true that the remedy was applied too late, but it was instrumental in precipitating the crisis before the strength of the colonists grew to such proportions as to make all opposition difficult, costly, and useless. In my opinion—and I say this with all sincerity—it is beyond all doubt that had not that administration been removed, had not the forces destined to make Mexican law respected in Texas been distracted from their aim, that territory would have been inseparably united to our country. The colonists were not as yet in a position to take up arms in open rebellion. The Mexican forces under the command of the distinguished General Terán, would have made our sovereignty effective to the very margins of the Sabine. But

God willed that our revolutionary ardor should reappear in 1832, and this year marks the accentuation of the imminent danger that threatens us with the loss of one of our richest departments.

After the exemption from payment of duties granted to the colonies in Texas expired, steps were taken to establish customs houses and to protect them with small military detachments. General Terán, in November, 1831, personally proceeded to Texas and with the prudence and moderation which characterized him, availed himself of the means at his command to stall the evils which he saw on every hand. The significance of the proclamation made in the town of Liberty, by which the *ayuntamiento* of that town dictated certain measures that are the prerogatives of our sovereign government, did not escape his penetrating mind. He knew before hand, in view of the rebellion promoted by Edwards in Nacogdoches in his attempt to establish the so-called Freedonian Republic, that there existed among the settlers a secret design to withdraw from the Mexican union. He pretended not to see what was apparent everywhere, taking advantage of the time gained to organize and locate the customs houses and to fortify the points most accessible to contraband trade. The alarm of the colonists at these measures and the violation of all our laws on the part of the ships engaged in this trade are unexplainable. The colonists declared that their rights were profaned by the presence of the revenue officers and the Mexican soldiers that were detailed to support them in the execution of their duties. The citizens of Anáhuac committed several outrages against the officers and the garrison of that town. When Col. Ugartechea tried to defend his position, the ungrateful John Austin, with a considerable number of armed men recruited in Brazoria, attacked and defeated him. The rebels then made their way to Nacogdoches, where the brave General José de las Piedras was killed.

Texas remained independent in fact, and the colonists tranquilly resumed possession, continuing their contraband trade. Since Tampico, which was the base from which General Terán drew his principal resources, had fallen into the hands of the revolutionists, he was obliged to turn his attention to the more immediate danger and was, therefore, unable to mete out with merited severity the chastisement which the Texans deserved. The fear of the loss of Texas weighed heavily upon his heart and, foreseeing the bitter and disastrous consequences to his beloved country, in a moment of despair he shot himself, July 3, 1832. Though both religion and society condemn suicide, the strong man who in a moment of delirium caused by the unbearable sufferings of his country won the name of the Mexican Cursius, will always be worthy of the compassion and tears of his countrymen. From that very moment the traitors of Texas took off their mask, believing, in their boundless pride, that Mexico possessed no other man of character capable of imposing our law upon them and restraining them in their daring. It was at this time that Don José Antonio Mejía appeared before Matamoros with a force which had embarked at Tampico. Although in a ridiculous agreement negotiated with Colonel José Mariano Guerra, he pledged himself to maintain the integrity of our national territory and to march to the subjection of the rebellious settlers the only result was to dissipate uselessly the resources that might have been used for that important purpose.

The colonists, having heard of the progress made by the revolution of Veracruz, decided to support it in order to justify, by these means, their rebellion. In the resolutions drawn up in Brazoria on June 10, the second article reads as follows:— *Approved: that we view with the greatest and deepest interest the Plan promoted by the heroic and distinguished General Santa Anna and the firm resistance offered to the numerous usurpations and infractions committed by the present administration against the institutions of our adopted and beloved country.* I have cited this article in order that it may be compared with the resolutions adopted in 1835 against General Santa Anna himself in which it is also stated that he has attacked the *institutions of their adopted and beloved country.* It is thus that they have skilfully taken advantage of all our political disturbances, making us, as a matter of fact, their tool and the butt of their criminal designs. The changes at last brought about by the revolution of 1832 filled them with joy, both because they succeeded in having our troops removed and because the mania of condemning every thing that had been done or that had ever been thought of by the previous administration having become general, the more prudent precautionary measures were abandoned. Even Article 11 of the wise law of April 6, 1830, was abrogated. These facts clearly point out whose is the immense responsibility that weighs upon the agents or accomplices of our national misfortune.

In April, 1833, a convention met in San Felipe de Austin, which drew up a constitution to erect Texas into a separate, independent and sovereign government, apart from Coahuila. Stephen F. Austin, the most prominent colonist as well as the first of rebels, was commissioned to proceed to this capital to prove to the government that the colony was strong and powerful enough to stand by itself, the provisions of the law of May 7, 1823, regarding separate statehood having been fulfilled. With the hypocrisy that characterized him, Austin presented himself and tried to put in motion all the influences which his audacity suggested. Inadvertently, certain expressions which amounted to threats escaped him and revealed his determination of supporting his petition by force if *what he called his rights* were not granted. When rebuked for his insolence he excused himself by stating that he was not thoroughly familiar with the language of the indulgent Mexicans. But his perfidy led him to issue instructions, on October 2nd, to the authorities of Texas to organize themselves as an independent government, against the wishes of the supreme government of the republic. The *Ayuntamiento* of Béxar not only replied to him indignantly, but also notified the government of his plans, as a result of which an order for his arrest was issued December 21, 1833, and executed on January 2, 1834. When Austin was taken back to Mexico City, he was placed at the disposal of the Commandancy General because of his military rank of colonel. The supreme court, however, declared that his case fell under the jurisdiction of the district court. This tribunal showed him every consideration and ordered him placed in liberty on bond, finally releasing him agreeable to the act of amnesty. General Santa Anna showed great interest in his favor. Certain unavoidable reflections arise from the facts related. At the time when Stephen Austin was promoting and encouraging the independence of Texas, the Mexican republic was under a federal government, its administration favored this system and carried it out with the greatest exaggeration. Why, then, was the project of making Texas independent conceived under such circumstances? It is evident that the subsequent rebellion seized upon the change in government merely as a pretext. The arrest and imprisonment of a man whom the nation had favored constantly was the inevitable outcome of his own criminal conduct. To justify the Texas rebellion as a result of this judicial case is the same as to admit that the colonists did not recognize a single principle of our legislation and that the only bond that could have held them united to the Mexican nation was the disregard of all their crimes.

Some of the Mexican settlers of Nacogdoches communicated to General Cós that the authorities of that place followed no law except their whim, and that in order to cause dissatisfaction among the Mexican colonists, foreign laws were enforced without paying any attention to those of our country. They stated that five Mexican citizens and a religious from Zacatecas, Fray Antonio Díaz, had recently been assassinated, all as a result of the hatred felt against the Mexican nation. The government, aware of these outrages, ordered the immediate enlistment of 500 men, of which 300, under the command of Colonel Ugartechea, marched to that department with the coming of spring to enforce our laws and to reestablish order in every sense of the word. It was provided that a reserve of 200 men should remain in Béxar for any contingency that might arise. For the purpose of cooperating with the revenue officers and the constituted authorities, a small detachment under the command of Captain Antonio Tenorio proceeded to Anáhuac. But the

colonists for whom contraband trade had become a habit refused
to recognize José González as administrator of the customs houses
and they denied Tenorio all supplies for the thirty-four men of
his company. From January 22nd on, the colonists had brazenly
manifested their determination not to pay any duties whatsoever.
They even went as far as to threaten him by stating that in
order to prevent the establishment of a permanent detachment of
Mexican troops, they would call to arms even the boys under
age. It was soon discovered that the vacant lands were being
sold without the consent of the national authorities to the adventurers who came in on every side, and that contraband trade
was generally carried on in all the ports and along the whole
frontier. In Matagorda, Santa Anna, and González, there were
considerable deposits of foreign merchandise and goods, none of
which had paid any duties. The revenue officers, with no other
backing than the small military force detailed to support them,
went to seize the ships that had just arrived at La Vaca. Here
they were promptly tied and the cargo was unloaded before
their very eyes. In order to foster the plan for a general uprising,
the news of which was publicly known, they tried to involve the
Tahuayase Indians and the Comanches, asking them to fall upon
San Antonio de Béxar and Bahía del Espiritu Santo, acting in
combination with the colonists who were to attack the detachment
of Tenorio. Early in the morning, on May 4th, the lumber that
was to be used to repair Davis's Fort was set on fire and there
was no investigation instituted to bring the culprits to justice.
This was but the prelude of a still greater conflagration already
being planned. Finally, on June 29th, the people of Anáhuac
rebelled, supported by 200 armed adventurers and two pieces
of artillery commanded by William Barret Travis. This band,
which was vastly superior to the detachment of Captain Tenorio,
succeeded in capturing him. The trying circumstances to which
this efficient officer was reduced, forced him to surrender his arms
with the exception of twelve rifles, but he succeeded in being
allowed to depart freely, receiving the necessary supplies for the
purpose. Fearful of the consequences of their small and insig-

nificant triumph, the rebels appointed a commission composed of eleven men to go to see General Cós to explain the circumstances. He replied with dignity, offering to respect the faithful and peaceful colonists, demanding the punishment of the instigators of the mutiny, and asking that Travis be turned over to him. The political chief of the Brazos district facilitated the escape of the latter, and even allowed four individuals who had captured the correspondence dispatched by General Cós to Captain Tenorio to go unpunished.

The legislature of Coahuila and Texas had authorized the governor, Agustin Viezca, to remove the supreme government of the State to the city of Béxar. Viezca had promised to comply with the law of March 31st providing for the reduction of the militia, and manifested a willingness to abide by the orders of the supreme government, all of which inspired confidence and concealed his ulterior designs; but on the 30th he fled to Texas. Therefore, the commandant general was obliged to issue orders for his arrest. This was executed on June 6th but, soon after, the prisoner again succeeded in escaping. It was not to be expected that the colonists, who were fully aware of their interests, would fail to take advantage of this excellent opportunity afforded them by unforeseen circumstances. They availed themselves of the incident to give their criminal conduct a veneer of legality. They immediately called a meeting at Columbia which appointed John A. Wharton, W. D. C. Hall, H. Smith, J. F. Perry, J. H. Bell, S. Whiting, G. B. McKinstry, W. C. White, P. D. McNeel, F. Bingham, J. A. Phelps, Edwin Waller, E. Andrews, J. P. Caldwell, E. G. Head, and Bird B. Caller [3] as a committee to determine the most convenient policy to be adopted in view of the supposed absence of a constituted government. The commission presented a plan consisting of eight articles in which very plausible arguments were advanced. The third of these, however, advised the establishment of a provisional independent government. This had always been the object of their aspirations. As in

[3] Cf. W. Brown, History of Texas, I, 293.

justice bound, General Cós rejected the creation of authorities
not recognized by the constituted government and pointed out
the errors under which the colonists labored in their biased
analysis regarding the general condition of the country. The
commandant general praised the peaceful conduct of some of the
citizens who condemned the disturbance of San Felipe and recommended to the political chief the reestablishment of law and order
and the consequent punishment of those who had the audacity to
attack the Mexican detachment. The lack of foresight with
which the authorities of Coahuila decided to move to Texas is
most surprising. They failed to realize that the department of
Texas was in general disorder and that the design of the colonists
was obviously separation from our country. In all justice
to patriotic motives, I will never admit that Mexican officials fell
so low as to be involved as accomplices in a plot to dismember
our territory. However, their indiscreet and ill-directed zeal
caused them to contribute to the success of the rebellion in a most
effective manner. In 1833, the colonists anxiously sought their
separation from Coahuila, alleging injustices on the part of its
authorities which were never committed nor proved. Yet now,
circumstances having changed, they justify their insurrection by
the abuses which they claim the national government has committed against those same hated authorities. It is necessary to
close one's eyes not to perceive that no other end has been sought
than final separation from the Mexican nation, the contradictory
reasons with which they have attempted to justify their continuous insurrections being advanced merely to fool those who
have not studied and consequently do not understand their restless character.

Instead of returning to make a report to the government on
the mission entrusted to him before His Majesty, the king of the
French, as duty and common decency demanded, Lorenzo Zavala
made his way directly to Texas from the United States in the
schooner San Felipe. The death of this Mexican who, because
of his great talent and vast knowledge might have been the glory
and pride of his country would keep me from referring to his

censurable conduct if the obligation which I have taken upon myself did not force me to recount the facts as they took place. According to the information of James H. C. Miller, Zavala made his way to Columbia where, together with Williams, Johnson, and Baker, he encouraged the decision taken by the colonists to revolt. He exaggerated to them the impotence of the republic to oppose their plans and he himself began to recruit troops and to organize the insurrection. History reserves a place in its pages for Zavala, but this place is the same one that has been accorded to Count Julian, Monk, the American General Benedict Arnold, and to Moreau. A glorious death in battle did not save the last of these from the shame of having used his genius against the interest of his country. *Quis talia fando . . . temperet a lacrymis?* [4]

It was inevitable that at the moment of setting out upon an enterprise of such magnitude, fear should constrain some of the colonists in spite of the unanimous approval of the decision taken, and the *ayuntamiento* of González, therefore, declared that it had implicit confidence in the good will of Congress and the President toward Texas; that it would refuse to obey the call of the governor against national troops, and that it would keep aloof from taking a part in the civil dissensions of the republic. This conduct, though insincere and of doubtful nature as shown by the subsequent acts of that *ayuntamiento* and its inhabitants, received the approval of the supreme government because it supported the idea of obedience and adherence by offering to firmly withstand the base requests of the rebels. On August 12th, the supreme government replied to the *ayuntamiento,* giving assurances that the National Congress would consider the needs of the inhabitants of Texas when it took up the constitutional reforms petitioned by almost all sections of the country, and that it would then provide a suitable remedy. The executive gladly assured them of his cooperation, promising to take the corresponding measures, provided that the colonists showed the good judgment and temperance which their adoption of this country as their own

[4] Who by prophesying such things . . . could refrain from tears?

presupposed. It reminded them that they must abide by the reforms made to the fundamental laws of the nation by the majority of its inhabitants, which the government would be obliged to maintain at all costs, lending its protection to the peaceful inhabitants and meting out exemplary punishment to those who promoted dissensions. The *ayuntamiento* of Gonzáles showed its appreciation by joining the rebels against the troops that were sent to take possession of a piece of artillery that was there for no purpose.

A meeting was held in Nacogdoches, September 14, presided over by Samuel Houston who in June, 1834, planned to invade our territory at the head of the war-like Creeks and who today is acting as the president of Texas. In this meeting where, as it was natural to suppose, they spoke of violated rights, of unfulfilled promises, and of the need of shaking off the detestable yoke, nine articles were approved, all of which I faithfully transcribe here because the transactions of that day may and should be considered as an actual declaration of independence.

"Resolved: 1st. That we are well disposed and determined to maintain peace and the best harmony, and that we shall not depart from this conduct unless we are compelled by force to defend and preserve our lives, our property, our liberty and our sacred rights.

"2nd. That having sworn loyalty and the observance of the Constitution and the laws under which we migrated to this country we promise religiously to fulfill our oath at all cost.

3rd. That we believe it is proper to submit this matter to all the inhabitants of Texas in order that the general opinion and judgment of the people may be ascertained.

"4th. That an election be held to select seven commissioners who may represent the rights of the Texans in the general assembly or convention to be called for the purpose and which is to meet in Washington or any other place that may be deemed convenient.

"5th. That Messrs. Solomon R. Peck and Whitaker be appointed judges to hold the said election, to count the votes and to issue the corresponding credentials to those who may be elected in order that these may in turn appoint other judges to do likewise in the other districts of the litoral of Texas. In case a vacancy occurs due to absence or any other motive it shall be the duty of the commission of vigilance or public security to fill the vacancy.

"6th. That this election be held in the city of Nacogdoches and in all the other places of the litoral of Texas the first day of October next, at ten o'clock in the morning.

"7th. That this assembly proceed to the appointment of a commission to be known as the commission of vigilance or public security, to be composed of William G. Logan, Vicente Cordoba, Richard Sparks, Whitaker, Joseph Durst, William Elliot, James Bradshaw, Solomon R. Peck, and Robert A. Irion.

"8th. That the duty of the commission shall be to find out and communicate immediately whatever news they can, to attend to all matters, and to give an account of everything as often as may be deemed proper:

"9th. That we are in sincere accord with the spirit and sentiments expressed in the foregoing resolutions." [5] John Allen proposed, and it was agreed, to name election judges for the election of a colonel to form a regiment.

To support the resistance offered by González to the delivery of the piece of artillery, a party of over a thousand men assembled at San Felipe, and Travis at the head of two hundred men and with two cannon attacked Goliad the night of the 9th of October, succeeding in capturing the commandant, Captain Salariego, and a small detachment which General Cós had left there on his way to Béxar. Hostilities were now generally recognized and, the colonists having declared unanimously for the insurrection, there was nothing left for the commandant general to do except to repel force with force and to uphold vigorously the rights of the nation and the decorum of her arms.

[5] Careful search for the original of these resolutions was made but it could not be found, either among published documents or in the Béxar and Nacogdoches archives.

The consultation called by the meeting of Nacogdoches, met in November and definitely declared for the independence of Texas from the magnanimous nation that had given shelter to the colonists, who had protected them with just and liberal laws, who had given them her best lands, and whom she had favored even more than her own children. The following decree was adopted by the convention;

"Whereas, General López de Santa Anna and other military chieftains have, by force of arms, overthrown the federal institutions of Mexico and dissolved the social compact which existed between Texas and other members of the Mexican confederacy; now the good people of Texas, availing themselves of their natural rights.

Solemnly Declare

"1st. That they have taken up arms in defense of their rights and liberties, which were threatened by the encroachments of military despots, and in defense of the republican principles of the federal constitution of Mexico of 1824.

"2nd. That Texas is no longer morally or civilly bound by the compact of union; yet, stimulated by the generosity and sympathy common to a free people, they offer their support and assistance to such of the Mexican confederacy, as will take up arms against military despotism.

"3rd. That they do not acknowledge that the present authorities of the nominal Mexican republic have the right to govern within the limits of Texas.

"4th. That they will not cease to carry on war against said authorities whilst their troops are within the limits of Texas.

"5th. That they hold it to be their right, during the disorganization of the federal system and the reign of despotism, to withdraw from the union, to establish an independent government, or to adopt such measures as they may deem best calculated to protect their rights and liberties; but that they will continue faithful to the Mexican government so long as that nation is governed by the constitution and laws that were formed for the government of the political association.

"6th. That Texas is responsible for the expenses of her armies now in the field.

"7th. That the public faith of Texas is pledged for the payment of any debts contracted by her agents.

"8th. That she will reward by donations in lands, all who volunteer their services in her present struggle, and receive them as citizens.

"These declarations we solemnly avow to the world and call God to witness their truth and sincerity, and invoke defeat and disgrace upon our heads should we prove guilty of duplicity. B. T. Archer, president.—P. B. Dexter, Secretary." The declaration was signed by the 57 members of the consultation.

The despicable adventurers admitted without disguise in this document that the constitution of 1824 had been invoked merely to gain time and to secure the sympathy of the Mexicans who were sincere in their adherence to this document; that it had been but a device thought of in their weakness, while opinion in favor of absolute independence became general; that they awaited only the help expected in response to the efforts of the commission sent to the United States by the promoters of the disturbances in May; and that they counted upon the supplies secured by Stephen Austin on his own personal credit. The victory obtained by forces three times as numerous as those of the isolated and weak detachments of our government encouraged them in their pride and made them believe that Mexico was unable to bring into the field a strong force to oppose their designs. Who constituted Texas an arbiter of the destinies of the nation, of which it is only a very insignificant part? This province might have had the right to change her system of government, but the exercise of such a privilege did not give her the right to confer or pass the right on to other states against the determined and unanimous will of the nation. But when the Texans proclaimed their independence, they made evident the low esteem in which they held our laws, and, having dared to declare that all civil and moral obligations on their part to maintain the union had ceased, they now offered to help any who might follow them in their example in an attempt to induce other departments to withdraw from the national authority which they called a military despotism. They referred to the officials of the republic as nominal authorities and declared that they would make war upon them as long as Mexican troops remained within the limits of Texas. And for what reason? In order *to establish an independent government, or to adopt the measures they might deem best calculated to protect their rights and liberties.* These words with a purposely doubtful meaning provide for the case of annexation, ever the object of the United States, the aim of all the intrigues of their cabinet which has manipulated everything to the present time, extending its protection to the most scandalous rebellion of our day. It is astonishing that those who, disregarding Mexican law, have opened a vast market of human flesh in Texas should dare to acclaim the sacred name of liberty. It is astonishing that those who have lived entirely without restraint should now clamor for their rights. They have not respected a single one of the laws that govern any well-regulated society. It is strange that those who have usurped the sovereign power of the nation should speak of property rights. In a word, it is incomprehensible that they should sponsor a war without quarter against the country that gave them lands, good homes, generous laws, and the blessings of their own civilization.

While Stephen Austin remained in this capital, he lost no time in establishing relations with the discontented, and even made overtures to outlaws such as from time to time disturb the peace of the republic with no clearly defined political principles and regardless of the powers that be, merely to violate personal property and lay waste the country where they operate. In the highlands of Aguililla a messenger was intercepted with letters from Austin to Gordiano Guzmán in which he proposed to him to join the uprising which was finally put down by the zeal of the ever watchful general Paredes. It is evident that if the Texas leader resorted to such unworthy means, in order to inflict losses

upon our country, he did not neglect others less censurable to
prevent the forces of the republic from reaching Texas and
maintaining our sovereignty by distracting their attention with
disturbances nearer at hand and apparently more urgent. It was
in the United States that he perfected the plans for the proposed
insurrection, and it is even known that he had relations with
persons of the highest rank who have since helped him in putting
his project into execution. No sooner did he land in Texas than
he was proclaimed general-in-chief. It was necessary for the
new leader to engage in a signal campaign to justify his appointment, increase his popularity, and attain the ultimate aim of his
desire. Therefore, he immediately gathered what forces he could
and set out for Béxar. Realizing that the force at his command
was insufficient to cope with a general rebellion, an incident not
foreseen, General Cós concentrated his troops in that city for
the purpose of defending himself. The garrison, which had to
stand against a force four times its number, was very unfortunate
in all its sallies. After a fifty-day siege, during which time supplies and munitions failed to reach the besieged due to the distance from the nearest base, the poor transportation facilities,
and the unfavorable season of the year, the town was forced to
capitulate. The efforts of Col. Ugartechea, who attempted by
forced marches, traveling as much as twenty-three leagues in one
day, to take reenforcements and supplies from Laredo to the
besieged, were unavailing, and the city surrendered on December 13.

The invasion of Tampico, led by General José Antonio Mejía
is really but a phase of the history of the Texas campaign. On
November 13, two officers, who had previously had an understanding, proclaimed the federal system, and by surprise took
possession of the artillery base. Fortunately, a company from
the active battalion of Tuxpan dispatched by the Minister of
War, arrived just at that moment, and with its help and the support of the sensible portion of the garrison, Commandant Gómez
succeeded in reestablishing order. The afternoon of the 14th,
three ships flying the national flag were sighted. Aboard them

were 200 adventurers who had embarked in New Orleans. Through the treachery of Col. Ortega, who commanded the fort at the bar, they succeeded in capturing it. Early in the morning of the following day they led a furious attack upon the town but were repelled and completely defeated by the well-organized defence and the heroic conduct of the troops and the citizens who were indignant when they found out that the enemy were foreigners, even though they were led in the charge by two spurious Mexicans. The pirates reembarked, leaving behind them a few prisoners upon whose heads fell the rigor of the law of nations, after the requisite investigations prescribed by law had been put into practice. Where is the Mexican who does not feel his blood boil at the injustice of this expedition, organized in the port of a nation that calls herself our friend, for the avowed purpose of assassinating our countrymen, violating their rights, and upsetting public order? If there are laws in the United States prohibiting such expeditions, it was a perfidy not to have enforced them. If such laws do not exist, that country is one of the most dangerous on the face of the globe, for no nation can feel safe against attacks which the executive of that country has no power to prevent or condemn. What the *Commercial Herald* says with regard to this and similar aggressions is particularly noteworthy and does honor to the truly independent spirit of its editor.

"What would be thought," he says, "if a group of men held a meeting and decided to proceed openly to raise and equip a body of troops in the United States with the avowed purpose of sending them, their arms, and their baggage to Ireland to cooperate with the Irish in their declaration of independence against England? Better still, in order to give a stronger example of the principle involved, what would we say if in Haiti, a public meeting decided to arm and equip a body of troops to be sent against us for the purpose of helping our colored population to shake off the yoke of slavery? Let us go a step beyond and ask what would be the feeling of indignation amongst us if we were to read in one of the dailies of Canada the proposal to raise a body of troops destined to help the Cherokees and to aid them in defending their territory against the efforts of Georgia? By placing ourselves in the position of the Mexicans, we should likewise realize how they look upon the conduct observed by our citizens in the United States who are trying to raise troops to help those who have rebelled against the constituted authorities of their provinces." Nothing need be added to this elucidating and impartial summary.

Finally a day arrived when, seduced by the happy coincidence of a thousand unforeseen circumstances, the Texas colonists sundered all ties and openly declared themselves independent from the Mexican nation. Their delegates assembled in Washington, in the District of Brazoria, drew up a declaration of independence, March 2, 1836. This is but the admission of a fact and the carrying out of a plan long since recognized. An attempt is made, however, to support this action by an astonishing jumble of impostures. It is stated that the Texans were invited and admitted subject to the observance of a contract by which assurances were given to maintain the written constitution; that this having been annulled, all their obligations ceased. Our country, with ill-advised generosity, acceded to their requests and took them into our midst because they asked and desired to be taken in. We have observed that at the time when the first grants were made the government of the nation was a monarchy and that subsequently several changes have been effected in the government none of which justify them in refusing their obedience because no specific form of government was stipulated in the contracts. An insolent minority cannot arrogate to itself the right of determining the form of government of the republic in violation of the wishes of the great majority. If such a minority was not in accord with the changes effected it was free to leave the country whenever the obligations imposed upon it became too great a burden or a menace to its liberties.

The rebels allege as the principal complaint that they were not permitted to organize themselves as an independent state of the union, governed by a constitution framed and designed by themselves. Granting the stability of the federal system, it was still very questionable whether Texas already possessed the necessary elements and resources to be organized as an independent entity. Furthermore, we cannot ignore the natural distrust which such a forward step inevitably inspired, when we consider the well-known aim of all the petitions of the colonists. A change in the administration of the country having taken place, the Texans should have waited the results of the principal innovations planned, in view of the fact that congress had raised Texas to the rank of a department, separting it from Coahuila to that extent.

They accuse us of having neglected primary education in Texas. This charge clearly shows their bad faith. As is well known, education is left by our laws to the respective *ayuntamientos*. The city councils of Texas not only exercised all the prerogatives allowed them but assumed many that are foreign to such bodies. Why then did they not look after education if it interested them so deeply? Furthermore, the Texas *ayuntamientos* imposed taxes and used their revenues without the least interference on the part of Mexican officials. If they failed to use them for the education of their children, it was clearly their fault. The people of Texas were represented in the legislature of the state. It was there that they should have presented their demands regarding this subject as they did with regard to lands, the prime object of their desires, the obvious aim of their insatiable greed.

The colonists bitterly complain of their having been sacrificed to the interest of Coahuila. This is but a typical untruth. The officers of the state inclined rather to the opposite extreme, indiscreetly favoring the Texans by assenting to their endless petitions. In the course of the preceding pages, the grants of lands made to them have been noted. It is particularly noteworthy, however, that among the grantees there were only two or three citizens of Coahuila, whose grants were in general usurped by other empresarios. The colonists sometimes curse Coahuila for her supposed injustices to them, and at others they curse the nation for its arbitrary acts against Coahuila.

The charges of oppression and tyranny brought against our military officers are false and unfounded. Far from this, our soldiers have, on the contrary, been exposed to the same libelous charges as all our public officers. They have been disarmed and driven from their posts while holding them in the discharge of their duties. Every attempt made to enforce law has been pointed out by the colonists as an attack, while the repression of crime has been called an insult and classed as an attempt upon individual liberties in their newly invented dictionary. Even now they maintain that trade has been hampered by unheard-of restrictions and vexations. During the first seven years they were exempt from paying duties on all goods imported into Texas. After the expiration of this privilege, there has been nothing but contraband trade along the entire coast and the whole frontier.

The prohibition against the erection of places of worship and the practice of other cults than the Roman Catholic was the law of the land at the time when the colonists came and they agreed to conform to it. Why didn't they stay in their own country to raise temples in the vast solitudes of the west? Nations adopt or reject restrictions with regard to religious practices as they see fit. To pretend to force us to promulgate religious toleration is to assume the exercise of a right over us even superior to that of conquest, for the religion and the customs of a conquered country have always been respected.

Lastly, the rebels have tried to justify their criminal uprising before God and before man as the result of the adoption of necessary repressive measures by the easygoing Mexican government. The use of force to restrain the restless, to punish the rebellious, and to maintain obedience is an inherent right of the sovereignty of nations. What other right can the United States invoke in support of the troops sent to Florida to chastise the Seminoles and the Creeks? What is right for one nation should be right for all: The attributes of sovereignty are identical in all nations. The civilized world has already passed judgment upon the usurpations of the Texans, refusing to admit the reasons advanced in support of their declaration of independence.

Convinced of the justice of its cause, and no less of its power to defend it, the government undertook to raise an army that should march to repair the reverses suffered by a handful of our troops, and to give a severe lesson to those who had dared to insult the Mexican name. The circumstances of the republic at that time could not have been more embarrassing or unfavorable. The constitution of 1824 had been abolished and a new one had not as yet been framed, all of which produced an uncertainty and restlessness which made the most resolute spirits fear for the future. The party opposed to the modification of the fundamental law was still strong, its leaders still enjoyed the influence and prestige of the power they had wielded for so long. Was it not natural to fear that, with the best troops of the government sent to the confines of Texas, the balance of power might incline towards those opposed to the existing order of things? Those unable to properly evaluate the force of Mexican honesty when the interests at stake are those of the country thought so. The government did not hesitate, however, preferring to remain defenseless in the heart of the country to the sad consolation of maintaining itself in power at the cost of national dishonor. I shall always remember with tears in my eyes the memorable reply of President Barragán, given to an individual who tried to exaggerate to him the dangers of our situation and the fear that the party of Valentín Gómez Farías might take the field again if the central part of the republic was drained of its best troops in order to send them against the rebellious colonists. "Gómez Farías," said he, "is a Mexican, and, if by returning to power he should lock me up in the cells of the inquisition, the dishonor would be his, but if Texas is not recovered, the shame will fall upon the entire nation." It is only human to rejoice at the response of the nation to the noble confidence placed in her disinterested patriotism. All efforts were directed to Texas and the government abandoned all fear of a serious disturbance in the interior. True it is that some Mexicans, though few in number, did not sacrifice their interests and their personal resentments upon the altar of their country. The great majority, however, supported the government which, with unerring foresight, had decided that the preservation of peace was essential, a policy which others considered the beginning of our downfall. It is thus that the spirit of a people is displayed during trying circumstances, and even though engaged in a struggle against fate itself, its constancy will sooner or later overcome the rigors of destiny.

The lack of resources was one of the obstacles that afflicted the government most. Our finances had reached the last stage of depletion as a result of a thousand causes too well known to make it necessary for me to enumerate. How could war be waged without money in such a far away country, without the barest essentials of life? The government, however, was not daunted by the difficulties. It made use of every penny its revenue afforded, and received the generous support of the Mexican people. But in spite of all the resources it was able to muster, our soldiers were still exposed to great privations. But the Mexican soldier has always known how to endure sufferings in silence when fighting for the sacred rights of his country. The revolutions of 1832 and 1833 had completely disorganized the army, and the executive had just begun its reorganization, when it was called upon to lead the newly assembled troops to the frontier. Companies were organized, instructed, and drilled while on the march, and many of the men fired their first shot against the enemy. It was indeed a glorious enterprise but strewn with difficulties, since the government was forced to supply everything on the spur of the moment: soldiers, equipment, supplies, and, in a word everything necessary for the unexpected campaign,

The supreme government entrusted the command of the army to His excellency, Antonio López de Santa Anna, President of the Republic. To-day, as then, I still maintain that his appointment was the most advisable at the time. The recent prestige of the glorious victory of Zacatecas was a potent stimulus to the soldier accustomed to follow in the path of glory of an accredited leader. In this campaign dangers and difficulties multiplied themselves with such astounding rapidity that it was most urgent to appeal to the enthusiasm of the masses, for though a furtive passion, it produces happy results when used opportunely. At the generals' council of war which I called in the capital, it was unanimously agreed that the appointment of one so favored by fortune was most desirable.

The general-in-chief arrived in Mexico towards the close of November, proceeding to San Luis Potosí early the following month, after issuing the corresponding orders for the march of the various divisions, the assembling of all army equipment, and the arrangement of everything that was necessary for beginning the campaign. The General displayed the greatest activity while in San Luis, both with regard to the increase of the divisions, the organization of the brigades, and the assembling of supplies and of practically everything that was needed. The government invested Santa Anna with authority to secure funds by pledging the revenue of the nation because the Minister of Finance had found all doors closed to his efforts, and was now at his wits end to secure the necessary resources. The advisability of such a measure was justified, as expected, by the results.

Towards the close of December, our forces assembled at San Luis Potosí, consisting of a little more than 6,000 men, began their march to Béxar, then held by the enemy. The General had deliberately planned to make it the base for his operations out of regard for the fact that being the only city in the territory of Texas whose population was Mexican in its entirety, it could be relied upon to lend that cooperation which can be expected only of friends. It was for this reason that he determined to cross 400 leagues of uninhabited deserts, enduring inconveniences and hardships that might have been avoided by choosing another route. The army underwent great privations during its march and consequently deserves the highest praise for its constancy and resignation, qualities characteristic of the Mexican soldier.

A division of the army was to surprise Béxar early the morning of the 23rd of February, 1836, but for some reason yet unknown the orders of the General were not carried out. It is a fact, however that the failure or the inability to comply with an order so evidently wise, was responsible for the loss of many lives later. On March 6th, at daybreak, the assault was made upon the fortress of the Alamo as agreed in a council of war. The blood of the conquerors and the conquered mingled in the engagement and our soldiers added new laurels to their accredited heroism. Party spirit has underestimated the true merit of the engagement. A fort that has artillery, a defence consisting of two separate walls, and whose capture required the loss of 70 killed and 300 wounded, cannot rightly be called an indefensible position.

Having succeeded in taking possession of Béxar, the General detailed a division to operate on Goliad, Cópano, and along the entire coast to Brazoria, placing it under the orders of the brave General José Urrea. Another under the command of General Antonio Gaona was to clear the way from Béxar to Bastrop, taking a position to the rear of the enemy in Nacogdoches. The third division, which we may call the central, marched between the first two with its objective being to secure the crossings on the Colorado where, according to information, the enemy had taken up a position.

General Urrea fulfilled the high hopes placed in his well-known courage and activity by overcoming Dr. Grant, forcing the rebels to evacuate Goliad, and finally capturing Fannin and his men at Encinal del Perdido. This series of uninterrupted victories led General Urrea to Brazoria, the objective of his operations as indicated by his orders. General Urrea and his division well deserve the gratitude of their country.

Gaona lost his way in the desert between Bastrop and San Felipe and was unable to reach Thompson until April 20th.

The officer in charge of the advance guard which was to capture one of the crossings on the Colorado notified the General-in-chief that he found himself in an extremely exposed position. The General immediately set out with the reserve forces, and on April 5th joined the army at Atascosito Crossing. The enemy did not wait, and the march was then continued to San Felipe de Austin. This town was found consumed by fire, the enemy having had no other recourse in their flight. The victories of the Alamo and Llano del Perdido, the occupation of the entire coastline to Brazoria, and the rapid and concerted marches of all our divisions had produced such dismay among the enemy that its only thought was to secure a place of refuge beyond the Sabine. Thompson's Crossing was occupied by our troops, and the rebels retreated to Groce's Place, while the leaders of the insurrection met in Harrisburg. Unfortunately, the efforts of our troops to capture them were frustrated in spite of their night's march, because the leaders, fearful of the lightning speed of our marches, fled beforehand. Col. Almonte captured a large supply of food in New Washington. These supplies were of inestimable value to the army at a time when it had practically nothing. The General-in-chief arrived in that city the 18th of April. The commander of a scouting party sent to Lynchburg gave notice of the approach of the enemy. After this nothing was thought of but immediately attacking it. Houston's force did not exceed 800 men and he had taken a position in the woods along the banks of Buffalo Bayou at the point where it joins the San Jacinto. His situation was desperate. The General-in-chief asked his second in command to send him a reenforcement of 500 picked troops in order to make the victory more certain. Of these only 400 arrived, the morning of the 21st, the greater part being recruits. Anxious to draw the enemy to a more advantageous position, the General-in-chief retired a thousand *varas* and pitched camp on a hill protected by heavy woods on the right and by an extensive plain on the left and front. The enemy skirmished with our forces while taking their position, but without compromising a general engagement or showing much spirit.

The night of the 20th, the forces were assigned their respective positions, a parapet was constructed, and due vigilance maintained. Three companies defended the woods, a battalion covered the center, while our cannon and the reserves formed our left. Let us quote from the General-in-chief, the disastrous effects of an unforeseen and unexplainable surprise.

"I placed my escort, reenforced by thirty-two men mounted

on officers' horses, in a strategic position from which it could observe the enemy and give protection to the already mentioned baggage. Hardly had an hour passed since the last disposition, when General Cós came to me to ask me, in the name of Captain Miguel Aguirre, commandant of the escort, *that he be permitted to allow his troops to eat and to water and feed* the horses which had not been fed since the day before. The pitiful tone in which this petition was made moved me to grant it, warning him, however, that as soon as the men were through, Captain Aguirre should immediately take up his position as ordered. His failure to do so contributed to the surprise that the enemy succeeded in effecting.

"Fatigued as a result of having spent the morning on horseback, and not having slept the night before, I lay down under the shade of some trees while the troops ate their rations. I sent for General Manuel Fernández Castrillón, who was acting as major general, and I ordered him to keep a close watch and to advise me of the slightest movement of the enemy. I also asked him to wake me up as soon as the troops had eaten, for it was necessary to take decisive action as soon as possible.

"As fatigue and long vigils provoke heavy slumber, I was sleeping deeply when the din and fire of battle awoke me. I immediately became aware that we were being attacked and that great disorder prevailed. The enemy had surprised our advance guard, a party attacked the three chosen companies that guarded the woods to our right and took possession of them, increasing the confusion with their unfailing rifles. The rest of the infantry of the enemy was making a front attack, protected by their two cannon, while their cavalry charged our left.

"Although the evil was done, I thought for a moment that it might be repaired. I ordered the permanent battalion of Aldama to reenforce that of Matamoros which was sustaining the battle; and hurriedly organized an attack column under orders of Colonel Manuel Céspedes, composed of the permanent battalion of Guerrero and detachments from Toluca and Guadalajara, which, simultaneously with the column of Colonel Luelmo, marched forward to check the principal advance of the enemy. My efforts were all in vain. The front line was abandoned by the two battalions that were holding it, notwithstanding the continuous fire of our artillery commanded by the brave Lieutenant Arenal. The two newly organized columns were dispersed, Colonel Céspedes being wounded and Captain Luelmo killed. General Castrillón, who ran from side to side to restore order among our ranks, fell mortally wounded. The recruits bunched themselves and confused the tried soldiers, and neither the first nor the second made any use of their weapons. In the meantime the enemy, taking advantage of the opportunity, carried their charge forward rapidly, and shouting madly, secured a victory in a few minutes which they did not dream was possible."

Those victories which are considered as certain beforehand too often prove, unfortunately, bitter and unexpected defeats. Napoleon looked upon his Russian campaign as the natural complement of his glory because every detail had been carefully planned and because he had at his command the entire resources of Europe. Fortune forsook him, alas, and all the resources of his fertile genius proved unavailing in courting the favors of the wilful dame. It was this same fickle goddess that turned her face from us at the very moment when the republic was to gain immense renown by the respect which her arms had exacted. A whim of fate was sufficient for victory to desert our standards and to perch herself on those of our spiritless adversaries. The capture of the General-in-chief, our President, exercised a greater influence than that which the colonists anticipated because, when the generals held a council of war, it was responsible for the decision to retreat with the entire army as far as Matamoros. Béxar was abandoned in view of the fact that the retreat of the army left its garrison in the obvious necessity of surrendering, isolated as it was and lacking food supplies. The success of San Jacinto has filled the Texans with a pride and insolence comparable only to the discouragement that possessed them before the fateful 21st of April. The memories left of the constancy and courage of the Mexican soldiers will not, however, be soon forgotten, and in a day not far distant we anxiously hope to be able to prove to the colonists our ability to reconquer our lost territory and to crown our efforts with victory.

The night of May 14th the government received the unexpected news of the defeat, all the more surprising in view of the antecedents which promised a complete success of all our efforts to save the integrity of our country. Under these critical and unexpected circumstances the government proved that it knew how to rise above misfortune and that no mishap could make it waver in the noble purpose of vindicating the rights of the nation. The orders countermanding the retreat, though issued without loss of time, were not received by the army until it was too late, and it was inevitable for our forces to take up their quarters in Matamoros.

It was then decided to organize a reserve force of 3000 men to embark from Tampico and Vera Cruz for Matamoros under orders of General Valencia. Various measures were dictated to carry out this resolution and the divisions that were to compose the expedition were organized, but prudence made it advisable to postpone their departure in order to attend to the more immediate needs of preserving peace and order in the interior of the republic. The recent developments in Texas, as was natural, had caused a great sensation in the republic and the enemies of peace began to show their face, encouraged by the false idea that with the fall of General Santa Anna, it would now be easy for them to regain their influence and power. They were deceived, however. The energy of the government proved sufficient to frustrate their designs. The consoling spectacle of a united people in support of their honor and their rights was again presented to the world.

The command of the second army, which was organized, fell to General Bravo, who, because of his prudence, his loyalty, and his patriotism, was worthy of being entrusted with the defence of our national cause. General Valencia was appointed quartermaster general. When the circumstances under which the government was forced to organize and completely equip this second

army are considered, the honor that accrues to it for having overcome the obstacles and difficulties that multiplied themselves on
every hand, cannot be denied. The transportation trains were
complete, the troops were armed and uniformed, and nothing
that had been taught by experience was neglected in order to
make the fate of the soldier more bearable. The elements of
nature that had begun to add to the hardships of our army ever
since the 27th of April seem to have combined against the troops
of the reserve force, inflicting equally heavy losses to the brigades
that marched by way of Leona Vicario and those that followed
the road to Victoria. In spite of these difficulties, 7000 men were
assembled in the towns of the north and in Matamoros. The
zeal displayed by the general-in-chief, the generals, and all ranking officers in their efforts to maintain discipline, to instruct the
troops, and to prepare them for the campaign, undertaken with
the greatest ardor and enthusiasm, is beyond exaggeration. A
pontoon bridge was sent from Yucatan to Matamoros, anticipating
the need of such equipment for the march of troops through a
country intersected by large rivers. The army had more than
sufficient supplies of every kind. Five war vessels had been acquired to deprive the enemy of the valuable help received from
the United States, and two more were to be bought. These vessels were also to facilitate the transportation of troops, if judged
advisable by the general-in-chief, from one place to another
along the coast. Why didn't our forces enter Texas again?
For lack of money and nothing else! Admitting that the new
Minister of Finance found resources to equip the troops and make
their departure possible, in spite of his predecessor's statement
in reply to my urgent demands that it was impossible to raise a
single *peso* to carry on the war against Texas, it is likewise
necessary to admit that the actual resources were overestimated
by the new optimistic minister. After promising that he would
place the necessary funds at my command in order to carry out
the great enterprise which was the object of all my thoughts and
efforts, he failed to do so, either because he was unable or unwilling to do it. Again victory, which seemed to be almost within

our grasp, fled from our midst, and we failed in our plans to reconquer that revolted territory. When at the price of a very
costly sacrifice to the country, a loan of 15,000 *pesos* monthly,
had been negotiated, the season that makes Texas an impenetrable waste set in, and the plans and efforts of the government
were again frustrated. It was under these circumstances that
the constitutional period of the administration under which I
served came to an end, the victory of the small Mexican fleet
over the Texan ships and the capture of the schooner *Independence* marking the close of our career. General Bustamante,
whom the government called from Europe as early as June in
order to entrust to his talent and military experience the command of the army, was declared to be the choice of the Mexican
nation for its government. The country rightly expects that she
will owe to his zeal and interest the avengeance of her honor
and the well-deserved chastisement of the many injuries received.

I am the first to condemn the unphilisophical spirit of those
who habitually excite national animosity. I have felt no small
embarrassment in fulfilling the sad task of retelling the series
of injustices with which the United States have repaid the candor
of an unexperienced nation in adopting their principles, a country
that to please them has sacrificed her beliefs and her traditions,
and who, without jealousy, took pride in the high rank which
they had assumed as a result of their power. But my country
stands above all other interests and even though the task was
repugnant, I have been obliged to point out the menace of the
snares set for us by her enterprising neighbor, the open disregard with which our friendship has been betrayed, their well-
known ambitions, the unswerving policy they have pursued, and
the shamelessness with which they have favored our enemies,
furnishing them men, arms and munitions and advancing their
cause by all the means which their unscrupulous diplomacy has
suggested.

From the state of Maine to Louisiana a call has been made

in the public squares to recruit volunteers for the ranks of the rebels in Texas.

Everywhere meetings have been held, presided over, as in New York, by public officials of the government, to collect money, buy ships, enlist men, and fan that spirit of animosity that characterizes all the acts of the United States with regard to Mexico. The newspapers, paid by the land speculators, without excepting the *Globe* of Washington, which is doubtless an official organ, have sponsored the insurrection of Texas with the same ardor they would have supported the uprising of 1776. Our character, our customs, our very rights have been painted in the darkest hues, while the crimes of the Texans have been applauded in the house of the President, in the halls of the capitol, in the marts of trade, in public meetings, in small towns, and even in the fields. The President of the Mexican republic was publicly executed in effigy in Philadelphia in an insulting and shameful burlesque. The world has witnessed all these incidents, of which we have become aware through the shameful accounts in the newspapers of the United States. Could greater insults, outrages, or indignities be offered us by an open declaration of war? Let national indignation answer the question.

The Anglo-Americans, not content with having supplied the rebels with battleships to prey upon our commerce, to deprive us of our property and to commit all the abuses of piracy upon the high seas and on our defenseless coast, have protected them with their fleet and have captured the ships of the Mexican squadron that have tried to prevent contraband trade in Texan waters. It is such acts that make our blockade ineffective. It was in no other way that Greece obtained her independence at Navarino. With the Turkish squadron vanquished, the Greeks were left without an enemy. On September 1, 1835, our schooner *Correo* was captured by a vessel of the United States. The papers and belongings of its commander and officers were pillaged and the men were taken to New Orleans and locked in the public jails of the city. Would not the United States have protested with unexcelled indignation if the schooner *Grampus,* or any other of their war vessels, had been captured by the *Correo* and brought at once with its entire crew to a Mexican port? A cry of indignation would have unanimously been raised throughout every state of the Union, and the bombardment of all our ports would have not been sufficient vengeance to atone for such an insult. Recently the war corvette *Natchez* of the United States captured an American ship engaged in war contraband trade, a practice condemned by all neutral nations. More scandalous still was the capture of the Mexican warship *General Urrea,* whose flag was run down and the ship immediately taken to an American port. It matters little that the ship has since been released, because no satisfaction has been given for this arbitrary act. Furthermore, the Americans have succeeded in their purpose by clearing Texan waters of vessels that hinder the arrival of aid for the Texan rebels. The Mexican government, with the right that pertains to all nations, declared her ports, bays, and inlets in a state of blockade and advised the accredited representatives of all friendly nations in this capital of the fact, without excepting, as was natural, the United States. Later, the United States was notified that, having the necessary maritime force to enforce the blockade, Mexico would take the necessary steps to make it effective. All nations have respected this inherent right of sovereignty of our country except the United States, who escort all ships going to the Texan coast with their Florida fleet. This enables such vessels to carry contraband of war such as arms, munitions, and volunteers for our enemies. Yet this nation demands of us the fulfillment of treaties so shamefully violated by herself!

The Texas question, whether considered from the point of view of a successful termination, or a forced subjection, has given the cabinet of the United States, every opportunity desired for the increase of her territory. Relying upon the inability of the Mexican republic to assemble the necessary resources for a definite and successful attempt to recuperate her lost territory and to vindicate her honor, nothing will be easier for the Ameri-

cans than to add one more star to their flag. After signing the
treaty of limits of 1819 and reaffirming it in 1832, they had no
grounds to extend the limits of the United States to the Río
Bravo or beyond. By encouraging an insurrection among the
inhabitants of Texas, however, by lending it their support and
influence, the same results will be obtained, proclaiming always
to maintain neutrality, but in reality assuming a policy similar
to that observed during the struggle of Spain and her colonies.
The Texans, by these we mean the citizens of the United States
temporarily living in Texas, will ask to be annexed to that republic, their independence will, as a matter of course, be recognized out of regard for what is emphatically termed *the rights
of a free people*, and annexation will follow soon after, for it
will not be possible for the United States to look with indifference upon the fate of this new son of Jonathan. Will this involve any violence? No! The United States have arrogated
to themselves, among other high principles, that of redeeming
humanity of its vexations and of favoring the weak whenever
there are no great obstacles.

But should the Mexican nation decide to use her numerous
resources for the prosecution of the shameful war in Texas,
succeeding thereby in reconquering it, the cabinet of the United
States will not lose the hope of acquiring, amidst the attendant
disorders, the territory which it still maintains is *contested*. Both
in Mexico, through the Chargé de Affaires, Mr. Butler, and in
Washington, through the Secretary of State, Mr. Forsyth, doubts
have been raised as to the true limits of the two republics, ignoring the generally recognized Sabine river, in order to extend the
boundary to the Natchez. General Gaines, who was stationed
at Natchitoches with a detachment, to observe the Texas campaign ever since its beginning, proposed, on the 29th of March,
to cross the imaginary line with his troops. On the 4th of May
he was authorized by the Secretary of War to advance *as far as
the old fort of Nacogdoches which is within the limits of the*
United States according to their claims. The 11th of July he
received fuller instructions for the occupation of that point
to which he finally moved. In the meantime the state depart-

ment tried to appease our minister, Señor Goroztiza, by sending him the copy of a letter written by the President of the United States to the governor of Tennessee, dated August 6th, in which he disapproved the call of General Gaines for militia reenforcements. But the President wrote to General Gaines on the 4th of September, 1836, as follows: "The United States are strictly committed to a policy of neutrality in the struggle of Texas. This neutrality must be observed and enforced by the commander of the forces of the United States on that frontier. It is the duty of Mexico to prevent the Indians that live within her territory from committing depredations against the citizens of the United States. If Mexico is unwilling or unable to comply with this duty, the United States are authorized by the law of nations and the right of self-defense to make effective this obligation of Mexico. If the commander of the American forces is convinced that any group of Indians is disturbing the peace of the frontier of the United States and that they receive help or protection in Mexican territory, it is not to be expected that Mexico will take offense if he adopts the most prompt and decisive measures to chastise such Indians, depriving them of the means of continuing their unlawful activities against the lives and property of American citizens. It will be advisable to take the most advanced position possible in view of these facts, one that shall be adequate to protect the frontier. You are furthermore hereby authorized to pursue the Indians wherever they may be found, *without regard for the Mexican limits or those which the Texans claim*." Gorostiza protested in the most energetic terms against the discretional authority given General Gaines to penetrate into Mexican territory with the pretext of restraining Indian hostilities. He manifested that no such hostilities had ever existed except *in the imagination of the Texans and their sympathizers*. He refuted the arbitrary interpretation placed upon article 33 of the treaty between Mexico and the United States. Gorostiza stated, with that keen perception that characterized him, that General Gaines had been ordered to act in conformity with the information he could gather, aware of the fact that, since all news would come from an enemy territory, the facts would be distorted by malice and hatred. Our envoy, convinced that his protests were disregarded, his arguments ignored, and his mission frustrated, requested his passports in order not to authorize by his presence the insults offered to his nation and the violation of her territory. Our government approved this conduct as the only honorable recourse under the circumstances. The action of Gorostiza, in view of the difficulty of his mission to the United States, does honor to his diplomatic talent, his wide experience in matters of this kind, and to the nation which prides herself in having unconquerable defendants of her sacred rights.

The coincidence of the march of General Gaines to the frontier with the uprising of Texas after the occupation of the territory by a Mexican army naturally gives rise to the suspicion that the object of his mission, as well as that of the increase of the army of the United States, was to help the rebels *in case of necessity,* and to occupy, in the midst of the consequent disorder, the territory still contested, reenforcing by the presence of troops the demands which were again being presented. The letter written by the President in September has no other object than to find a new pretext for trespassing the limits. The Indians kept aloof during the entire conflict without making the least move. Had they taken the warpath, it is only natural to suspect that they would have done it at the instigation of interested agents who desired to create a pretext for intervention. The United States and Mexico had agreed to repress Indian hostilities within their respective territories, but it was never understood that the United States were thereby authorized to penetrate into Mexican territory whenever the Indians assumed hostilities, nor that Mexico had the right in turn to do likewise within the United States whenever they were afflicted by similar disturbances. Such an interpretation is obviously absurd. Will the United States admit that we have the rights to cross over into Arkansas whenever the Apaches decide to incommode the inhabitants of that district? Such an interpretation of Article 33 would result in an immediate declaration of war against Mexico. In view of such a scandalous violation of the limits guaranteed by two treaties and supported by the good faith of the contracting parties, I leave it to the good judgment of every honorable Mexican to decide what is our duty if we value our self-esteem.

Throughout the course of the incidents related, the policy of General Jackson is easily discernible in his evident desire to acquire Texas. The old general has always felt a deep sympathy for the South where he was born, where he holds his property, and where he enjoys the greatest popularity. It is in that section that the hateful traffic in slaves is still practiced, and it is that section that is interested in securing a new market where human beings may be sold. The greater part of the colonists of Texas came from the southern states. Likewise, the land speculators, among whom General Jackson has many intimate friends such as the so-called president Houston, came from there. By annexing Texas to the Union, the number of senators and representatives in Congress who support the maintenance and protection of slavery would be increased. In case that, as has been clearly indicated in all their recent transactions, a separation should be effected between the North and the South and two republics be erected, the latter would enhance her power greatly by the acquisition of Texas as an integral part of its territory. Neither within the United States nor abroad has anybody ignored the fact that in the events that have taken place in Texas, motives more powerful than mere sympathy for the adventurers and speculators have been brought into play. Mr. Morfit's mission to the revolted colony, with instructions to report to the cabinet in Washington on the political conditions in Texas, its resources for securing independence, and its ability to maintain it, had no other object than to get the desired information for the purpose of presenting it to Congress to justify the proposal of the government to recognize the independence of the province. An excerpt from the message of President Jackson to Congress, December 6th, 1836, clearly outlines his policy with regard to Mexico and to Texas.

"It is already known to you, by the correspondence between

OF THE TEXAN REVOLUTION 365

the two Governments communicated at your last session, that our conduct in relation to that struggle is regulated by the same principles that governed us in the dispute between Spain and Mexico herself, and I trust that it will be found on the most severe scrutiny that our acts have strictly corresponded with our professions. That the inhabitants of the United States should feel strong prepossessions for the one party is not surprising. But this circumstance should of itself teach us great caution, lest it lead us into the great error of suffering public policy to be regulated by partiality or prejudice; and there are considerations connected with the possible result of this contest between the two parties of so much delicacy and importance to the United States that our character requires that we should neither anticipate events nor attempt to control them. The known desire of the Texans to become a part of our system, although its gratification depends upon the reconcilement of various and conflicting interests, necessarily a work of time and uncertain in itself, is calculated to expose our conduct to misconstruction in the eyes of the world. There are already those who, indifferent to principle themselves and prone to suspect the want of it in others, charge us with ambitious designs and insidious policy. You will perceive by the accompanying documents that the extraordinary mission from Mexico has been terminated on the sole ground that the obligations of this Government to itself and to Mexico, under treaty stipulations, have compelled me to trust a discretionary authority to a high officer of our Army to advance into territory claimed as part of Texas if necessary to protect our own or the neighboring frontier from Indian depredation. In the opinion of the Mexican functionary who has just left us, the honor of his country will be wounded by American soldiers entering, with the most amicable avowed purposes, upon ground from which the followers of his Government have been expelled, and over which there is at present no certainty of a serious effort on its part being made to reestablish its dominion. The departure of this minister was the more singular as he was apprised that the sufficiency of the causes assigned for the advance of our troops by the commanding general had been seriously doubted by me, and there was every reason to suppose that the troops of the United States, their commander having had time to ascertain the truth or falsehood of the information upon which they had been marched to Nacogdoches, would be either there in perfect accordance with the principles admitted to be just in his conference with the Secretary of State by the Mexican minister himself, or were already withdrawn in consequence of the impressive warnings their commanding officer had received from the Department of War. It is hoped and believed that his Government will take a more dispassionate and just view of this subject, and not be disposed to construe a measure of justifiable precaution, made necessary by its known inability in execution of the stipulations of our treaty to act upon the frontier, into an encroachment upon its rights or a stain upon its honor."

Who does not see in these words the design to excuse the sympathy of the Anglo-American people for the rebels of Texas? Who does not see the attempt to prepare public opinion for the instructions issued to General Gaines regarding the occupation and violation of our territory? Who does not see the desire of winning the favor of Congress for the recognition of independence? As a matter of fact, in spite of the protests of neutrality and of the President's explanation that it was not yet time to enter fully into the details of this thorny question, a few days later he assumed an entirely different attitude, removing the transparent veil of his heretofore guarded policy by forcing one of the Houses of Congress to a violent and unjust declaration. But Jackson did more. He did not leave the presidency without conferring one last benefit upon Texas by appointing an accredited agent to that government. In his retirement in the Hermitage he will now have time for serious meditation upon the disastrous consequences that are more than likely to follow the abandonment of the advice and principles of Washington concerning the preservation of peace and harmony with other nations.

In the course of the observations set down in the present

book it has been noticed that the measures adopted by the United States with regard to Texas were analogous to those used for the acquisition of the Floridas. In the present case, as in the former, claim upon claim of exaggerated or imaginary injuries have been piled up and the opportune moment awaited to present them together. In the meantime the stage has been set by deft diplomatic negotiations and the Texas revolution. The coincidence of their demands with the developments in Texas, the irritating tone of the message of General Jackson, his threat to regard us as was customary to regard the pirates of the Barbary Coast, leave no room for a favorable interpretation of their motives, even granting our unwillingness to recognize the hurriedly prepared claims now presented for the first time. A cursory reading of the message of February 6th of the present year will persuade the most credulous that the cabinet of the United States has anticipated us in making public their injuries in order to win the ear of the civilized world and make the denunciation of the series of injustices, insults, and usurpations committed against us, fall upon deaf ears. Without examining the claims presented by citizens of the United States who allege to have suffered injuries at the hands of our government, without submitting them to the most common laws of logic, without taking sufficient time for an analysis of the grievances described, many of which are unfounded or greatly exaggerated, Mr. Powhatan Ellis, the chargé de affaires of the United States, has demanded that we humbly recognize the claims, offer immediate reparations, and make a complete and servile apology. Reply has been made that the data at hand are insufficient, and a promise given that all possible additional information will be secured as soon as circumstances permit, but this has not satisfied him. Without any grounds for withdrawing, he threatened to ask for his passport if a satisfactory reply in accordance with his instructions was not given immediately. Finally, he asked for his passport and left the country accompanied by some of his countrymen fully armed to act as a bodyguard against any attempt upon his person while enroute, ignoring the fact that the government had taken care to provide him with an adequate military escort to Veracruz. None of those means dictated by an unscrupulous policy have been spared to justify an incident unparalleled by the outrages committed in the dark ages when force and violence alone determined the rights of nations. Its equal can only be found in the history of the United States. If in these negotiations better faith were shown, they would find the Mexican government more than kindly disposed to attend to their requests whenever supported by principles of equity and justice. But there is no doubt that their well-known aim is and has been to demand as indemnization a sum, arrived at by that incomprehensible art of American calculations, that will equal the price of Texas, just as in the case of the Floridas they demanded a similar sum from Spain. The only difference between that transaction and the one for the acquisition of Texas is that in the former, Spain's claims against Miranda's expedition organized in New York to invade Venezuela were admitted, while in the present case the expenses incurred in the organization of expeditions equipped in the United States to support our first struggles for independence are included. Where can we find greater shamelessness or a more inconsistent and scandalous policy?

The Anglo-Americans have never failed, whenever possible, to inflict damages upon our country. In Upper California their navy supported an insurrection of Americans against our government. Such an insurrection would never have been attempted had not the leaders felt certain of the approval and support of the United States. The bloody revolution of New Mexico is, no doubt, due to the activities of secret agents of the United States, further proof of which is seen in the fact that the leaders of this sanguinary revolt took refuge in American territory. It is an indisputable fact that Americans long to acquire possessions on the Pacific coast. Such designs, unnoticed by European powers while their attention is engaged in solving more immediate problems at home, will doubtless bring forth later inevitable protests in defense of their menaced rights.

The bare outline we have just hastily sketched of the un-

scrupulous policy of the United States should serve as a warning
to Mexicans, making them realize the dangers that threaten them.
It is but natural to expect that when they come to a full realization of these acts of oppression and violence, their indignation
will know how to average them. The imagination of the Anglo-
Americans is stimulated by their own vanity, and in their dreams
of grandeur, they look upon us as pigmies, objects deserving of
their pity. They consider our possessions but a fair prize of their
greed. While the attention of humanity has been held by other
problems, while the world has turned its energy to their solution,
they have exercised, through their might, a pernicious influence.
"All nations," says a certain noted writer, "seem to have approached their natural limits, but the United States continue to
sail rapidly on their course, without halting, towards a goal which
the human eye cannot discern." We ,the Mexicans, cannot afford
to stand by as idle spectators. Perhaps in the high designs of
Providence it may be written that we are called to redeem the
New World from the degradation and slavery which threatens
it. *Quod praecor eveniet . . . et Leus optanit, prospera signa
dedit.*

The decree of Congress, providing for the vigorous prosecution of the war in Texas, is no more than our national honor
demands. Our honor—unsoiled during twenty-seven long years
of constant strife,—the self-respect of the nation,—that can be
preserved only by the defence of her rights with dignity and determination, our very political existence are at stake. Mexico cannot give up her territory nor can it consent that a rival power
should establish itself upon a strategic position in her rear, ab-
sorbing part of her provinces and menacing the others. It is impossible for us to give up more than 200 leagues of coastline,
depriving ourselves of our most extensive facilities for the construction of shipyards, the shortest and most advantageous commercial routes, the most fertile lands of the republic, and the best
resources of the nation. If Mexico should consent to such baseness, she would lose her position as a first-class nation among
American powers and descend to an unworthy level that would

force her to buy, through a series of continuous humiliations, a costly and precarious existence. The loss of Texas would reduce the value of our lands; real estate throughout the rest of the republic would be worth a fourth of its present value. It would become necessary to renounce the building up of an independent industry, capable of supporting our eight millions of inhabitants, because within a few years, our grain, sugar, and all foodstuffs would have to be imported from Texas. The cost of fortifying the new frontier to defend it against the Colossus of the North, brought so much nearer, would be a hundredfold the cost of the present struggle. It would be impossible for us to stop contraband trade along a widespread and uninhabited frontier. This would result in the ruin of our maritime resources, the chief and only means from which we derive the revenue necessary for the expenses of administration. The loss of Texas will inevitably result in the loss of New Mexico and the Californias. Little by little our territory will be absorbed, until only an insignificant part is left to us. Our destiny will be similar to the sad lot of Poland. Our national existence, acquired at the cost of so much blood, recognized after so many difficulties, would end like those weak meteors which, from time to time, shine fitfully in the firmament and disappear. It is for this reason that General Terán wrote the government, "Whoever consents to and refuses to oppose the loss of Texas is a despicable traitor, worthy of being punished with a thousand deaths."

Such is the opinion of all good Mexicans. The general who to-day holds in his hands the destinies of the nation is guided by this same conviction. The resources of the country now available are more than sufficient to humble the pride of those who, not knowing how to defend their territory, obtained a victory at San Jacinto by a mere whim of fortune, that fickle goddess that seems to rejoice in disappointing those who place too much confidence in her favors. Five thousand infantry and 500 cavalry would be enough, more than enough, to put an end to the high hopes of the Texans, to drive them to the banks of the Sabine, and to reconquer the favors of destiny. The superiority of the Mexican soldier over the mountaineers of Kentucky and the hunters of Missouri are well known. He knows how to endure all privations with serene calmness, and how to overcome hunger and conquer death herself. Veterans, seasoned by twenty years of wars, cannot be intimidated by the presence of an enemy, ignorant of the art of war, incapable of discipline, and renowned for insubordination. General Bustamante has been called to the highest office of the nation by the unanimous vote of his countrymen. They have raised him to this high position with the expressed condition that he must give his immediate attention to Texas, using all the enthusiasm that brought him to our shores out of an unjust exile to avenge the deep wounds of his betrayed country. He counts upon the support of all parties, because even those who oppose the changes introduced by the system implanted in 1834 are not insensible to the wounded pride of the country and the threatened loss of part of her territory. This truth is borne out by the preservation of peace during the long period in which the country, governed without a constitution, has willingly upheld the executive in spite of the weakness to which circumstances have reduced it. Is there anything impossible to a united people, willing to place national dignity above all interests, and actuated by a common motive?

The fear that we will find ourselves involved in a war against the United States if we refuse to subscribe to the terms demanded is not without foundation. If their diplomacy has been dictated by a preconceived plan,—and this cannot be doubted by those who have observed the skill with which the cabinet in Washington directs its affairs—it is obvious that their aim has been to acquire possession of the disputed territory by force if necessary. This will involve us in more serious difficulties than even those presented by the Texas question itself. War with the United States, however, need not be feared, for our final salvation may depend upon it.

War is the greatest scourge that may afflict nations. It is a calamity that must be avoided if possible, whenever independent political existence and the inherent rights of sovereignty are not at stake. War among the nations of America is an attempt against their own happiness, and is contrary to those high aims which the New World should try to realize by maintaining peace, while the nations of Europe solve the serious problems confronting them. Therefore, the American nation that provokes the war will be responsible for an attempt against the political ideals of this continent as opposed to the system of government prevailing in Europe. Up to the present, we have given ample proof of our patience, and the judgment of the civilized world cannot help but absolve us of any charge of aggression against the United States. Consequently, the blame will fall upon them alone, and this will not be favorable to their designs. Some of their statesmen have foreseen the consequences and admitted them, rising above the prejudices of their contemporaries and defending the noble cause of justice. Ex-president John Quincy Adams is worthy of special mention for what he said in the House of Representatives on May 25, 1836, when he made the following remarkable statements.

"Your war, sir, is to be a war of races—the Anglo-Saxon American pitted against the Moorish-Spanish Mexican American —a war between the northern and southern halves of North America; from Passamaquoddy to Panama. Are you prepared for such a war? And again, I ask, what will be your cause in such a war? Aggression, conquest, and the reestablishment of slavery where it has been abolished. In that war, sir, the banners of freedom will be the banners of Mexico; and your banners, I blush to speak the word, will be the banners of slavery.

"Sir, in considering these United States and the United Mexican States as mere masses of power coming to collision against each other, I cannot doubt that Mexico will be the greater sufferer by the shock. The conquest of all Mexico would seem to be no improbable result of the conflict, especially if the war should extend no further than to the two mighty combatants. But will it be so confined? Mexico is clearly the weakest of the two Powers; but she is not the least prepared for action. She has the more recent experience of war. She has the greatest number of veteran warriors; and although her highest chief has just suffered a fatal and ignominious defeat, yet that has happened often before to leaders of armies too confident of success and contemptuous of their enemy. Even now, Mexico is better prepared for a war of invasion upon you, than you are for a war of invasion upon her. There may be found a successor to Santa Anna, inflamed with the desire, not only of avenging his disaster, but what he and his nation will consider your perfidious hostility. The national spirit may go with him. He may not only turn the tables upon the Texan conquerors, but drive them for refuge within your borders, and pursue them into the heart of your own Territories. Are you in a condition to resist him? Is the success of your whole Army, and all your veteran generals, and all your militia calls, and all your mutinous volunteers against a miserable band of five or six hundred invisible Seminole Indians, in your late campaign, an earnest of the energy and vigor with which you are ready to carry on that far otherwise formidable and complicated war?—complicated, did I say? And how complicated? Your Seminole war is already spreading to the Creeks, and, in their march of desolation, they sweep along with them your negro slaves, and put arms into their hands to make common cause with them against you; and how far will it spread, sir, should a Mexican invader, with the torch of liberty in his hand, and the standard of freedom floating over his head, proclaiming emancipation to the slave and revenge to the native Indian, as he goes, invade your soil? What will be the condition of your State of Louisiana, of Mississippi, of Alabama, or Arkansas, of Missouri, and of Georgia? Where will be your negroes? Where will be that combined and concentrated mass of Indian tribes, whom by an inconceivable policy, you have expelled from their widely distant habitations, to embody them within a small compass on the very borders of Mexico, as if on purpose to give that country a nation of natural allies in their hostilities against you? Sir, you have a Mexican, an Indian, and a negro war upon your hands, and you are plunging yourself into it blindfold; you are talking about acknowledging the independence of the Republic of Texas, and you are thirsting to annex Texas, ay, and Coahuila, and Tamaulipas, and Santa Fé, from the source to the mouth of the Rio Bravo to your already over-distended dominions. Five hundred thousand square miles of the territory of Mexico, would not even now quench your burning thirst for aggrandizement.

"But will your foreign war for this be with Mexico alone? No, sir. As the weaker party, Mexico, when the contest shall have once begun, will look abroad, as well as among your negroes and your Indians, for assistance. Neither Great Britain nor France will suffer you to make such a conquest from Mexico; no, nor even to annex the independent State of Texas to your Confederation, without their interposition. You will have an Anglo-Saxon intertwined with a Mexican war to wage. Great Britain may have no serious objection to the independence of Texas, and may be willing enough to take her under her protection, as a barrier both against Mexico and against you. But as aggrandizement to you, she will not readily suffer it; and above all, she will not suffer you to acquire it by conquest, and the reestablishment of slavery. Urged on by the irresistible, overwhelming torrent of public opinion, Great Britain has recently, at a cost of $100,000,000, which her people have joyfully paid, abolished slavery throughout all her colonies in the West Indies. After setting such an example, she will not—it is impossible that she should—stand by and witness a war for the reestablishment of slavery where it had been for years abolished, and situated thus in the immediate neighborhood of her islands. She will tell you that if you must have Texas as a member of your Confederacy, it must be without the taint or the trammels of slavery; and if you will wage a war to handcuff and fetter your fellow-man, she will wage the war against you to break his chains. Sir, what a figure in the eyes of mankind would you make, in deadly conflict with Great Britain—she fighting the battles of emancipation, and you the battles of slavery; she the benefactress and you the oppressor of human kind! In such a war, the enthusiasm of emancipation, too, would unite vast numbers of her people in aid of the national rivalry, and all her natural jealousy against our aggrandizement. No war was ever so popular in England as that war would be against slavery, the slave trade, and the Anglo-Saxon descendant from her own loins."

In the speech of this famous American the reasons that may be advanced to restrain the United States in its imprudent and ambitious policy have been summarized with admirable skill. Perhaps the irresistible force of truth will bring to their senses those who, encouraged by the success of their enterprises, have never stopped to meditate upon the disastrous consequences.

Although the population of the United States exceeds that of the Mexican republic by three million inhabitants, the former is disseminated over an area of 174,306 square leagues, according to the best figures available, while the latter occupies an area of 75,830 square leagues. Consequently, our relative population per square mile is greater than that of the United States, where there are 58 persons per square league as compared to 90 in Mexico. A compact population offers greater advantages for defensive and offensive war when we consider the facilities for recruiting troops. Our long struggle for independence and the subsequent civil strife have made practically every man in the republic become a soldier. We might say that our entire male population is trained in military service. These conditions do not prevail in the United States where, as a result of a long era of peace, the population has dedicated itself to tasks not conducive to the development of a war-like people. Therefore, we find that their regular troops do not exceed a fourth of our armed strength. Although the scientific education of officers is not neglected in the United States, it may be affirmed that they are ignorant of maneuvers in a large scale, for seldom, if ever, have their various units been assembled to act as a whole. Their national militia, though excellent for the protection of their homes, would be of little use in an aggressive war. The United States could muster, at the most, 6000 regular troops, without being able to exceed this number. Is this force sufficient to intimidate the Mexican nation? No. The Mexicans defeated a veteran Spanish force of more than 20,000 men, formidably entrenched within the country, enjoying the prestige of defending an established government, the advantages of deep-rooted prejudices, and the glamour of long established power.

A nation that does not possess a navy needs not fear the United States. A war between England or France and that country might be very harmful to those maritime powers, but to Mexico it could do nothing for it is evident that one cannot lose that which one does not possess. A blockade of our ports could be maintained only at the cost of untold difficulties, for our coasts are unapproachable during one entire season of the year and deadly at all times on account of their climate. By fortifying and defending such poor ports as we have on our coast, the fleet of the United States would find itself constantly exposed without shelter to the fury of our tropical storms. Furthermore, the number of ships necessary to blockade 600 leagues of coast line must be taken into account, if a rigorous blockade is to be maintained. Such a blockade would inevitably be made ineffective by the ships of the nations that trade with the republic. The merchant vessels of the United States themselves would not be the least in violating it, since in that country everything is sacrificed to commercial interests. It is doubtful whether England and France would respect such a blockade in view of the valuable trade relations with our republic, which is one of the chief markets for their manufactures and the acquisition of the precious metals so much in demand in Europe; it is more than probable that those two great powers will not be indifferent to a question that jeopardizes their interests for an indefinite time. Such a policy would in fact deprive them of all connections with a considerable part of the Mexican Gulf.

The good will shown by Great Britain in all her political and commercial relations with our country, her extensive and valuable investments, our great debt to her—the payment of which depends on the improvement of our internal and external situation —all seem to indicate that that great power, arbiter of the destinies of the world for several centuries, will not permit the United

States to extend her power at the cost of our republic, where England has always found one of her best markets, where she enjoys deep-rooted sympathy, and where her subjects have received the kindest treatment. If the abolition of slavery continues to be one of the chief aims of the enlightened administration of England, she will not fail to realize how detrimental to the realization of her object will be the possibility of the United States increasing their territory, which would result in the extension of that vast market where human beings are bought and sold. The similarity of our views upon this serious and humanitarian question will no doubt greatly incline England in our favor, considering that our laws surpass even the most philanthropic legislation enacted by other nations for the protection of human liberty.

France has joined England in her efforts to abolish slavery. The character of the French people has so many points in common with that of our own, the advantages of a reciprocal trade are so marked, and her interests in maintaining the balance of power both in the old and new worlds so great, that she can not very well make an exception in her magnanimous and humane policy, by abandoning Mexico to a doubtful fate.

Considering the acute commercial crisis through which the United States is passing, prudence alone will restrain them from war against a nation that is one of the main outlets not only for their manufactures but for their raw materials as well, furnishing in return the precious metal so essential to the reestablishment of their credit on a sound basis, at a time when it has been so seriously affected. It is true that our navy is weak and will not be able to compete with that of the United States. But we can issue letters of marque to private vessels to prey and harrass her commerce not only in Mexican waters but in the far distant Indian Ocean, a practice that will prove most lucrative to those who may agree to fly the Mexican flag.

I have impartially analyzed the policy of the United States, supported by the facts I have presented, for the calm examination of the reader. More than once, I have applauded the progress of the institutions of that republic, prosperous because of its industry and its public spirit. I have never ceased to feel grateful for the many considerations extended to me by her inhabitants while attending to an important mission entrusted to me by my country before their government. I owe to my country, however, the fruit of my experience and of my observations, and it is because of this duty, as sweet as it is sacred, that I have been obliged to relate the events as they have occurred, expressing my fears and my hopes as I see them. The Mexican nation can never consent to the loss of a considerable part of her territory, without soiling her honor and being humiliated. She stands ready to buy peace at any cost, except that of her honor. Let the motive for the many complaints against the United States be removed, and our well-founded fears that force alone is responsible for the injustices offered will disappear.

Jose Maria Tornel

INDEX

build barges, 173; Filisola at, 173; Urrea ordered to, 183.

Austin, John, drives Ugartechea out, 331.

Austin, Moses, heads American colonization, 308; death of, 309.

Austin, Stephen F., advice to Santa Anna, 42, 87, 135; spreads news of letter to Jackson, 45, 87; succeeds father in colonization grant, 309; grants to, 311, 313, 318; takes petition to Mexico, 333; arrest and imprisonment of, 333–334; released, 334; secures supplies in United States, 342; correspondence with Guzman, 343; campaign against San Antonio, 344.

Ayllón, Lucas Vásquez de, early explorer of Texas, 303.

Bachiller, Miguel, takes special mail to Santa Anna, 79; his capture, 79; not a special messenger, 119.

Badillo, D. N., escorts mysterious travelers, 108.

Balderas, Luis, part in execution at Goliad, 256; defeats Tarancahuaces, 240.

Ballesteros, José María, wounded at Encinal, 229.

Baltimore, expeditions organized at, 296.

Bara, D. N., capture of men at Cópano, 106.

Barragán, Marcos, sent to Lynchburg, 23; gives notice of approach of enemy, 23; detailed to watch Lynchburg, 75; reports Houston in sight, 75.

Barragán, Miguel, acting president, 10; disapproval of loan, 10; letter of Santa Anna to, 52, 152; characteristic reply of, 349.

Batres, ——, money deposited by, 54; part in San Luis loan, 99.

Beales, John C., grants to, 319, 320; member of the *Mexican Company*, 320.

Belle, La Salle's ship, 301.

Berthier, Alexander, Louisiana negotiations, 291.

Béxar (San Antonio), importance of 12–13, 351; surprise frustrated, 13; capture of Alamo, 14, 153; made base, 15; news of surrender of Cos at, 99; no terms offered Travis, 153; condition of country between San Antonio and Rio Grande, 177; ordered reoccupied, 281; surrender of Cos at, 344.

Blanco, Victor, grant to, 317.

Bonaparte, Napoleon, sale of Louisiana, 291.

Booty, sale of, 107; Urrea gathers booty, 187; supplies found at Columbia, 241–242; at Brazoria, 243, 277.

Boundary, negotiations with Mexico, 306; contested territory, 361.

Bradburn, John Davis, goes to Brazo de Santiago, 259.

Bravo, Nicolás, in command of second army, 356–357.

Brazoria, steamboat at, 141; Urrea at, 182; force, 195–196; Urrea sets out for, 241; citizens well disposed, 242; boats sent to Columbia, 244; resolutions of, 322.

Brazos de Santiago, 186; threatened, 256; Bradburn in, 259; wounded taken to, 276.

Brazos River, skirmish on, 73; difficulties in crossing, 73; unable to cross at San Felipe, 73, 173; exploration of right bank, 74; capture of Thompson's Crossing, 74; Urrea crosses, 243.

Bringas, Juan, aide to Santa Anna, 78; at the Alamo, 102.

Brutus, schooner on patrol duty, 141.

Buffalo Bayou, Houston's position on, 24.

Burnet, David G., Santa Anna writes to, 87; reply of, 87; visit to Santa Anna, 128; grant to, 313.

Burr, Aaron, conspiracy of, 324.

Bustamante, Anastacio, election of, 95.

Cameron, John, grants to, 313, 315.

Campos, Juan Vicente, representative

Grande, Mariano, grant to, 317.

Grant, Dr. James, overcome by Urrea, 16, 169, 216, 170; news of, 216, grant to, 320.

Grants, of land in Texas, 311–321; annulled, 321.

Grayson, P. H., member of Texan Cabinet, 128; questions Martínez Caro, 128.

Green, Thomas J., in command of New Orleans volunteers, 87, 133.

Groce's Crossing, Texans at, 21; 73.

Guadalupe River, difficulty of crossing, 72.

Guerra, José Mariano, agreement with Mejía at Matamoros, 332.

Guerrero, ayuntamiento in sympathy with Texans, 212.

Gutiérrez, Bernardo, expedition of, 324.

Guzmán, Gordiana, relations with Austin, 343.

Hardeman, Bailey, member of Texas Cabinet, 128; questions Martínez Caro, 128; appointed commissioner to Mexico, 133.

Harrisburg, leaders of Texan revolution at, 22, 74; capture of, 22, 74; reasons for capture, 29–30, 74; Martínez Caro's comments, 121; Santa Anna sets out for, 173.

Harrison, Dr., sent on special mission, 239, effects of, 241–242.

Hewetson, James, grant to, 314.

Holzinger, Juan José, negotiator of Fannin's surrender, 60, 62, 228; account given to Texans, 105; ordered to fortify Matagorda, 239.

Hospital Corps, 100–101.

Houston, Sam, came from New Orleans, 17; his force reduced, 21, 75, 242; position on Buffalo Bayou, 23, 76; Santa Anna brought before him, 33, 83–84; Houston blushes, 34; Santa Anna's opinion of, 37–38; position at Groce's Crossing, 73; orders colonists to abandon homes, 74–75, 123; conciliatory policy of, 85; leaves for New Orleans, 85; questions Martínez Caro,

118; opposes Santa Anna being placed on board steamboat, 130; policy of, 174–175, 242–243; not popular with colonists, 243; his force, 262; tries to introduce Creeks in Mexico, 327; presides at Nacogdoches meeting, 339.

Iberri, Castillo, sent to Filisola for reenforcements, 122.

Iberville, M., establishes fort on Mississippi, 302.

Independence, declaration of, 339, 341, 346.

Independence, schooner on patrol duty, 141; capture of, 358.

Indians, trade with, 66–67; settlement of in Texas, 68–69, 327; in revolt, 199; skirmish with Tarancahuases, 240; grant of land to Sewane, 311; ruthless policy of United States towards, 326–327; invited to attack Béxar and Bahia, 335; Gaines instructed to pacify, 362.

Infante, D. N., sick, 253.

Inquisition, establishment of, in Urrea's division, 277.

Intrigue, to discredit Filisola, 276–277.

Invincible, boarded by Santa Anna, 41, 86, 133; on patrol duty, 141.

Iraeta, Mariano, position between Victoria and Goliad, 221.

Jackson, Andrew, sympathy for Texans, 42; letter to, 43, 87, 135; interpretation of, 46, 88; relations with Santa Anna, 88–89; instructions to Gaines, 362; interest in Texas, 364; excerpt from message to Congress, 364–366; send accredited representative to Texas, 366.

Jefferson, Thomas, advocate of expansion policy, 287–288.

Joutel, M., account of La Salle's second voyage, 301–302.

Juntas, las, Urrea spends night at, 232.

INDEX

387

Nuestra Señora del Pilar de los Adaes, northeastern boundary of Texas, 298.

Nuevo Leon, contribution to army, 11.

Núñez, Gabriel, almost killed by mistake, 87; a companion of Santa Anna in prison, 87; brings Legoff back to Mexico, 148; detailed to meet enemy, 219; fight of Encinal, 224.

Occeano, brings volunteers from New Orleans, 133.

Old Fort, Santa Anna at, 173; Gaona at, 182, 261; Woll wishes to make it rallying point, 275.

Onís, Luis de, Spanish minister to United States; 298; Spain's claims to Texas, 298–300.

Orozimba, only house in, 136; Patton returns to, 142.

Padilla, Juan Antonio, grant to, 318.

Padre Ballí, island of, 259.

Pagés, Bartolomé, plan for Santa Anna's escape, 134–135; frustrated, 136–140; arrested, 140; impracticability of plan, 140–143.

Panama, Isthmus of, designs on, 287.

Pánuco, claimed as limit by moderates, 288.

Paredes, General, puts down Guzmán's uprising, 343.

Patton, William, comes from Victoria to take charge of Santa Anna, 87; arrival of, 134; investigation of Pagés, 140; return to Orozimba, 142; release of Martínez Caro, 142.

Peralta, Col., killed at San Jacinto, 124.

Perdido River, east boundary desired, 292.

Perdido, plain of, fight, 223–228, surrender of Fannin, 57–59, 170, 228–229.

Pérez Arze, Juan, wounded at Refugio, 220.

Phelps, Dr. J. A., Santa Anna and companions in house of, 136.

Piedras, José de las, killed at Nacogdoches, 331.

Pinckney, Charles, American minister, 292.

Pole, captured, 240.

Ponce, Juan, early explorer, 303.

Portilla, José Nicolás de la, responsible for manner of execution at Goliad, 63, 105–106; left at Santa Gertrudis, 215; order to execute all prisoners, 234; excerpt from Diary of, 236; not responsible, 235–237.

Postscript, appended to Urrea's Diary, 283.

Powell's, Mrs., concentration at, 174, 182–183; location of, 182; council of war, 184–185; Urrea at, 241, 247.

Powers, James, grant to, 314.

Pretalia, Rafael, ordered to surprise enemy, 215; capture of Refugio, 218–220; shoots prisoners at Victoria, 231; sent as special messenger, 245.

Prisoners, exchange of, 177–178; shot at Victoria, 231; at Goliad; 16–20, 63, 106, 128, 234–235; surgeons spared, 234.

Public lands, mismanagement of, 288.

Quintana, Santa Anna lands in, 134.

Ramírez, Antonio, part in execution at Goliad, 236.

Ramírez y Sesma, General, on Colorado, 28, 170, 173; instructions to, 71; joins Santa Anna, 74; sent to San Antonio, 97, 101; report of, 172; at Mrs. Powell's, 174; made second in command, 182; march to Colorado, 274.

Ramón, Domingo, expedition of, 299.

Ramos Arizpe, Miguel, grant to, 316.

Ratas Creek, ambush on, 217; failure of, 217.

INDEX

176–180, 194, 181; plight of, 21, 40–41.

Thompson's Crossing, capture, 22, 111.

Thorn, Frost, grant annulled, 321.

Tocqueville, M. Alexis C. H. M., psychology of people in United States, 307.

Tola, Luis, taken to Matamoros, 188.

Toledo, Alvárez, expedition of, 324.

Tolsa, Eugenio, instructions to, 71; in command of second brigade, 99; leaves San Luis, 99; reenforces Sesma, 170; at Mrs. Powell's, 174.

Tornel, José María, letter of Santa Anna to, 64–70; correspondence with Filisola, 176, with Urrea, 277; biography, 284; defence of appointment of Santa Anna, 350–351; his account of the campaign, 351–356; efforts to reconquer Texas, 357–358; end of his term in office, 358.

Travelers, the mysterious, 108.

Travis, William Barret, refuses to surrender, 14; no terms offered, 153; attack of Anáhuac, 335; Goliad, 340.

Treaty of Limits, 288, 306.

Treaty of San Ildefonso, 293–294.

Tres Palacios Creek, 238.

Trevino, Col., killed at San Jacinto, 124.

Trial by Jury, establishment of, in Texas, 323.

Trollope, Mrs. Frances M., criticism of Indian policy, 326–327; remarks on slavery, 328.

United States, desire for expansion, 287–288, 307; ingratitude of, 290; purchase of Louisiana, 291–292; policy of, 294–297, 306–308, 325; unscrupulous claims, 304; 367–368; boundary disputes, 306; Indian policy, 326–327; slavery, 328–329; designs on Texas, 343, 363–364; violation of neutrality, 345, 358–361; intervention, 363–364, 368; danger of war, 371–72; blame of, 372–375.

United States Cabinet, attitude of, 46–47.

Ugartechea, Col. Domingo, driven out, 331; sent to Texas, 334; efforts to reenforce General Cos, 344.

Urquijo, Luis, Spanish minister, 291.

Urrea, José; review of operations, 15–20; Fannin's surrender, 57–62; 223–229, 234–236; secret report, 165–166, 182, 187–198; at Mrs. Powell's, 174, 247; criticism of, 181, 197; demand for trial, 198, 207; Diary of his operations, 211–256; defence of himself, 230, 232–233, 327–355, 271–279; condemnation of retreat, 257–268; arrest of Texan commissioners, 270; appointed to supersede Filisola, 280–281; recall to Mexico, 282; summary of activities, 352.

Vara, Rafael de la, ordered to Santa Rosa, 214; in charge of baggage and wounded, 221.

Vehlein, Joseph, grant to, 312, 316.

Velasco, farewell to citizens, 133, 157; disembarkation, 134, 141; agreements of, 38–42, 44–45, 85–87, 131–132, 176–177.

Veracruz, rebellion of, 332.

Victoria, Rusk at, 135, scouts sent to, 222; Urrea sets out for, 229; capture of, 230–231; supplies, 232; Alavez left in command, 237; reoccupation of, 281.

Volunteers, arrived from New Orleans, 86–87, 133–134.

Wallace, B. C., Fannin's surrender, 61–62.

Ward, Col., surrender of, 231–232; sent to Goliad, 234.

Washington (on the Brazos), Almonte at, 28, arrival of Santa Anna, 23; convention of, 346.

Watchman, schooner, in Cópano, 259.

Wavell, Arthur G., grant annulled, 321.

Webster, Daniel, 296.

THE CHICANO HERITAGE

An Arno Press Collection

Adams, Emma H. **To and Fro in Southern California.** 1887

Anderson, Henry P. **The Bracero Program in California.** 1961

Aviña, Rose Hollenbaugh. **Spanish and Mexican Land Grants in California.** 1976

Barker, Ruth Laughlin. **Caballeros.** 1932

Bell, Horace. **On the Old West Coast.** 1930

Biberman, Herbert. **Salt of the Earth.** 1965

Casteñeda, Carlos E., trans. **The Mexican Side of the Texas Revolution (1836).** 1928

Casteñeda, Carlos E. **Our Catholic Heritage in Texas, 1519-1936.** Seven volumes. 1936-1958

Colton, Walter. **Three Years in California.** 1850

Cooke, Philip St. George. **The Conquest of New Mexico and California.** 1878

Cue Canovas, Agustin. **Los Estados Unidos Y El Mexico Olvidado.** 1970

Curtin, L. S. M. **Healing Herbs of the Upper Rio Grande.** 1947

Fergusson, Harvey. **The Blood of the Conquerors.** 1921

Fernandez, Jose. **Cuarenta Años de Legislador:** Biografia del Senador Casimiro Barela. 1911

Francis, Jessie Davies. **An Economic and Social History of Mexican California** (1822-1846). Volume I: Chiefly Economic. Two vols. in one. 1976

Getty, Harry T. **Interethnic Relationships in the Community of Tucson.** 1976

Guzman, Ralph C. **The Political Socialization of the Mexican American People.** 1976

Harding, George L. **Don Agustin V. Zamorano.** 1934

Hayes, Benjamin. **Pioneer Notes from the Diaries of Judge Benjamin Hayes, 1849-1875.** 1929

Herrick, Robert. **Waste.** 1924

Jamieson, Stuart. **Labor Unionism in American Agriculture.** 1945

Landolt, Robert Garland. **The Mexican-American Workers of San Antonio, Texas.** 1976

Lane, Jr., John Hart. **Voluntary Associations Among Mexican Americans in San Antonio, Texas.** 1976

Livermore, Abiel Abbot. **The War with Mexico Reviewed.** 1850

Loyola, Mary. **The American Occupation of New Mexico, 1821-1852.** 1939

Macklin, Barbara June. **Structural Stability and Culture Change in a Mexican-American Community.** 1976

McWilliams, Carey. **Ill Fares the Land:** Migrants and Migratory Labor in the United States. 1942

Murray, Winifred. **A Socio-Cultural Study of 118 Mexican Families Living in a Low-Rent Public Housing Project in San Antonio, Texas.** 1954

Niggli, Josephina. **Mexican Folk Plays.** 1938

Parigi, Sam Frank. **A Case Study of Latin American Unionization in Austin, Texas.** 1976

Poldervaart, Arie W. **Black-Robed Justice.** 1948

Rayburn, John C. and Virginia Kemp Rayburn, eds. **Century of Conflict, 1821-1913.** Incidents in the Lives of William Neale and William A. Neale, Early Settlers in South Texas. 1966

Read, Benjamin. **Illustrated History of New Mexico.** 1912

Rodriguez, Jr., Eugene. **Henry B. Gonzalez.** 1976

Sanchez, Nellie Van de Grift. **Spanish and Indian Place Names of California.** 1930

Sanchez, Nellie Van de Grift. **Spanish Arcadia.** 1929

Shulman, Irving. **The Square Trap.** 1953

Tireman, L. S. **Teaching Spanish-Speaking Children.** 1948

Tireman, L. S. and Mary Watson. **A Community School in a Spanish-Speaking Village.** 1948

Twitchell, Ralph Emerson. **The History of the Military Occupation of the Territory of New Mexico.** 1909

Twitchell, Ralph Emerson. **The Spanish Archives of New Mexico.** Two vols. 1914

U. S. House of Representatives. **California and New Mexico:** Message from the President of the United States, January 21, 1850. 1850

Valdes y Tapia, Daniel. **Hispanos and American Politics.** 1976

West, Stanley A. **The Mexican Aztec Society.** 1976

Woods, Frances Jerome. **Mexican Ethnic Leadership in San Antonio, Texas.** 1949